The Martin Buber Reader

The Martin Buber Reader
Essential Writings

Edited by
Asher D. Biemann

THE MARTIN BUBER READER
© Asher D. Biemann, 2002.

All rights reserved. No part of this book may be used or reproduced in any manner whatsoever without written permission except in the case of brief quotations embodied in critical articles or reviews.

First published 2002 by
PALGRAVE MACMILLAN™
175 Fifth Avenue, New York, N.Y. 10010 and
Houndmills, Basingstoke, Hampshire, England RG21 6XS
Companies and representatives throughout the world.

PALGRAVE MACMILLAN is the global academic imprint of the Palgrave Macmillan division of St. Martin's Press, LLC and of Palgrave Macmillan Ltd. Macmillan® is a registered trademark in the United States, United Kingdom and other countries. Palgrave is a registered trademark in the European Union and other countries.

ISBN 0–312–24051–1 hardback
ISBN 0–312–29290–2 paperback

Library of Congress Cataloging-in-Publication Data

Buber, Martin, 1878–1965.
  [Selections. English. 2002]
  The Martin Buber reader: essential writings/edited by Asher Biemann.
     p. cm.
  Includes bibliographical references and index.
  ISBN 0–312–24051–1—ISBN 0–312–29290–2 (pbk.)
    1. Philosophy. 2. Bible. O.T.—Criticism, interpretation, etc. 3. Judaism. 4. Hasidism. 5. Relationism. 6. Philosophy and religion. 7. Community—Philosophy. 8. Zionism. I. Biemann, Asher. II. Title.

B3213.B82 E52 2002
296.3—dc21   2002016924

A catalogue record for this book is available from the British Library.

Design by Newgen Imaging Systems (P) Ltd., Chennai, India.

First edition: September, 2002
10 9 8 7 6 5 4 3 2 1

Printed in the United States of America.

CONTENTS

Introduction	1
Part I Bible	**21**
The Election of Israel: A Biblical Inquiry (1938)	23
Biblical Leadership (1933)	33
What are we to do about the Ten Commandments? Reply to an Inquiry (1929)	43
Biblical Humanism (1933)	46
The Man of Today and the Jewish Bible (1936)	51
Part II Hasidism	**61**
Spirit and Body of the Hasidic Movement (1935)	63
The Life of the Hasidim (1908)	72
Hasidism and Modern Man (1956)	85
Part III Judaism and Jewish Religiosity	**95**
The Faith of Judaism (1929)	97
Two Foci of the Jewish Soul (1932)	107
Jewish Religiosity (1923)	115
Heruth: On Youth and Religion (1919)	125
On the [Jewish] Renaissance (1903)	139
The Renewal of Judaism (1911)	145
Hebrew Humanism (1941)	158
Part IV Dialogue and Anthropology	**167**
From *Religion as Presence* (1922)	169
From *I and Thou*	181
From *Dialogue* (1932)	189
Distance and Relation (1950)	206
Genuine Dialogue (1954)	214

Part V Philosophy and Religion   217

Philosophical and Religious World View (1928)   219
Religion and Philosophy (1951)   223
Teaching and Deed (1934)   234

Part VI Community   241

Comments on the Idea of Community (1931)   243
Community (1919)   247
How Can Community Happen? (1930)   252
Three Theses of a Religious Socialism (1928)   258

Part VII Zionism and Nationalism   261

Concepts and Reality (1916)   263
Nationalism (1921)   268
Zionism and Nationalism (1929)   277
The National Home and National Policy
   in Palestine (1929)   281
Zionism and "Zionism" (1948)   289

Bibliographical Guide   293

Index   295

The Martin Buber Reader

Introduction

What are Martin Buber's essential writings? The editor is confronted with a body of work that spans a creative period of more than 65 years and that appears in a variety of literary genres and methods combining poetry, fiction, playwriting, translation, philosophy, and narrative, with subjects ranging from Viennese literature to Christian mysticism, from the Hebrew prophets to Taoism, from philosophy to art, and from Hasidism to capital punishment. Martin Buber (1878–1965) was nothing short of a humanist in a Renaissance manner, a universal scholar in the tradition of the classical Goethe, whose *Bildung* (education) became an icon for many German-speaking Jews and remained their ideal long after it was abandoned by their German fellow citizens.[1] In this, Buber stood at the climax of a development that had begun with the European Enlightenment and its Jewish manifestation, the *Haskalah,* embracing education as the single catalyst for political and social emancipation, and which continued throughout the nineteenth century with Jews enthusiastically immersing themselves in their cherished German culture and not seldomly disappearing in it.

At the time of Buber's birth in Vienna in 1878, Jews lived relatively undisturbed in the Hapsburg lands under Franz Joseph and in the new German empire under Wilhelm I, but their Judaism was fractioned into irreconcilable religious denominations, or indifference, or even self-hatred. Buber came from a typical assimilated, urban Jewish family of considerable wealth and education with roots in Galicia, then a province of Austria–Hungary. With a father studying Darwin in his youth and a grandfather back in Lemberg (Lvov) defending the ideals of the *Haskalah* while editing a widely respected compendium of Midrashic literature, Buber's heritage was not only one of classic German–Jewish culture but also one that stood at the passage between Eastern European Jewry, whose ritual life was still intact in largely autonomous communities, and the fragmented, individualized modern West.[2] Buber spent the better part of his adolescence at the traditional home of his grandparents where he also came into tangential contact with local Hasidic, or "pious" communities that combined Jewish mysticism, folk traditions, and an often supernatural style of leadership. Between the ages three and fourteen, Buber lived as a fully observant Jew whose everyday languages were Yiddish and Polish (in addition to Hebrew, German, and French), and who received comprehensive instruction in the classical Jewish literature. Like many of his contemporaries, however, Buber, by his own account, soon became increasingly "estranged" from both Hasidism and Judaism.[3] When, in an attempt to reopen this passage of his youth, he turned to the study of Hasidism later in his life,[4] he did so as a fully acculturated Jew in search of the community, authenticity, and religiosity that he was unable to find in the highly sophisticated societies of Vienna, Berlin, Leipzig, and Zurich, the centers of his formative years.[5] In Buber's writings on Judaism, both Hasidism and *Haskalah* are repeatedly invoked as the path-breaking forces of Jewish self-discovery, self-liberation, and an impending rebirth of Judaism (see On the [Jewish] Renaissance [1903] p. 139 in this volume). Buber's German adaptations of Hasidic narratives—most famously the legends of Rabbi Nachman of Bratzlav (1906), the Baal-Shem (1908), and the collection of Hasidic tales (1946)—had such an impact on his generation that even remote Jews, the philosopher Ernst Bloch and the statesman Walter Rathenau among them, began to feel pride in their Jewishness after reading them.[6] It was with the renderings of Hasidism, congenial with the then prevailing *zeitgeist* (intellectual, moral, and cultural state of an era),[7] that Buber first reached a wide audience, Jews and non-Jews, disenchanted with what was frequently perceived as a lifeless, unspiritual, and mechanical West.

Yet, the first impulse of Buber's "self-liberation" did not come from Hasidism but from Zionism.[8] By the time Buber discovered Hasidism for himself and for German culture, he had already become the leading ideologue of a movement that he helped create, around 1900, and that was no less a distinct expression of the spirit of modernity: the Jewish Renaissance, the rerooting and recasting of Judaism in a cultural-spiritual mold that invariably pointed to the philosopher Friedrich Nietzsche whose cult-like spell over young Jews and non-Jews of this time is well known.[9] The Renaissance movement was essentially an offshoot of the young Buber's active role in the early stages of Zionism, and, as offshoots tend to be, a critique of it. Unlike Zionism, itself a restorative phenomenon that had just gained momentum under the leadership of Theodor Herzl, the Jewish Renaissance conceived of itself as a suprapartisan and ultimately supranational movement whose primary concern was not the physical resurrection of the Jewish people but the respiritualization of Judaism. As such, the Jewish Renaissance was directed toward an immediate, inner revival of Judaism in the Diaspora, rather than a postponed, material revival in the land of Israel. For Buber, who ultimately withdrew from Zionist activities in 1904, the Jewish Renaissance did not mean an ideological subdivision of Zionism but Zionism in its truest form. As early as 1899, when speaking at the Third Zionist Congress in Basel, Buber maintained that Zionism was not a matter of "partisanship"

(*Parteisache*) but a comprehensive "worldview."[10] Two years later, together with the young chemist Chaim Weizmann, the writer Berthold Feiwel, the mathematician Leo Motzkin, the artist Ephraim Moses Lilien, and other intellectuals—many of them young Russian Zionists—Buber was instrumental in drafting the Democratic Fraction, a group that was much indebted to the "spiritual" Zionism of Ahad Ha'am, demanding a commission devoted to the advancement of "Jewish culture."[11] Ironically the very question of "culture," a source of uneasiness for the Zionist leadership as well as the religious camp, broke Herzl and Buber apart, leading to the dismantling of the Democratic Fraction after 1903.

The fundamental difference between Herzl's Zionism and Buber's lay, at its core, in the perception of what made the Jewish national movement urgent: To Herzl, it was an external threat, from the pogroms in Russia and the rise of urban, modern anti-Semitism in the most enlightened of all nations—France, Austria–Hungary, and Germany; to Buber, it was an internal threat marked by assimilation, alienation, and spiritual emptiness—in short, a crisis of culture. The former strove for "normalization" of the Jewish people; the latter, for the renewal of Judaism. One might indeed wonder why Buber, who returned to Vienna from Galicia in 1896 to study at the capital's university, did not seem to be overly alarmed by the anti-Semitic populism of the Pan-Germanist Georg V. Schönerer and the Christian Socialist Karl Lueger that was raging through the city at exactly this time. But for Buber, anti-Semitism, a word rarely even mentioned in his writings, was not a reality that could inspire the revival of Judaism but one that only served as a pretext for national egotism under a Jewish flag.[12] With the Hapsburg model of multiculturalism falling apart into a jumble of ethnic national alliances, leaving Jews soaring between the phantom Austria–Hungary and the phantom of a Jewish state, Buber recoiled from any self-sufficiency of political nationalism and placed his own nationalism in a tradition of national humanism and later, Jewish socialism, echoing the voices of the proto-Zionist Moses Hess, the pioneer of labor Zionism Aaron David Gordon, and the socialist pacifist Gustav Landauer, to mention a few. Shaped by their ideas, Buber's lifelong attitude toward mainstream Zionism remained one of critique, yet not necessarily opposition.[13] Invoking the Italian Renaissance, at least in its neoromantic interpretation, Buber envisioned the Jewish national Renaissance as a "branch of the stream of the new [human] renaissance... a rebirth in which every person and every people will participate, each according to his kind and his values: a rebirth of humanity, a rule of 'new lands.' "[14] What stood at the center of this renaissance was again a deeply humanistic conception with learning and self-awareness as the anchors of a national rebirth. In another sense, the renaissance project was really about Jewish "re-education"—about educating Jews back to Judaism by offering them a cultural alternative to religion and assimilation.[15]

The problem of "culture" concerned Buber both in theory and practice. In a short essay of 1901, he commented on the debate on culture and its decline into civilization that was familiar to his time through the writings of Jakob Burckhardt, Nietzsche, and his teachers at the Friedrich Wilhelms University of Berlin, Wilhelm Dilthey and Georg Simmel.[16] Still in 1943, Buber defined "culture" as "creation" and "fulfillment of life" whose essence means particularity and uniqueness, whereas civilization "is occupied with a world that already exists and that can only be discovered."[17] Jewish culture, therefore, and Jewish creativity were essentially identical, and Buber's influence on the discussion of Jewish art,[18] the conception of a Hebrew University, and the establishment of a publishing house devoted to Jewish culture (the Berlin-based Jüdischer Verlag) must be viewed in the context of an aesthetic resurrection of Judaism. In fact, just as we can see Buber's Jewish Renaissance as the expression of his Zionism, it is legitimate to call his Zionism a "form of cultural politics."[19]

In his autobiographical remarks, however, Buber points to another aspect of his Zionism: "Zionism," he writes, "meant for me the restoration of the connection—the renewed taking root [*Einwurzelung*] in the community."[20] Like the debate of culture and civilization, the problematization of community and society was a characteristic fin de siècle phenomenon, raised in Ferdinand Tönnies's book of 1887, *Community and Society*, and reflected (in different ways) in the works of Georg Simmel and Max Weber. The discussion reached back to the origins of utopian socialism and communism in the mid-nineteenth century—to the Saint-Simonists (followers of the social reformer Claude Henri de Rouvroy) in France and the young revolutionaries in Germany and in Italy. But by the turn of the century, much of the revolutionary urge of socialism had faded, leaving the utopian mood even more pronounced. Communes and agricultural colonies inspired by German nationalism (Karl Eugen Dühring), social utopianism (Theodor Hertzka, Franz Oppenheim), or anarchism (Gustav Landauer) appeared in Germany as early as the 1890s.[21] They were, for the better part, upper-class expressions of counterculture, fusing the ideas of humanism, mysticism, vitalism, health consciousness, and aestheticization of manual labor. Among them was the circle of the brothers Heinrich and Julius Hart, the *Neue Gemeinschaft* (New Community); their accompanying worldview promised total "harmony," the creation of a "man of fulfillment" (*Mensch der Erfüllung*), who "is the god and artist of [H]is own universe," and a community that would realize the "highest ideals of culture."[22] Buber lectured in this circle at least twice, between 1899 and 1900, once on the Christian mystic Jakob Böhme, and once on "Old and New Community."[23] It was within this circle that Buber not only developed a close friendship with Gustav Landauer but also his first, albeit still vague and visionary, thoughts on community, the individual, and society. The description of the "new" community as a "living interaction of whole, refined human beings," whose sole purpose is "life," in contrast to the "old" communities whose purpose is religion and commerce; the distinction between community and society, directly borrowed from Tönnies, rendering community "postsocial," as "transcending society and its norms;" and, finally, the experience of the "great Thou" as the communion with the universe—these motifs recur, though much purified from the mystical, vitalist language, in Buber's later writings on Judaism, social philosophy, and dialogue.

With culture and community being the elementary components and concerns in Buber's Zionism and reconnection with Judaism, we must perceive the larger Jewish Renaissance also as a cultural and social critique. Judaism, itself, as Buber imagines it, using the model of Hasidism, becomes a critique of his time, of European culture and society, of Eurocentric Zionism, and of Judaism. Conversely, Buber's later writings became a critique of his earlier work, particulary the "mystical" phase that permeated his thought throughout the first decade of the twentieth century.

Between his graduation from the University of Vienna in 1904 and World War I was a period of utmost versatility in Buber's work: Aside from the renditions of Hasidism, there are translations from Yiddish (David Pinski's *Eisik Scheftel,* 1905), a collection of mystical thinkers (*Ecstatic Confessions,* 1909), German adaptations of Tshuang Tse (1910), Chinese ghost and love stories (1911), the Finnish national epic (*Kalewala,* 1914), Celtic legends (*Vier Zweige des Mabinogi,* 1914), and Buber's own contribution to mythical thinking, his *Daniel* of 1913.

There is also Buber's role as the editor of a series of "sociopsychological" monographs, *Die Gesellschaft* (Society), for the publisher Rütten & Loening. Between 1906 and 1912 (Buber was then living in Berlin), forty volumes appeared with leading European intellectuals contributing titles such as *Revolution* (Gustav Landauer), *State* (Franz Oppenheimer), *Language* (Fritz Mauthner), *Custom* (Ferdinand Tönnies), *Eroticism* (Lou Andreas-Salomé), *Dilettantism* (Rudolf Kassner), and *Religion* (Georg Simmel). In his preface to the series of 1906, Buber first introduced the concept of the "interhuman" (*das Zwischenmenschliche*) as the principal function of society and community. Sociology, in his definition, is the "science of the forms of the interhuman," and to the extent that society has to be understood as an "experience of souls" (*Erlebnis von Seelen*), sociology has to be psychological: "Its object is social life, which is to be regarded as a psychical process."[24] Buber's dialogical philosophy, which he developed about ten years later, again seized on the term of the "interhuman" and should, perhaps, be seen as a commentary on this concept.

The analytical, descriptive, and critical aspects that emerged from Buber's *Gesellschaft* seem slightly at odds with the enigmatic tone and mythical aura in his own writings of the same period. If we had to name a common theme in these writings, it would be the struggle for and *with* unity—a struggle that Buber saw as progression from otherworldly ecstatism to down-to-earth realism. "Since then," Buber wrote of his "conversion," which occurred shortly before World War I, "I have given up the 'religious' which is nothing but the exception, extraction, exaltation, ecstasy.... I possess nothing but the everyday out of which I am never taken."[25] Not by accident is the subtitle of Buber's *Daniel,* "Gespräche von der Verwirklichung" (Dialogues on Realization), a reverberation of the Young-Hegelian philosophies of "realization" and "deed," particularly Ludwig Feuerbach's *Philosophy of the Future* (1843). In a radical antitheological move, Feuerbach sought to "re-introduce philosophy from the realm of 'extracted souls' into the realm of physical, living souls, from the divine, self-sufficient bliss of thought into the human misery."[26]

Buber, who critically engaged with Feuerbach's work as early as 1900 and considered him a precursor of the dialogical principle,[27] gradually performed Feuerbach's "realization" of religion himself, and ultimately followed Feuerbach's transformation of philosophy into anthropology, mediated through the prevailing *Lebensphilosophie* (philosophy of life) of his teacher Wilhelm Dilthey. In his mature interpretation of Hasidism, the mystical element, although still prominent, is directed *toward* the world, not turned away from it; the fundamental difference between the sacred and the profane is overcome, because the sacred, in Feuerbach's language, has been "realized."[28] Similarly, what is stressed in Buber's early speeches on Judaism, which are, in essence, variations on his Hasidic principle, is the "realization" of Judaism as a religion—its transformation into "religiosity" through human action. "Genuine religiosity," Buber wrote in 1923, "is *doing.* It wants to sculpt the unconditioned out of the matter of this world. The countenance of God reposes, invisible, in an earthen block."[29]

But Buber's "doing" differs radically from Jewish orthopraxy (the "correct" observation of Jewish law, or *Halakha*). There is a clear distinction between "religion" and "religiosity" (which Buber adopted directly from his teacher Georg Simmel)[30]—the former was concerned with "organization" and "preservation," and the latter, with "creativity" and "renewal." But there is also a balance and creative tension between them, between priest and prophet, tradition and revolution. Religiosity, Buber admitted, "needs forms."[31] Indeed, although Buber shared his disdain for Talmudic Judaism with other Jewish reformers, revolutionaries, and secular Zionists, he tried not to abrogate Jewish laws and doctrines associated with "religion" outright but wanted to see them imbued "with new and incandescent meaning, so that they will seem to have been revealed to every generation anew."[32] Buber believed that the Law, too, needed to be "realized," "fulfilled" to the extent that "every man, by living authentically, shall himself become a Torah, a law."[33] The renewing force of religiosity, as the example of Hasidism seems to demonstrate, is possible also in a traditional society and, as Buber ultimately failed to see, may even require such a society. But as a force of renewal, true religiosity is always a subversion of religion—not a mere reform but a thorough revolution. In the end, Buber's attitude toward *Halakha,* which invites comparison to the radical antitraditionalist Micha Berdichevski, remained ambiguous at best and found its most undiplomatic expression in his speech "Heruth" of 1919 (p. 125 in this volume). This speech prompted the famous discourse on the question of Jewish law with the neo-observant Jewish philosopher and close friend of Buber, Franz Rosenzweig.[34]

The critical theme in Buber's early addresses on Judaism, delivered at the Prague Zionist chapter Bar Kochba, is the renewal and reformulation of Jewish identity. As such, they form a link between Buber's first Zionist expressions, the Jewish Renaissance, and his study of Hasidism and mysticism. In contrast to Reform Judaism at that time, Buber's religiosity, although emancipating and self-empowering the individual, was not relegated to the personal sphere or to the satisfaction of personal spirituality and rationality, but became the building agent of unity and, by extension, community. Just as the realization of God, for Buber, amounted to the realization of humankind, the renewal of Judaism amounted to the renewal of Jewish peoplehood. The same theme continues as an undercurrent in Buber's later speeches on Judaism as well, whose audience was not always a Zionist or even a Jewish group, as in the apologetic The Two Foci of the Jewish Soul (1932) (p. 107 in this volume), an address delivered in March 1930 at one of the Protestant *Judenmissionsgesellschaften* (Societies for the Mission of the Jews) in Stuttgart. And it comes to a closure in Buber's essay, "Hebrew Humanism" (p. 158 in this volume) of 1941, in which "Hebrew" replaces "Jewish" and "humanism" replaces "renaissance," tying together the national and the supranational, the classical and the revolutionary. Unlike the "Jewish Renaissance," "Hebrew Humanism" is an open critique of Zionism, an outspoken "opposition" to Jewish "national egoism," and an implicit reaffirmation of occidental, primarily German, humanism—the kind that reared the young Buber half a century before, in the light of the unfolding catastrophe in Europe. "[W]e Jews from Germany," Buber wrote, "must contribute to the education of our people in Palestine who are striving for regeneration...." (ibid., p. 159). The re-education of Jews in the Diaspora to Judaism is now a re-education of Jews in Palestine to humanism. But in truth, Buber maintained that they are two sides of the same process—a process that leads to the "concrete transformation" of the "life of the individual as well as that of the community" (ibid., p. 161). The progression in Buber's Jewish writings, therefore, is not simply one from mysticism to Judaism, to humanism, but one of defining humanism through Judaism and Judaism through humanism, which, in the final analysis, is even closer to the vision of the late *Haskalah* than to Nietzsche and neoromanticism.

The context of Buber's renewal of Judaism lies also behind the widely popular journal, self-confidently called *Der Jude*,[35] which he founded and edited from 1916 to 1924, creating a uniquely Pan-Jewish forum of discourse that still remains the most comprehensive document of German–Jewish culture of that era. Unique was also the interconfessional journal *Die Kreatur*, which Buber edited between 1926 and 1930, together with the Catholic theologian Joseph Wittig and the Protestant psychotherapist and intellectual Viktor von Weizäcker. Both enterprises testify to Buber's inclusive, yet not unpolemic vision of Judaism.

A certain process of universalization still must be observed in Martin Buber's thought. Appearing in the line of self-confessed mysticism, Hasidism, and Judaism is a shift toward religion in general, whereas in the line of Zionism, nationalism, and (religious) socialism there appears to be a shift toward the phenomenon of community. Both are changes in perspective, rather than content, which coincide with Buber's turn (or return) to philosophy and theory as well as his turn to academic life.

Becoming an academic teacher was a choice neither envisioned nor seriously prepared for by Buber. His doctoral dissertation, submitted to the University of Vienna in 1904 after a relatively long course of study, was never published,[36] and a habilitation (a second and larger dissertation qualifying one to teach at a university) in art history was never begun.[37] After his university studies (in philosophy and art history) and a year of research and rest in Florence, Buber turned to freelance writing and occasional editing as a profession, living first in Berlin (from 1906 to 1916), and then in Heppenheim, a small picturesque town in the heart of Germany. In 1923, when Buber was offered a lectureship in Jewish religious studies (*jüdische Religionswissenschaft*) and ethics, which was later converted into an adjunct professorship in the general study of religion at the University of Frankfurt, the personal files still listed his profession as "*Schriftsteller*" (writer).[38]

At the University of Frankfurt, Buber taught a variety of courses on the general theory of religion and biblical Judaism from 1924 until April 1933, when he resigned from his post before being officially suspended by the National Socialists in October of the same year.[39] How seriously Buber took the systematic, if not strictly academic, study of religion became evident from his plans as early as January 1916[40] to develop the foundations of a "social- and religious-philosophical system" in a five-volume work, whose "Prolegomena" and first volume was to be a slim book published in December 1922—*I and Thou* (see p. 181 in this volume). At that time, the dialogical principle, so central to his work and indeed Buber's entire frame of thought, was still subordinate—even though essential—to his general understanding of religion. This is also true of a series of earlier lectures, "Religion as Presence" (see p. 169 in this volume), that Buber delivered between January and March 1922 at the Frankfurt Lehrhaus, the leading institution of Jewish adult education at the time. Although the audience was predominantly Jewish, the tenor in the lectures was no longer "renewal" in the charged language of Jewish youth movements but one of historical and comparative study introducing the dialogical element as an explanatory model in the theory of religion. The problem of mystical experience was transformed into one of religious encounter, a deliberate self-critique of Buber's earlier approach, anticipating the fundamental ideas of *I and Thou,* which was completed precisely during that time. Despite the primarily theoretical concerns, however, the audience and reader of both texts could hardly ignore the strong normative impetus already inherent in Buber's conception of dialogue, as well as its groundedness in biblical Jewish thinking.[41]

Together with the search for principles in the religious experience, and the reevaluation of the term "experience" itself, the most dramatic shift Buber made in *I and Thou* was a conscious turn toward language. With the "realization" of religion and the hauling in of the mystical union to the sphere of concrete "presence" (*Gegenwart*), which, in German, connotes both "presence" and "present time," Buber arrived at a conception of religious encounter that occurs in the temporal space of language—that is language and can only be represented through a process of thought that remains within the concrete temporality of language—*Sprachdenken*. Dialogue, for Buber, became the format of revelation, with God addressing the human individual as a "You" in the concrete flow of time, rendering revelation itself time bound. In this sense, "religiosity" is the temporalization of religion; and for Buber, just as true dialogue is free of content, religiosity is content-free and necessarily free of timeless laws and doctrines. By analogy, human encounter can be conceived as an act of speech operating with the two basic "word-pairs" that determine our attitude toward the world we live in—"I-You" and "I-It." For Buber, the human "I" is never a single "I" but always in relation: "Saying I and saying one of the two basic words are the same" (From *I and Thou,* p. 182 in this volume). In speaking one of the basic words, we determine our relation as one of subject-object ("I-It"), which can be lifted out of time, recorded, and described because it is essentially static, or as one of "meeting" ("I-You"), which must remain in time, for there is no permanence but only "becoming" (*werden*). It is in speaking "I-You" that the "I" becomes "I," and it is in our encounter with the "spoken word" of God that God becomes God. The human condition, which, for Buber, was an essentially interhuman one, is defined by a duality of attitude (*Grundhaltung*) expressed in the basic word-pairs and the creative tension between them. Ontologically, our choice of attitude reflects a form of being. The "I" of "I-It" is not the same as the "I" of "I-You." Just as we cannot live permanently in the "I-You" act of speech, we cannot live authentically in the "I-It" speech of observation. And just as mysticism and ecstasy remove the individual, now dissolved in a cosmic unity, from its social responsibilities, the "response-ability" of the "I," its individuality fully affirmed, becomes the single moral imperative in the social sphere of the interhuman.

One may look at Buber's dialogical philosophy as a logical extension of his antithetical themes of culture/civilization, community/society, and religion/religiosity. The focus on language, however, though a bit blurry compared to the synchronous philosophies of Franz Rosenzweig and Ferdinand Ebner, is a conspicuous turn in Buber's development in the 1920s. Only in the late 1920s, perhaps not untouched by the rise of existentialism and an increasing I-Thou discourse permeating philosophy and Christian theology,[42] did Buber develop his dialogical thought as an area independent, though not detached, from his scholarship in religion.

The shift from a primarily religious to a more philosophical orientation is apparent in both content and form. His essay "Philosophical and Religious World View" (p. 219 in this volume) appeared in 1928; "Religion and Philosophy" (p. 223 in this volume) in 1929; and *Eclipse of God,* Buber's most systematic engagement with twentieth-century philosophy, in 1952. Using an overall philosophical terminology, Buber problematized philosophy, truth, and epistemology, applying dialogical categories. In contrast to *I and Thou,* written in the magical, visionary style of German literary expressionism,[43] Buber's later dialogical writings, *Dialogue* of 1929 (p. 189 in this volume), *The Question to the Single One* of 1936, and *Elements of the Interhuman* of 1954 (p. 214 in this volume), resorted to a relatively unassuming language, combining elements of philosophical existentialism (which Buber, like many other existentialists, rejected), contemporary German philosophy, and of course his own unique linguistic twists. In this capacity, Buber's later writings on dialogue served as clarifications and reinterpretations of the rather poetic *I and Thou,* expanding its social and anthropological dimensions; and similar to most interpretative traditions, it befits Buber to be read backwards.

With regard to Buber's Jewish writings, his appointment at the University of Frankfurt and the shift toward the study of religion and philosophy seemed to be a move away from particular Jewish concerns. Although Buber's appointment was in what would be "Jewish studies" today, his lectures avoided specifically Jewish sources like Rabbinics and liturgy and approached Judaism from the angles of comparative religion, history, or philosophy, but most frequently from a biblical view all of which were perfectly accessible to students of a Christian background.[44]

In these years, Buber emerged both as a biblical scholar and a translator of the Bible. Approached by the young publisher Lambert Schneider in 1925 to revise the existing translations of the "Old Testament," Buber, together with Franz Rosenzweig, undertook the famous *Verdeutschung* of Hebrew Scripture, following a model of recreating the poetic rhythm, stylistic and linguistic peculiarities, and "spokenness" and dialogical quality of the Hebrew original in German. The translation itself was primarily an attempt at reconnecting a largely assimilated Jewish readership, illiterate in Hebrew, with a genuine Hebrew tradition; but it also aimed at correcting the image imprinted on German readers by the still prevalent Luther Bible. With Rosenzweig's untimely death in 1929, Buber continued the project by himself, constantly revising the earlier drafts and printed versions, until it was completed in Jerusalem in 1961.

It is important to remember that Buber's scholarship on the Hebrew Bible also coincided with the rise of National Socialism in Germany. In 1933, the year of Hitler's ascent to power, Buber published his essays, "Biblical Leadership" (p. 33 in this volume) and "Biblical Humanism" (p. 46 in this volume), as well as an excerpt from his translation of Isaiah, "The Consolation of Israel," the first volume of the widely popular Schocken Bücherei. In 1936, a year after the proclamation of the

Nuremberg Laws completing the disfranchisement of Jews in Germany, Buber published a translation of 23 Psalms (*Aus Tiefen rufe ich Dich*), a second, expanded edition of *Kingship of God,* and an essay, "The Man of Today and the Jewish Bible" (p. 51 in this volume). In 1938, the year of *Kristallnacht* (crystal night) and his emigration, Buber published an essay, "The Election of Israel" (p. 23 in this volume). Given this historical context, one must view Buber's biblical scholarship not only as a corollary of his Bible translation but also as a veiled commentary on and intellectual resistance to Nazism. Using the Bible as a source common to Jews and Christian Germans, Buber's essays invoke biblical values against the idols of nationalism, and biblical humanism against the destruction of humanity. Hidden from an all-pervasive censorship, their subtexts served as vehicles of accusation and hope, calling upon a community in fear to resist and remain true to its past: "This stormy night," wrote Buber in 1933, "these shafts of lightning flashing down, this threat of destruction—do not escape from them into a world of logos, of perfected form! Stand fast, hear the word in the thunder, obey, respond!" (Biblical Humanism [1933], p. 50).

In retrospect, Buber's tone of defiance and unswerving adherence to humanistic ideals seemed tragically unwise. But in the years between 1933 and 1938, Buber exercised immense influence on a subculture of Jewish learning that had hitherto been unparalleled.[45] Forced to leave his home in Germany in 1938, Buber immigrated to Palestine and settled in Jerusalem. An outwardly secular but also an antitraditional Jew, albeit with a strong Jewish identity and religious commitment, Buber was barred from teaching religion at the still young Hebrew University of Jerusalem because of a "veto" by a group of Orthodox Jews, who were rightly disconcerted about his radical reinterpretation of Judaism.[46] Buber was offered a position in social philosophy instead, which he filled from 1938 until his retirement in 1951. During that time he became not only the first chairman of sociology but also the first president of the Israel National Academy of Sciences and Humanities. Always vocal and controversial, Buber remained a fixture in Jerusalem who was made an honorary citizen and received birthday greetings from his "friend, admirer, and opponent" David Ben-Gurion, the first prime minister of Israel.[47]

During his appointment at the Hebrew University, two further shifts can be observed in Martin Buber's thought. First, there was a turn toward the study of social philosophy which, quite naturally, followed from Buber's academic teaching and his earlier concerns with the possibility of community. We have seen that Buber's concept of community could not readily be detached from his concept of religiosity. For a short period of time, Buber even toyed with the idea of establishing a group of "Jewish religious socialists" modeled after similar Christian groups, and in April 1928 he and the Swiss Protestant theologian Leonhard Ragaz organized a convention to this effect in Heppenheim, under the heading, "Socialism through Faith" (*Sozialismus aus dem Glauben*) (see Three Theses of a Religious Socialism [1928], p. 258 in this volume). In contrast, Buber's approach to social philosophy at the Hebrew University seemed much more historical, analytical, descriptive, and in line with his editing of *Die Gesellschaft*. But there was also a practical tendency in Buber's academic work, as his student and later eminent Israeli sociologist Shmuel N. Eisenstadt remembers: The students were encouraged to conduct empirical studies on the social structure of the *Yishuv* (the Jewish community in Palestine) and the cooperative settlements (Moshavim and Kibbutzim) to test their validity for authentic human relationships.[48]

In a second, parallel turn, Buber began to develop a philosophical, "integrative" anthropology[49] of his own. *The Problem of Man,* a collection of seminars on the history of philosophical anthropology conducted in 1938 at the Hebrew University, appeared first in Hebrew in 1943.[50] "Distance and Relation" (p. 206 in this volume), which Buber considered the first foundation (*Begründing*) of his anthropology, appeared in 1950; *Man and His Image-Work,* an anthropology of art, in 1955; "What Is Common to All," in 1956; "Guilt and Guilt Feelings," in 1957; and "The Word That Is Spoken," in 1960. Together, these texts form a rather loose segment in Buber's collected works of 1962 under the heading, "Philosophical Anthropology."[51] Significantly, Buber, then 83 years of age, described himself as an anthropological thinker, or philosophical anthropologist, whose work and thought were devoted to an understanding of the "fact of man."[52] The dialogical principle, then, became once more part of a larger methodological framework. Anthropology, the science of man, is now concerned not with human nature and species, not with the "existence" of the individual nor with the fabric of the collective, but with man insofar as man is possible in relation to other beings. "Only the man who realizes in his whole life with his whole being the relations possible to him helps us to know man truly," wrote Buber in 1947.[53] In 1963, Maurice Friedman edited Buber's anthropological essays in English under the title The *Knowledge of Man,* introducing the volume as the completion of the "last and one of the most significant stages in the development of his [Buber's] philosophical thought, and in particular his philosophical anthropology, his study of what is peculiar to man as man."[54] The book, redacted by Buber, appeared in 1965, the year of his death.

There is a third aspect that emerges from Buber's life in Jerusalem. Although Buber had left the Zionist platform decades before, he still remained a Zionist in his own way and a relentless critic of what he deemed Zionist *Realpolitik,* as opposed to his own "*Wirklichkeitszionismus*" (Zionism of reality), in which the category of "realization" still resonated. Hence, it was possible for Buber in 1916 to defend Zionism against the "fictitious Judaism" of liberalism embodied by the Marburg philosopher, Hermann Cohen (see Concepts and Reality [1916], p. 263 in this volume) while, at the same time, to attack the Zionism of a *sacro egoismo* (see Zionism and Nationalism [1929], p. 277 in this volume). In 1925, when the right-wing, militant party of Revisionism was formed under Vladimir Ze'ev Jabotinsky in response to the mounting friction between Arabs and

Jews under the British mandate power, a group of Jewish intellectuals led by Arthur Ruppin founded B'rith Shalom (Peace Association) to promote Arab–Jewish dialogue and understanding "on the basis of absolute political equality of two cultural autonomous peoples."[55] Buber, whose ideas informed much of the German chapter of the association, actively joined B'rith Shalom while still in Germany and later (in 1942) became one of the founding members of *Ichud* (Union), a group associated with the League for Jewish–Arab Rapprochement and Cooperation (which Buber also helped found in 1939); the group promoted a model of cultural, social, political, and economic union between Jews and Arabs—nothing short of a "revival of the whole Semitic world."[56] As such, the *Ichud* rejected outright the partition into separate Jewish and Arab states (models of which were proposed by Victor Jacobson in 1932, the Peel Commission in 1937, and the United Nations in 1947) and also clashed with the Biltmore Program of May 1942 that David Ben-Gurion had initiated to facilitate the mass immigration of Jewish refugees from Europe—an urgent necessity at the time—with effective partition in mind.[57] In May 1948, when the Yishuv, led by David Ben-Gurion, unilaterally proclaimed independence and statehood, Buber revisited the act as one of "national assimilation," mere satisfaction of the "protective" tendency in Zionism, a yearning for sovereignty rather than true independence, and ultimately a blaspheming of the name of Zion (see Zionism and "Zionism" [1948], p. 289 in this volume) Yet, as a Zionist of "*Wirklichkeit*" (reality), Buber was well aware that the war that had broken loose could become a war of national survival at any moment: "Thus against my will I participate in it with my own being, and my heart trembles like that of any other Israeli" (see Zionism and "Zionism" [1948], p. 291). But Buber added: "I cannot, however, be joyful in anticipating victory, for I fear lest the significance of Jewish victory be the downfall of Zionism" (see Zionism and "Zionism" [1948], p. 291). Clutching to the ideal of Hebrew humanism and prophetic history, which were bound together by the reality of an ever new, unpredictable situational encounter, Buber continued to believe in Zionism as a "greater" task and in the possibility of true coexistence between Arabs and Jews until the end of his life.

The question of what is essential in Martin Buber's writings can now be addressed again. We have seen that Buber was a man of extraordinary versatility who continuously reinvented himself and was able to embark on parallel trains of thought. With the formulation of the dialogical principle, Buber became an increasingly systematic, unsystematic thinker, applying the model of dialogue to virtually all areas of thought. On the other hand, as readers of his work, we, too, are tempted to apply the model of dialogue to all of his writings, even before it was created.

As a "philosopher of dialogue" Buber was also introduced to an American audience in the early 1950s. Buber himself visited the United States on three separate lecture trips, once in 1951–1952, then in 1957, and again in 1958. His dialogical philosophy left strong impressions with the Protestant theologian Reinhold Niebuhr, and the young Jewish thinkers Will Herberg and Arthur Cohen, to mention only a few, but also with the psychotherapists Leslie H. Farber and Carl R. Rogers.[58]

For about two decades Martin Buber's ideas were vividly discussed in philosophy departments and divinity schools, together with the reception of existentialist thought and, in fact, frequently as a "Jewish" exponent of it.[59] With the gradual waning of the existentialist mood at American and European universities, however, Buber all but vanished from the platform of academic philosophy while his dialogical writings continued to inform many liberal Christian thinkers, theologians, and interfaith programs in America and Europe.[60] But this development should not obscure the fact that Buber's ideas anticipated and, as an undercurrent, still sustain much of the philosophical discourse on the "Other," human rights, conflict solution, education, and mental therapy. Likewise, Buber's addresses on Judaism have lost none of their appeal for many young Jews in America and still play a critical role for Jewish spirituality and renewal movements in our days.[61]

The current scholarly interest in Buber has shifted from general philosophy to Jewish studies, particularly history. Indeed, the intellectual history of early twentieth century Europe, the history of Zionism, and the history of the State of Israel would be substantially incomplete without reference to Buber's work, as would be the study of Hasidism and biblical criticism. Recent scholarship has made available many earlier sources that had been neglected under the focus on Buber's dialogical period and that can now help us paint a more differentiated image of Buber's thought.[62]

The Buber who emerges at the center of this image is a dynamic thinker of great intellectual elasticity and complexity, shaped by an evolving vision of humanism and humanity, or what might be called normative anthropology. The insight that humanity is an unscripted process of interhuman events was Buber's major contribution to twentieth-century thought. In essence, Buber could be described as an eminent *public intellectual* whose deeply felt, unconventional Jewishness was a source of pride, open-mindedness, and moral commitment, and whose work felt most at home outside the walls of the academy as well as, it should be noted, outside the walls of synagogues.[63]

In this volume, "essential" is understood as a collection of representative writings in the most pronounced areas of Martin Buber's productivity that can be viewed together in a coherent manner. These areas are in thematical rather than historical order: Bible, Hasidism, Judaism and Jewish religiosity, dialogue and anthropology, philosophy and teaching, community, and Zionism. The list is obviously incomplete, for there are also the areas of aesthetics, psychology and psychotherapy, mysticism, and literary interpretation; nor can the plotting of areas be a distinct separation. On the contrary, such a separation would necessarily be at odds with Buber's organic style of thought. Furthermore, since maintaining a certain coherence always involves a process of censorship, many of

Buber's earlier writings that have been mentioned above could not be included, for they are so far removed from the central body of his work that their significance is apparent often only to the specialist. This collection, nonetheless, tries to incorporate some of the quasi-apocryphical texts to the extent that they are consistent and compatible with Buber's mature thought. Many of the sources had to be carefully condensed and reedited. Omitted passages are marked with ellipses ("..."), and significant variants in text and translation (all existing translations have been reviewed) are indicated in the accompanying notes. The format of this volume, however, does not allow it to be a textual-critical edition. An editor's note has been provided where contextual understanding is necessary. Notes that were included by Buber in the original text are marked (M.B.); if they were provided by other editors, the name of the editor will appear in parentheses. The bibliographical information for each selection generally includes the first printing in the original language and the actual English source used for this volume. It should also be noted that the use of "man" for the German *Mensch* in earlier translations generally indicates a gender-inclusive reading.

I would like to thank Judith Buber-Agassi, the executer of the Martin Buber estate, whose initiative and vision have made this collection possible. My thanks to Rick Balkin, our agent, who has represented the book and its author with great knowledge and enthusiasm. I am also grateful to the staff at Palgrave for their professional assistance and conscientious, thoughtful copyediting of the manuscript. To Paul Mendes-Flohr I should express my deep gratitude for his critical and constructive advice in the final stages of the book. I am indebted to my wife, Dalia, for her careful reading of the text, and to our children, Natan and Gidon, whose patience and impatience have made it possible to complete the reader.

Asher D. Biemann
Cambridge, Massachusetts
November 2001

Notes

1. On the concept of *Bildung* among German Jews, see especially George L. Mosse, *German Jews Beyond Judaism* (Bloomington and Cincinnati: Indiana University Press and Hebrew Union College Press, 1985). That Buber was fully aware of this tradition becomes obvious in his essay "Goethe's Concept of Humanity," written for the 1949 Goethe Bicentennial Convocation at Aspen, Colorado ("Das Reinmenschliche," in *Pointing the Way. Collected Essays,* ed. and trans. Maurice Friedman [New York: Harper & Brothers, 1957], pp. 74–80). Since Buber was unable to attend, the essay was read by Ernst Simon, who contributed an essay himself to the convocation, "Goethe und der religiöse Humanismus" (English) in Goethe and the Modern Age, ed. Arnold Bergstrasser (Chicago: Henry Regnery, 1950), pp. 304–25.

2. On Buber's own account of his childhood and heritage, see his "Autobiographical Fragments," in *The Philosophy of Martin Buber* (Library of Living Philosophers, vol. 12), eds. Paul A. Schilpp and Maurice Friedman (La Salle, Ill.: Open Court, 1967), pp. 3–39. For comprehensive biographical

information, see Hans Kohn, *Martin Buber—Sein Werk und seine Zeit. Ein Beitrag zur Geistesgeschichte Mitteleuropas 1880–1930,* with a postscript by Robert Weltsch, "Martin Buber 1930–1960" (Cologne: Joseph Melzer, 1961); Maurice Friedman, *Martin Buber's Life and Work* Detroit: Wayne State University Press, 1988); on Buber's earlier years, see Gilya Gerda Schmidt, *Martin Buber's Formative Years: From German Culture to Jewish Renewal, 1897–1909* (Tuscaloosa and London: University of Alabama Press, 1995); for recent scholarship, see Martin Treml's introduction to the *Martin Buber Werkausgabe,* vol. 1 (Frühe kulturkritische und philosophische Schriften, 1891–1924) (Gütersloh: Gütersloher Verlagshaus, 2001).

3. Cf. Martin Buber, "My Way to Hasidism," in *Hasidism and Modern Man,* ed. and trans. Maurice Friedman (New York: Horizon Press, 1958), p. 55. Buber stopped putting on his *tefillin* (small ritual leather boxes worn during prayer) at age 14 and never returned to them. See Buber's letter to Franz Rosenzweig of 1 October 1922, translated in Franz Rosenzweig, *On Jewish Learning* (New York: Schocken, 1965), p. 110.

4. Beginning in 1905 with "Der Rabbi und sein Sohn—Eine Legende, dem Rabbi Nachman von Bratzlaw nacherzählt" (*Ost und West* 5, July–August 1905).

5. Buber enrolled at the University of Vienna in 1896 but went on to study in Leipzig (winters 1897–98 and 1898–99), then Zurich (summer 1899), Berlin (winters 1899–1900 and 1900–01), and then again in Vienna, where he graduated in 1904.

6. On the reception of Buber's Hasidic writings, see Paul Mendes-Flohr, "Begegnungen und Vergegnungen: Die Rezeption Martin Bubers im Judentum," in *Martin Buber (1878–1965). Internationales Symposium zum 20. Todestag,* eds. Werner Licharz and Heinz Schmidt (Arnoldshainer Texte, vol. 57), vol. 1 (Frankfurt/M.: Haag & Herchen, 1989), p. 242. Along with Bloch and Rathenau, Mendes-Flohr mentions Georg Lukàcs, as well as the American counterculture icon Norman Mailer.

7. Hasidism indeed became a preferred subject for young Jewish rebels, as well as neo-Romantic intellectuals at that time. As early as 1862, Moses Hess referred to Hasidism as a "transition from mediaeval Judaism to a regenerated Judaism" and expected an incalculable "great good which will result from a combination of Chasidism with the national movement." See Moses Hess, *Rome and Jerusalem, the Last Nationalist Question,* trans. Meyer Waxman (London and Nebraska: University of Nebraska Press, 1995 [reprint]), p. 247f., Note 5. Likewise, the historian Simon Dubnow and the revolutionary Hebrew publicist Micha Yosef Berdichevski began to value Hasidism in their work at about the same time as Buber did. Berdichevski, in fact, contacted Buber about a "society for the collection of Jewish legends and fables (see letter to Buber, 28 February 1909, in *Martin Buber. Briefwechsel aus sieben Jahrzehnten,* ed. Grete Schaeder [Heidelberg: Lambert Schneider, 1973] [henceforth referred to as *Briefwechsel I, II, or III*], vol. 1, p. 273). Buber also intended to coedit a *Corpus Hasidicum* with the Hebrew writer Samuel Yosef Agnon, which was, however, abandoned after Agnon's collection of Hebrew sources went up in flames in 1924. The preface to Buber's *The Great Maggid* (1923), however, still credits Agnon with supplying at least some of the material. Note also S. Schechter, *Die Chassidim. Eine Studie über jüdische Mystik* (Leipzig: Jüdischer Verlag, 1909) and Samuel A. Horodezky's *Religiöse Strömungen im Judentum, mit besonderer Berücksichtigung des Chassidismus* (Bern: E. Bircher, 1920).

On the resurgent interest in Hasidism, see also Paul Mendes-Flohr: "Fin de Siècle Orientalism, the *Ostjuden* and the Aesthetics of Self-Affirmation," in *Divided Passions: Jewish Intellectuals and the Experience of Modernity* (Detroit: Wayne State University Press, 1991); Michael Brenner: *The Renaissance of Jewish Culture in Weimar Germany* (New Haven and London: Yale University Press, 1996). See also the essay by Barbara Galli, "Nathan Birnbaum's Reaction to Buber's Retelling of rabbi Nachman of Bratslav's Tales," in *The Journal of Jewish Thought & Philosophy,* vol. 10, no. 2 (2001): 313–39.

8. Cf. Buber, "My Way to Hasidism," p. 57.

9. On the intellectual roots of Buber's Jewish Renaissance, see Paul Mendes-Flohr, "Zarathustra's Apostle: Martin Buber and the Jewish Renaissance," in *Nietzsche and Jewish Culture,* ed. Jacob Golomb (London and New York: Routledge, 1997); also Asher D. Biemann, "The Problem of Tradition and Reform in Jewish Renaissance and Renaissancism," in *Jewish Social Studies* 8, no. 1 (Spring 2002): 58–87.

10. "Referat," *Stenographisches Protokoll der Verhandlungen des III. Zionistenkongresses,* Basel, 15–18 August 1899 (Vienna: Eretz Israel, 1899). Quoted in Kohn, *Martin Buber,* p. 27. This idea was especially emulated by the members of the Prague student group Bar Kochba, where Buber delivered his first addresses on Judaism (1909–11). In 1911 Hugo Bergman, on whose initiative

Buber had been invited, proposed the idea of a "greater Zionism" that could form "a living community to which nothing human is alien" ("Größerer Zionismus," in Bergman, *Jawne und Jerusalem. Gesammelte Aufsätze* [Berlin: Jüdischer Verlag, 1919], p. 10). In an essay of 1918, he writes, "If the Jewish movement ought to be more than a multiplication of existing nationalisms, if it ought to become a force in human history, then it must aim for a Jewish worldview." (*Jerubbaal: Zeitschrift der jüdischen Jugend* 1 [1918–19], p. 38). Meir Wiener, in the same publication, demands an "enlightened [*geläuterte*] Zionist worldview" (ibid., p. 71). A few years later Max Brod and Felix Weltsch collaborated on a volume entitled *Zionism as Worldview* (*Zionismus als Weltanschauung* [Mährisch/Ostrau: R. Färber, 1925]).

11. On the Democratic Fraction, see Gideon Shimoni, *Zionist Ideology* (Hanover and London: Brandeis University Press, 1995), p. 213; 281f.; Michael Berkowitz, *Zionist Culture and Western European Jewry before the First World War* (Chapel Hill and London: University of North Carolina Press, 1996), p. 43f.
12. See, for example, Buber's "Ways to Zionism" of 1901, in *The First Buber: Youthful Zionist Writings of Martin Buber*, ed. and trans. Gilya Gerda Schmidt (New York: Syracuse University Press, 1999), pp. 105-9.
13. On Buber's Zionism, see Paul Mendes-Flohr, "Das Volk des Bundes und seine politisch-moralische Verantwortung. Bubers Zionismus und der Staat Israel," in *Martin Buber (1878–1965)*, vol. 2, eds. Licharz and Schmidt, pp. 203-21. That Buber's attitude toward nationalism was not one of clearly defined national humanism until after World War I was indicated by Hans Kohn (cf. *Martin Buber*, p. 163) and demonstrated by Paul Mendes-Flohr, who sees in Gustav Landauer's harsh criticism of Buber's initially enthusiastic response to the war (shared with many other German Jews) a turning point in Buber's attitude toward nationalism and Zionism (cf. Paul Mendes-Flohr, *Von der Mystik zum Dialog. Martin Bubers geistige Entwicklung bis hin zu "Ich und Du"* [Königstein/Ts: Jüdischer Verlag, 1978]. English: *From Mysticism to Dialogue* [Detroit: Wayne State University Press, 1989], especially chapter 5). An article on Buber's early Zionism is Martina Urban, "In Search of a 'Narrative Anthology': Reflections on an Unpublished Buber-Manuscript," in *Jewish Studies Quarterly* 7 (2000): 252–88.
14. Martin Buber: "Jewish Renaissance" (1901), in *The First Buber*, ed. Schmidt, p. 32; 34.
15. See also Brenner, *The Renaissance of Jewish Culture*, p. 220.
16. "Kultur und Zivilisation—Einige Gedanken zu diesem Thema," *Kunstwart* 4, no. 15 (May 1901).
17. "Al Mahuta shel ha-Tarbut" (Hebrew, 1943), in Martin Buber, *Pnei Adam: Bechinot be-Anthropologia pilosofit* (Jerusalem: Mosad Bialik, 1962), p. 378.
18. On Buber's impact on the creation of Jewish art, see Gavriel D. Rosenfeld, "Defining 'Jewish Art' in Ost und West, 1901–1908. A Study in the Nationalisation of Jewish Culture," in *Leo Baeck Institute Yearbook*, 39 (1994): pp. 83–110.
19. Cf. Mendes-Flohr, *From Mysticism to Dialogue*, p. 11.
20. Buber, "My Way to Hasidism," p. 57.
21. See Ulrich Linse, ed., *Zurück o Mensch zur Mutter Erde: Landkommunen in Deutschland 1890–1933* (Munich: Deutscher Taschenbuch Verlag, 1983).
22. Heinrich and Julius Hart, *Das Reich der Erfüllung*, no. 2 (Leipzig: Eugen Diederichs, 1900), p. 92. Quoted in Kohn, *Martin Buber*, p. 294.
23. "Alte und neue Gemeinschaft," manuscript; now, Paul R. Flohr and Bernard Susser in *Association of Jewish Studies Review* 1 (1976): pp. 50–6. In English translation as appendix to Mendes-Flohr, *From Mysticism to Dialogue*.
24. Martin Buber, "Preface to 'Die Gesellschaft'," in *On Intersubjectivity and Cultural Creativity*, ed. and introduction by Eisenstadt (Chicago and London: Chicago University Press, 1992), p. 94f.
25. Buber, "Autobiographical Fragments," p. 26.
26. Ludwig Feuerbach, *Grundsätze der Philosophie der Zukunft* (Zurich and Winterthur: Verlag des literarischen Comptoirs, 1843), Preface.
27. Martin Buber, "Ein Wort über Nietzsche und die Lebenswerte," *Die Kunst im Leben* 1, no. 2 (December 1900): 13; also, "Zur Geschichte des dialogischen Prinzips," in Martin Buber, *Werke I* (Schriften zur Philosophie) (Munich: Kösel and Lambert Schneider, 1962), p. 291f.
28. Cf. Hasidism and Modern Man (1956) (pp. 87 and 92 in this volume).
29. Cf. Jewish Religiosity (1923) (p. 123 in this volume).
30. Cf. Georg Simmel, *Die Religion* (Die Gesellschaft, Band II) (Frankfurt/M.: Rütten & Loening, 1906).
31. Jewish Religiosity (1923) (p. 121 in this volume).
32. Ibid., p. 115.

33. Ibid., p. 122.
34. On the Buber-Rosenzweig debate on Jewish law, see Benny Kraut, "The Approach to Jewish Law of Martin Buber and Franz Rosenzweig," *Tradition* 12 (1972): 49–71; Zvi E. Kurzweil, "Three Views on Revelation and Law," *Judaism* 9 (Fall 1960): 291–98. On Buber's specific view on *Halakha* see Gershom Scholem, "Martin Buber's Conception of Judaism," in *On Jews and Judaism in Crisis. Selected Essays,* ed. Werner Dannhauser (New York: Schocken Books, 1976), pp. 126–71; Arthur Cohen, "Revelation and Law. Reflections on Martin Buber's Views on Halakha," *Judaism* 1 (July 1952): 250–56.
35. As early as 1903, Buber and Chaim Weizmann had planned to edit a journal called *Der Jude* (The Jew), but the project did not materialize. In an announcement of 1904, the objectives were outlined: "To the present generation, which experiences the people in its heart, Judaism is not a past that has come to a conclusion, not an ossified formula, but the living peoplehood (*Volkstum*) in its entire breadth and depth, in the multiplicity of all its forms and expressions.... An attempt is to be made to demonstrate the destiny and nature (*Bestimmung*) of the [Jewish] people and, based on this knowledge, to ignite its will for the future" (quoted in Hans Kohn, *Martin Buber,* p. 297). It should be noted that a journal, *The Jew,* already existed in the nineteenth century as Gabriel Riesser's emancipatory organ, *Der Jude. Periodische Blätter der Religion und Gewissensfreiheit,* which appeared from 1831 to 1833.
36. *Beiträge zur Geschichte des Individuationsproblems bei Nicolaus von Kues und Jakob Böhme,* unpublished and incomplete manuscript, Martin Buber Archives (Jerusalem), Ms.Var. 350. 2/aleph. An excerpt was published through Franz Rosenzweig in *Aus unbekannten Schriften. Festgabe für Martin Buber zum 50. Geburtstag* (Berlin: Lambert Schneider, 1928). For an analysis of the dissertation, see Mendes-Flohr, *From Mysticism to Dialogue.*
37. Cf. Grete Schaeder, "Martin Buber: Ein biographischer Abriß," in *Briefwechsel I,* p. 22.
38. The position was first offered to Frankfurt Rabbi Nehemia Nobel, and then, upon Nobel's sudden death in 1922, to the young Jewish philosopher and director of the Frankfurt Lehrhaus, Franz Rosenzweig, whose illness, however, prevented him from accepting it. As an entirely secular Jew, Buber was not immediately ratified by the local Jewish community. On the controversy around Buber's appointment, see Willy Schottroff, "Martin Buber an der Universität Frankfurt (1923–1933)," in *Martin Buber (1878–1965),* vol. 1, eds. Licharz and Schmidt, p. 49f. On the title "Schriftsteller," see p. 65, note 5.
39. For a list of lectures Buber delivered at Frankfurt, see ibid., p. 20f.
40. In Buber's own testimony. See "Zur Geschichte des dialogischen Prinzips," in *Das Dialogische Prinzip* (Heidelberg: Lambert Schneider, 1984), p. 308 (English as afterword in *Between Man and Man,* ed. Maurice Friedmann, trans. Ronald G. Smith [New York: Macmillan, 1965], p. 210). The first edition of *I and Thou* included a postscript by Buber, probably to clarify his place between two other works of similar ideas—Franz Rosenzweig's *Star of Redemption* and Ferdinand Ebner's *The Word and the Spiritual Realities* (both of 1921)—dating the conception of his work to spring 1916 and the first complete draft to fall 1919. The book was published de facto in December 1922. In January 1919, Buber shared the idea of a five-volume project with Hugo Bergmann (cf. Martin Buber, *Briefwechsel II,* no. 17; also ibid., no. 81; see also Schottroff, "Martin Buber an der Universität Frankfurt," p. 26f.). On the question as to whether and to what extent Buber was familiar with Rosenzweig's and Ebner's work before he wrote the final version of *I and Thou* see Rivka Horwitz, *Buber's Way to "I and Thou": The Development of Martin Buber's Thought and his "Religion as Presence" Lectures* (Philadelphia, New York, Jerusalem: Jewish Publication Society, 1988), p. 133ff. Also *Briefwechsel II,* p. 54f., note 1.
41. On the Jewish sources of *I and Thou* see Emil Fackenheim, "Universal and Jewish Aspects of the I-Thou philosophy," in *Jewish Philosophers and Jewish Philosophy,* ed. Michael L. Morgan (Bloomington: Indiana University Press, 1996), pp. 75–88.
42. In addition to Franz Rosenzweig and the Catholic philosopher Ferdinand Ebner (see Note 40 above), dialogical conceptions were developed in the 1920s and 1930s also by the Protestant thinkers Hans Ehrenberg, Eugen Rosenstock-Huessy, Friedrich Gogarten, Karl Heim, Emil Brunner, the Catholic philosopher Gabriel Marcel; then Theodor Litt, Karl Löwith, Ernst Grisebach, Karl Jaspers, Karl Barth, and Mikhail Bakhtin.
43. Referring to *I and Thou,* Buber acknowledged that he wrote "in an overpowering inspiration" at the expense of exactness ("Replies to my Critics," in *Philosophy of Martin Buber,* p. 706). Walter Kaufmann, in his essay, "Bubers Fehlschläge und sein Triumph" (in Johanan Bloch and Haim

Gordon, eds., *Martin Buber—Bilanz seines Denkens* [Freiburg: Herder, 1983], p. 28), charges the book with the "oracle-like tone of a false prophet."
44. Exceptions were his tutorials on Maimonides, Aggadic, and Hasidic texts. See Schottroff, "Buber an der Universität Frankfurt," p. 20f.
45. See Rivka Horwitz, "Buber als Lehrer und Erzieher der deutschen Juden zur Zeit des Nationalsozialismus," in *Martin Buber (1878–1965)*, vol. 1, eds. Licharz and Schmidt, pp. 96–115.
46. Cf. Robert Weltsch, "Martin Buber 1930–1960," in Hans Kohn, *Martin Buber*, p. 450. On Buber's life in Jerusalem see also Schalom ben Chorin, "Martin Buber in Jerusalem," in *Martin Buber 1878–1978*, ed. Wolfgang Zink (Bonn: Hohwacht, 1978), p. 95f.
47. Ben-Gurion to Buber (5 February 1963), in *Briefwechsel II*, p. 572.
48. See Eisenstadt's introduction to *On Intersubjectivity and Cultural Objectivity* (Chicago and London: Chicago University Press, 1992), pp. 5, 17.
49. On Buber's anthropological method (integrative anthropology), see *Philosophical Interrogations*, eds. Sidney and Beatrice Rome (New York, Chicago, San Francisco: Holt, Rinehart, and Winston 1964), p. 59.
50. *Ba'ayat ha-Adam—Iyunim be-Toldoteiha* (Tel Aviv: Machbarot le-sifrut, 1943). English as *Between Man and Man* (London: Routledge & K. Paul, 1947; New York: Macmillan, 1965).
51. Cf. Martin Buber, *Werke*, vol. 1 (Schriften zur Philosophie) (München and Heidelberg: Kösel and Lambert Schneider, 1962), p. 409f.
52. Cf. Martin Buber, "Replies to my Critics," p. 690. A preliminary version of Buber's "Replies" was first published in 1961.
53. Martin Buber, *Between Man and Man* (New York: Macmillan, 1965), p. 199.
54. Martin Buber, *The Knowledge of Man*, ed. Maurice Friedman (London: George Allen & Unwin, 1965), p. 11.
55. B'rith Shalom: Statutes, in *A Land of Two Peoples: Martin Buber on Jews and Arabs*, with commentary by ed. Paul Mendes-Flohr (New York: Oxford University Press, 1983), p. 74f.
56. "Declaration of the Association 'Union' (Ichud)" (September 1942), in *A Land of Two Peoples*, p. 149.
57. See Buber's "Dialogue on the Biltmore Program" of October 1944, in *A Land of Two Peoples*, pp. 161–64.
58. On Buber's trips to America and his influence, see Robert Weltsch, "Martin Buber 1930–1960," p. 461f.; Maurice Friedman, *Martin Buber's Life and Work, Later Years*, p. 184f.; Paul Mendes-Flohr, "Martin Buber's Reception among Jews," *Modern Judaism* 6, no. 2 (May 1986): 111–26.
59. Most prominently, Malcolm L. Diamond, *Martin Buber: Jewish Existentialist* (New York and Evanston: Harper & Row, 1960). See also the discussion of Buber in Paul Roubiczek, *Existentialism—For and Against* (London and New York: Cambridge University Press, 1964), pp. 139–60; and Jean Wahl, "Martin Buber and the Philosophies of Existence," in *Philosophy of Martin Buber*, pp. 475–510. Will Herberg, in *Judaism and Modern Man* (New York: Farrar & Straus, 1951), confessed that he owed his "existentialist approach" to Buber. Eugene Borowitz, too, places Buber, together with Rosenzweig, in the context of religious existentialism (*Choices in Modern Jewish Thought. A Partisan Guide* [West Orange, N.J.: Behrman House, 1983], pp. 143–65).
60. Buber's influence on Protestant theology extended from Friedrich Gogarten, Emil Brunner, Karl Heim, to Dietrich Bonheoffer, Rudolf Bultmann, and Paul Tillich. The Swiss theologian Hans Urs von Balthasar and the German educator and, later, psychotherapist Wilhelm Michel, are prominent examples on the Catholic side. Significantly, in 1966, Buber appears in the series *Makers of Modern Contemporary Theology*, "designed to introduce laymen and theologians who dominate Christian thought today" (Richmond, Va.: John Knox Press, 1966) in a volume written by Ronald Gregor Smith, the first English translator of *I and Thou*.
61. Michael Lerner, for instance, makes extensive use of Buber's essay "Renewal of Judaism" in his book, *Jewish Renewal: A Path to Healing and Transformation* (New York: Harper, 1995), p. vif. On Buber's influence on liberal Jewish movements in America see, Joshua Haberman, "Martin Buber and Reform Judaism," *European Judaism* 12, no. 2 (winter 1978); and Yitzchak Ahren and Jack Nusan Porter, "Martin Buber and American Counterculture," *Judaism* 29, no. 3 (summer 1980).
62. For reference to works see the Bibliography at the end of this volume.
63. Hence, an anthology entitled "Buber for Atheists" (*Buber für Atheisten*, ed. Thomas Reichert [Gerlingen: Lambert Schneider 1996]) does not seem out of place.

PART I
Bible

The Election of Israel: A Biblical Inquiry (1938)

In the prophecies of Amos, the man who forecast a devastating storm under the clear historical skies of Samaria, we find two passages (Amos 3:2 and 9:7) that seem to contradict each other.... In reality, the verses complement one another: Each of the two gains its truth only in connection with the other.

Interpretation must begin with the second. "Are ye not as the children of the Ethiopians unto me, O children of Israel? Have not I brought up Israel out of the land of Egypt, and the Philistines from Caphtor, and Aram from Kir?" As a historical people, Israel enjoys no precedence over any other. Like Israel, the other peoples were all wanderers and settlers; they all came "up" from a land of want and servitude into their present homeland. The one God, the Redeemer and Leader of the peoples, strode before all of them upon their way—even the hostile neighboring peoples—protecting them by His might. He guided their steps, gave them power, let them "inherit" the soil of a people that had been ruined by its sins and abandoned by history.[1] Some of them may have felt the guiding force and addressed it in prayer by the name of a tribal god, whereas others became only dimly and uncertainly aware of what was happening to them. Yet during that early period they shared a common formative destiny. The *national* universalism of the first of the literary prophets teaches that, historically, Israel enjoys no precedence over the others.

However, "You only have I known of all the families of the earth; therefore I will visit upon you all your iniquities." "Know" (*yada*), in its precise biblical sense (only as a result of which the verb can be used to designate a union of love between a man and a woman), means that the knowing being draws the known out of the abundance of creatures and that a particular and exclusive relationship is established between the two of them.[2] The kind of relationship that is intended here is told us by the second part of the sentence beginning with "therefore": Its content is established by just this relationship. "Visit upon" (*paqad*) in its precise sense means that someone is given what he deserves—either good or ill, reward or punishment. Israel alone has God set into such a relationship with Him that it can fail in this relationship and that all its failings are judged and punished in accordance with this relationship. As we learn from the great speech of rebuke (Amos 1:3–2:3), the other peoples must also atone for the historical iniquities they have committed in their national lives. But *their* faithlessness (*pesha*) consists in their pridefully doing evil to *one another* when they were put into their new lands to live together peacefully. Israel alone can at the same time offend against *God* by repudiating His teaching (Torah), for Israel alone has received it (Amos 2:4). Only Israel, during its wanderings, learned through revelation that its guiding power was not *its* God but *God:* the "God of hosts" (nine times in Amos), who guides the hosts of the cosmic powers as He guides the hosts of Israel, who as Creator also creates the spirit of man and as Revealer tells him what His intention is (Amos 4:13). However, this revelation did not befall Israel as a noncommitting announcement of the state of things but as entry into a *berith* with this God, into a covenant, a bond, an unconditionally committing union with Him. Historically, Israel enjoys no precedence over the others; superhistorically, it has precedence over them in this covenant, this subjection, this unconditional commitment in all commissions and omissions. In consequence thereof, any offense against the *berith* is "visited upon" it. That is the election of Israel. Only the call to a new generation leads out of the unconditionality of the judgment on the heaped-up offense: "Hate evil, and love the good, and establish justice in the gate; it may be that the Lord, the God of hosts, will be gracious unto the remnant of Joseph" (Amos 5:15).

When God addresses the shepherd Moses from the Burning Bush of Sinai (Exod. 3), He first reveals to him that He is the God of the Fathers (Exod. 3:6). But then He begins the speech in which He sends Moses forth with the words, "I have surely seen the affliction of *my people* (*ammi*) that are in Egypt" (Exod. 3:7), and He finishes it with the words, ". . . that thou mayest bring forth *my people* the children of Israel out of Egypt!" (Exod. 3:10). Repetition at the beginning and end of a speech calls special attention to the significance of a word as a "key word."[3] For the first time since the promises to the Fathers, Scripture has God speaking about the people, and for the very first time about them already existing. The covenant has not yet been made, the people have not yet come "to Him" (Exod. 18:5), the encounter has not occurred; and yet, in anticipation, He already calls it His own, He already binds Himself to it.

But the dialogue at the Burning Bush continues, and the first key word, *ammi,* is followed by a second, which is brought into much sharper prominence than the first. In reply to Moses's objection that he is too weak and insignificant for such a mission (Exod. 3:11), God answers: "*Ki ehyeh imakh,* certainly I will be there with thee" (Exod. 3:12). This *ehyeh im* [I will be with], as assurance of God's direct support, recurs in two places (Exod. 3:12 and 4:15), and between them (Exod. 3:14) the word *ehyeh* is spoken another three times to reveal the meaning of the mysterious name of God. He who speaks the *ehyeh* to you, who promises you that He will be there with you, who is with you wherever you are—He is the God of the Fathers, whose name Abraham called out throughout the land of Canaan when he built his altars there.

But the assurance is decisively limited so that no security can be gained from it. *Ehyeh asher ehyeh* is what it says: "I shall be there as whom [or however] I shall be there," God will be there, but He reserves to His will the manner and the action of His presence at any given time.[4] That is, you, my people, need not despair, God announces to Israel, for I am with you. But you may not forget your responsibility and rely on your being my people and on my being with you. For as soon as you do that, you are no longer my people and my being with you will turn into consuming fire. Thus, it happens, in fact, after each transgression of the people. And immediately after the first—the sin of the golden calf—it happens in a piercingly clear pronouncement. No longer "my people," says God in His remonstrance to Moses (Exod. 32:7–10); rather, "your people" (v. 7), and, scornfully, "this people" (v. 9): It is no longer His people, and the divine presence henceforth means destruction (v. 10). Only when Moses pleads with God to remember His oath of promise and repeats "your people" (Exod. 32:11–12), does God let Himself be moved to partial forbearance (Exod. 32:14, cf. Exod. 32:35), and the narrator may once again call Israel the people of God (v. 14).

And again it is the prophet—the interpreter of the great dialogue between the divine and the human, which is called history—who expresses the message in its complete form. The marriage that Hosea is commanded to enter into with a harlot figuratively represents the marriage of God with "the land" (Hos. 1:2). The last child of that union is called *lo ammi*, ("not my people"), for the word of God that commanded the giving of the name sounded thus: "You are not my people and I am not *ehyeh* to you." The statement refers to the two key words of the Burning Bush speeches. Their *ammi* is voided by this *lo ammi*, their *ehyeh* by this *lo ehyeh*; that is, you are no longer my people and so my non-voidable being there is not a guiding and protecting being with you—no longer a standing by you. In the divine response to the enormous offenses of the people, God's *ehyeh*, His bond, is dissolved and rendered inoperative by His *asher ehyeh*, His awful freedom.

And yet, even Hosea, like Amos, ends with a promise of redemption (unquestionably genuine). Amos closes with "I will turn the captivity of my people Israel" (Amos 9:14), and Hosea, with "I will heal their *turnings* away" (Hos. 14:5). The crucial presupposition is stated by Hosea: "*Turn* to Him!" (Hos. 14:3).

The designation "my people" is not the most exalted we find. Again, it is a prophet who announces the significance of the story of the Exodus: "Out of Egypt I called my son" (Hos. 11:1).

This divine word, too, refers to one in the Exodus story itself: "My first-born son is Israel" (Exod. 4:22).

What does this birthright mean? If one wants to picture the nations as God's children, then Israel surely cannot count as first born since it was not even in existence when the nations were divided after the Tower of Babel. Therefore, only an act of divine favor can be meant. For not only can God elevate a person to be His "son" by an act of divine adoption (2 Sam. 7:14; Ps. 2:7), He can also make him His "firstborn!" (Ps. 89:28), with special duties and privileges—and so likewise His people. But once again, what does this act mean in relation to Israel? What duties and privileges does it confer upon it?

For this, too, we have a prophetic explanation. Jeremiah says, "Israel is the Lord's hallowed portion (*qodesh,* selected for God), His first fruits of the increase! all that devour him shall be held guilty, evil shall come upon them" (Jer. 2:3). The offering to God of the earliest yield of corn, wine, and oil is called "first fruits" (*reshit*). It is a part selected from the whole for a sacred purpose, a hallowed portion. What is meant by the prophet's designating Israel as such?

To understand it properly we must peer into the depths of the picture. God receives whatever has been harvested first, and that is Israel. Why does it count as having been harvested first? There must be some special significance. If something is harvested first, it would no doubt be for the special reason that it ripened first. But had Israel already ripened in the early period of which the prophet is speaking? Was there already in the world of nations—for only this world can be the whole increase, the fruits of which are mentioned—a part that was worthy of being presented to God? The whole story of the Exodus is evidence to the contrary. The designation of Israel as *qodesh,* as *reshit,* manifestly cannot be based on the past but only on the destiny that was announced to it in its early period. Because of its destiny (which thus far it has not attained) Israel is sanctified first fruits; God has chosen it for that purpose.

This election, however, did not occur for the first time at Horeb. Like Jeremiah in his mother's womb, so Israel was "known" by God before it had yet been born. The time in which it was planted is the period after the division of the nations (Gen. 11). At that time it was planted to become *reshit:* beginning and preparing to fulfill the purpose of the human seed. At that time the as yet unborn Israel was elevated to become the "first-born son," with an office and a privilege. We can now move ahead to an understanding of what this office and this privilege were.

Endowed with the divine image as a sign of his delegated authority, man in the beginning was set upon the earth to rule it and all living things in the name of God (Gen. 1:27f.). The gift of the *zelem* (God's image, Gen. 1:27) and the delegation of the power to govern [*statthalterliche Gewalt*] belong together. God desires to rule over the earth through man; the second creation story presents this when it has man, not God, give the animals the proper names that express and establish their essence

(Gen. 2:19f.). But man is disobedient and faithless and he is expelled from his seat as a "delegate." And yet his office is not taken away from him; the path of toil upon which he is sent (Gen. 3:17ff.) should manifestly guide him in learning to fulfill it. But mankind in exile fails the second precondition of the office as well: harmony with one another. The story of the exile begins with fratricide, and the earth is filled with iniquity (Gen. 6:11). The Flood washes away this generation; from those that are saved a new humanity is to arise, but it fails like the first. To be sure, men now combine, but only for defiance and rebellion against the Lord who had intended for them the office of ruling in His stead. What they want is clear: not to serve as delegated governors upon earth but to take their places in heaven—and themselves, through magical power (that is the meaning of "name" in Gen. 11:4), rule the world. This, their perverse harmony, is now destroyed; this united multitude is severed into nations of different languages and thus scattered over the face of the earth. No longer is a single humanity possible. Just as human history began with the fratricide, so the history of nations began with the Tower of Babel; humanity can now be composed, if at all, only of nations, no longer of individual men. Even now man is not divested of his office, but he will be able to fulfill it only when the nations, preserving their irrevocable division, yet bind themselves together in a single humanity, which realizes God's dominion upon earth through power delegated to man.

How shall this new situation come about? One people must set an example of harmony in obedience to God for the others. From a mere nation, from the biological and historical unity of a *goy* (cf. *geviyah:* corpse, body), it must become a community, a true *am* (cf. *im:* [joined to...]; *umma* [side by side]) whose members are connected not merely by origin and common lot but are also bound to one another by just and loving participation in a common life. But it can do this only as an *am elohim,* a people of God, in which all are bound to one another through their common tie to a divine center. A pseudocommunity that lacks the center (Gen. 11:6) must fall apart. For men become brothers only as they become children of one father. That fratricide and that building of the Tower of Babel can only be atoned for and overcome together.

But this people, which is to be a living example to the other peoples, cannot be one of those that was dispersed; none of them is fit for the new task. A new people must arise.

In the cosmic hour after the Tower of Babel, God calls to the man "Abram" (Gen. 12:1) and brings him forth from his land, his kindred, and his father's house, from all ties to people and national life, into a new land that he may there beget a new people. Its task is told to him when the people he is to engender is addressed in his, "Abram's," name: From the blessing with which it is blessed is to come a blessing. "Be thou a blessing!..." (Gen. 12:2) God, who "knows" Abraham, is aware that Abraham will bid the people he begets to adhere to the way of the God who strides before them by its practice of righteousness and its proof of worth (Gen. 18:19).

The principle of the imitation of God is here established decisively for all time. This is what becoming a blessing for the other peoples means: setting a living example of a true people, a community. At the turn of the epoch, the prophet reflects upon the overwhelming imperative. Israel has not yet become a blessing, but he, Isaiah, does not repeat the imperative. Whatever he may demand of the people, he expects the fulfillment of becoming a blessing from grace. "In that day" little Israel, between the two world powers, will become "a blessing in the midst of the earth" (Isa. 19:24).

In a later, postexilic hour, the stirring memory of that command to Abraham again seizes a prophet. Israel has not become a blessing but a curse among the nations, yet the election must be fulfilled. The word of God breaks out from the prophet's lips: "So will I save you, and ye shall be a blessing!" (Zech. 8:13).

Jewish faith knows no "salvation by works alone." It teaches the mysterious *meeting* of human repentance and divine mercy.

With the words from the Burning Bush, "My people—I will be with thee," God confirms His covenant with the patriarchs as progenitors of the people that has now come to be.... Now Israel is to be brought from Egypt and come to "this mountain." Here, with the sealing of a final covenant, it is to "become of service to God" (Exod. 3:12); it is to quit the service (*avodah*) of the oppressor and enter the service (*avodah*) of the Redeemer.

Israel camps at Sinai, opposite the mountain (Exod. 19:2). God and His people stand opposite one another. Moses "goes up to God" (Exod. 19:3). And now God calls out to him the all-embracing message. Thus, He commands him to say to "the house of Jacob": "Ye have seen what I did unto the Egyptians, and how I bore you on eagles' wings, and brought you unto myself. Now therefore, hearken unto my voice indeed, and keep my covenant, then ye shall be mine own special treasure from among all peoples; for all the earth is mine, but ye shall be unto me a royal dominion of *kohanim,* a holy *goy*" (Exod. 19:4f.).

An explanation of some of the vocabulary in the passage is indispensable:

> (1) "Unto myself" *(elai)* does not mean "to my abode" (that would be expressed differently); rather, to meeting with me: God was indeed present in Egypt with Moses (cf., e.g., Exod. 5:22), but the meeting with the *people* was to follow only at Sinai.
> (2) Special treasure *(segulah)* is a possession set apart from the common property of the tribe for special disposition and use.
> (3) *Mamlakhah* does not mean "kingdom" let alone "government," but rather designates the unmediated sphere of the king's dominion, in which he announces his will.
> (4) *Kohanim* here does not mean "priests," rather (as, e.g., 2 Sam. 8:18; 1 Kings 4:5) the servants who "stand ready" to carry out the orders of the king—his adjutants through whom he announces his will.[5]

(5) The peoples are spoken of here, not in a biological sense but in a sociological one, as *ammim,* for in *this* sense Israel is chosen from among them. But Israel is to be holy *(qadosh)* as a *goy,* that is, with its whole biologically determined corporeality. (For this reason Franz Rosenzweig[6] was even inclined to translate here, "a holy body," which, however, might have aroused alien associations.) Where, later, the text proceeds from this point (as often in Deuteronomy), it avoids the ambiguity of the mystery and says "*am qadosh.*"

(6) For *qadosh* it is necessary to proceed from the passages dealing with the imitation of the holiness of God (Lev. 11:44f. inter alia). Here it designates a withdrawal that must not, however, be understood as a separation: As God is withdrawn from the world and yet is present and active in it, so is Israel to be in its relation to the surrounding nations; it is to be a *berakhah,* a "blessing" to them.

...

The Book of Deuteronomy, in particular, has assumed the task of elucidating the eagle passage in the powerful ancient *midrash* that the Bible presents. In four sermons and introductions to laws (Deut. 4:1–40; 7:1–11; 14:1f.; 26:16–19) it interprets the passage and especially the concept of "special treasure." It is a unique and incomparable thing, it says, that God has brought you forth unto Himself, has torn this people *(goy)* out of the bowels of a people *(goy),* out of the midst of the nations, has brought you out of the iron furnace of Egypt where you were smelted into suitable metal, and has now taken you as the people of His possession[7] and set you under His law. But not because of your eminence and importance has He chosen you—for you are of little consequence (Deut. 7:7)—rather out of gracious love. He has raised you unto Himself as sons; you are plighted to Him and He to you; He has entrusted you with high office as a people (that, and not rank, is meant by *elyon* in Deut. 26:19 and 28:1). But all of this depends upon your walking in His ways—your following after Him.

Toward the end of the book, however, a song tells (Deut. 32:11f.) how the being borne "on eagles' wings" should be understood. The newly fledged eaglets, as yet not daring to fly, huddle together in the aerie. Then the eagle rouses his nest, stirs his young to flight, and with gentle flapping of his wings, hovers over them—the God-eagle over the nations, as once at the beginning of creation his spirit hovered[8] over the face of the waters. But then the eagle spreads his wings and sets *one* of the young upon his pinion, carries it away, and, by throwing it into the air and catching it, teaches it to fly freely. Why the one? Why else but that it may fly ahead, leading the way for the others!

Election without obligation appears only in two places in the Bible, and they are connected with each other in content....

God sends Nathan to David to explain to him why he has not been called upon to build the sanctuary in Jerusalem. One of the most remarkable things about Nathan's speech (2 Samuel, chapter 7)—one of the strongest and most important speeches of God in Scripture—is that it (and it alone) takes up again, together, the two key words of the Burning Bush speech: "my people" and "I will be with thee" (*ammi* three times [2 Sam. 7:10 and 11]; *ehyeh imkha* [2 Sam. 7:9]). In his direct answer to God, David takes up the matter of the threefold *ammi* with threefold *amkha* and exclaims, "Who is like Thy people (*am*), like Israel, a nation (*goy*) one in the earth, whom God went to redeem unto Himself for a people (*am*)! . . . Thou didst establish to Thyself Thy people Israel to be a people unto Thee forever!" (2 Sam. 7:23f.). This untroubled royal glorification of the people gives not a word to the acceptance of obligation at Sinai and to the binding character of the *berith*.

The building of the Temple is complete; the ark has been brought into the Sanctuary in a great procession. Solomon (1 Kings 8:22–53) utters the broadly encompassing prayer in which he entreats God's response to all, even to the strangers who shall at some time pray turned toward this house; but, finally, also for Israel when, at some future time, the anger of God shall bring about its defeat, and in complete heartfelt repentance, it will pray from its exile, turned toward this land and toward this house. And Solomon concludes with the plea to God that He then forgive the people. "For they are Thy people, and Thine inheritance (*nahalah*), which Thou broughtest forth out of Egypt, from the midst of the furnace of iron. . . . For Thou didst set them apart from among all the peoples of the earth, to be Thine inheritance, as Thou didst speak by the hand of Moses Thy servant, when Thou broughtest our fathers out of Egypt, O Lord God!" (1 Kings 8:51ff.). The Solomonic speech—unlike the Davidic—recognizes as well the sinfulness of the people, "all their transgressions, wherein they have transgressed against Thee" (v. 50); but that does not imply the people's breaking the covenant between God and people; rather, only general and unavoidable human sinfulness, "for there is no man that sinneth not" (v. 46).

The fourth chapter of Deuteronomy, in particular, answers both speeches, providing significant correction and completion. At first it sounds like an antiphony to David's prayer: "For what great nation (*goy*) is there, that hath God so nigh unto them, as the Lord our God is whensoever we call upon Him!" (Deut. 4:7). But immediately thereafter we have what is missing in the king's speech: "And what great nation is there, that hath statutes and ordinances so righteous as all this law." Then a Solomonic motif appears: "But you hath the Lord taken and brought forth out of the iron furnace, out of Egypt, to be unto Him a people of inheritance" (Deut. 4:20). But here, too, there follows the corrective completion: "Take heed unto yourselves, lest ye forget the covenant of the Lord your God, which He made with you!" (Deut. 4:23). And again it sounds like an antiphony to David's prayer: "Or hath God assayed to go and take Him a nation from the midst of another nation. . . . according to all that the Lord your God did for you in Egypt!" (Deut. 4:34). But again what is missing there is expressed here: "Thou shalt keep His statutes, and

His commandments!" (Deut. 4:40). There is no security in the covenant if it is not fulfilled; God is a devouring fire (Deut. 4:24). Israel is chosen only when it realizes the election by its life as a community.

Here, too, a prophet expresses the message in its ultimate, historically true form. The time is after the fateful battle at Megiddo; the leaders comfort the people by reference to the Temple as unconditional security for the life of the people. Jeremiah, who on other occasions was accustomed to preaching in the marketplace, enters the court of the Temple on a solemn holiday and delivers his speech against the Temple to the surprised people and priesthood (Jer. 7:1–15; cf. 26:1–6). They come to the Sanctuary from all their wicked dealing and trust in the fact that God's name is called upon this house—thus certainly no evil can befall them! But God grants no security. If the house wherein His name dwells has become a robbers' den and there is no repentance, then it will be given over to destruction.... God, the King of Israel, leaves His throne and abandons it to destruction because Israel has not taken His kingdom seriously. It has known only the King's protective power and not submission of its own lived communal life to the truth of the King's covenant. But Israel is elected only when it realizes its election.

And yet—this is the consoling paradox of our existence—the Rejector can never cease being the Elector. One day God will make a new covenant with the house of Israel that will overcome the contradiction of their stubborn or indolent hearts. "I will put my law in their inward parts, and in their heart will I write it; and I will be their God, and they shall be my people" (Jer. 31:33).

Notes

Source: "Die Erwählung Israels—Eine Befragung der Bibel," first in *Almanach des Schocken Verlags für das Jahr 5699* (Berlin: Schocken, 1938). Also in, Michael A. Meyer, trans., *On the Bible: Eighteen Studies by Martin Buber* (New York: Schocken, 1968), pp. 80–92.

Editor's note: Founded in 1931 by the entrepreneur Salman Schocken, the Schocken Verlag quickly became the leading Jewish publishing house in Germany until it was closed down by the National Socialists in 1938. At the end of 1933, Schocken started an immensely popular series of short, handsomely crafted monographs (Schocken Bücherei) featuring a wide range of contemporary and classical Jewish literature, thought, and history. The first volume, *The Consolation of Israel,* was a bilingual edition of Isaiah, chapters 40–55, with a translation by Martin Buber and Franz Rosenzweig. The first Almanach appeared in September 1933 (Jewish New Year) with the famous programmatic statement by Martin Buber: "The Jewish person of today is an innermost exposed human being of our time. The forces of this era have chosen this very moment to demonstrate their power and to test if humanity can resist. They are measuring their strength with the Jew. Can the Jew withstand? Will he break into pieces? . . . Can he pass the test?" (Martin Buber: "Der jüdische Mensch von heute," *Schocken Almanach auf das Jahr 5694* [1933–34], p. 5). "The Election of Israel" appeared in the last Almanach to be published. What begins as a Biblical inquiry becomes a critique of "true" and "false" election in response to the mounting pressure of Nazism and the perversion of Israel's election into rejection.

1. The unquestionably genuine, in fact, necessary, verse, Amos 9:8, must be considered together with Amos 2:10, and both with Gen. 15:16, a specifically "prophetic" verse (M.B.).
2. Cf. Jer. 1:15 (N. Glatzer). On the Hebrew *yada* see also Philosophical and Religious World View (1928), (p. 219 in this volume).

3. On the concept of "key words" (*Leitwortstil*), see Martin Buber and Franz Rosenzweig, *Die Schrift und ihre Verdeutschung* (Berlin: Schocken, 1936). There, Buber defines a key word as a "word or root of a word that suggestively repeats itself in a text, a sequence of texts, or in the context: Whoever follows these repetitions will unlock the meaning of the text, or see it more clearly and with greater intensity."
4. Cf. The Faith of Judaism (1929) (p. 103 in this volume).
5. In our passage the concept of *kohanim* as those who are allowed to "come near" (Exod. 19:22) manifestly includes the seventy elders, as follows from chapter 24 (v. 1f. and v. 9). At this stage of the narrative there are as yet no priests (M.B.).
6. Franz Rosenzweig (1886–1929): German–Jewish philosopher, author of the *Star of Redemption* (1921), which anticipates many ideas of Martin Buber's dialogical thinking. In 1920, Rosenzweig became the director of the Freies jüdisches Lehrhaus in Frankfurt, which offered nonacademic courses on classical and modern Judaism and operated until it was closed down by the National Socialist regime in 1938. From 1925 until his death in 1929, Rosenzweig collaborated with Buber on a new German translation of the Hebrew Bible. The Buber–Rosenzweig translation was completed by Buber in 1961.
7. *Am nahalah* (Deut. 4:20). The *nahalah* passages express a different, more exclusive and particularistic tendency of interpretation than do the *segulah* passages, which preserve the language of the original spoken word (M.B.).
8. The verbal form *merahef* (hover), significantly, occurs only in these two passages (the verb as such only once more) (M.B.).

Biblical Leadership (1933)

I do not imagine that you will expect me to give you any so-called character sketches of biblical leaders. That would be an impossible undertaking, for the Bible does not concern itself with character, nor with individuality, and one cannot draw from it any description of characters or individualities. The Bible depicts something else, namely, persons in situations. The Bible is not concerned with the difference between these persons, but the difference between the situations in which the person, the creaturely person, the appointed person, stands his test or fails is all important to it.

But neither can it be my task to delve beneath the biblical account to a picture more historically trustworthy—to actual data from which I can piece together a historically useful picture. This too is impossible. It is not that the biblical figures are unhistorical. I believe that we are standing at the beginning of a new era in biblical studies; whereas the past era was concerned with proving that the Bible did not contain history, the coming era will succeed in demonstrating its historicity. By this, I do not mean that the Bible depicts men, women, and events as they were in actual history; rather, its descriptions and narratives serve as organic, legitimate ways of giving an account of what existed and what happened. I have nothing against calling these narratives myths and sagas, as long as we remember that myths and sagas are essentially memories that are actually conveyed from person to person. But what kind of memory manifests itself in these accounts? Note the word memory; not imagination. It is an organic memory molding its material. We know of it today, because occasionally—though indeed in unlikely and indeed in incredible ways—the existence of great poets with such organic memories still extends into our time. If we want to distinguish between a great narrator and one who is simply very talented, the best way is to consider how each of them handles the events of his own life. The great narrator allows the events to drop into him as they happen—careless, trusting, with faith. Then, memory does its part: What has thus been dropped into it, it molds organically, unarbitrarily, unfancifully into a valid account and narrative; a whole on which admittedly a great deal of conscious work must be done, but the distinguishing mark has been put upon it by the unarbitrarily shaping memory. The less than great narrator registers and makes an inventory in what he also calls the memory, but it is really something quite different; he preserves the events while they are happening to be able to draw them forth unaltered when needed. This less talented narrator will certainly draw them forth from the preservative, unaltered and fit for use to a degree, and then he may do with them what he can.

And so the great poets show us in their way how the nascence of myths and sagas takes place. Each myth—even the myth that we usually call the most fantastic of all—is creation around a memory core, around the kernel of the organically shaping memory. It is not that people to whom something as monumental as the Exodus from Egypt has happened subsequently improvise events, allowing their fancy to add elements that they do not remember and to "embroider" on what occurred. What happened continues to function; the event itself is still active and at work in their souls, but these souls—and this community soul [*Gesamtseele*]—is so made that its memory is formative and myth-creating. Thus, the task before the biblical writers is to work on the product of this memory. Nowhere is the arbitrary observed or the alien element allowed to interfere; there is no juggling.

This being the case, we cannot disentangle the historical from the biblical. The power of biblical writing, which springs from this shaping memory, is so great, the elemental nature of this memory so mighty, that it is quite impossible to extract any so-called historical matter from the Bible. The historical matter thus obtained would be unreal, amorphous, and without significance. But it is also impossible to distill "the historical matter" from the Bible for another reason. In contrast to the sacred historiography of other nations, in the case of Israel there is no evidence from profane parallels by which one might correct the sacred documents; there is no historiography of another tendency than that which resides in this shaping memory, and this shaping memory stands under a law. It is this law that I shall try to elucidate by the examples with which I deal today.

To bring out more clearly and exactly what I have in mind, I shall ask you to recall one of the nations with which Israel came into historical contact and dispute; I do so for the purpose of considering the aspect under which this nation must have regarded one of the biblical leaders. Let us try to imagine how Abraham must have been regarded by one of the nations against whose kings he fought, according to Genesis, chapter 14, a chapter whose fundamental historical character seems to me beyond doubt. Undoubtedly, Abraham was a historical figure to this nation in the same sense in which we usually speak about history today; but he was no longer Abraham. What is important for us to know about Abraham, what makes him a biblical character, a "Father," why does the Bible tells us about Abraham—that is no longer embraced under this historical aspect;

the significance of the figure has vanished. Or, take, for instance, the Egyptians and Moses, and imagine how an Egyptian historian might have described Moses and his cause. Nothing essential would be left; a skeleton would take the place of the living person.

All we can do, therefore, is refer to the Bible—to that which is characteristic of the biblical leader, as the Bible, without discretion, tells of him and thinks of him, under the law of its conception of history, *its* living of history, which is unlike everything that we regard as history. But from this law, from this biblical way of regarding leader and leadership—which is different from all other ways in which leader and leadership have been considered—has Judaism arisen.

As I wish to investigate the question of the essence of biblical leadership, I must exclude from the inquiry all those figures who are not *biblical* leaders in the strict sense of the term. This means, characteristically enough, that I must exclude all those figures who appear as continuators, all those who are not called, elected, appointed anew, as the Bible says, directly by God, but who enter upon a task already begun without such personal call—whether it is a disciple to whom the person who is not permitted to finish the task hands over his office, breathing, as it were, toward his disciple the spirit that breathes upon him; or whether it is a son who succeeds an elected, originally anointed king, without receiving any other anointing than the customary official one—which is thus no longer the anointing that comes upon a person and turns him into another man....

Only the elected, only those who begin, are then included under the biblical aspect of leadership. A new beginning may also occur within a sequence of generations, as, for instance, within those called the generations of the patriarchs; this is clearly seen in the case of Jacob, with whom something new begins, as indicated by the particular way in which revelation comes to him.

I will first attempt a negative characterization of the essential features of biblical leadership, which goes beyond both nature and history. To the men who wrote the Bible, nature, as well as history, is of God—in such a way that the biblical cosmogony relates each separately: In the first chapter the creation of the world is described as the coming of nature into being; in the second chapter this same creation of the world is described as the rise of history. Both are of God, but then the biblical event goes beyond them, God goes beyond them; not in the sense that they—nature and history—come to be ignored by God, but in the sense that time and again God's hand thrusts through them and interferes with what is happening—it so chooses, so sends, and so commands, as it does not seem to accord with the laws of nature and history to send, to choose, and to command.

I shall show by two particularly clear examples what I mean by this. First of all, it is the weak and the humble who are chosen. By nature it is the strong—those who can force their cause through—who are able and therefore chosen to perform the historical deeds. But in the Bible it is often precisely the younger sons who are chosen—from Abel, through Jacob, Joseph and Moses, to David; and this choosing is accompanied by a rejection—often a very emphatic rejection—of the older sons, or those who are chosen were born out of wedlock or of humble origin. And if it happens that a strong man like Samson appears, a man who does not have all of these limitations, then his strength is not his own; it is only loaned, not given, and he trifles it away and squanders it, as the Bible tells us, to get it back only in order to die.

A different but no less telling expression of what is meant by this peculiar election against nature is represented by the battle and victory of Gideon. The Bible has him do the strangest thing any commander ever did. He has an army of ten thousand men, and he reduces its numbers again and again, until only three hundred men remain with him; and with these three hundred men he does battle and conquers (Judges, chapter 7).

It is always the same story. The purpose of God is fulfilled, as the Bible itself says in one place (Zech. 4:6), not by might, nor by power, but "by my *ruah*,"[1] a word that defies translation and should, perhaps, be rendered "breath" rather than "spirit."

It is "against nature" that in one way or another the leaders are mostly the weak and the humble. The way in which they carry out their leadership is "contrary to history." It is the moment of success that determines the selection of events that seem important to history. "World history" is the history of successes; the heroes who have not succeeded but who cannot be excluded from it because of their very conspicuous heroism serve only as a foil, as it were. True, the conquered also have their place in "world history;" but if we scrutinize how it treats the conquerors and the conquered, what is of importance to history becomes abundantly clear....

The Bible knows nothing of this intrinsic value of success. On the contrary, when it announces a successful deed, it is duty-bound to announce in complete detail the failure involved in the success. When we consider the history of Moses, we see how much failure is mingled in the one great successful action, so much so that when we set the individual events that make up his history side by side, we see that his life consists of one failure after another, through which runs the thread of his success. True, Moses brought the people out of Egypt, but each stage of this leadership was a failure. Whenever he comes to deal with this people, he is defeated by them—regardless of how often God may interfere and punish them. And the real history of his leadership is not the history of the Exodus, but that of the wandering in the desert. The personal history of Moses's own life, too, does not point back to his youth and to what grew out of it; it points beyond, to death—to the death of the unsuccessful man, whose work, it is true, survives him, but only in new defeats, new disappointments, and continual new failures—and yet his work survives also in a hope that is beyond all these failures.

Or let us consider the life of David. As far as we are told, it consists essentially of two great stories of flight. Before his accession to the throne there are manifold accounts of his flight from Saul, followed by an interruption that is not trifling in terms of length and its value for profane history but in the account appears paltry enough; and after that is the flight from Absalom, which is painted for us in detail. And even where the Bible recounts David's triumph, as, for instance, with the entry of the Ark into Jerusalem, the triumph is clearly described as a disgrace in a worldly sense; this is very unlike the language of "world history." What Michal, his wife, says to David of his triumph—how he ought to have felt ashamed of it, behaving as he did in front of his people (2 Sam. 6:20)—that is the language of profane history, that is of history par excellence. To history such a royal appearance is not permitted, and, rightly so, seeing that history is what it is.

And, finally, this glorification of failure culminates in the long line of prophets whose existence is failure through and through. They live in failure; it is for them to fight and not to conquer. It is the fundamental experience of biblical leadership, of the leadership described by one of them, a nameless prophet whose words are preserved in the second part of the Book of Isaiah in which he speaks in the first person of himself as "the servant of the Lord," and says of God:

> He hath made my mouth like a sharp sword,
> In the shadow of His hand hath He hid me;
> And He hath made me a polished shaft,
> In his quiver hath He concealed me! (Isa. 49:2)

This existence in the shadow, in the quiver, is the final word of the leaders in the biblical world; this enclosure in failure, in obscurity, even when one stands in the blaze of public life, in the presence of the whole national life. The truth is hidden in obscurity and yet does its work, though indeed in a way far different from what is known and lauded as effective by world history.

Biblical leadership falls into five basic types, not according to differences in the personality and character of the leader—I have already said that personality and character do not come into consideration—but according to the difference in the successive situations, the great stages in the history of the people that the Bible describes, the stages in the dialogue between God and the people. For what the Bible understands by history is a dialogue in which man—in which the people—is spoken to and fails to answer, yet in which the people in the midst of its failure continually rises up and tries to answer. It is the history of God's disappointments, but this history of disappointments constitutes a way, one that leads from disappointment to disappointment and beyond all disappointments; it is the way of the people, the way of man—yes, the way of God through mankind. I said that there are five basic types in accordance with the successive stages of the situations in the dialogue: (1) the patriarch; (2) the leader in the original sense of one who leads the wandering; (3) the so-called judge; (4) the king, but of course not the king who is a successor or a member of a dynasty, but the founder of the dynasty, called the first anointed; and (5) the prophet. All of these types constitute different forms of leadership in accordance with the different situations.

The Patriarch

This is a current conception that is not quite correct. No rulership is here exercised, and, when we understand the conception in its accurate sense, we cannot speak of any leadership, for there is as yet no people to lead. The conception indicates a way along which the people are to be led, beginning with these men. They are fathers. It is for them to beget a people. It is the peculiar point in biblical history in which God, as it were, narrows down His original plan for the whole of mankind and causes a people to be begotten, that is, called to do its appointed work toward the completion of the creation, the coming of the kingdom. The fathers of this people are the men of whom I speak. They are fathers, and nothing else. Patriarch expresses too much. They are the real fathers; they are those from whom this tribe, this people, proceeds; and when God speaks to them, when God blesses them, the same thing is always involved: conception and birth, the beginning of a people. And the great story that stands in the middle of the story of the patriarchs—the birth and offering of Isaac—makes exactly this point, in a paradoxical manner. Kierkegaard has presented this paradox very beautifully in the first part of his book, *Fear and Trembling*.[2] This paradoxical story of the second in the line of the patriarchs, of his being born and very nearly being killed, shows what is at stake: a begetting, but the begetting of a people standing at the disposal of God; a begetting, but a begetting commanded by God.

The Leader

We have a people, and the people is in bondage. A man receives the charge to lead it out. That is he whom I have described as the leader in the original meaning of the word. It is he who serves in a human way as a tool for the act that God pronounces, "I bore you on eagles' wings, and brought you unto myself" (Exod. 19:4). I have already spoken of his life. But in the middle of his life the event takes place in which Moses, after the passage through the Red Sea, intones the song in which the people joins, and which is the proclamation of a king. The words with which the song ends proclaim it, "King shall the Lord be for ever and ever" (Exod. 15:18). The people has here chosen God Himself for its king, and that means that it has made a vital and experienced truth out of the tradition of a divine kingdom that was common to all Semitic tribes but never had been taken quite seriously. The Hebrew leaders are so much in earnest about it that after the land has been conquered they undertake to do what is "contrary to history:" They try to build up a society without a ruling power save only that of God. It is that experiment in primitive theocracy that the Book of Judges tells and that degenerates into anarchy, as is shown by the examples given in its last part.

The Judge

The so-called judge constitutes the third type of leadership. This type is to be understood as the attempt made by a leading group among the people that are dominated by the desire to make actual the proclamation of God as king, and try to induce the people to follow them. This attempt miscarries time and again. Repeatedly, the people, falls away from God, to use the biblical phrase. But we can also express this in the language of history: Time and again the people fall apart; it is one and the same thing whichever language we use. The attempt to establish a society under no other dominion than God's—this too can be expressed in the language of history, or if one likes, in the language of sociology: The attempt to establish a society on pure voluntarism fails over and over again. The people falls away. This is always succeeded by an invasion by one of the neighboring peoples, and Israel, from a historical point of view—fallen apart and disunited—does not stand firm. But in its conquered state it again makes itself subject to the will of God, resolves anew to accept God's dominion, and again a divine mission occurs; there is always a leader whom the spirit lays hold of as it laid hold of Moses. This leader, whose mission it is to free the people, is "the Judge," or more correctly, "he who makes right" [*Rechtschaffer*]; he makes this right exist in the actual world for the people, which after its return to God again has right on its side, by defeating the enemy. This is the rhythm of the Book of Judges; it might almost be called a tragic rhythm, were it not that the word tragic is so foreign to the spirit of biblical language.

The King

But in this Book of Judges there is also something being prepared. The experience of failure, of the inability to bring about this intended, naive, primitive theocracy becomes ever deeper; ever stronger grows the demand for a human kingdom. Judges itself is in its greater part written from an antimonarchical standpoint. The kings of the peoples file before one in a way determined by this point of view, which reaches its height in that ironic fable of Jotham's (Judges, chapter 9). But in its final chapters, the Book of Judges has to acknowledge the disappointment of the theocratic hope, because the people is as it is, because men are as they are. And so kingship is demanded under Samuel, and it is granted by God. Previously, I said that the way leads through the disappointments. Thus, the demand of the people is, as it were, laid hold of and consecrated from above; for by the anointing of the king a man is transformed into the bearer of a charge laid upon him. But this is no longer—as was the case with the Judge—a single charge, the completion of which brings his leadership to an end; it is a governor's charge that goes beyond individual acts; indeed, beyond the life of individual men. Anointing may also imply the beginning of a dynasty, when the king is not rejected by God, as Saul was.

The kingdom is a new stage in the dialogue—a new stage of attempt and failure—but in this stage the account lays the burden of the failure on the king and no longer, as in the Book of Judges, on the whole people. It is no longer those who are led but the leader himself who falls, who cannot stand the test of the charge, who does not make the anointing come true in his own person—a crucial problem in religious history. The history of the great religions, and in general all great history, is bound up with the problem: How do human beings stand the test of what here is called anointing?

The history of the kings is the history of the failure of he who has been anointed to realize the promise of his anointing. The rise of messianism—the belief in the anointed king who realizes the promise of his anointing—is to be understood only in this context.

The Prophet

But now in the situation of the failure of kings the new and last type of leader in biblical history arises, the leader who above all other types is "contrary to history"—the prophet—he who is appointed to oppose the king, and even more, history. When God says to Jeremiah, "I have made thee...a brazen wall against the whole land" (Jer. 1:18), it is really so; the prophet stands not only against the ruler but against the people itself. The prophet is the man who has been set up against his own natural instincts that bind him to the community, and who likewise sets himself up against the will of the people to live on as they have always lived, which, naturally, for the people is identical with the will to live. It goes without saying that not only the rulers but also the people treat the prophet as their enemy in the way in which, as a matter of history, it falls to the lot of such men to be treated. These experiences of suffering that thus come upon the prophet join together to form that image of the servant of the Lord, of his suffering and dying for the sake of God's purpose.

When the Bible then tries to look beyond these manifestations of leadership to one that no longer stands amidst disintegration and failure, when the idea of the messianic leader is conceived, it means nothing else by it than that at last the answer shall be given: From out of mankind itself the word shall come, the word that is spoken with the whole being of man, the word that answers God's word. It is an earthly consummation that is awaited, a consummation in and with mankind. But this precisely is the consummation toward which God's hand pushes through that which He has created, through nature and through history. This is what the messianic belief means, the belief in the real leader, in the right handling and timely coming [*Zurechtkommen*][3] of dialogue, in God's disappointment being at an end. And when a fragment of an apocryphal gospel has God say to Jesus, "In all the prophets have I awaited thee, that thou wouldst come and I rest in thee, for thou art My rest,"[4] this is the late elaboration of a truly Jewish conception.

The biblical question of leadership is concerned with something greater than moral perfection. The biblical leaders are the foreshadowings of the dialogical man, of the man who commits his whole being to God's dialogue with the world and who stands firm throughout this dialogue. The life of those people to whom I have referred is absorbed in this dialogue, whether the dialogue comes about through an intervention, as in Abraham's talk with God about Sodom, or Moses's after the sin of the golden calf, whether it comes about through a resistance they offer against that which comes upon them and tries to overpower them—but their resistance ends in submission, which we find documented from Moses to Jeremiah—or whether the dialogue comes about through the struggle for a purpose and a task, as we know from the dialogue that took place between David and God: Whatever the way, man enters into the dialogue again and again; imperfect entry, yet one that is not refused—an entry that is determined to persevere in the dialogical world. All that happens is experienced as dialogue, what befalls man is taken as a sign, what man tries to do and what miscarries is taken as an attempt and a failure to answer, as a stammering attempt to respond as well as one can.

Because this is so, biblical leadership always means a process of being led. These men are leaders insofar as they allow themselves to be led, that is, insofar as they accept what is offered to them, insofar as they take upon themselves the responsibility for what they have been entrusted with, insofar as they make real what has been laid upon them from outside of themselves—make it real with the free will of their own being, in the "autonomy" of their person.

As long as we remember this, we can make the lives of these leaders clear. Almost always what we see is the taking of a man out of the community. God lifts the man out of the community, cuts him off from his natural ties; from Abraham to Jeremiah, he must go forth out of the land in which he has taken root, away to the place where he has to proclaim the name of God; it is the same story, whether it is wandering over the earth like Abraham, or becoming utterly alone in the midst of the people like the prophets. They are drawn out of their natural community; they fight with it; they experience in this community the inner contradiction of human existence. All of this is intensified to the utmost precisely in the prophets. The great suffering of the prophets, preserved for us by Jeremiah himself in a small number of (in the highest sense of the word) autobiographical sayings, is the ultimate expression of this condition.

But this ever-widening gulf between leader and community, the ever-greater failure of the leader, the leader's ever greater incompatibility with "history"—this means, from the biblical standpoint, the gradual overcoming of history. What we are accustomed to calling history, is from the biblical standpoint, only the facade of reality. It is the great failure [*Versagen*],[5] the refusal to enter into the dialogue, not the failure in the dialogue, as exemplified by biblical man. This great refusal [*Sich-Versagen*] is sanctioned with the imposing sanction provided by so-called history. The biblical point of view repudiates with ever-increasing strength this two-dimensional reality, most strongly in the prophets; it proclaims that the way, the real way, from the Creation to the Kingdom is trod not on the surface of success, but in the depths of failure. The real work, from the biblical point of view, is the late recorded, the unrecorded, the anonymous work. The real work is done in the shadow, in the quiver. Official leadership fails more and more; leadership devolves more and more upon the secret. The way leads through the work that history does not write down and that history cannot write down, work that is not ascribed to he who did it but which possibly at some time in a distant generation will emerge as having been done, without the name of the doer—the secret working of the secret leadership. And when the biblical writer turns his eyes toward the final, messianic overcoming of history, he sees how the outer history becomes engulfed, or rather how both the outer history and the inner history fuse, how the secret that the leadership had become rises up out of the darkness and illuminates the surface of history, how the meaning of biblical history is consummated in the whole reality.

Notes

Source: Biblisches Führertum (lecture delivered in Munich in 1928), first in *Kampf um Israel—Reden und Schriften, 1921–1932* (Berlin: Schocken, 1933). Greta Hort, trans., in *Israel and the World: Essays in a Time of Crisis* (New York: Schocken, 1948) pp. 119–33; also in Michael A. Meyer, trans., *On the Bible: Eighteen Studies by Martin Buber* (New York: Schocken, 1968), pp. 137–50.

Editor's note: Buber delivered the lecture in 1928 before a small group of pacifists whose most memorable member was the writer Thomas Mann. The theme of leadership returns in Buber's inaugural address of 25 April 1938, at the Hebrew University, "Die Forderung des Geistes und die Geschichtliche Wirklichkeit" (in English, as "Plato and Isaiah," in *Israel and the World*). In 1933 (the year of Hitler's rise to power), when the lecture was published in a collection entitled, *The Struggle for Israel* (*Kampf um Israel—Reden und Schriften, 1921–1932* [Berlin: Schocken, 1933]), the question of leadership had assumed a new urgency.

1. G. Hort ends here with ". . . but by my 'spirit.' "
2. Søren Kierkegaard (1813–1855), Fear and Trembling (1843) (Princeton, N.J.: Princeton University Press, 1983); Buber is referring to the chapters "Exordium" and "Eulogy on Abraham."
3. The German *zurechtkommen* means both, "to manage" and "to be on time." G. Hort: ". . . in the setting right of dialogue."
4. Quoted in Jerome, Comm. in Isa. 11:2 (N. Glatzer).
5. The German *Versagen* is used here as "failure" and "mis-saying." See also *Sich-Versagen* in the sentence that follows.

What are we to do about the Ten Commandments? Reply to an Inquiry (1929)

You want to know what I think should be done about the Ten Commandments to give them a sanction and validity that they no longer possess.

In my opinion the historical and present status of the Decalogue derives from a twofold...fact.

1. The Ten Commandments are not part of an impersonal codex governing an association of men. They were uttered by an *I* and addressed to a *Thou*. They begin with the *I* and every one of them addresses the *Thou* in person. An *I* "commands," and a *Thou*—every *Thou* who hears this *Thou*—"is commanded."

2. In the Decalogue, the word of He who issues commands is equipped with no executive power effective on the plane of predictable causality. The word does not enforce its own hearing. Whoever does not wish to respond to the Thou addressed to him can apparently go about his business unimpeded. Though He who speaks the word has power (and the Decalogue presupposes that He had sufficient power to create the heavens and the earth), He has renounced this power sufficiently to let every individual actually decide for himself whether he wants to open or close his ears to the voice, and that means whether he wants to choose or reject the I of "I am." The person who rejects Him is not struck down by lightning; the person who elects Him does not find hidden treasures. Everything seems to remain just as it was. Obviously God does not wish to dispense either medals or prison sentences.

This, then, is the situation in which "faith" finds itself. According to all criteria of predictable causality, the hearing of what there is to hear does not pay. Faith is not a mere business enterprise that involves risk balanced by the possibility of incalculable gain. It is a venture pure and simple—a venture that transcends the law of probability. This holds especially for those hardened believers whose idea about death and what comes after death is that it will all be revealed in due time but cannot be anticipated by the imagination—not even by "religious" imagination.

Human society—and by that I mean the living community at any definite period—as far as we can recognize the existence of a common will [*Gesamtwille*] in its institutions, has at all times had an interest in fostering and keeping the Ten Commandments. To be sure, human society is less interested in those commandments that refer to the relationship to God, but it certainly wants the rest to be kept, because it would not be conducive to the welfare of society if murder, for example, ceased to be a crime and became a vice. To a certain extent this holds even for the prohibition against adultery, at least as long as society believes that it cannot get along without marriage, and indeed it never has gotten along without it, not even in its "primitive" stages of polyandry and polygamy. And as long as society cares about maintaining the connection between generations and transmitting forms and contents in a well-regulated manner, it must respect the command to honor one's parents. The Soviet Union has proven that even a society built up to achieve communistic goals must care about honoring that commandment.

It is understandable that society does not want to base a matter so vital on a foundation as insecure as faith—on wanting or not wanting to hear. So, society has always endeavored to transfer those commands and prohibitions it considered important from the sphere of "*religion*" to that of "*morals*"—to translate them from the language that uses the personal imperative to the impersonal formulation of "musts." Society wishes these commandments to be upheld by public opinion, which can to a certain extent be controlled, rather than by the will of God whose effectiveness cannot be predicted or counted on. But since even the security of opinion is not entirely dependable, the commands and prohibitions are once more transferred, this time to the sphere of "law," that is, they are translated into the language of "if formulations." For example, if someone should do this or that, then such and such a thing shall be done to him. And the purpose of the threat of "such and such a thing" is not to limit the freedom of action of the law breaker but to punish him. God scorned to regulate the relation between what a man does and what, as a result of his doing, is done to him, by exact mathematical rules; but that is exactly what society attempts. To be sure, society certainly has the personnel to carry out its rulings—a personnel that, at least in principle, has well-defined work to perform: the courts, the police, jailers, and hangmen. Oddly enough, however, the result is still far from satisfactory. Statistics, for example, do not show that the death penalty has had the effect of diminishing the number of murders.

For the sake of clarity, I have oversimplified the situation. In history, all of these processes are far more circumstantial and interconnected. All of this is not reprehensible as long as the "translation" [*Übertragung*] does not claim to be a translation.[1] Plagiarism is legitimate here, but citation is not. Provided society does not insist that the moral and legal forms into which it has transformed the Ten Commandments, that the product that is an I-and-Thou deprived of the I and the Thou, is still the Ten Commandments, its activities are unobjectionable; it is as a matter of fact impossible to imagine how society could exist without them. But nothing of its vast machinery has anything to do with the situation of the human being who in the midst of a personal experience hears and feels himself addressed by the word "thou." "Do not carry [*tragen*] HIS, your God's name into delusion" (Exod. 20:7), or "Speak not against your comrade as a witness of lies" (Exod. 20:13).[2] The vast machinery of society has nothing to do with the situation that prevails between the all-powerful Speaker who avoids exerting His power and he who is spoken to; and it has nothing to do with the daring, catastrophic, redeeming situation of faith. But if society were to have the temerity to pretend that its voiceless morals and its faceless law are really "the word" adapted to the times and extricated from the husk of superstitions and outmoded ideas—something would take place that has not yet happened in the history of mankind. And then it would, perhaps, be too late for society to discover that there is "One" who rejects jailers and hangmen as executors of His will.

Now, provided you have not given me up as someone who is simply behind the times, but ask me more insistently than before what should be done with the Ten Commandments, I shall reply, Do what I am trying to do myself: Lead up to them—not to a scroll, not even to the stone tablets on which "the finger of God" (Exod. 31:18) once wrote the commandments after they had been uttered, but to the "spoken word."

Notes

Source: "Was soll mit den zehn Geboten geschehen?" first in *Die Literarische Welt* 7(6), (1929). Olga Marx, trans., in *Israel and the World Essays in a Time of Crisis* (New York: Schocken, 1948), pp. 85–8; also in Michael A. Meyer, trans., *On the Bible: Eighteen Studies by Martin Buber* (New York: Schocken, 1968), pp. 118–21.

Editor's note: The reply should be read as a commentary to and indeed careful revision of Buber's earlier speech, Heruth (1919) (p. 125 in this volume), in which the question of the law is addressed in still predialogical language. Buber was forced to clarify his standpoint concerning the law in response to Franz Rosenzweig's letter "Builders" ("Die Bauleute," 1923), which sparked the famous correspondence on "Law," later published in *Schocken Almanach auf das Jahr 5697* (1936–37), (Berlin: Schocken, 1937). The basic ideas of the 1929 piece are repeated in Buber's *Moses* of 1945: "The soul of the Decalogue ... is to be found in the word 'Thou.' Here nothing is either stated or confessed; but orders are given to the one addressed, to the listener." (*Moses. The Revelation and the Covenant* [Oxford: East and West Library, 1946], p. 130). See also Buber's short reflection, "Die zweiten Tafeln," *Insel-Almanach auf das Jahr 1919* (Leipzig: Insel Verlag, 1919), pp. 148–9.

1. The homonymy of the German "*Übertragung*" (literally, transferral, translation, metaphor) cannot be fully recreated in English. Buber uses "*Übertragung*" twice here (hence "translation" in both cases), but it should probably read "transferral" (or reference) and "translation."
2. The English follows the Buber–Rosenzweig translation: "Trage nicht SEINEN deines Gottes Namen auf das Wahnhafte," and "Aussage nicht gegen deinen Genossen als Lügenzeuge." (*Die Fünf Bücher der Weisung* [Berlin: Lambert Schneider, 1930], pp. 231–2). O. Marx follows the King James version.

Biblical Humanism (1933)

In 1913, I assembled and headed a small circle of Jews interested in education.[1] As we formulated plans for a Jewish school of advanced studies (which World War I prevented from materializing), I proposed that the course of studies of the prospective institution be guided by the concept of a Hebrew humanism. By this I meant that just as the West has for centuries drawn educative vigor from the language and the writings of antiquity, so does the pivotal place in our system of education belong to the language and the writings of classical Israel. It is for these forces that we must win new focal influence; that they may, out of the raw materials of contemporary life and its tasks, fashion a human being with new Jewish dignity.

Sixteen years later I attended the Sixteenth Zionist Congress. When I wished to convey, in brief, what I thought was missing in the educational system of Jewish Palestine and what I hoped for, I again found no better designation for it than "Hebrew humanism, in its truest meaning."[2] This newly added phrase, "in its truest meaning," encompassed my experience of three decades with the Jewish national movement. This movement had activated the people as a people, had revived the language as a language; but in neither case, its history or its literature, had it distinguished with prophetic awareness and prophetic demand true values from false, nor drawn order and direction for the inherited material. It had failed to understand that the archetype of this people sprang from the ordering and direction-giving deed; that the great document of this language was grounded in the ordering and directing word; that a *formal* "Renaissance" is inflated nonsense; that, rather, the future of a community beginning anew on the soil of the old homeland depends on the *rebirth of its normative primal forces*. Hebrew humanism means fashioning a Hebrew man, and a Hebrew man is not at all the same as a Hebrew-speaking man.

In an important treatise that attempts to determine the basic nature of Western humanism, Konrad Burdach has very rightly pointed to a maxim in Dante's *Convivio:* "The greatest desire Nature has implanted in everything from its beginning is the desire to return to its origins."[3] In conformity with these words, Burdach sees as the goal of the spiritual movement we are accustomed to call humanism a "return to the wellsprings of humanity, not by way of speculative thought, but by way of a concrete *transformation* of the total inner life."[4] It is not antiquity in its totality as historical matter that the humanist receives; he receives that part of it which by its nature seems capable of furthering the "return." Thus, Goethe in Rome, "in the presence of the sculptural creations of the ancients," feels himself "led back to man in his purest condition."[5] Similarly, a Hebrew humanism can rise only from a sensitive selection that out of the totality of Judaism discerns the Hebrew person in his purest state. Thus our humanism is directed to the Bible.

To be sure, a Hebrew man is not a biblical man. The "return" that is meant here cannot in the nature of things mean a striving for the recurrence or continuation of something long past, but only a striving for its renewal in a genuinely contemporary manifestation. Yet only a man worthy of the Bible may be called a Hebrew man. Our Bible, however, consists of instruction, admonition, and dialogue with the Instructor and Admonitor. Only that man who wishes to do and hear what the mouth of the Unconditioned commands him is a man worthy of the Bible. Only that man is a Hebrew man who lets himself be addressed by the voice that speaks to him in the Hebrew Bible and who responds to it with his life.

Manifestly, the two concepts are not identical. Manifestly, too, the converse of the proposition that every Hebrew man must be worthy of the Bible is not valid. The Hebrew man is that individual who lets himself be addressed by the voice that speaks to him in the Hebrew language. That is the meaning of biblical humanism.

Humanism moves from the mystery of language to the mystery of the human person. The reality of language must become operative in a man's spirit. The truth of language must prove itself in the person's existence. That was the intent of humanistic education, as long as it was alive.

Biblical humanism moves from the mystery of the Hebrew language to the mystery of the Hebrew being. Biblical humanistic education means fulfillment of the one in the other. Its intent is to lead the Jew of today back to his origins. But his origins are there where he hears the voice of the Unconditional resounding in Hebrew.

Biblical humanism is concerned with a "concrete transformation" of our total—and not alone our inner—lives. This concrete transformation can only follow upon a rebirth of the normative primal forces that distinguish right from wrong, true from false, and to which life submits itself. The primal forces are transmitted to us in the word—the biblical word. Some, like myself, will not let the biblical word usurp the place of the voice; they will not acknowledge the word as that voice's absolute, sufficing, immutably valid expression. Yet even they must feel certain that we can truly retrieve the normative only as we open ourselves to the biblical word, wherein it appears as a primal force. This primal force enables a community to perceive and comply with what has been proclaimed to it; it enables the leader to proclaim to this community as revealed word what they ought to perceive and comply with, for the leader may not in any way consider himself to be the source of such proclamation. We are no longer a community capable of this. But if we will open ourselves to the biblical word, if the individual will let it affect his personal life and open himself to the authority of the normative, then we may hope that the persons so affected—in various ways, yet all as one—will once again coalesce into a community in the primal meaning of the concept.

Here, however, when I speak of the biblical word, I mean not its content but the word itself—essential in only the original word in the mystery of its spokenness [*Gesprochenheit*]: If we quote it, it must retain its character as a word spoken here and now. The biblical word is translatable, for it encloses a content with which it issues forth to man. It is not translatable, for it encloses a mystery of language with which it issues forth to Israel. At the center of biblical humanism stands the service due the untranslatable word.

I have chosen to call our province of education a humanism because here too the building blocks for the structure of personality must be produced from the depths of language. The adjective "biblical" changes everything basically. For the biblical language is, at base, not only a different language, it is a different manner of speaking and a different mode of expression.

The word of Greek antiquity is detached and formally perfected. It is removed from the block of actual spokenness, sculpted with the artful chisel of thought, rhetoric, and poetry—removed to the realm of form. It would be considered crude and useless—barbarian—were it to retain any immediacy. It is valid only when it becomes pure form.

The purity of the Hebrew Bible's word resides not in form but in originality [*Ursprünglichkeit*]. Whenever it was subjected to a consciously artistic adaptation it was polluted. Its full biblical force is present in the biblical word only when it has retained the immediacy of spokenness. It is essential to the biblicality of the biblical word that a psalm is an outcry and not a poem, that a prophetic speech is an appeal and not properly a formal elocution. In the Bible the voice of the speaker is not transformed; it remains as is. Yet it seems removed from anything incidental; it is purely original [*ursprünglich*]. That is why it also became possible in the domain of this word for the humanized voice of God, resounding in human idiom and captured in human letters, to speak not *before us*, as does a character in the role of a god in the epiphanies of Greek tragedy, but *to us*.

Because the word of Greek antiquity is worked over and hammered into shape—because it is a product—it tends to be monological. The atmosphere of the solitary, sculpting spirit still encompasses it on the platform. That an Athenian orator plans and practices his speeches does not reduce his stature; a prophet who did likewise would be effaced. Socratic irony conceals an elemental immutability in communication; in the Bible, when an idea is expressed, the speaker regards the listener with concern. Whoever is addressed by the tragic chorus—men or gods—is, ultimately, not addressed at all; its foreboding song attains fulfillment by itself. But the psalmodic chorus, which has prayed, "Save us for Thy mercy's sake!" (Ps. 6:5), then listens in the stillness to hear whether its prayer has been granted. Untransfigured and unsubdued, the biblical word preserves the dialogical character of living reality.

Just as the nature of the word differs essentially in these two instances, so too is its apprehension essentially different: It is taught or reported [*berichtet*] in a basically different manner. The Greek Logos (word) is; it possesses eternal being (Heraclitus). Although the prologue of the hellenizing Gospel of John, like the Hebrew Bible, begins with "In the beginning," it immediately continues with the totally un-Hebraic "*was* the Word." In the beginning of the Bible's account of creation, there is no word: It comes to be; it is spoken. In this account there is no "word" that is not spoken; the only being of a word resides in its being spoken. But then all being of things that are comes from having been spoken, from the primary word being spoken: "He Himself spoke and it was." The Greeks teach the word; the Jews report it.

This essential difference carries over into the educational area. Western humanism conceives language as a formation [*Gebild*], and so it proceeds to "a liberation of the truly formative powers of man" (Konrad Burdach); the "spiritual empire" that he wants to establish "might be called the Apollonian." The power of giving shape is set above the world. The highest faculty of the spirit is the formative one: It wants to *form* the person as perfectly as possible; it wants to *form* the *polis* (society, state) as perfectly as possible.

The law of a biblical humanism must be different. It conceives language as an event [*Geschehen*]—an event in mutuality. Therefore, it must aim at an event—more concretely, at an event in mutuality. Its intent is not the person who is shut up within himself, but the open one; not the form, but the relation; not mastery of the secret, but immediacy in facing it; not the thinker and master of the word, but its listener and executor, its worshipper and proclaimer. Nor is its intent the perfected structure of the *polis,* nor the free and disciplined interplay of the limbs of a political body; its intent is the *edah*,[6] the present intercommunity of this entire body of people, true immediacy of "justice" and "love," of "esteem" and "faithfulness" between men. But this *edah* is the "*edah* of God," for in fulfilling itself as a community, these people provide the proper response to the address of their Master: They fulfill the word. The word is fulfilled, by way of individual man and the people, not in a perfected form [*Gebild*] but in a proof of self [*Bewährung*].

But this proof does not possess the permanence of the formed work; it exists only in the factual moment. Biblical humanism cannot, as does its

Western counterpart, raise the individual above the problems of the moment; it seeks instead to train the person to stand fast in them, to prove himself in them. This stormy night, these shafts of lightning flashing down, this threat of destruction—Do not escape from them into a world of *logos,* of perfected form! Stand fast, hear the word in the thunder, obey, respond! This terrifying world is the world of God. It lays claim upon you. Prove yourself in it as a man of God!

Thus would biblical humanism declare a rebirth of the normative primal forces of Israel.

Notes

Source: "Biblischer Humanismus," first in *Der Morgen* 9(4), (October 1933). Also in, Michael A. Meyer, trans., *On the Bible: Eighteen Studies by Martin Buber* (New York: Schocken, 1968), pp. 211–16.

Editor's note: For a later and substantially different version of this essay see Hebrew Humanism (1941) (p. 158 in this volume).

1. The group was organized by Martin Buber, Erich Kahler, and Arthur Salz and met on 30 March 1913, at the Hotel Savoy in Berlin (see also Hans Kohn, *Martin Buber—Sein Werk und seine Zeit* [Cologne: J. Melzer, 1961], p. 150, no. 1).
2. Cf. Zionism and Nationalism (1929) (p. 279 in this volume).
3. Dante, *Convivio,* 4, v. 12. Cf. Konrad Burdach, "Über den Ursprung des Humanismus" (1914), in *Reformation, Renaissance, Humanismus* (1918) (Darmstadt: Wiss. Buchgesellschaft, 1963), p. 157.
4. Ibid., p. 158.
5. Ibid., p. 189.
6. Hebrew: community of common origin. Buber is playing with the Hebrew double meaning of "community" and "witness."

The Man of Today and the Jewish Bible (1936)

Biblia (books) is the name of a book—one composed of many books. It is really one book, for one basic theme unites all the stories and songs, sayings and prophecies contained within it. The theme of the Bible is the encounter between a group of people and the One without Name [*Namenloser*] who, in the course of history, in the sequence of events occurring on earth, will address the group and be addressed by it, and whom the group has dared to call by name.[1] Whether openly or by implication, the stories are reports of encounters. The songs lament the denial of the grace of encounter—plead that it may be repeated, or give thanks because it has been vouchsafed. The prophecies summon man who has gone astray to turn—to return to the region where the encounter took place, promising him that the torn bond shall once more be made whole. If this book transmits cries of doubt, it is the doubt that is the destiny of man who after having tasted nearness must experience distance and learn from distance what it alone can teach. When we find love songs in the Bible, we must understand that these are not reinterpretations of later time,[2] but that the love of God for His world is revealed through the depths of love that human beings can feel for one another.

Since this book came into being, it has confronted generation after generation. Each generation must struggle with the Bible in its turn and come to terms with it. The generations are by no means always ready to listen to what the book has to say and to obey it; they are often vexed and defiant: Nevertheless, the preoccupation with this book is part of their life and they face it in the realm of reality. Even when generations negated the book, that very negation confirmed the book's claim upon them; they bore witness to the book in the very act of denying it.

The picture changes when we shift to the man of today, and by this, I mean the "intellectual" man of our time, the man who holds it important for intellectual values to exist, and admits—yes, even himself declares that their reality is bound up with our own power to realize them. But if we were to question him and probe down to truth—and we do not usually probe that far down—he would have to own that his feeling about the obligations of the spirit is in itself only intellectual. It is the signature of our time that the spirit imposes no obligations. We proclaim the rights of the spirit, we formulate its laws, but they enter only into books and discussions, not into our lives. They float in midair above our heads, rather than walk the earth in our midst. Everything except everyday life belongs to the realm of the spirit. Instead of union, a false relationship obtains between the spirit and everyday life. This relationship may shape up as spurious idealism, toward which we may lift our gaze without incurring any obligation to recover from the exigencies of earth; or it may present itself as spurious realism, which regards the spirit as only a function of life and transforms its unconditionality into a number of conditional characters: psychological, sociological, and others. It is true that some contemporaries realize all of the corroding consequences of this separation of two interdependent entities—a corrosion that is bound to penetrate into deeper and deeper strata until the spirit is debased into a willing and complacent servant of whatever powers happen to rule the world. The men of whom I am speaking have pondered over how this corrosion can be halted and have appealed to religion as the only power that is still capable of bringing about a new union between spirit and world. But what goes by the name of religion nowadays will never bring about such a union. For today, "religion" itself is part of the detached spirit. It is one of the subdivisions—one that is in high favor, to be sure—of the structure erected over and above life, one of the rooms on the top floor, with a very special atmosphere of its own. But this sort of religion is not an entity that includes all of life and, in this its present status, can never become one. It has lost its unity and so it cannot lead man to inner unity. It has adapted to this twofold character of human existence. To exert an influence on contemporary man, religion itself would have to return to reality. And religion was always real only when it was free of fear, when it shouldered the load of concreteness instead of rejecting it as something belonging to another realm, when it made the spirit incarnate, and sanctified everyday life.

The so-called Old Testament constitutes the greatest document of such reality. Two traits, which are however interrelated, set it apart from the other great books of the world religions. One trait is that in the "Old Testament" both events and words are placed in the midst of the people, of history, of the world. What happens does not happen in a vacuum existing between God and the individual. The Word travels by way of the individual to the people, so that they may hear and translate it into reality. What happens is not superior to the history of the people; it is nothing but the secret of the people's history made manifest. But that very fact places the people acted upon in opposition to the nations that represent, in their own eyes, an end in themselves, to groups concerned only with their own welfare, to the "breath of world history." These people are called upon to weld their members into a community that may serve as a model for the many different nations. The historical continuity of "seed" and "earth" is bound up with the "blessing" (Gen. 12ff.), and the blessing with the mission. The "Holy" permeates history without divesting it of its rights.

The second trait is that in the Bible the law is designed to cover the natural course of man's life. Eating meat is connected with animal sacrifice; matrimonial purity is sanctified month after month: Man is accepted as he is with all of his urges and passions and included in holiness, lest his passions grow into a mania. The desire to own land is not condemned, and renunciation is not demanded, but the true Lord of the land is God, and man is nothing but a "sojourner" in His midst. The Landlord makes a harmonious balance of property ownership, lest inequality arise, grow, and break the bond between the members of the community. Holiness penetrates nature without violating it. The living spirit wishes to spiritualize and quicken life; it wishes spirit and life to find the way to one another; it wishes spirit to take shape as life, and life to be clarified through spirit. The spirit wishes creation to attain perfection through itself. The function of this book is to bear witness to the spirit's will to perfection and to the command to serve the spirit in its search for union with life. If we accept the Old Testament as merely "religious writing," as a subdivision of the detached spirit, it will fail us, and we must fail it. If we seize upon it as the expression of a reality that comprises all of life, we really grasp it, and it grasps hold of us. But contemporary man is scarcely capable of this grasp any longer. If he "takes any interest" at all in the Scriptures, it is an abstract, purely "religious" interest, and more often not even that, but an interest connected with the history of religion or civilization—or an aesthetic interest, or the like—at any rate it is an interest that springs from the detached spirit with its numerous autonomous domains. Man of today is not like the generations of old, who stood before the biblical word to hearken to or to take offense at it. He no longer confronts his life with the Word; he locks life away in one of many unholy compartments, and then he feels relieved. Thus, he paralyzes the power, which of all powers, is best able to save him....

To understand the situation fully, we must picture the complete chasm between the Scriptures and the man of today.

The Jewish Bible has always approached and still does every generation with the claim that it must be recognized as a document of the true history of the world, that is, of the history according to which the world has an origin and a goal. The Jewish Bible demands that the individual fit his own life into this true history, so that "I" may find my own origin in the origin of the world, and my own goal in the goal of the world. But the Jewish Bible does not set a past event as a midpoint between origin and goal. It interposes a movable, circling midpoint that cannot be pinned to any set time, for it is the moment when I, the reader, the hearer, the man, catch through the words of the Bible the voice, which from earliest beginnings has been speaking in the direction of the goal. The midpoint is this mortal and yet immortal moment of mine. Creation is the origin; redemption, the goal. But revelation is not a fixed, dated point poised between the two. The revelation at Sinai is not this midpoint itself, but the perceiving of it, and such perception is possible at any time. That is why a psalm or a prophecy is no less "Torah," that is, instruction [*Weisung*], than the story of the Exodus from Egypt. The history of this people—accepting and refusing at once—points to the history of all mankind, but the secret dialogue expressed in the psalms and prophecies points to my own secret.

The Jewish Bible is the historical document of a world swinging between creation and redemption, which, in the course of its history, experiences revelation, a revelation that *I* experience *if I am there*. Thus, we can understand that the resistance of the man of today is that of his innermost being.

The man of today has two approaches to history. He may contemplate it as a freethinker, and participate in and accept the shifting events, the varying success of the struggles for power, as a promiscuous agglomeration of happenings. To him, history will seem a medley of the actions and deaths of people, of grasping and losing, triumph and misery—a meaningless hodgepodge to which the mind of man, time and again, gives an unreliable and unsubstantial semblance of meaning. Or he may view history dogmatically, derive laws from past sequences of events and calculate future sequences, as though the "main lines" were already traced on some roll that needs to merely unroll; as though history were not the vital living, growing of time, constantly moving from decision to decision, of time into which my time and my decisions stream full force. He regards history as a stark, ever-present, inescapable space.

Both of these approaches are a misinterpretation of historic destiny, which is neither chance nor fatality. According to biblical insight, historic destiny is the secret correlation [*Wechselhaftigkeit*] inherent in the current moment—the confrontation [*Aneinandergeraten*] of here and there.[3] When we are aware of origin and goal, there is no meaningless drift; we are carried along by a meaning we could never think up for ourselves, a meaning we are to live—not to formulate. And that living takes place in the awful and splendid moment of decision—your moment and mine no less than Alexander's and Caesar's. And yet your moment is not yours but, rather, the moment of your encounter.

The man of today knows of no beginning. As far as he is concerned, history ripples toward him from some prehistorical cosmic age. He knows of no end; history sweeps him on into a posthistorical cosmic age. What a violent and foolish episode this time between the prehistorical and the posthistorical has become! Man no longer recognizes an origin or a goal because he no longer wants to recognize the midpoint. Creation and redemption are true only in the premise that revelation is a present experience. Man of today resists the Scriptures because he cannot endure revelation. To endure revelation is to endure this moment full of possible decisions—to respond to and to be responsible for every moment. Man of today resists the Scriptures because he does not want to accept responsibility any longer. He thinks he is venturing a great deal, yet he industriously evades the one real venture, that of responsibility.

Insight into the reality of the Bible begins with drawing a distinction between creation, revelation, and redemption. Christianity withdrew from such insight—and thus from the grounds of the "Old Testament"—in its earliest theology, which fused the essentials of revelation and the essentials of redemption in the Christ. It was entirely logical for Marcion to dispute the value of a creation, which from his point of view was bound to seem nothing but a premise, and to brand it as the blunder of another, inferior god. With that act, the essence of time, which was closely allied to the essence of our spirit, was abandoned; time that distinguishes between past, present, and future—structures in the Bible that reach their most concrete expression in the three structures of creation, revelation, and redemption. The only gate that leads to the Bible as a reality is the faithful distinction between the three, not as hypostases or manifestations of God, but as stages, actions, and events in the course of His intercourse with the world, and thus also as the main directions of His movement toward the world. But such distinction must not be exaggerated to mean separation. From the point of view of the Bible, revelation is, as it were, focused in the "middle," creation in the "beginning," and redemption in the "end." But the living truth is that they actually coincide—that "God every day renews the work of the Beginning,"[4] but also every day anticipates the work of the end. Certainly both creation and redemption are true only in the premise that revelation is a present experience. But if I did not feel creation as well as redemption happening to myself, I could never understand what creation and redemption are.

This fact must be the starting point for the recurring question, if and how the chasm between man of today and the Scriptures can be bridged. We have already answered the question whether the man of today can believe, by saying that while he is denied the certainty of faith, he has the power to hold himself open to faith. But is not the strangeness of biblical concepts a stumbling stone to his readiness to do so? Has he not lost the reality of creation in his concept of "evolution," that of revelation in the theory of the "unconscious," and that of redemption in the setting up of social or national goals?

We must wholly understand the very substantial quality of this strangeness, before we can even attempt to show that there is still an approach, or rather, *the* approach.

And again we must begin with the center.

What meaning are we intended to find in the words that God came down in fire—to the sound of thunder and horn, to the mountain that smoked like a furnace—and spoke to His people? It can mean, I think, one of three things. Either it is figurative language used to express a "spiritual" process; or if biblical history does not recall actual events, but is metaphor and allegory, then it is no longer biblical and deserves no better fate than to be surrendered to the approach of modern man—the historical and aesthetic, and such. Or it is the report of a "supernatural" event, one that severs the intelligible sequence of happenings that we term natural by interposing something unintelligible. If that is the case, man of today in deciding to accept the Bible would have to make a sacrifice of intellect that would cut his life irreparably in two, provided he does not want to lapse into the habitual, lazy acceptance of something he does not really believe. In other words, what he is willing to accept would not be the Bible in its totality including all of life, but only religion abstracted from life.

But there is a third possibility: It could be the verbal trace [*Wortspur*] of a natural event, that is, an event that took place in the world of the senses common to all men and fitted into connections that the senses can perceive. But the assemblage of people that experienced this event experienced it as revelation vouchsafed to them by God and preserved it as such in the memory of generations—an enthusiastic, spontaneously formative memory. Experience undergone in this way is not self-delusion on the part of this assemblage; it is what they see, what they recognize and perceive with their reason, for natural events are the carriers of revelation, and revelation occurs when he who witnesses the event and sustains it experiences the revelation it contains. This means that he listens to that which the voice, sounding forth from this event, wishes to communicate to him—its witness to his constitution, to his life, to his sense of duty. It is only when this is true that man of today can find the approach to biblical reality. I, at any rate, believe that it is true.

Sometimes we have a personal experience related to those recorded as revelations and capable of opening the way for them. We may unexpectedly become aware of a certain apperception within ourselves, which was lacking but a moment ago and whose origin we are unable to discover. The attempt to derive such apperception from the famous unconscious stems from the widespread superstition that the soul can do everything by itself, and it fundamentally means nothing but this: What you have just experienced always was in you. Such notions build up a temporary construction that is useful for psychological orientation but collapses when one tries to stand upon it. But what occurred to me was otherness—the touch of the other. Nietzsche says it more honestly, "You take, you do not ask who it is that gives."[5] But I think that as we take, it is of the utmost importance to know that someone is giving. He who takes what is given him and does not experience it as a gift is not really receiving; and so the gift turns into theft. But when we do experience the giving, we find out that revelation exists. And we set foot on the path that will reveal our life and the life of the world as a sign communication. This path is the approach. It is on this path that we shall meet with the major experience that is of the same kind as our minor experience.

The perception of revelation is the basis for perceiving creation and redemption. I begin to realize that in inquiring about my own origin and goal I am inquiring about something other than myself and something other than the world. But in this very realization I begin to recognize the origin and goal of the world.

What meaning are we intended to find in the statement that God created the world in six days? Certainly not that He created it in six ages, and that "create" must mean "come into being"—the interpretation of those who try to contrive an approach to the Bible by forcing it into harmony with current scientific views. But just as inadequate for our purposes is the mystic interpretation, according to which the acts of creation are not acts, but emanations. It is in keeping with the nature of mysticism to resist the idea that for our sake, God assumed the lowly form of an acting person. But divest the Bible of the acting character of God, and it loses its significance, and the concepts of a Platonic or Heraclitean system—concepts born from the observation of reality—are far preferable to the homunculus-like principles of emanation in such an interpretation. What meaning, then, are we intended to find? Here, there can be no question of verbal traces of an event, because there was no one to witness it. Is access then barred to everyone who cannot believe that the biblical story of creation is the pure "word of God"? The saying of our sages (Babylonian Talmud, Tractate *Berakhot* 31b) to the effect that the Torah speaks the language of men hides a deeper seriousness than is commonly assumed. We must construe it to mean that what is unutterable can only be uttered, as it is here expressed, in the language of men. The biblical story of creation is a legitimate stammering account. Man cannot but stammer when he lines up what he knows of the universe into a chronological series of commands and "works" from the divine workshop. But this stammering of his was the only means of doing justice to the task of stating the mystery of how time springs from eternity, and world comes from that which is not world. Compared to this, every attempt to explain cosmogony "scientifically"—to supply a logical foundation for the origin of all things—is bound to fail.

If, then, the man of today can find the approach to the reality of revelation in the fact that it is our life that is being addressed, how can he find the approach to the reality of creation? His own individual life will not lead him straight to creation as it does to revelation, which he can find so readily because, as we have seen, every moment we live can in itself be its midpoint. Nevertheless the reality of creation can be found, because every man knows that he is an individual and unique. Suppose it were possible for a man to make a psycho-physical inventory of his own person—to break down his character into a sum of qualities; and suppose it were possible for him to trace each separate quality and the concurrence of all back to the most primitive living creatures, and in this way make an uninterrupted genetic analysis of his individuality by determining its derivation and reference—then his form, his face, unprecedented, comparable to none, unique, his voice never heard before, his gestures never seen before, his body informed with spirit, would still exist as the untouched residue, underived and underivable, an entity that is simply present and nothing more. If, after all this futile effort, such a man had the strength to repeat the question, he would in the final analysis discover himself simply as something that was created. Because every man is unique, another first man enters the world whenever a child is born. By being alive—everyone groping like a child back to the origin of his own self—we may experience the fact that there is an origin—that there is creation.

And now to the third, the last, and the most difficult problem: How are we to understand the concept that "in the end of days" everything in the world will be resolved, that the world will be so perfectly redeemed, as it is written, that there will be "a new heaven and a new earth"? (Isa. 66:22) Here, again, two opposite interpretations must be avoided. We must not regard the tidings in the light of another world to come. They mean that this, our world, will be purified to the state of the Kingdom, that creation will be made perfect, but not that our world will be annulled for the sake of another world. Neither do the tidings refer to a more righteous order, but to "righteousness;" not to mankind grown more peaceful, but to "peace."

Here, too, the voice we hear stammers legitimately. The prophet, who is overwhelmed by the divine word, can only speak in the words of men. He can speak only as one who is able to grasp from what and whence he is to be redeemed, but not for what and whither. And the man of today? Must not this he hears be strangest to him, exactly because it is closest to his fathomless yearning? He dreams of change but does not know transformation. He hopes that if not tomorrow, then the next day things will be better; but the idea that truth will come means nothing to him. He is familiar with the idea of development and the overcoming of obstacles, but he can realize neither that a power wishes to redeem him and the world from contradiction, nor that because of the existence of this power it is demanded of him that he turn with the whole of his being. How can we mediate between this man and the biblical message? Where is the bridge?

This is the most difficult of all. The lived moment leads directly to the knowledge of revelation, and thinking about birth leads indirectly to the knowledge of creation. But in his personal life probably not one of us will taste the essence of redemption before his last hour. And yet, here too, there is an approach. It is dark and silent and cannot be indicated by any means, save by my asking you to recall your own dark and silent hours. I mean those hours in the lowest depths when our soul hovers over the frail trapdoor which, at the very next instant, may send us down into destruction, madness, and "suicide" at our own verdict. Indeed, we are astonished that it has not opened up until now. But suddenly we feel a touch, as of a hand. It reaches down to us, it wishes to be grasped—and yet what incredible courage is needed to take the hand, to let it draw us up out of the darkness! This is redemption. We must realize the true nature of the experience proffered us: It is that our "redeemer liveth" (Job 19:18), that he wishes to redeem us—but only by our own *acceptance* of his redemption with the turning of our whole being.

Approach, I said. For all this still does not constitute a rootedness in biblical reality. But it is the approach to it. It is a beginning....

Notes

Source: Der Mensch von Heute und die jüdische Bibel (lecture of 1926), first in Martin Buber and Franz Rosenzweig: *Die Schrift und ihre Verdeutschung* (Berlin: Schocken, 1936). Olga Marx, trans., in *Israel and the World: Essays in a Time of Crisis* (New York: Schocken, 1948), pp. 89–102; also in Michael A. Meyer, trans., *On the Bible: Eighteen Studies by Martin Buber* (New York: Schocken, 1968), pp. 1–13.

1. O. Marx: ". . . and the Lord of the world in the course of history, the sequence of events occurring on earth."
2. O. Marx: ". . . understand that the love of God for his world . . . "
3. O. Marx ends with: ". . . in the current moment."
4. From the Siddur (Hebrew prayer book).
5. Friedrich Nietzsche (1844–1900), *Ecce Homo* (1888), "On Zarathustra," section 3. The passage reads: "One hears—one does not seek; one takes—one does not ask who gives: A thought suddenly flashes up like lightening, it comes with necessity, without faltering—I have never had any choice in the matter." (Anthony M. Ludovici, trans., *Ecce Homo* [New York: Russell & Russell, 1964], p. 102).

PART II

Hasidism

Spirit and Body of the Hasidic Movement (1935)

Spirit

Movements that strive for a renewal of society mean, for the most part, that the axe should be laid at the root of the existing order; they set in contrast to what has come into being a fundamentally different product of willed thought. Not so the religious movements that proceed from a renewal of the soul. However much the principle that is advocated by a genuine religious movement may be diametrically opposed to the prevailing religious status of the environment, the movement experiences and expresses this opposition not as one to the essential original content of the tradition; it feels and explains itself rather as summoned to purify this original content of its present distortions—to restore it, to "bring it back." But from this same starting point the religious movements can progress very differently in their relation to the prevailing faith. On the one hand, the old-new principle may set its own message in bodily opposition to and as the original state of the late stage of the tradition. It presents its message, therefore, as the obscured original truth, rescued and brought to light, represented by the central man "come" to restore it, and actually identical with him. Then the complete transformation and separation soon takes place. Such movements may be designated as founding ones. On the other hand, the principle may simply return to an older stage of the tradition—to the "pure word" that it has to liberate and whose distortion it combats. Then a partial separation takes place so that the mythical-dogmatic and magical-cultic fundamentals remain for the most part untouched; and, despite the organizational separation, the spiritual unity essentially continues. These movements are called reforming ones.

There is, however, a third possibility. The principle may accept the tradition in its present state with undiminished value; its teachings and precepts may be recognized in their full present extension without examining their historical credentials and without comparing them with an original form; but the principle creates a new *illumination* of the teachings and precepts; it makes it possible for it to win in this light a new soul, a new meaning; it renews the vitality of the teachings without changing them in their substance. Here no separation takes place, although here too the battle between the old and the new must break out and can take on the most violent forms: The new community remains within the hereditary one and seeks to penetrate it from within—a measuring of two forces against each other, the moving force and the conserving force, a measuring that is soon carried over to the ground of the new community itself and continues among its members, indeed, within the heart of each individual.... Among the movements of this type is the Hasidic which, around the middle of the eighteenth century, began in Podolia and Wolhynia, by the turn of the century had taken possession of the Jewry of the whole Polish kingdom as well as important parts of North East Hungary and Moldavia, and by the middle of the nineteenth century had developed into a structure benumbed in spirit but mighty in numbers that continues in existence to this day.

Genuine religious movements do not offer man the solution of the world mystery but equip him to live from the strength of the mystery; they do not instruct him about the nature of God but show him the path on which he can meet God. But among them, the third type of which I spoke is most especially concerned not with a universally valid knowledge of what is and what ought to be but only about the here and now of the human person—the eternally new shoot of the eternal truth. Just for this reason, this movement can take over, unchanged, a system of general dogmas and precepts from the contemporary stage of the tradition; its own contribution cannot be codified, it is not the material of a lasting knowledge or obligation but only light for the seeing eye, strength for the working hand, appearing ever anew. This announces itself especially clearly in Hasidism....

Hasidism took over and united two traditions without adding anything essentially different to them other than a new light and a new strength: a tradition of religious law—next to the Vedic sacrificial teaching, the most comprehensive structure of spiritual commands—the ritual formation of Judaism; and a tradition of religious knowledge, which was inferior to gnosis in the power of its images and superior to it in systematization—the Kabbalah.

These two streams of tradition were, of course, individually united in each Kabbalist, but their real fusion into one reality of life and community first took place in Hasidism.

The fusion took place through the old-new principle that it represented: the principle of the responsibility of man for God's fate in the world. Responsibility, not in a conditioned, moral sense but in an unconditioned, transcendent sense; the mysterious, inscrutable value of human action, the influence of the acting man on the destiny of the universe, even on its guiding forces—that is an ancient idea in Judaism....

This idea was elaborated in the development of the Kabbalah to the central and sustaining role in which it came forward in Hasidism; through the Kabbalistic concept of God's fate in the world.

Mythically living in the consequences of Iranian religiousness, conceptually outlined in many kinds of gnosis, the conception appears to us of the divine soul imprisoned in the material world, from which it must be redeemed.... The Kabbalah has taken over the conception of the exiled divine soul but has reforged it in the fire of the Jewish idea of unity, which excludes a primal duality. The fate of the Glory of God, the "Indwelling" (Shekhinah), now no longer befalls it from its opposite, not from the powers of matter alienated from or in enmity to God, but from the necessity of the primal will itself; it belongs to the meaning of the creation.

How is the world possible? That is the basic question of the Kabbalah, as it was the basic question of all gnosis. How can the world be since God still is? Since God is infinite, how can anything exist outside Him? Since He is eternal, how can time endure? Since He is perfect, how can imperfection come into being? Since He is unconditioned, why the conditioned?

The Kabbalah... answers: God contracted Himself to world because He, nondual and relationless unity, wanted to allow relation to emerge; because He wanted to be known, loved, and wanted; because He wanted to allow to arise from His primally one Being, in which thinking and thought are one, the otherness that strives to unity.... God willed a freely existing, in freedom knowing, in freedom loving, in freedom willing otherness; *He set it free* [*gab sie frei*]. This means the concept of *tsimtsum* (contraction).[1] But while this power, taken away from eternal being, was accorded its freedom, the limitation of its freedom was set by nothing other than its own consequences; it flooded forth beyond its God-near purity. Becoming broke forth out of being; what the Kabbalah calls "the mystery of the Breaking of the Vessels" took place.... As the light from the highest plunged into the lower spheres and shattered them, light sparks from the primordial being in the immediate presence of God—the genius-natured Adam Kadmon[2]—have fallen into the imprisonment of the material things. God's *Shekhinah* descends from sphere to sphere, wanders from world to world, banishes itself in shell after shell until it reaches its furthest exile: us. In our world, God's fate is fulfilled.

But our world is in truth the world of man.

...The Kabbalah posits the Adam Kadmon in the beginning of the world's becoming as the figure of God and the archetype of the universe, God's light his substance, God's name his life, the still quiescent elements of the spheres his limbs, all the opposites joined in him as right and left. The coming asunder of his parts is the coming to be of the world; it is also a sacrifice. But at its end—at the rim of that which has become, the event of all the breaking and darkening of the primordial light, grown out of the exuberant growth of the spheres, all opposites in him fallen apart into male and female—there stands again man, the mixed work of the elements, this earthly, singled-out individual, named, metabolically changing, innumerably born and dying, man. In him the otherness that is left to its freedom has worked itself out to its last consequences, in him it has concentrated, and he, the latest, the most burdened of creatures, has from among them all, received the full heritage of freedom.... Here, the decision takes place.

In other teachings, the God soul, sent or released by heaven to earth, could be called home or freed to return home by heaven; creation and redemption take place in the same direction, from "above" to "below." But this is not so in a teaching that, like the Jewish, is so wholly based upon the double-directional relation of the human I and the divine Thou, on the reality of reciprocity, on the *meeting*. Here, man, this miserable man is, by the very meaning of his creation, the helper of God. For his sake, for the sake of the "chooser," for the sake of he who can choose God, the world was created.... From him, from "below" the impulse toward redemption must proceed. Grace is God's *answer*.

None of the upper, inner worlds, but only this lowest and most external world, is capable of providing the thrust to transformation in the *Olam Ha-Tikkun*[3] (the world of completion), in which "the figure of the *Shekhinah* steps out of the hiddenness." For God has contracted Himself to the world, He has set it free; now fate rests on its freedom. That is the mystery of man....

What Hasidism strives for as regards the Kabbalah is the "deschematization" of the mystery. The old–new principle that it represented is, restored in purified form, that of the cosmic-metacosmic power and responsibility of man. "All worlds depend on his works, all gaze at and long for the teaching and the good deeds of man." This principle, which, by virtue of the pure intensity of Hasidism became a religious movement,[4] is no new element of teaching, as in general, Hasidism included no new element of teaching; only here it has become—through suppression (not extirpation) of the violences, formal beliefs, and mystical theories that manifoldly clung to it—a center of a life form and of a community. The eschatological impulse did not perish; the longing for the messianic redemption found at times an even more personal expression in conjuring words and storming undertakings. But the work for the sake of the end subordinated itself to the continual working on the inner worlds through the hallowing of all action....

Hasidism wants to "reveal God in this low, undermost world, in all things and at the same time in man that in him there be no limb and no movement in which God's strength might not be hidden, and none with which he could not accomplish unification." To the question of what service should come first, the Baal-Shem, the founder of Hasidism, answered: "For the spiritual man this is the first: love without mortification; for the others this is the first: to learn to see that in all corporality is a holy life and that man can lead everything back to this its root and can hallow it."

... One shall not mortify himself; "he who does harm to his body, does harm to his soul." The ascetic ecstasy is "from the other side," not of a divine, but of a demonic, nature. One shall not murder the "evil urge," the passion in oneself, but serve God with it; it is the force that shall receive direction from man ("You have made the urge evil," God already says to man in the Midrash). The "alien thoughts," the lusts that come to man are pure ideas that are corrupted in the "Breaking of the Vessels" and now desire to be raised again by man. "Even the noblest bitterness touches on melancholy, but even the most common joy grows out of holiness." One cannot reach the kernel of the fruit except through the shell....

... It is the teaching of the hallowing of the everyday. It is of no value to aspire to a new type of action that is sacral or mystical according to its material; what matters is that one does the allotted tasks—the ordinary and obvious ones—in their truth and in their meaning, and that means in the truth and the meaning of all action.

Even one's works are shells; he who performs them with the right dedication, embraces, in essence, the boundless.

On the basis of this view, it is understandable why Hasidism had no incentive to break loose any stick from the structure of the traditional law, for according to the Hasidic teaching nothing could exist that was not to be fulfilled with intention or whose intention could not be discovered. But it is also understandable how just thereby the conserving force secretly remained superior to the moving and renewing one and finally conquered it within Hasidism itself....

Body

A teaching that places the unspecifiable "how" of an act high above the codifiable "what" is not able to hand down what is peculiar to it through writing; it is communicated ever again through life, by the leader to the community but, preferably, from teacher to disciple. Not as though the teaching were divided into a part accessible to all and an esoteric realm; it would contradict its meaning, the work for man, if it concealed a secret drawer with hieratic inscription. Rather, the mystery that is handed down is just that which is also proclaimed by the enduring word; only, true to its nature as a "how" it is only pointed to by the word, but in its substantial truth it can only be presented through authentication [*Bewährung*].

Hence, a "hidden *zaddik*" said of the rabbis who "say Torah," that is, interpret the word of the Scriptures, "What is it that the Torah says? Man shall heed that all his conduct should be a Torah and himself a Torah."...

The men in whom "being a Torah!" fulfills itself are called *zaddikim*, "the righteous," the legitimate ones. They bear the Hasidic teaching, not only as its apostles, but as its working reality. They are the teaching....

The *zaddik* is not a priest or a man who renews in himself an already accomplished work of salvation or transmits it to his generation, but the man who is more concentratedly devoted than other men to the task of salvation that is for all men and all ages—the man whose forces, purified and united, are directed toward the one duty. He is, according to the conception of him, the man in whom transcendental responsibility has grown from an event of consciousness into organic existence. He is the true human being—the rightful subject of the act in which God wants to be known, loved, and wanted. In him, the "lower," earthly man realizes his archetype—the cosmic primordial man who embraces the spheres. He is the turning of the great flood; in him the world returns to its origin....

A true man is more important than an angel because the latter is "one who stands," but he is "one who walks;" he advances, penetrates, and ascends. Constant renewal is the characteristic life principle of the *zaddik*. In him, creation's event of becoming concentrates itself into creative meaning, the genuine meaning, wholly free from arbitrariness and self-seeking, which is nothing other than the turning of the creation to the Creator. The *zaddik* incessantly beholds directly the bodily renewal of all and "is moved at each moment by the renewal of the creature;" his being answers with the renewal of the spirit. And as the bodily renewal in nature is always accompanied by a submersion, a dissolution, a sleep of the elements, so there is no true spiritual becoming without a ceasing to become.... The symbolic act that corresponds to this event of deep inwardness is the immersion bath.[5] Primeval symbol of rebirth (which is only genuine when it includes death and resurrection), ... it is practiced by the *zaddikim* with a high and joyous passion that has nothing of the ascetic in it. It is told of many *zaddikim,* how during the most severe frost of winter they broke the ice of the stream to immerse themselves in flowing water; and the meaning of this fervor is revealed in the statement of a Hasid that one could replace the immersion bath by a spiritual act—that of the "stripping away of bodiliness." What is here expressed in the action is preparation and readiness to enter into the "condition of the nothing" [*Beschaffenheit des Nichts*], in which alone the divine renewal can take place.

In this ever-new exercise of the "receiving power" of the *zaddik,* the ever-new dedication of his acting power takes place. Armed with rejuvenated strength, he goes ever again to his work—to his daily work: to the thousandfold work of "unification," the *yihud....*

It is of fundamental importance to contrast the characteristic conception of yihud with magic action. The magic act means the influence of a subject on an object, of a man versed in magic on a "power"—a divine or demonic, personal or impersonal, power, appearing in the world of things or concealed behind it. Thus, it is a constitutive duality of elements of which the one, the human, is, by its fundamental nature, the weaker. But by virtue of this man's magic ability, it becomes the stronger, the most compelling. It compels the other, the divine or the demonic, into human service, into human intention, into human work. The man from whom the act proceeds is also its goal and end; the magic act is an isolated, circular causal process that turns back in on itself. *Yihud* signifies not the influence [*Einwirkung*] of a subject upon an object but the working out [*Auswirkung*] of the objective with subjectivity and through it, of existing being in and through what is becoming—a true, serious, and complete working out; indeed, so that what is becoming is not a tool that is moved but a self-mover that is freed, free, acting out of freedom—world history is not God's game, but God's fate. *Yihud* means the ever-new joining of the spheres striving to be apart, the ever-new marriage of the "majesty" with the "Kingdom"—through man; the divine element living in man moves from him to God's service, to God's intention, to God's work; God, in whose name and by whose command of creation the free *yihud* takes place, is his goal and end, with he himself turning not into himself but to God—not isolated but swallowed in the world process, not circular but the swinging back of the divine strength that was sent forth.

This distinction explains why magic must include a qualitative special action that is supposed to produce the special effect: gestures and speeches of a particular nature alien to other men and other moments. *Yihud,* in contrast, means no special formula or procedure—nothing other than the ordinary life of man, only concentrated and directed to the goal of unification....

...All formulas and arts are patchwork; the true unification rises beyond them. "He who in his prayer," says the Baal-Shem, "employs all the *kavanot*[6] that he knows, effects only just what be knows. But he who speaks the word with great binding to God, for him all *kavanah* enters of itself into each word." What matters is not what can be learned; what matters is giving oneself to the unknown....

It becomes clear here that *yihud* means a risk, *the* risk. The unification of God shall take place in the world; man shall work on God's unification out of his own unification—the human, earthly salvation, earthly understanding, earthly life must be risked for the divine. This is manifested most powerfully in prayer. It is told of one *zaddik* that every day before he went to pray, he ordered his household as if he were going to die.... The Baal-Shem-Tov compared the ecstatic movements of the Hasid, who prayed with his whole body, to the movements of a drowning man....

...Here, in genuine prayer, there appears most clearly the essential meaning of *yihud*—that it is not a "subjective" happening but the dynamic form of the divine unity itself. "The people imagine," said Rabbi Pinhas of Koretz, "that they pray before God. But this is not so. For prayer itself is the essence of divinity."

Of such kind is the lonely service of the *zaddik*. But he who remains satisfied with this is not a true *zaddik*. Man's bond with God authenticates and fulfills itself in the human world....

There are three circles in which the love of the *zaddik* is authenticated.

The first and broadest encompasses the many who come to the *zaddik* from a distance, partly—especially on the high holidays—to spend a few days near him, "in the shadow of his holiness," and partly to ask help from him for their bodily and spiritual needs. In this pilgrimage there is something of that faithful and trusting spirit with which the Palestinians once went to the temple in Jerusalem three times a year, through sacrifice, to free themselves from evil and join themselves with the divine: "the *zaddik* takes the place of the altar." ...

The second, middle circle includes those who live in the neighborhood of the *zaddik*. This represents, in general, only a part of the Jewish community of that place, the rest consisting of the "opponents" (*Mitnagdim*) and the indifferent, whose official spiritual leader is the "*rav*." Inside the Jewish community, which is a "compulsory community," stands the Hasidic—a free, a "chosen community," with the *zaddik*, the "*rebbe*" at its head (yet several *zaddikim* have also exercised the functions of the *rav* in the Hasidic-dominated communities and have borne his title). This difference corresponds to that between the legitimation of the *rav* and that of the *rebbe*. The qualification of the *rav* is the knowledge of the law demonstrated in its Talmudic roots and in the whole fullness of its rabbinical ramifications. The qualifications of the *rebbe* are the spontaneously acknowledged leadership of souls, the depth of his "fear of God," that is, the dominant feeling of the *presence* of God, and the fervor of his "heart service," that is, the shaping of his whole life to active prayer.

This in no ways means, of course, that these qualities were to be found only among the *zaddikim* and not also among the traditional rabbis, nor does it mean that many of the *zaddikim* did not possess a comprehensive and independently developing knowledge of *Halakha* (Jewish law).... One must guard against comprehending pragmatically instead of dialectically the antithesis that is inevitable in the contemplation of the inner history; the movement of the spirit takes place in contradiction, but it does not embody itself in it. With this qualification, the Hasidic community may be regarded as the social representation of the principle of spontaneity; the *zaddik* as the representative of autonomous leadership....

The third, narrowest circle is that of the disciples, of whom several are usually taken into the household community of the *zaddik*. This is the proper sphere of the transmission—the communication of the teaching from generation to generation....

The three circles in which the love of the *zaddik* is authenticated—the crowd, streaming to and fro, those seeking help; the community, bound together in the connection of space and life; and the strong ring of souls of the disciples—exhibit the forces that generated the vitality of the Hasidic movement. Its spiritual structure was founded upon the handing down of the kernel of the teaching from teacher to disciple—not as if something inaccessible to everyone was transmitted to him, but because in the atmosphere of the master, in the spontaneous working of his being, the inexpressible "how" descended, swinging and creating. The very same teaching, only blended and less condensed, was communicated in the word of counsel and instruction and was developed in the customs and brotherly life of the community. This absence of rank in the sphere of its teaching—this antihierarchical position—ensured Hasidism its popular power. As it did not abolish from without the precedence of possession, but removed its value from within through uniting rich and poor as equal members, before God and the *zaddik,* of a community of reciprocal outer and inner help—a community of love—so it overcame, in its highest moments fully, the far stronger (in Judaism elementally strong) precedence of learning—the Talmudic but also the Kabbalistic. The "spiritual" man—the man who works with his brains—is by nature no closer to the divine; indeed, as long as he has not gathered the multiplicity and ambiguity of his life into unity, as long as he has not subdued the violence of his pains to composure, he is further from the divine than the simple man who, with the simple trust of the peasant, leaves his cause to heaven.

This combination of purity of teaching and popular character is made possible by the basic content of Hasidic teaching—the hallowing of everything worldly. There is no separation within the human world between the high and the low; to each, the highest is open, each life has its access to reality, each nature its eternal right, from each thing a way leads to God, and each way that leads to God is *the* way.

Notes

Source: "Geist und Leib der chassidischen Bewegung," first as Introduction to *Der große Maggid und seine Nachfolge* (Frankfurt/M.: Rütten & Loening, 1922). Maurice Friedman, trans., in *Hasidism* (New York: Philosophical Library, 1948). Also in *The Origin and Meaning of Hasidism* (New York: Horizon Press, 1960) pp. 114-149.

Editor's note: The title "The Great Maggid" (literally, narrator, also preacher) refers to Dov Baer of Mezritch (d. 1772), a disciple of the Baal-Shem. When Buber, after a long period of withdrawal from his Hasidic work, edited the legends of "The Great Maggid" in 1921, he prefaced the collection by stating that he had matured as a re-narrator and interpreter. In the Preface, Buber also strengthened his dialogical interpretation of Hasidism, distinguishing between myth (the divine and the human are interwoven), story [*Sage*] (the divine and the human are separate), and legend in which "the world is expressed as separation, but what is told is an interaction between sphere and sphere, dialogue, mutuality" (Martin Buber, *Die chassidischen Bücher* [Berlin: Schocken 1927], p. 333). As one of Buber's most important reflections on Hasidism, "Spirit and Body of the Hasidic Movement," appeared as an independent piece in *Deutung des Chassidismus—Drei Versuche* (Berlin: Schocken, 1935).

1. M. Friedman: contradiction.
2. Hebrew: literally, primal man.
3. Buber translates *tikkun* here as "completion" (*Vollendung*), rather than "repair" or "healing."
4. M. Friedman: meeting (probably a misreading of *Bewegung* for *Begegnung*).
5. Ritual bath (*mikvah*), which requires full imersion in flowing water. Note that the word *mikvah* is also related to the Hebrew word for "hope" (*tikvah*).
6. Hebrew: intentions (plural of *kavanah*). See also The Life of the Hasidim (1908) (p. 78 in this volume).

The Life of the Hasidim (1908)

Hitlahavut: Ecstasy

Hitlahavut[1] is "the inflaming"; the ardor of ecstasy. It is the goblet of grace and the eternal key.

A fiery sword guards the way to the tree of life. It scatters into sparks before the touch of *hitlahavut,* whose light finger is more powerful than it. To *hitlahavut* the path is open, and all boundaries vanish before its boundless step. The world is no longer its place: It is the place of the world.

Hitlahavut unlocks the meaning of life. Without it even heaven has no meaning and no being. "If a man has fulfilled the whole of the teaching and all the commandments but has not had the rapture and the inflaming, when he dies and passes beyond, paradise is opened to him, but because he has not felt rapture in the world, he also does not feel it in paradise."

Hitlahavut can appear in all places and at all times. Each hour is its footstool and each deed its throne. Nothing can stand against it, and nothing can hold it down; nothing can defend itself against its might, which raises everything corporeal to spirit. He who is in it is in holiness. "He can speak idle words with his mouth, yet the teaching of the Lord is in his heart at this hour; he can pray in a whisper, yet his heart cries out in his breast; he can sit in a community of men, yet he walks with God: mixing with the creatures yet secluded from the world." Each thing and each deed is thus sanctified. "When a man attaches himself to God, he can allow his mouth to speak what it may speak and his ear to hear what it may hear, and he will bind the things to their higher root."

Repetition, the power that weakens and decolors so much in human life, is powerless before ecstasy, which catches fire again and again from precisely the most regular, most uniform events. Ecstasy overcame one *zaddik* in reciting the Scriptures, each time he uttered the words, "And God spoke." A Hasidic wise man who told this to his disciples added, "But I think also, if one speaks in truth and one receives in truth, then one word is enough to uplift the whole world and to purge the whole world from sin." To the man in ecstasy the habitual is eternally new. A *zaddik* stood at the window in the early morning light and cried, trembling, "A few hours ago it was night and now it is day—God brings up the day!" And he was full of fear and trembling. He also said, "Every creature should be ashamed before the Creator: Were he perfect, as he was destined to be, then he would be astonished and awakened and inflamed because of the renewal of the creature at each time and in each moment."

But *hitlahavut* is not a sudden sinking into eternity: It is an ascent to the infinite from rung to rung. To find God means to find the way without end. The Hasidim saw the "world to come" in the image of this way, and they never called that world a Beyond. One of the pious saw a dead master in a dream. The latter told him that from the hour of his death he went each day from world to world. And the world that yesterday was stretched out above his gaze as heaven is today the earth under his foot; and the heaven of today is the earth of tomorrow. And each world is purer and more beautiful and more profound than the one before.

The angel rests in God, but the holy spirits go forward in God. "The angel is one who stands, and the holy man is one who travels on. Therefore, the holy man is higher than the angel."

Such is the way of ecstasy. If it appears to offer an end, an arriving, an attaining, an acquiring, it is only a final no, not a final yes: It is the end of constraint, the shaking off of the last chains, the detachment that is lifted above everything earthly. "When man moves from strength to strength and ever upward and upward until he comes to the root of all teaching and all command, to the I of God, the simple unity and boundlessness—when he stands there, then all the wings of command and law sink down and are as if destroyed. For the evil impulse is destroyed since he stands above it." . . .

In ecstasy all that is past and future draws near to the present. Time shrinks, the line between the eternities disappears; only the moment lives, and the moment is eternity. In its undivided light appears all that was and all that will be, simple and composed. It is there as a heartbeat and becomes manifest as such.

The Hasidic legend has much to tell of those wonderful ones who remembered their earlier forms of existence, who were aware of the future as of their own breath, who saw from one end of the earth to the other and felt all the changes that took place in the world as something that happened to their own bodies. All this is not yet that state in which *hitlahavut* has overcome the world of space and time. We can perhaps learn something of this latter state from two simple anecdotes that supplement each other. It is told of one master that he had to look at a clock during the hour of withdrawal to keep himself in this world; and of another that when he wished to observe individual things he had to put on spectacles to restrain his spiritual vision; "for otherwise he saw all the individual things of the world as one."

But the highest rung that is reported is that on which the withdrawn one transcends his own ecstasy. When a disciple once remarked that a *zaddik* had "grown cold" and censored him for it, he was instructed by another, "There is a very high holiness; if one enters it, one becomes detached from all being and can no longer become inflamed." Thus, ecstasy completes itself in its own suspension....

But the truest life of the man of ecstasy is not among men. It is said of one master that he behaved like a stranger, according to the words of David, the King: "A sojourner [*Gastsasse*][2] am I in the land. Like a man who comes from afar, from the city of his birth. He does not think of honors nor of anything for his own welfare; he only thinks about returning home to the city of his birth. He can possess nothing, for he knows: That is alien, and I must go home." Many walk in solitude, in "the wandering."...

There are still more profoundly solitary ones whose *hitlahavut*, for all that, is not yet fulfilled. They become "unsettled and fugitive." They go into exile "to suffer exile with the *Shekhinah*. It is one of the basic conceptions of the Kabbalah that the *Shekhinah*, the exiled glory of God, wanders endlessly, separated from her "lord," and that she will be reunited with him only in the hour of redemption. So these men of ecstasy wander over the earth, dwelling in the silent distances of God's exile—companions of the universal and holy happening of existence. The man who is detached in this way is the friend of God, "as a stranger is the friend of another stranger because of their strangeness on earth." There are moments in which he sees the *Shekhinah* face to face in human form, as that *zaddik* saw it in the holy land "in the shape of a woman who weeps and laments over the husband of her youth."

But not only in faces out of the dark and in the silence of wandering does God give Himself to the soul afire with Him. Rather, out of all the things of the earth His eye looks into the eye of him who seeks, and every being is the fruit in which He offers Himself to the yearning soul. Being is unveiled in the hand of the holy man. "The soul of him who longs very much for a woman and regards her many-colored garment is not turned to its gorgeous material and its colors but to the splendor of the longed-for woman who is clothed in it. But the others see only the garment and no more. So he who in truth longs for and embraces God sees in all the things of the world only the strength and the pride of the Creator who lives in the things. But he who is not on this rung sees the things as separate from God."...

Avodah: Service

Hitlahavut is envelopment in God beyond time and space. *Avodah*[3] is the service of God in time and space.

Hitlahavut is the mystic meal. *Avodah* is the mystic offering. These are the poles between which the life of the holy man swings.

Hitlahavut is silent since it lies in the heart of God. *Avodah* speaks, "What am I and what is my life that I wish to offer you my blood and my fire?"

Hitlahavut is as far from *avodah* as fulfillment is from longing. And yet *hitlahavut* streams out of *avodah* as the finding of God from the seeking of God....

Between seeking and finding lies the tension of a human life; indeed, the thousandfold return of the anxious, wandering soul. And yet the flight of a moment is slower than the fulfillment. For God wishes to be sought, and how could he not wish to be found?

When the holy man brings ever new fire that the glowing embers on the altar of his soul may not be extinguished, God Himself says the sacrificial speech.

God governs men as He governed chaos at the time of the infancy of the world. "And as when the world began to unfold and He saw that if it flowed further asunder it would no longer be able to return home to its roots, then He spoke, 'Enough!'—so it is that when the soul of man in its suffering rushes headlong, without direction, and evil becomes so mighty in it that it soon could no longer return home, then His compassion awakens, and He says, 'Enough!'"

But man too can say "Enough!" to the multiplicity within him. When he collects himself and becomes one, he draws near to the oneness of God—he serves his Lord. This is *avodah*.

It was said of one *zaddik*, "With him, teaching and prayer and eating and sleeping are all one, and he can raise the soul to its root."

All action bound in one and the infinite life carried into every action: This is *avodah*. "In all the deeds of man—speaking and looking and listening and going and remaining standing and lying down—the boundless is clothed."

From every deed an angel is born, a good angel or a bad one. But from half-hearted and confused deeds that are without meaning or without power, angels are born with twisted limbs or without a head or hands or feet....

This is not to be understood, however, as if there were in this kind of service a cleavage between the earthly and the heavenly deed. Rather, each motion of the surrendered soul is a vessel of holiness and of power. It is told of one *zaddik* that he had so sanctified all his limbs that each step of his feet wed worlds to one another. "Man is a ladder, placed on earth and touching heaven with its head. And all his gestures and affairs and speaking leave traces in the higher world."

Here, the inner meaning of *avodah* is intimated, coming from the depths of the old Jewish secret teaching and illuminating the mystery of that duality of ecstasy and service—of having and seeking.

God has fallen into duality through the created world and its deed: into the essence of God, *Elohut* [*Gotteswesen*],[4] which is withdrawn from the creatures, and the presence of God, the *Shekhinah*, which dwells in things, wandering, straying, scattered. Only redemption will reunite the two in eternity. But it is given to the human spirit, through its service, to be able to bring the *Shekhinah* near to its source, to help it to enter it....

This is the meaning of service. Only the prayer that takes place for the sake of the *Shekhinah* truly lives. "Through his need and his want he knows the want of the *Shekhinah,* and he prays that the want of the *Shekhinah* will be satisfied and that through him, the praying man, the unification of God with His presence will take place." Man should know that his suffering comes from the suffering of the *Shekhinah*. He is "one of her limbs," and the stilling of her need is the only true stilling of his.... "I am prayer," speaks the *Shekhinah*. A *zaddik* said, "Men think they pray before God, but it is not so, for prayer itself is divinity."...

Prayer may be held down in two different ways: if it is spoken without inner intention and if the earlier deeds of the praying man spread themselves like a thick cloud between him and heaven. The obstacle can only be overcome if the man grows upward into the sphere of ecstasy and purifies himself in its grace, or if another soul who is in ecstasy sets the fettered prayers free and carries them upward along with his own. Thus, it is told of one *zaddik* that he stood silent and without movement for a long time during communal prayer and only then began to pray, "just as the tribe of Dan lay at the end of the camp and gathered all that was lost." His word became a garment to whose folds the prayers that were held below would cling and be borne upward. This *zaddik* used to say of prayer, "I bind myself with the whole of Israel, with those who are greater than I that through them my thoughts may ascend, and with those who are lesser than I that they may be uplifted through me."

But this is the mystery of community: Not only do the lower need the higher, but the higher also need the lower. Here lies another distinction between the state of ecstasy and the state of service. *Hitlahavut* is the individual way and goal; a rope is stretched over the abyss, tied to two slender trees shaken by the storm: It is trod in solitude and dread by the foot of the venturer. Here, there is no human community, neither in doubt nor in attainment. Service, however, is open to many souls in union. The souls bind themselves to one another for greater unity and might. There is a service that only the community can fulfill.

The Baal-Shem told a parable: "Some men stood under a very high tree. And one of the men had eyes to see. He saw that in the top of the tree stood a bird, glorious with genuine beauty. But the others did not see it. And a great longing came over the man to reach the bird and take it; and he could not go from there without the bird. But because of the height of the tree this was not in his power, and a ladder was not to be found. Still out of his great and powerful longing he found a way. He took the men who stood around him and placed them on top of one another, each on the shoulder of a comrade. He, however, climbed to the top so that he reached the bird and took it. And although the men had helped him, they knew nothing of the bird and did not see it. But he, who knew it and saw it, would not have been able to reach it without them. If, moreover, the lowest of them had left his place, then those above would have fallen to the earth. 'And the Temple of the Messiah is called the bird's nest in the book Zohar.'"

But it is not as if only the *zaddik's* prayer is received by God or as if only this prayer is lovely in his eyes. No prayer is stronger in grace and penetrates in more direct flight through all the worlds of heaven than that of the simple man who does not know anything to say and only knows to offer God the unbroken promptings of his heart....

A villager who, year after year, attended the prayer house of the Baal-Shem in the "Days of Awe"[5] had a boy who was dull in understanding and could not even learn the shape of the letters, let alone understand the holy words. His father did not take him to the city on the "Days of Awe," for he knew nothing. Still when the boy was thirteen years old and of age to receive God's law, the father took him with him on the Day of Atonement that he might not eat something on the day of penance through lack of knowledge and understanding. Now the boy had a small whistle that he always played during the time he sat in the field and pastured the sheep and calves. He had brought it with him in his pocket without his father knowing it. The boy sat in the prayer house during the holy hours and did not have anything to say. But when the *Mussaf*[6] prayer was begun, he spoke to his father, "Father, I have my whistle with me, and I wish to play on it."

Then the father was very disturbed and commanded him, "Take care that you do not do so."

And the boy had to hold himself in. But when the *Mincha*[7] prayer came, he spoke again, "Father, allow me now to take my whistle."

When the father saw that his son's soul desired to play the whistle, he became angry and asked him, "Where do you keep it?" And when the boy showed him the place, his father laid his hand on the pocket and guarded the whistle. But then the *Neila*[8] prayer began, and the lights burned, flickering in the evening, and the hearts burned like the lights, unexhausted by the long waiting. And through the house the Eighteen Benedictions[9] strode once again, weary but erect. And the great confession returned for the last time and, before the evening descended and God judged, the worshippers lay yet once more before the Ark of the Lord, their foreheads on the floor and their hands extended. Then the boy could no longer suppress his ecstasy; he tore the whistle from his pocket and let its voice resound powerfully. All stood startled and bewildered. But the Baal-Shem raised himself above them and spoke, "The judgment is suspended, and wrath is dispelled from the face of the earth."

Thus, every service that proceeds from a simple or a unified soul is sufficient and complete. But there is yet a higher one. For he who has ascended from *avodah* to *hitlahavut* has submerged his will in it and receives his deed from it alone, having risen above every separate service.... He who thus serves in perfection has conquered the primeval duality and has brought *hitlahavut* into the heart of *avodah*. He dwells in the kingdom of life, and yet all walls have fallen, all boundary stones are uprooted, all separation is destroyed. He is the brother of the creatures and feels their glance as if it were his own, their step as if his own feet walked, their blood as if it flowed through his own body. He is the child[10] of God and lays his soul anxiously and securely in the great hand beside all the heavens and earths and unknown worlds, and stands on the flood of the sea into which all his thoughts and the wanderings of all beings flow. "He makes his body the throne of life, and life the throne of the spirit, and the spirit the throne of the soul, and the soul the throne of the light of God's glory, and the light streams round about him, and he sits in the midst of the light and trembles and rejoices."

Kavanah: Intention

Kavanah[11] is the mystery of a soul directed to a goal.

Kavanah is not will. It does not think of transplanting an image into the world of actual things—of making fast a dream as an object so that it may be at hand, to be experienced at one's convenience in satiating recurrence. Nor does it desire to throw the stone of action into the well of happening that its waters may for awhile become troubled and astonished, only to return then to the deep command of their existence, nor to lay a spark on the fuse that runs through the succession of the generations, that a flame may jump from age to age until it is extinguished in one of them without sign or leave-taking. It is not the meaning of *Kavanah* that the horses pulling the great wagon should feel one impulse more or that one building more should be erected beneath the overfull gaze of the stars. *Kavanah* does not mean purpose, but goal.

But there are no *goals,* only *the goal*. There is only one goal that does not lie, that becomes entangled in no new way, only one into which all ways flow, before which no byway can forever flee: redemption.

Kavanah is a ray of God's glory that dwells in each man and means redemption.

This is redemption, that the *Shekhinah* shall return home from its exile: "That all shells may withdraw from God's glory and that it may purify itself and unite itself with its owner in perfect unity." As a sign of this the Messiah will appear and make all beings free.

To many a Hasid, it is, for the whole of his life, as if this must happen here and now. For he hears the voice of becoming as it roars in the gorges and feels the seed of eternity in the ground of time as if it were in his blood. And so he can never think otherwise than that this moment, and now this one, will be the chosen moment. And his imagination compels him ever more fervently, for ever more commandingly speaks the voice and ever more demandingly swells the seed....

Others, however, are aware of the progress of the stride, see the place and hour of the path and know the distance of the Coming One. Each thing shows them the uncompleted state of the world; the need of existence speaks to them, and the breath of the winds bears bitterness to them. The world in their eyes is like an unripe fruit. Inwardly they partake in the glory—then they look outward: All lies in battle.

When the great *zaddik*, Rabbi Menachem, was in Jerusalem, it happened that a foolish man climbed the Mount of Olives and blew the *shofar* (ram's horn trumpet). No one had seen him. A rumor spread among the people that this was the *shofar* blast that announced the redemption. When it came to the ears of the rabbi, he opened a window and looked out into the air of the world. And he said at once, "Here is no renewal."

This is the way of redemption: that all souls and all sparks of souls that have sprung from the primeval soul and have sunk and become scattered in all creatures at the time of the original darkening of the world or through the guilt of the ages should conclude their wandering and return home purified....

It is not only souls that are everywhere imprisoned but also sparks of souls. Nothing is without them. They live in all that is. Each form is their prison.

And this is the meaning and mission of *kavanah*: that it is given to men to lift up the fallen and to free the imprisoned. Not only to wait, not only to watch for the Coming One: Man can work toward the redemption of the world.

Just that is *kavanah*: the mystery of the soul that is directed to redeem the world....

Each man has a sphere of being, far extended in space and time, which is allotted to him to be redeemed through him. Places that are heavy with unraised sparks and in which souls are confined wait for the man who will come to them with the word of freedom....

However, though it is only the blessed ones who can plunge tranquilly into the darkness to aid a soul that is abandoned in the whirlpool of wandering, it is not denied to even the least of persons to raise the lost sparks from their imprisonment and send them home.

The sparks are to be found everywhere. They are suspended in things such as in sealed-off springs; they stoop in the creatures as in walled-up caves, they inhale darkness and they exhale dread; they wait. And those that dwell in space flit hither and thither around the movements of the world, like light-mad butterflies, looking to see which of them they might enter to be redeemed through them. They all wait expectantly for freedom....

But the liberation does not take place through formulas of exorcism or through any kind of prescribed and special action. All this grows out of the ground of otherness, which is not the ground of *kavanah*. No leap from the everyday into the miraculous is required. "With his every act man can work on the figure of the glory of God that it may step forth out of its concealment." It is not the matter of the action, but only its dedication that is decisive.... He who prays and sings in holiness, eats and speaks in holiness, in holiness takes the prescribed ritual bath, and in holiness is mindful of his business—through him the fallen sparks are raised and the fallen worlds are redeemed and renewed.

Around each man—enclosed within the wide sphere of his activity—is laid a natural circle of things which, before all, he is called to set free. These are the creatures and objects that are spoken of as the possessions of this individual: his animals and his walls, his garden and his meadow, his tools and his food. Insofar as he cultivates and enjoys them in holiness, he frees their souls. "For this reason a man should always have mercy on his tools and all his possessions."

But also in the soul itself there appear those that need liberation. Most of these are sparks that have fallen through the guilt of this soul in one of its earlier lives. They are the alien, disturbing thoughts that often come to man in prayer. "When man stands in prayer and desires to join himself to the Eternal, and the alien thoughts come and descend on him, these are holy sparks that have sunken and that wish to be raised and redeemed by him; and the sparks belong to him, they are kindred to the roots of his soul: it is his power that will redeem them." . . .

This is the *kavanah* of receiving: that one redeems the sparks in the surrounding things and the sparks that draw near out of the invisible. But there is yet another *kavanah*, the *kavanah* of giving. It bears no stray soul rays in helpful hands; it binds worlds to one another and rules over the mysteries, it pours itself into the thirsty distance, it gives itself to infinity. But it too has no need of miraculous deeds. Its path is creation [*Schaffen*], and it is the word that comes before all other forms of creation.

From time immemorial speech was for the Jewish mystic a rare and awe-inspiring thing. A characteristic theory existed that dealt with the Hebrew letters as with the elements of the world and with their intermixture as with the inwardness of reality. The word is an abyss through which the speaker strides. "One should speak words as if the heavens were opened in them. And as if it were not so that you take the word in your mouth, but rather as if you entered into the word." He who knows the secret melody that bears the inner into the outer—*kavanah*: intention, who knows the holy song that merges the lonely, shy letters into the singing of the spheres—he is full of the power of God, "and it is as if he created heaven and earth and all worlds anew." He does not find his sphere before him as does the freer of souls; he extends it from the firmament to the silent depths. But he also works toward redemption. "For in each letter are the three: world, soul, and divinity. They rise and join and unite themselves, and they become the word, and the words unite themselves in God in genuine unity, since a man has set his soul in them, and worlds unite themselves and ascend, and the great rapture is born." Thus, the acting person prepares the final unificiation[12] of all things [*All-Einung*].

And as *avodah* flowed into *hitlahavut*, the basic principle of Hasidic life, so here too *kavanah* flows into *hitlahavut*. For creating means to be created: The divine moves and overcomes us. And to be created is ecstasy: Only he who sinks into the Nothing of the Absolute receives the forming hand of the spirit. This is portrayed in parable. It is not given to anything in the world to be reborn and to attain to a new form unless it comes first to the Nothing, that is, to the "form of the in-between [*Gestalt des Dazwischen*]." No creature can exist in it; it is the power before creation and is called chaos.... "And this is called wisdom, that is, a thought without revelation. And so it is: If man desires that a new creation come out of him, then he must come with all his potentiality to the state of nothing, and then God brings forth in him a new creation, and he is like a fountain that does not run dry and a stream that does not cease to flow."

Thus, the will of the Hasidic teaching of *kavanah* is twofold: that enjoyment—the internalizing of that which is without—should take place in holiness, and that creation—the externalizing of that which is within, should take place in holiness. Through holy creation and through holy enjoyment the redemption of the world is accomplished.

Shiflut: Humility

God never does the same thing twice, said Rabbi Nachman of Bratzlav.

That which exists is unique, and it happens but once. New and without a past, it emerges from the flood of returnings [*Wiederkünfte*], takes place, and plunges back into it, unrepeatable. Each thing reappears at another time, but each is transformed. And the throws and falls that rule over the great world creations, and the water and fire that shape the form of the earth, and the mixings and unmixings that brew the life of the living, and the spirit of man with all its trial-and-error relation to the yielding abundance of the possible—none of these can create an identical thing nor bring back one of the things that has been sealed as belonging to the past. It is because things happen but once that the individual partakes in eternity. For the individual with his inextinguishable uniqueness is engraved in the heart of the all and lies forever in the lap of the timeless as he who has been created thus and not otherwise.

Uniqueness is thus the essential good of man that is given to him to unfold. And just this is the meaning of the return [*Wiederkehr*], that his uniqueness may become ever purer and more complete; and that in each new life the one who has returned may stand in ever more untroubled and undisturbed incomparability. For pure uniqueness and pure perfection are one, and he who has become so entirely individual that no otherness any longer has power over him or place in him has completed the journey and is redeemed and rests in God....

But as man seeks God in lonely fervor—yet there is a high service that only the community can fulfill—and as man accomplishes enormous things with his everyday actions—yet does not do so alone but needs for such action the world and the things in it—so the uniqueness of man proves itself in his life with others. For the more unique a man really is, so much more can he give to the other and so much more will he give to the other. And this is his one sorrow, that his giving is limited by the one who takes. For "the bestower is on the side of mercy and the receiver is on the side of rigor. And so it is with each thing. As when one pours out of a large vessel into a goblet: The vessel pours from out of its fullness, but the goblet limits the gift."

The individual sees God and embraces Him. The individual redeems the fallen worlds. And yet the individual is not a whole, but a part. And the purer and more perfect he is, so much more intimately does he know that he is a part and so much more actively there stirs in him the community of existence. That is the mystery of humility.... To feel the universal generation as a sea and oneself as a wave—that is the mystery of humility.

But it is not humility when one "lowers himself too much and forgets that man can bring down an overflowing blessing on all the world through his words and his actions." This is called impure humility. "The greatest evil is when you forget that you are the son of a king." He is truly humble who feels the other as himself and himself in the other.

Haughtiness means to contrast oneself with others. The haughty man is not he who knows himself but he who compares himself with others. No man can presume too much if he stands on his own ground since all the heavens are open to him and all worlds devoted to him. The man who presumes too much is the man who contrasts himself with others, who sees himself as higher than the humblest of things, who rules with measure and weights and pronounces judgment.

"If Messiah should come today," a *zaddik* said, "and say, 'You are better than the others,' then I would say to him, 'You are not Messiah.'"

The soul of the haughty lives without product and essence; it flutters and toils and is not blessed. Thoughts whose real intent is not what is thought, but which refer to themselves, are, along with their brilliance, merely shadows. The deed that has in mind not the goal but the profit has no body, only surface; no existence, only appearance. He who measures and weighs becomes empty and unreal like measure and weight. "In him who is full of himself there is no room for God."...

The humility that is meant here is no willed and practiced virtue. It is nothing but an inner being, feeling, and expressing. Nowhere in it is there a compulsion, nowhere a self-humbling, a self-restraining, a self-resolve. It is indivisible as the glance of a child and as simple as a child's speech.

The humble man lives in each being and knows each being's manner and virtue. Since no one is to him "the other," he knows from within that none lacks some hidden value; he knows that there "is no man who does not have his hour." For him, the colors of the world do not blend with one another; rather, each soul stands before him in the majesty of its particular existence. "In each man there is a priceless treasure that is in no other. Therefore, one shall honor each man for the hidden value that only he and none of his comrades has."...

Living with the other as a form of knowing [*Erkennen*] is justice. Living with the other as a form of being is love. For the feeling that is called love among men—the feeling of being near and of wishing to be near a few—is nothing other than a recollection from a heavenly life: "Those who sat next to one another in Paradise and were neighbors and relatives, they are also near to one another in this world." But in truth, love is all comprehensive and sustaining and is extended to all of the living without selection and distinction. "How can you say of me that I am a leader of the generation," said a *zaddik*, "when I still feel in myself a stronger love for those near me and for my seed than for all men?"...

Thus, it is held that the love of the living is the love of God, and it is higher than any other service. A master asked one of his disciples, "You know that two forces cannot occupy the human mind at the same time. If, then, you rise from your couch tomorrow and two ways are before you—the love of God and the love of man—which should come first?" "I do not know," the disciple answered. Then spoke the master, "It is written in the prayer book that is in the hands of the people, 'Before you pray, say the words, Love thy companion as one like thyself.' Do you think that the venerable ones commanded that without purpose? If someone says to you that he has love for God but has no love for the living, he speaks falsely and pretends that which is impossible."

Therefore, when one has departed from God, the love of a man is his only salvation. A father complained to the Baal-Shem, "My son is estranged from God—what shall I do?" He replied, "Love him more."

This is one of the primary Hasidic words: to love more. Its roots sink deep and stretch out far. He who has understood this can learn to understand Judaism anew. There is a great moving force therein....

The essence of love[13] lives in a kingdom greater than the kingdom of the individual and speaks out of a knowing deeper than the knowing of the individual. It exists in reality between the creatures, that is, it exists in God. Life covered and guaranteed by life, life pouring itself into life; thus, first do you behold the soul of the world. What the one is wanting, the other makes up for. If one loves too little, the other will love more.

Things help one another. But helping means to do what one does for its own sake and with a collected will. As he who loves more does not preach love to the other, but himself loves and, in a certain sense, does not concern himself about the other, so the helping man, in a certain sense, does not concern himself about the other but does what he does out of himself with the thought of helping. That means that the essential thing that takes place between beings does not take place through their intercourse, but through each seemingly isolated, seemingly unconcerned, seemingly unconnected action performed out of himself. This is said in parable: "If a man sings and cannot lift his voice and another comes to help him and begins to sing, then this one too can now lift his voice. And that is the secret of co-operation [*Verbindung*]."

To help one another is no task, but a matter of course, the reality on which the "life together" of the Hasidim is founded. Help is no virtue but an artery of existence....

He who lives with others in this way realizes with his deed the truth that all souls are one; for each is a spark from the original soul, and the whole of the original soul [*Urseele*] is in each.

Thus lives the humble man, who is the righteous,[14] loving man and the helper—mixing with all and untouched by all, devoted to the multitude and collected in his uniqueness, fulfilling on the rocky summits of solitude the bond with the infinite and in the valley of life the bond with the earthly, flowering out of deep devotion and withdrawn from all desire of the desiring. He knows that all is in God and greets His messengers as trusted friends. He has no fear of the before and the after, of the above and the below, of this world and the world to come. He is at home and never can be cast out. The earth cannot help but be his cradle, and heaven cannot help but be his mirror and his echo.

Notes

Source: "Das Leben der Chassidim," first in Martin Buber, *Die Legende des Baalschem* (Frankfurt/M.: Rütten & Loening, 1908). Earlier versions of *"Kavanah"* and *"Shiflut"* appeared in *Die Welt* 11, no. 23 (1907) and 11, no. 48 (1907), respectively. Maurice Friedman, trans., *The Legend of the Baal-Schem* (New York: Harper, 1955); also *Hasidism and Modern Man* (New York: Horizon Press, 1958), pp. 74–122.

Editor's note: The present text is one of Buber's earliest interpretations of Hasidism. Note that Buber's language is still under the spell of predialogical mysticism. At the same time, however, we cannot but observe the progression from ecstasy (*hitlahavut*) to humility (*shiflut*) as one from solitude to co-operation (*Verbindung*). Note also the rudimentary distinction between "living with the other as a form of knowing" and "living with the other as a form of being," which recurs in Buber's philosophy of dialogue.

1. Hebrew: enthusiasm, inflaming (*lehava:* flame).
2. Buber translates the Hebrew *ger* literally as "temporary resident" (cf. Pss. 39:12, 119:19).
3. In Hebrew, *avodah* can mean both work and worship.
4. M. Friedman: *Elohim*.
5. The days between the Jewish New Year (Rosh Hashanah) and the Day of Atonement (Yom Kippur).
6. Additional prayer on special days
7. Afternoon prayer.
8. Concluding prayer on Yom Kippur.
9. Eighteen Benedictions prayer (*Amidah,* standing prayer): Central prayer in Jewish worship service.
10. M. Friedman: son
11. Hebrew: intention; literally, being-in-direction; directedness.
12. M. Friedman: oneness
13. M. Friedman: It is the love of a being who lives...
14. M. Friedman:... the loving man...

Hasidism and Modern Man (1956)

Life and Legend[1]

It has been more than fifty years since I began to acquaint the West with the religious movement known as Hasidism, which emerged in the eighteenth century but extends into our time. If, today, reporting and clarifying, I wish to speak of that work as a whole, it is not—I think I can say this with confidence—for the sake of my personal endeavors. In producing this work I had nothing else in mind other than carrying out a commission to the best of my ability, as an honest artisan would. I speak for the sake of what my work wished and wishes to point to. Much in it has at times been misunderstood and needs clarification.

Commission, I said—but is this comparison accurate? Was there someone who commissioned? No, there certainly was not; no one told me that he needed what I made. Yet, it has not been a literary project either. There was something that commanded me, yes; which even took hold of me as an instrument at its disposal. What was it? Perhaps, just Hasidism itself? No, it certainly was not this. Hasidism works exclusively within the boundaries of Jewish tradition and concerns no one outside of these boundaries. It was—I might even venture to express—something that hid itself in Hasidism and would, or rather should, go out into the world. And I was not unsuited to help it do this.

At that time, I was still, to be sure, an immature man; the so-called *zeitgeist* still had power over me. Together with my readiness to make an adequate testimony to the great reality of faith disclosed to me through books and men was something of the widespread tendency of that time to display the contents of foreign religions to readers who wavered between desire for information and sheer curiosity. Furthermore, I did not yet know how to hold in check my inner inclination to transform poetically the narrative material. I did not bring in any alien motifs; still I did not listen attentively enough to the crude and ungainly but living "folk tone" that could be heard from this material. At work in me, too, was a natural reaction against the attitude of most Jewish historians of the nineteenth century toward Hasidism, in which they found nothing but wild superstition. The need, in the face of this misunderstanding, to point out the purity and loftiness of Hasidism led me to pay all too little attention to its popular vitality. Thus, today I can still affirm these early attempts, to some extent, as a piece of work; as fulfillment of the task placed upon me. However, these efforts have long since ceased to satisfy me. The representation of the Hasidic teaching that I gave was essentially faithful; but where I retold the legendary tradition, I still did so as the Western author that I was.

Only in the course of the decade that followed the first publications did my authorship become a service, even though its independence could naturally only grow and not lessen.

In the year before World War I, the approach of the first stage of a catastrophe in the most exact sense of the term became evident to me.

At that time, I gradually began to realize what later, after the end of the war, fulminated within me to certainty: that the human spirit is either bound to existence [*existenzverbindlich*] or, even though it is of the most astonishing caliber, it is nothing before the decisive judgment. Note well, this was not a question of a philosophical conviction; it was not a question of what is usually described as existentialism. Rather, it was a question of the claim of existence itself, which had grown irresistible. The realization that grew in me at that time—that of human life as the possibility of a dialogue with being—was only the intellectual expression of just this certainty or just this claim.

At the same time, but in a special osmosis with it, my relationship to Hasidism was basically transformed ever more. To be sure, I knew from the beginning that Hasidism was not a teaching that was realized by its adherents in this or that measure, but as a way of life, to which the teaching provided the indispensable commentary. But it became overpoweringly clear that this life was involved in a mysterious manner in the task that had claimed me. I could not become a Hasid. It would have been an unpermissible masquerading had I taken on the Hasidic manner of life—I who had an entire other relation to Jewish tradition, since I must distinguish in my innermost being between what is commanded to me and what is not commanded to me. It was necessary, rather, to take into my own existence as much as I actually could of what had been truly exemplified for me there, that is, of the realization of that dialogue with being whose possibility my thought had shown me. I say, to be sure, "task," and I say, "It needed to be done." But in truth there was never anything like an intention or a project—it happened only as it happened....

Out of these transformations the work has taken shape in the special form in which I have now, for the most part, retold the crude and shapeless traditional material. It is, in my opinion, a valid form of literature, that I call legendary anecdote. It has not developed out of literary presuppositions on the path of literary attempts but out of the simple necessity to create a verbal expression adequate to an overpowering objective reality. It was the reality of the exemplary lives—of the lives reported as exemplary—of a great series of leaders of Hasidic communities. They were not reported in a connected biography but in a tremendous series of instances—limited events in which something was at times spoken but often, only done, only lived. Yet even the dumb happening spoke: It told the exemplary. And, indeed, it did not tell it didactically; no "moral" was attached to the event, but it spoke, even as a life event speaks. And if a saying was included, its effect too was like that of a life event. But since the whole was handed down in crude formlessness, the new teller was obliged to reconstruct the pure event—nothing less but also nothing more. Thus grew the form of the legendary anecdote. They are called anecdotes because each one of them communicates an event complete in itself, and legendary because at the base of them lies the stammering of inspired witnesses who witnessed what befell them, what they comprehended, as well as what was incomprehensible to them; for the legitimately inspired has an honest memory that can nonetheless outstrip all imagination.

This form has enabled me to portray the Hasidic life in such a way that it becomes visible as at once reality and teaching. Even where I had to let theory speak, I could relate it back to the life.

But I became more and more aware of a fact that has become of utmost significance to me: that the kernel of this life is capable of working on men even today, when most of the powers of the Hasidic community itself have been given over to decay or destruction, and it is just on the present-day West that it is capable of working in a special manner. After the rise and decline of that life in the Polish, Ukrainian, and Lithuanian ghettos, this kernel has entered into a contemporaneity, which is still surely only reminiscent—only an indication in the spirit—but even so can accomplish something in this manifestation that was basically foreign to the reality of that time. From here comes an answer to the crisis of Western man that has become fully manifest in our age. It is a partial answer only, not an ideological one, however, but one stemming directly out of reality and permeated by it. That life arose once as the reply of the primal Jewish faith [*urjüdischer Glaube*] to the utterly unfruitful exaltation of the pseudomessianic movements of the seventeenth and eighteenth centuries that confounded redemption and liberation, even as they confounded the divine and the human. To this salvational confusion it offered resistance of a hallowing of the everyday in which the demonic was overcome through being transformed.

Sacred and Profane

What is of greatest importance in Hasidism, today as then, is the powerful tendency, preserved in personal as well as in communal existence, to overcome the fundamental separation between the sacred and the profane.

This separation has formed a part of the foundations of every religion. Everywhere the sacred is removed and set apart from the fullness of the things, properties, and actions belonging to the universal, and the sacred now forms in its totality a self-contained holiness outside of which the diffused profane must pitch its tent.

The consequence of this separation in the history of man is a twofold one. Religion is thereby assured a firm province whose untouchableness is ever again guaranteed it by the representatives of the state and society, not, for the most part, without compensation. But at the same time, the adherents of religion are thereby enabled to allow the essential application of their relation of faith to fulfill itself within this province alone, without the sacred being given a corresponding power in the rest of life, and particularly in its public sphere.

In Judaism, the border between the two realms appears at first glance to be drawn with utmost clarity. To one coming from the outside, the great mass of rituals appears like something existing for itself. Moreover, even from within much testifies to the sharpness of this separation: thus, the invocation of God spoken at the end of the Sabbath as that which separates the sacred from the profane.[2] One need only note how many everyday actions are introduced by a blessing, however, to recognize how deep the hallowing reaches into what is in itself unsanctified. One not only blesses God every morning on awakening because He has allowed one to awaken but also when one begins to use a new house or piece of clothing or tool because one has been preserved in life to this hour. Thus, the simple fact of continued earthly existence is here sanctified on each occasion that offers itself and thereby also the occasion itself. The concept is progressively formed, however, that the separation between the realms is only a provisional one. The commands of the religious law, accordingly, only delimit the sphere that is already claimed for hallowing—the sphere in which the preparation and education for every action becoming holy takes place. In the messianic world, all shall be holy. In Hasidism, this tendency reaches a highly realistic consummation. The profane is regarded only as a preliminary stage of the holy; it is the not yet hallowed. But human life is destined to be hallowed in all its natural, that is, its created, structure. "God dwells where one lets Him in," says a Hasidic adage; the hallowing of man means this letting in. Basically, the holy in our world is nothing other than what is open to transcendence, as the profane is nothing other than what at first is closed off from it, and hallowing is the event of opening out.

Here, a misunderstanding must be avoided. One readily ascribes to Judaism a "religious activism" that does not know the reality of grace and pursues vain self-hallowing or self-salvation. In reality, in Judaism, the relation between man's action and God's grace is guarded as a mystery, even as that between human freedom and God's all-knowing—a mystery that is ultimately identical with that of the relation between God and man. Man cannot take himself in hand, so to speak, to hallow himself; he is never in his own hand. But there is something that he has retained as a creature; something that is given over just to him and expected just from him. It is called the beginning. A saying explains the opening word of the Hebrew Bible, the word *bereshit* ("in the beginning"), in this fashion: The world was created for the sake of the beginning, for the sake of making a beginning, for the sake of the human beginning ever anew. The fact of creation means an ever-renewed situation of choice. Hallowing is an event that commences in the depths of man, where choosing, deciding, and beginning take place. The man who thus begins enters into the hallowing. But he can only do this if he begins just as man and presumes to no superhuman holiness. The true hallowing of a man is the hallowing of the human in him. Therefore, the Biblical command, "Holy men shall you be unto me" has received Hasidic interpretation thus, "*Humanly* holy shall you be unto me."

In life, as Hasidism understands and proclaims it, there is, accordingly, no essential distinction between sacred and profane spaces, between sacred and profane times, between sacred and profane actions, between sacred and profane conversations. At each place, in each hour, in each act, in each speech, the holy can blossom forth. As an example that rises to symbolic heights, I cite the story of Rabbi Shmelke's sleep.[3] So that his study in the holy books should not suffer too long an interruption, Rabbi Shmelke slept in a sitting position, with his head on his arm; but between his fingers he held a burning candle that awakened him as soon as the flame touched his hand. When Rabbi Elimelech visited Rabbi Shmelke and recognized the still imprisoned might of his holiness, he carefully prepared for him a couch and induced him with much persuasion to stretch himself out on it for awhile. Then he shut and darkened the window. Rabbi Shmelke only awoke when it was already broad daylight. He noticed how long he had slept, but it did not bother him; for he felt an unknown, sunlike clarity. He went into the prayer house and prayed before the community, as was his custom. To the community, however, it appeared as if they had never before heard him, so did the might of his holiness compel and liberate all. When he sang the song of the Sea of Reeds,[4] they had to pull up their caftans so that the waves rearing up to the right and the left would not wet them.

Here the antiascetic character of Hasidic teaching also finds expression. No mortification of the urges is needed, for all natural life can be hallowed: One can live it with holy intention. The Hasidic teaching likes to explain this intention in connection with the Kabbalistic myth of the holy sparks. With the "breaking of the world vessels," which in the era before creation could not withstand the creative overflow, sparks have fallen into all things and are now imprisoned in them until once again a man uses a thing in holiness and thus liberates the sparks that it conceals. "All that man possesses," says the Baal-Shem, "conceals sparks which belong to the root of his soul and wish to be elevated by him to their origin." And he says further, "Therefore one should have mercy on his tools and all his possessions; one should have mercy on the holy sparks." Even in food there dwell holy sparks, and eating can be holier than fasting: The latter is only the preparation for hallowing; the former can be hallowing itself.

What Hasidism here expresses mythically is a central knowledge that is communicable only in images, not in concepts. But it is by no means exclusively bound to this one mythical tradition. The same teaching is expressed in a wholly different, biblically based image: "Every creature, plant and animal offers itself to man, but by man all is offered to God. When man with all his limbs purifies and hallows himself to an offering, he purifies and hallows the creature." Here, the concept becomes still clearer that man is commissioned and summoned as a cosmic mediator to awaken a holy reality in things through holy contact with them.

The same basic thought attains expression, not in such traditional form but in a wholly personal way, in the conversation that has been preserved for us of a great *zaddik* with his son. He asks the son, "With what do you pray?" The son understands the meaning of the question as, On what meditation do you base your prayer? He replies, "Everything of great stature shall bow before Thee."[5] Then he asks the father, "And with what do you pray?" "With the floor," answers the father, "and with the bench." This is no metaphor; the word "with" is now meant quite directly: In praying, the rabbi joins himself to the floor on which he stands and the bench on which he sits. They, the things that are surely made by human hand, yet like all things have their origin in God, help him to pray. And he helps them pray, indeed; he raises them—the wooden floor and the wooden bench—to origin; to their origin, he "elevates" them.

But this "elevation" is by no means to be understood as removing the worldly character of things or spiritualizing the world, although something of this is to be found in Hasidic doctrine. The life of which I speak, the exemplary life, has proved itself stronger than the thought, and in the measure that the teaching became the commentary of this life, it had to adapt itself to it. What is ultimately in question here finds naive yet true expression in another narrative. It is told of a *zaddik* that once the people spoke before him of the great misery of the human race. Sunk in grief, he listened. Then he raised his head. "Let us," he cried, "draw God into the world, and all will be stilled." One must not understand this bold speech as if a presumptuous "activism" comes to words in it. It stems rather from the same spirit as the saying that we have already quoted, "God dwells where one lets Him in." God wants—that is the meaning of it—to dwell in the world, but only when the world wants to let Him in. Let us, the Hasidic rabbi says to the world, prepare for God a dwelling place [*Wohnstatt*] into which He desires to enter; when it is prepared by us, by the world of its own will, we let God in. The hallowing of the world will be this letting in. But grace wants to help the world to hallow itself.

None of this presupposes, however, that God does not dwell in his creation. That would indeed contradict that verse of the Scriptures in which it is said of God, He makes His dwelling "with them in the midst of their uncleanness," a verse that does not speak, to be sure, of a permanent dwelling—that would be described otherwise—but simply of a temporary residing. Also the postbiblical conception of the *Shekhinah*[6]—later given manifold mythical development by the mystics and intimately familiar to Hasidism—the conception of the divine "indwelling" [*Einwohnung*]—a hypostasis or emanation that joins itself to the human race exiled from Paradise, or to Israel driven out of its land, and wanders with it over the earth—it too means only the divine participation in the destiny of His sinful and suffering creation: The work of the "stilling" of this suffering, of which the Hasidic tale speaks, is no longer of a historical nature. Here, as ever again in Hasidism, the eschatological conception breaks into the lived hour and permeates it.

We must, therefore, distinguish within Hasidic life and Hasidic teaching between two kinds of "letting God in." This distinction can be clarified through looking once more at two different sayings.

The one is attached to the conception of the *Shekhinah*. The verse of the Psalm, "A passing guest am I on the earth, do not conceal from me your commandment,"[7] was expounded thus by a *zaddik:* "You are, like me, a guest on the earth and your indwelling has no resting place: So do not withdraw yourself from me, but disclose to me your commandment so that I can become your friend." God helps with His nearness the man who wants to hallow himself and his world.

To understand correctly what manner of existence is meant here, we would do well to place another saying of the same *zaddik* by its side: "The sparks which fell down from the primal creation into the covering shells and were transformed into stones, plants, and animals, they all ascend to their source through the consecration of the pious who works on them in holiness, uses them in holiness, consumes them in holiness." Thus is the man created who calls himself a guest on earth.

The second saying stems from a later *zaddik:* "The peoples of the earth also believe that there are two worlds; 'in that world,' they say. The difference is this: They understand the two worlds to be removed and cut off from each other. But Israel believes that the two worlds are one in their ground and that they shall become one in their reality."

Only the two sayings taken together give us the basic content of Hasidic faith.

Western Man

The central example of the Hasidic overcoming of the distance between the sacred and the profane points to an explanation of what is to be understood by the fact that Hasidism has its word to speak in the crisis of Western man....

Modern thinkers have attempted to give a causal explanation of the crisis through various partial aspects: Karl Marx, through the radical "alienation" of man caused by the economic and technical revolutions, and the psychoanalysts, through individual or even collective neuroses. But none of these attempts at explanation nor all of them together can yield an adequate understanding of what concerns us. We must take the injured wholeness of man upon us as a life burden to press beyond all that is merely symptomatic, and grasp the true sickness through which those motifs receive the force to work as they have worked. Those who instead contemplate the cruel problematic as a subject of unsurpassable interest—who know how to describe and even perhaps to praise it—contribute, at times with the highest gifts, to the massive decisionlessness whose true name is the decision for nothing.

An especially threatening trait of the crisis is the secularized form of the radical separation between the sacred and the profane. The sacred has become in many cases a concept empty of reality—one of merely historical and ethnological significance. But its character of detachment has found an heir. One no longer knows the holy face to face; but one believes that one knows and cherishes its heir, the "spiritual," without, of course, allowing it the right to determine life in any way.... No false piety has ever attained this concentrated degree of inauthenticity.

Only now has one basically gotten rid of the holy and the command of hallowing.

Against the behavior of present-day man, Hasidism sets the simple truth that the wretchedness of our world is grounded in its resistance to the entrance of the holy into lived life. The spirit was not spun in the brain; it has been from all eternity, and life can receive it into human reality. A life that does not seek to realize what the living person, in the ground of his self-awareness, understands or glimpses as the right is not merely unworthy of the spirit; it is also not worth being lived.[8]

Especially important within the secularized division between the above and the below is the sickening of our contact with things and beings. The thinking of the age knows how to speak about things and beings in an illuminating fashion, but the great insight that our relations to things and beings form the marrow of our existence seems to have become alien to life. The Hasidic teaching of the holy engagement [*Umgang*] with all existing beings opposes this corrosion of the living power of meeting [*Begegnungskraft*] as the progressive evasion of man before the meeting with God in the world.

The Message of Hasidism

I have not converted the message of Hasidism into solid concepts; I am concerned with preserving its mythical as well as its epic essence. I cannot concur with the postulate of the hour—to demythologize religion. For myth is not the subsequent clothing of a truth of faith; it is the unarbitrary testimony of the image-making vision and the image-making memory, and the conceptual cannot be refined out of it. No sermonic teaching can replace the myth, but there can certainly be sermonic teachings that are able to renew it through bearing it uninjured into the present. That this may be possible, where myth has taken on a gnostic nature, that is, where it has been employed to represent the mystery of transcendent being as knowable, it must, of course, be freed from this nature, this unnatural state, and restored to its original condition. Such restoration and renewal was accomplished by Hasidism with the myths permeated by gnosis that it took over from the Kabbalah. My transmission of the Hasidic message is no speculative theology; where myth is here perceivable, it is one that has entered into the lived life of seven generations, as whose late-born interpreter I function.

In this form I have sought, in a lifelong work, to introduce the Hasidic life teaching to present-day Western man. It has often been suggested to me that I should liberate this teaching from its "confessional limitations," as people like to put it, and proclaim it as an unfettered teaching of mankind. Taking such a "universal" path would have been for me pure arbitrariness. To speak to the world what I have heard, I am not bound to step into the street. I may remain standing in the door of my ancestral house: Here, too, the word that is uttered does not go astray.

The Hasidic word says that the worlds can fulfill their destiny of becoming one through man's life becoming one. But how can that be understood? Is then a completed unity of living thinkable anywhere else than in the transcendence itself? Israel's confession of the oneness of God says, indeed, not merely that outside of Him there is no God, but also that He alone is unity. Here, the interpreter must enter in. If man can become "humanly holy," that is, become holy as man, in the measure and in the manner of man, and, indeed, as it is written, "to Me,"[9]—in the face of God—then he, the individual man, can also—in the measure of his personal ability and in the manner of his personal possibility—become one in the sight of God. Man cannot approach the divine by reaching beyond the human; he can approach Him through becoming human. To become human is what he, this individual man, has been created for. This, so it seems to me, is the eternal core of Hasidic life and of Hasidic teaching.

Notes

Source: "Der Chassidismus und der abendländische Mensch," first in *Merkur* 10, no. 10 (October 1956). Maurice Friedman, trans., in *Jewish Heritage* 1, no. 1 (1957); *Hasidism and Modern Man* (New York: Horizon Press, 1958); also in Alexander Altman, ed., *Between East and West* (London: East and West Library, 1958).

Editor's note: The present essay is one of Buber's latest and most popular statements on Hasidism, speaking directly to the moral and intellectual crisis of post-World War II Germany, where it also appeared under the title "Hasidism and the *Crisis* of Western Man" (Hans Jürgen Schütz, ed., *Juden, Christen, Deutsche* [Stuttgart: Kreuz Verlag, 1961]). Buber uses the essay to comment on the failure of Western philosophy, psychology, and even religion to create a sacred space for the "human" within the process of secularization; but he also uses the essay to create a self-critique as well as justification of his interpretative approach to Hasidism, which had been subject to a long scholarly quarrel with the religious historian and expert on Jewish mysticism, Gershom Scholem, dating back to the first edition of the *Great Maggid* (*Der grosse Maggid und seine Nachfolge* [Frankfurt/M.: Rütten & Loening, 1922]) and culminating in the "Hasidism controversy" of the early 1960s.

1. Subheadings are not in the original.
2. The reference is to the concluding blessing of the *Havdalah* service marking the end of the Sabbath.
3. Rabbi Shmelke of Nikolsburg (d. 1778), disciple of the "great Maggid."
4. Exod. 14:30–15:19.
5. Neh. 9:7. From the Siddur (Hebrew prayer book).
6. See also The Life of the Hasidim (1908) (p. 75 in this volume).
7. Ps. 119:19; see also The Life of the Hasidim (1908) (p. 74 in this volume).
8. M. Friedman: ... unworthy of life.
9. Exod. 19:6.

PART III
Judaism and Jewish Religiosity

The Faith of Judaism (1929)

The Way of Faith

My subject is not the religion but only the faith of Judaism. I do not wish to speak to you about cult, ritual, and moral-religious standards, but about faith—faith taken in its strictest and most serious sense. Not the so-called faith that is a strange mingling of assumptions and cognitions, but the faith that means trust and loyalty. It follows that I do not start from a Jewish theology but from the actual attitude of faithful Jews from the earliest days up until our own time. Even though I must of necessity use theological concepts when I speak of this realm of faith, I must not for a moment lose sight of the nontheological material from which I draw these concepts: the popular literature and my own impressions of Jewish life in Eastern Europe—but in the East there is nothing that cannot be found in the West, as well.

When I refer to this popular material, people often say to me, "You mean, I take it, Hasidism?" That is a question that is natural enough, only it is not primarily Hasidism that I have in mind. In Hasidism I see merely a concentrated movement—the concentration of all those elements that are to be found in a less condensed form everywhere in Judaism, even in "rabbinic" Judaism. Only, in rabbinic Judaism this movement is not visible in the structure of the community but holds sway over the inaccessible structure of the personal life. What I am trying to formulate may be called the *theologoumena* (religious doctrines) of a popular religion.

It is impossible to trace any of these *theologoumena* back to any one epoch; my intention is to present the unity to be found in the changing forms. Religious truths are generally of a dynamic kind; they are truths that cannot be understood on the basis of a cross section of history but only when they are seen in the whole line of history—in their unfolding, in the dynamic of their changing forms. The most important testimony to the truth of this conception comes from the way in which these truths clarify and fulfill themselves and from their struggle for purity.

The truth of the history of religion is the growth of the image of God, the *way* of faith. Though my subject does not impose the historical form on me, it is still about the *way* of the Jewish faith that I must speak.

The Dialogical Situation

The question has often been raised whether Jewish dogmatics does or does not exist. The emphasis should rather fall on the question of the relative power of dogma in Judaism. There is no need to prove that there is dogma, in view of the incorporation of the thirteen articles of faith of Maimonides[1] into the liturgy. But dogma remains of secondary importance. In the religious life of Judaism, primary importance is not given to dogma but to the remembrance and the expectation of a concrete situation: the encounter of God and men. Dogma can only arise in a situation in which detachment is the prevailing attitude to the concrete, lived moment—a state of detachment that becomes easily misunderstood in dogmatics as being superior to the lived moment itself. Whatever is enunciated in abstract in the third person about the Divine, on the thither side of the confrontation of I and Thou, is only a projection onto the conceptual construct plane which, though indispensable, proves itself again and again to be inessential.

It is from this point of view that we must regard the problem of so-called monotheism. Israel's experience of the Thou in the direct relationship, the purely singular experience, is so overwhelmingly strong that any notion of a plurality of principles simply cannot arise. In contrast with this stands "the heathen," the man who *does not recognize* God in his manifestations. Or, rather, a man is a heathen to the extent to which he does not recognize God in his manifestations.

The fundamental attitude of the Jews is characterized by the idea of the *yihud,* the "unification," a word that has been repeatedly misunderstood.[2] *Yihud* involves the continually renewed confirmation of the unity of the Divine in the manifold nature of God's manifestations, understood in a quite practical way. Again and again, this recognition [*Erkennung*], acknowledgment [*Anerkennung*], and rediscernment [*Wiedererkennung*][3] of the divine unity is brought about through human perception and verification [*Bewährung*] in the face of the monstrous contradictions of life and especially in the face of the primal contradiction that shows itself in multitudinous ways, which we call the duality of good and evil. But the unification is brought about not despite these contradictions, but in the spirit of love and reconciliation; not by the mere profession of the unification, but by the fulfillment of the profession. Therefore, the unification is contained in no pantheistic theorem, but in the reality of the impossible, in translating the image [*Ebenbild*] into actuality [*verwirklichen*], in the *imitatio Dei*. The mystery behind this fact is fulfilled in martyrdom, in the death with the cry of unity on one's lips, the "Hear, O Israel,"[4] which at this point becomes testimony in the most vital sense.

A wise man of the Middle Ages said, "My God, where can I find you, but where can I not find you?"[5] The Eastern European Jewish beggar of today softly and unfalteringly whispers his *Gotenyu* in the trembling and dread of his harshest hour; the pet name is untranslatable and naive but, in its saying, becomes rich in meanings. In both, there is the same recognition, the same reacknowledgment of the One.

It is the dialogical situation in which the human being stands that finds its sublime or childlike expression.

Judaism regards speech as an event that grasps beyond the existence of mankind and the world. In contradiction to the static of the idea of *logos*, the "word" appears here in its complete dynamic as "that which happens." God's act of creation is speech, but the same is true of each lived moment. The world is given to the human beings who perceive it, and the life of man is itself a giving and receiving. The events that occur to human beings are the great and small untranslatable but unmistakable signs of their being addressed; what they do and fail to do can be an answer or a failure to answer. Thus, the whole history of the world—the hidden, real world history—is a dialogue between God and his creature; a dialogue in which man is a true, legitimate partner, who is entitled and empowered to speak his own independent word from his own being.

In no way do I contend that the conception and experience of the dialogical situation are confined to Judaism. But I am certain that no other community of human beings has entered with such strength and fervor into this experience as have the Jews.

The Human Action

What is presupposed when one is serious about the lived dialogue, regarding the moment as word and answer, is, of course, that one is serious about the appointment of man to the earth.

In strong contrast to the Iranian conception[6] with all its later ramifications, the Jewish conception is that the happenings of this world take place not in the sphere between two principles, light and darkness or good and evil, but in the sphere between God and men—these mortal, brittle human beings who yet are able to face God and withstand His word.

The so-called evil is fully, and as a primary element, included in the power of God, who "forms the light, and creates darkness" (Isa. 45:7). The divine sway is not answered by anything that is evil in itself but by individual human beings, through whom alone the so-called evil—the directionless power—can become real evil. Human choice is not a psychological phenomenon but utter reality, which is taken up into the mystery of the One who is. Man is truly free to choose God or to reject Him, and to do so not in a relationship of faith that is empty of the content of this world but in one that contains the full content of the everyday. The "fall" did not happen once and for all and become an inevitable fate, but it continually happens here and now in all of its reality. In spite of all past history, in spite of all his inheritance, every man stands in the naked situation of Adam: To each, the decision is given. It is true that this does not imply that further events are deducible from that decision; it only implies that the human being's choice is the side of reality that concerns him as one called upon to act.

It is only when reality is turned into logic and A and non-A dare no longer dwell together that we get determinism and indeterminism, a doctrine of predestination and a doctrine of freedom, each excluding the other. According to the logical conception of truth, only one of two contraries can be true, but in the reality of life as one lives it they are inseparable. The person who makes a decision knows that his deciding is no self-delusion; the person who has acted knows that he was and is in the hand of God. The unity of the contraries is the mystery at the innermost core of the dialogue.

I said above that "evil" is to be taken only as a primary element; humanly speaking, as passion. Passion is only evil when it remains in the directionless state, when it refuses to be subject to direction, when it will not accept the direction that leads toward God—there is no other direction. In Judaism the insight recurs again and again in many forms that passion, "the evil urge," is simply the elemental force that is the sole origin of the great human works, including the "holy." The verse in the Scriptures that says at the end of the last day of creation God allowed Himself to see His work "that it was very good" (Gen. 1:31) has been taken by tradition to refer to the so-called "evil urge." Of all the works of creation, it is passion that is the very good, without which man cannot serve God or truly live. The words, "And thou shalt love the Lord thy God with all thine heart" (Deut. 6:5) are interpreted, "With both thy Urges," with the evil, undirected, elemental urge, as well as the good—because it is directed—urge.[7] It is of this so-called Evil Urge that God says to man, "You have made it evil."

Consequently, "inertia" is the root of all evil. The act of decision implies that man is not allowing himself any longer to be carried along on the undirected swirl of passion but that his whole power is included in the move in the direction toward which he has decided—and man can decide only toward the direction of God. The evil, then, is only the "shell," the wrapping, the crust of the good—a shell that requires active piercing.

Some time ago a Catholic theologian saw in this conception a "Jewish activism" to which grace is unknown. But it is not so. We are not less serious about grace because we are serious about the human power of deciding, and through decision the soul finds a way that will lead it to grace. Here, man is not given complete power; rather, what is stressed is the ordered perspective of human action—an action that we may not limit in advance. It must experience limitation as well as grace in the very process of acting.

The great question that agitates man today more and more deeply is, How can we act? Is our action valid in the sight of God, or is its very foundation broken and unwarranted? The question is answered as far as Judaism is concerned by our being serious about the conception that man has been appointed to this world as an originator of events—as an actual partner in the real dialogue with God.

This answer implies a refusal to have anything to do with all separate ethics—any concept of ethics as a separate sphere of life—a form of ethics that is all too familiar in the spiritual history of the West. Ethical life has entered into religious life and cannot be extracted from it. There is no responsibility unless there is One to whom one is responsible, for there is no reply where there is no appeal. In the last resort, "religious life" means concreteness itself—the whole concreteness of life *without reduction*—grasped dialogically, included in the dialogue.

Thus, man has a real start in the dialogue over and over again. However mysteriously, something has been allotted to man, and that something is the beginning. Man cannot finish, and yet he must begin, in the most serious, actual way. This was once stated by a Hasid in a somewhat paradoxical interpretation of the first verse of Genesis: " 'In the beginning'— that means: for the sake of the beginning; for the sake of beginning did God create heaven and earth."[8] For the sake of man's beginning; that there might be one who would and should begin to move in the direction of God....

The Turning

This "beginning" by process of man manifests itself most strongly in the act of the turning [*Umkehr*].[9] It is customary to call it "repentance," but to do so is a misleading attempt to psychologize; it is better to take the word in its original, literal meaning. For what it refers to is not something that happens in the secret recesses of the soul, showing itself outwardly only in its "consequences" and "effects;" it is something that happens in the immediacy of the reality between man and God. The turning is as much a "psychic" event as is a man's birth or death; it comes upon the whole person, is carried out by the whole person, and does not take place as a man's self-intercourse but as the plain reality of primal mutuality [*Ur-Gegenseitigkeit*].[10]

The turning is a human fact, but it is also a world-embracing power. We are told that when God contemplated creating the world and sat tracing it on a stone, in much the same way as a master builder draws his ground plan, He saw that the world would have no stability. He then created the turning, and the world had stability. For from that time on, whenever the world was lost in the abyss of its own self, far away from God, the gates of deliverance were open to it—a deliverance that it was mercifully permitted to bring about through its own movement leading it to its complete turning back.

The turning is the greatest form of "beginning." When God tells man, "Open me the gate of the turning as narrow as the point of a needle, and

I shall open it so wide that carriages can enter it;" or when God tells Israel: "Turn to me, and I shall create you anew,"[11] the meaning of human beginning becomes clear as never before. By turning, man arises anew as God's child.[12]...

Again we see that there is no separate sphere of ethics in Judaism. This, the highest "ethical" moment, is fully received into the dialogical life existing between God and man. The turning is not a return to an earlier "sinless" state; it is the revolution of the whole being [*Wesensumschwung*]—in whose process man is projected onto the way of God. This, *he hodòs tou theou*,[13] however, does not merely indicate a way that God enjoins man to follow; it indicates that He, God Himself, walks in the person of His *Shekhinah,* His "indwelling," through the history of the world; He takes the way—the fate of the world upon himself. The man who turns finds Himself standing in the traces of the living God....

And when we remember this, we can also understand how the following sentence is linked to the beginning of the sermon: "For *he basileia ton ouranon*[14] is at hand," which, according to the Hebrew or Aramaic usage of the time cannot have meant the "Kingdom of Heaven" in the sense of "another world;" *shamayim* (Heaven) was at that time one of the paraphrases for the name of God: *Malkhut shamayim,*[15] *he basileia ton ouranon*, does not mean the Kingdom of Heaven but the Kingdom of God, which wills to fulfill itself in the whole of creation and wills thus to complete creation. The Kingdom of God is at the hand of man; it wills him to grasp and realize it, not through any theurgical act of "violence" but through the turning of the whole being; and not as if he were capable of accomplishing anything through so doing but because the world was created for the sake of his "beginning."

Against Gnosis and Magic

The two spiritual powers of gnosis and magic, masquerading under the cloak of religion, threaten more than any other powers the insight into the religious reality, into man's dialogical situation. They do not attack religion from the outside; they penetrate into religion, and once inside it, pretend to be its essence. Because Judaism has always had to hold them at bay and to keep separate from them, its struggle has been largely internal. This struggle has often been misunderstood as a fight against myth. But only an abstract theological monotheism can do without myth and may even see it as its enemy; living monotheism needs myth, as all religious life needs it, as the specific form in which its central events can be kept safe and lastingly remembered and incorporated....

The tribes of Jacob could only become Israel by disentangling themselves from both gnosis and magic. He who imagines that he knows and holds the mystery fast can no longer face it as his "Thou;" and he who thinks that he can conjure it and utilize it is unfit for the venture of true mutuality.

The gnostic temptation is answered by "the Instruction," the Torah, with the truly fundamental cry, "The secret things belong unto the Lord our God; but the things that are revealed belong unto us and to our children for ever, that we may do all the words of this instruction" (Deut. 29:28). Revelation does not deal with the mystery of God but with the life of man. And it deals with the life of man as that which can and should be lived in the face of the mystery of God; and turning toward that mystery, even more, the life of man is so lived when it is his true life.

The magical temptation is confronted with the word of God from out of the Burning Bush. Moses expected the people in their distress to ask him what was the name of the god as whose messenger he spoke (not, what was the name of the "God of their Fathers!" [cf. Exod. 3:13]). For according to the usage common to primitive peoples, once they seized the secret of the name, they could conjure the god and thus coerce him to manifest himself to them and save them. But when Moses voices his scruple as to what reply he should give to the people, God answers him by revealing the sense of the name, for He says explicitly in the first person that which is hidden in the name in the third. Not "I am that I am," as alleged by the metaphysicians—God does not make theological statements—but the answer that His creatures need and that benefits them: "I shall be there as I there shall be" (Exod. 3:14). That is, you need not conjure me, for I am here, I am with you; but you cannot conjure me, for I am with you time and again in the form in which I choose to be with you time and again; I myself do not anticipate any of my manifestations; you cannot learn to meet me; you meet me, when you meet me....

It is also in the light of its own inner battle against the infiltration of gnosis and magic that the dynamic of later Judaism must be understood, and especially that vexatious Talmud. We can only grasp some of its apparently abstract discussions when we keep in mind this constant double threat to the religious reality—the threat from gnosis taking the form of the late Iranian teaching of the double principles and the intermediary substances, and the threat from magic taking the form of the Hellenistic practice of theurgy. Both of these amalgamated inside Judaism and became the Kabbalah, that uncannily powerful undertaking by the Jew to wrest himself free of the concreteness of the dialogical situation.

The Kabbalah was overcome because it was taken just as it was into the primal Jewish conception of the dialogical life. This overcoming of the Kabbalah is the significant work of Hasidism. Hasidism caused all intermediary substances to fade before the relationship between God's transcendence, to be named only "the unlimited," the suspension of all limited being, and his immanence, his "indwelling." The mystery of this relationship is, however, no longer knowable but is applied directly to the pulsating heart of the human person as the *yihud,* the unification that man must profess and verify [*bewähren*] in every moment of his life and in his relationship to all things of the world. On the other hand, Hasidism drains theurgy of its poison, not by attempting to deny the influence of humanity on deity, but by proclaiming that far above and beyond all formulas and gestures, above all exercises, penances, preparations, and premeditated actions, the hallowing of the whole of the everyday is the one true bearer of the human influence. Thus, it dissolves the technique of theurgy, and leaves no "practicable," specific means behind—no means that are valid once and for all and applicable everywhere. In this way, Hasidism renews the insight into the mutuality in which the whole of life is put unreservedly at stake; the insight into the dialogical relationship of the undivided human being to the undivided God in the fullness of this earthly present, with its unforeseeable, ever-changing and ever-new situations; the insight into that differentiation between "secret" and "revelation," and the union of both in that unknowable but ever to be experienced "I shall be there;" the insight into the reality of the divine-human meeting.

Gnosis misunderstands that meeting; magic offends it. The meaning of revelation is that it is to be prepared; Hasidism interprets that revelation is to be prepared in the whole reality of human life.

The Triad of World Time

The insight that Judaism has with regard to the dialogical situation or, rather, the fact that it is completely imbued with the dialogical situation, gives Judaism its indestructible knowledge of the threefold chord in the triad of time: creation, revelation, redemption.

Within early Christianity the Gospel according to John was the first to try to substitute a duad for the triad by weaving revelation and redemption into one. The light that shone in darkness and was not received by the darkness, the light enlightening the whole man, which comes into the world—that light is at the same time revelation and redemption; by his coming into the world, God reveals Himself, and the soul is redeemed. The Old Testament shrinks into a prologue to the New Testament.

Marcion[16] went further: He tried to substitute a monad for the duad by banishing creation from religious reality; he tore God the Creator apart from God the Redeemer and declared that the former was not worthy of being adored. The "alien" God, who reveals himself in redeeming the world, redeems the soul from the cosmos and simultaneously from the builder of the cosmos, who becomes merely the "righteous"—not the "good"—God of the Jews, the demiurge, the lawgiver, the sham god of this aeon. The Old Testament was rejected as being anti-God.

Marcion's work has not been accepted by the Christian Church, which has indeed fought a great battle against it. The extent to which Marcion's influence has persisted in Christian thought, however, is shown by Adolf von Harnack's[17] marcionizing thesis, which is only one of many evidences. In his thesis, while accepting the prophets as religiously valid,[18] Harnack stamps the "preservation" of the Old Testament as a canonical document in Protestantism as "the consequence of religious and ecclesiastical paralysis." But more would be gained with the victory of this thesis than the separation of two books and the profanation of one for

Christendom: Man would be cut off from his origin, the world would lose its history of creation, and with that its creaturely character; or creation would itself become the "fall." Existence would be divided not only cosmologically, but in the last resort it would be divided religiously beyond possibility of redress into a "world" of matter and moral law, and an overworld of spirit and love. Here, the Iranian teaching of dual principles reaches its Western completion, and the duality of man, estranged from his natural, vitally trustful faith, finds its theological sanction. No longer does redemption crown the work of creation; redemption vanquishes creation. The world *as such* can no longer become the Kingdom of God. "The Unknown" who is worshipped at this point is the spirit of *reduction*.

For Western people such an issue would have meant only a threat of disintegration; for Judaism it would have meant certain dissolution. What saved Judaism is not, as the Marcionites imagine, the fact that it failed to experience "the tragedy," the contradiction in the world's process, deeply enough, but, rather, that it experienced that "tragedy" in the dialogical situation, that is, it experienced *the contradiction as theophany*. This very world, this very contradiction—unabridged, unmitigated, unsmoothed, unsimplified, unreduced—this world shall not be overcome, but consummated. It shall be consummated in the Kingdom, for it is that world, and no other, with all its contrariety, in which the Kingdom is a latency such that every reduction would only hinder its consummation, whereas every unification of contraries would prepare it. It is a redemption not from the evil, but of the evil, as the power that God created for his service and for the performance of His work.

If it is true that the whole world—all the world process, the whole time of the world, unsubtracted—stands in the dialogical situation; if it is true that the history of the world is a real dialogue between God and His creature, then the triad, as which this history is perceived, becomes not a man-made device for his own orientation, but actual reality itself. What comes to us out of the abyss of origin and into the sphere of our uncomprehending grasp and our stammering narrative is God's cry of creation into the void. Silence still lies brooding before Him, but soon things begin to rise and give answer—their very coming into existence is answer. When God blesses His creatures and gives them their appointed work, revelation has begun; for revelation is nothing other than the relation between giving and receiving, that is, it is also the relation between desiring to give and failing to receive. Revelation lasts until the turning creature answers and his answer is accepted by God's redeeming grace. Then the unity emerges, formed out of the very elements of contrariety, to establish amidst all the undiminished multiplicity and manifoldness the communion of creatures in the name of God and before His face.

Just as God's cry of creation does not call to the soul, but to the wholeness of things, as revelation does not empower and require the soul, but all of the human being, so it is not the soul, but the whole of the world that is meant to be redeemed in the redemption. Man stands created, a whole body, ensouled by his relation to the created, enspirited by his relation to the Creator. It is to the whole man, in this unity of body, soul, and spirit, that the Lord of Revelation comes and upon whom He lays His message. So it is not only with his thought and his feelings, but with the sole of his foot and the tip of his finger as well, that he may receive the sign language of the reality taking place. The redemption must take place in the whole corporeal life. God the Creator wills to consummate nothing less than the whole of His creation; God the Revealer wills to actualize nothing less than the whole of His revelation; God the Redeemer wills to draw into His arms nothing less than the all in need of redemption.

Notes

Source: "Der Glaube des Judentums" (lecture), first in *Volk und Reich der Deutschen,* ed. Bernhard Harms (Berlin: R. Hobbing 1929). Greta Hort, trans., in *Mamre: Essays in Religion* (Melbourne: Melbourne University Press, 1946); slightly revised in *Israel and the World: Essays in a Time of Crisis* (New York: Schocken, 1948), pp. 13–27.

Editor's note: The lecture was commissioned in 1928 by the staatswissenschaftlichen Kurse in Reichenhall, but delivered only a year later at the Weltwirtschaftliches Institut in Kiel. Written for a predominantly non-Jewish audience, the lecture is devoid of the normative tone in Buber's earlier addresses; rather, it is one of Buber's most systematic and mature interpretations of Judaism. Note that Buber already makes full use of his dialogical philosophy.

1. On the 13 Principles of Maimonides see Herut: On Youth and Religion (1919) (p. 132, in this volume).
2. On the concept of *yihud* see Spirit and Body of the Hasidic Movement (1935) (p. 68 in this volume).
3. G. Hort: reacknowledgement (*Israel and the World*), re-finding (*Mamre*).
4. Deut. 6:4
5. Yehuda Halevi (1085–1140): Jewish philosopher and Hebrew poet.
6. Zoroastrianism, named after its founder Zoroaster (seventh century B.C.E), maintains a conception of ethical dualism.
7. Berakhot 54a.
8. Cf. Hasidism and Modern Man (1956) (p. 89 in this volume).
9. What Buber has in mind here is the Hebrew term *teshuvah* whose triple meaning of "turning," "repentance," and "response" plays a central role in his dialogical philosophy. Thus, the terms *Hinwendung* (turning toward the other) and *Rückbiegug* (bending back) developed in Dialogue (1932) (p. 197 in this volume) can well be understood from the juxtaposition of "turning to" (*lashuv*) and "turning away" (*lasur*) as it appears in the liturgy of *Yom Kippur* (Day of Atonement).
10. G. Hort (*Mamre*): ur-reciprocity.
11. Zech. 1:3.
12. G. Hort (*Mamre*): Paragraph missing.
13. Greek, literally, the way of God. The reference is to Mark 12:14.
14. Greek: the kingdom of Heaven. The reference is to Matt. 5:3.
15. Hebrew, literally, kingdom of the heavens.
16. Marcion (d. 160 C.E.): Christian theologian, whose dualistic conception of God and new canonization of the New Testament was rejected by most of Orthodox and Catholic Christianity. To Marcion, the God of the "Old Testament" (the "Demiurge") was entirely diffent from the "God of Love" in the New Testament and had to be abandoned altogether. Marcion was excommunicated in 144.
17. Adolf von Harnack (1851–1930), German Protestant theologian whose lectures, *Das Wesen des Christentums,* at the University of Berlin (1899–1900) prompted Leo Baeck's *Das Wesen des Judentums* (1905). Bubert takes issue here with Harnack's book *Marcion—Das Evangelium vom fremden Gott* (1921).
18. Not in G. Hort.

Two Foci of the Jewish Soul (1932)*

You have asked me to speak to you about the soul of Judaism. I have complied with this request, although I am against the cause for which you hold your conference,¹ and I am against it not "just as a Jew," but also truly as a Jew, that is, as one who waits for the Kingdom of God, the Kingdom of Unification, and who regards all such "missions" as yours as springing from a misunderstanding of the nature of that kingdom and as a hindrance to its coming. If, in spite of this, I have accepted your invitation, it is because I believe that when one is invited to share one's knowledge, one should not ask, "Why have you invited me?" but should share what one knows as well as one can, and that is my intention.

There is, however, one essential branch of Judaism about which I do not feel myself called upon to speak before you, and that is "the Law." My point of view with regard to this subject diverges from the traditional one; it is not a-nomistic, but neither is it entirely nomistic. For that reason I should attempt neither to represent tradition nor to substitute my own personal standpoint for the information you have desired of me. Besides, the problem of "the Law" does not seem to me to be part of the subject about which I was asked to speak. It would be a different matter were it my duty to present the teaching of Judaism. For the teaching of Judaism comes from Sinai; it is Moses's teaching. But the soul of Judaism is pre-Sinaitic; it is the soul that approached Sinai, and there received what it did receive; it is older than Moses; it is patriarchal, Abraham's soul, or more truly, as it concerns the product of a primordial age, it is Jacob's soul. Jewish law put on the soul, and the soul can never again be understood outside of "the Law;" yet the soul itself is not of "the Law." If one wishes to speak of the soul of Judaism, one must consider the transformations it underwent through the ages until this very day; but one must never forget that in

---

* An address delivered in 1930.

every one of its stages the soul has remained the same and gone on in the same way.

This qualification, however, only makes the task more difficult. "I should wish to show you Judaism from the inside," wrote Franz Rosenzweig in 1917 to a Christian friend of Jewish descent, "in the same 'hymnal' way as you can show Christianity to me, the outsider; but the very reasons which make it possible for you to do so make it impossible for me. The soul of Christianity may be found in its outward expressions; Judaism wears a hard protective outer shell and one can speak about its soul only if one is within Judaism."[2] If, therefore, I still venture here to speak about the soul of Judaism from the outside, it is only because I do not intend to give an account of that soul but only some indication of its fundamental attitude.

It is not necessary for me to labor the point that this fundamental attitude is nothing less than the attitude of faith, viewed from its human side. "Faith," however, should not be taken in the sense given to it in the Epistle to the Hebrews (Heb. 11:6), as faith that God exists. That has never been doubted by Jacob's soul. In proclaiming its faith, its *emunah,* the soul only proclaimed that it put its trust in the everlasting God, *that He would be present* to the soul, as had been the experience of the patriarchs, and that it was entrusting itself to Him, who was present (see Gen. 28:20; 35:3).[3] The German romantic philosopher Franz Baader did justice to the depth of Israel's faith relationship when he defined faith as "a pledge of faith [*Geloben*], that is, as a tying of oneself, a betrothing of oneself, an entering into a covenant."[4]

The fealty [*Angelobtsein*] of the Jew is the substance of his soul. The living God to whom he has pledged himself appears in infinite manifestations in the infinite variety of things and events; and this acts both as an incentive and as a steadying influence upon those who owe Him allegiance. In the abundance of His manifestations they can always recognize the One to whom they have entrusted themselves and pledged their faith. The crucial word that God Himself spoke of, this rediscovery of His presence that was spoken to Moses from the midst of the Burning Bush: "I shall be there as I there shall be" (Exod. 3:4). He is ever present to His creature but always in the form peculiar to that moment, so that the spirit of man cannot foretell in the garment of what existence and what situation God will manifest Himself. It is for man to recognize Him in each of his garments. I cannot straightaway call any man a pagan; I know only of the pagan in man. But insofar as there is any paganism, it does not consist in not discerning God but in not recognizing Him as ever the same; the Jewish in man, on the contrary, seems to me to be the ever renewed rediscernment of God.

I shall therefore speak to you about the Jewish soul by making a few references to its fundamental attitude; I shall regard it as being the concretion of this human element in a national form and consider it as the nation-shaped instrument of such a fealty and rediscernment.

Two Foci of the Jewish Soul (1932)

I see the soul of Judaism as elliptically revolving around two centers.

One center of the Jewish soul is the primeval experience [*Urerfahrung*] that God is wholly raised above man, that He is beyond the grasp of man, and yet that He is present in an immediate relationship with these human beings who are absolutely incommensurable with Him, and that He faces them. To know both of these things at the same time, so that they cannot be separated, constitutes the living core of every believing Jewish soul; to know both "God in heaven," that is, in complete hiddenness, and man "on earth," that is, in the fragmentation of the world of his senses and his understanding; God in the perfection and incomprehensibility of His being, and man in the abysmal contradiction of this strange existence from birth to death—and between both, immediacy! When the naively pious Jew in Eastern Europe—not unlike the pious Jews of pre-Christian times (e.g., Wisdom of Salomo 2:16)—calls this God "Little Father" ["*Väterlein*"] today, he does not repeat something that he has learned, but he expresses a realization that he has come upon himself of the fatherhood of God and the sonship of man. It is not as though these men did not know that God is also utterly distant; it is rather that they know at the same time that however far away God is, He is never unrelated to them, and that even the man who is farthest away from God cannot cut himself off from the mutual relationship....

"Fear of God," accordingly, never means to the Jews that they ought to be afraid of God, but that, trembling, they ought to be aware of His incomprehensibility. The fear of God is the creaturely knowledge of the darkness to which none of our spiritual powers can reach, and out of which God reveals Himself. Therefore, the "fear of God" is rightly called "the *beginning* of knowledge" (Ps. 111:10; Prov. 1:7). It is the dark gate through which man must pass if he is to enter into the love of God. He who wishes to avoid passing through this gate, he who begins to provide himself with a comprehensible God—constructed thus and not otherwise—runs the risk of having to despair of God in view of the actualities of history and life, or of falling into inner falsehood. Only through the fear of God does man enter so deeply into the love of God that he cannot again be cast out of it.

But the fear of God is just a gate; it is not a house in which one can settle down comfortably—he who should want to live in it in adoration would neglect the performance of the essential commandment. God is incomprehensible, but He can be known through a bond of mutual relationship. God cannot be fathomed by knowledge, but he can be imitated. The life of man who is unlike God can yet be an *imitatio Dei*. "The likeness" [*Gleichnis*] is not closed to the "unlike" [*Ungleichen*]. This is exactly what is meant when the Scripture instructs man to walk in God's way and in His footsteps. Man cannot by his own strength complete any way or any piece of the way, but he can enter on the path, he can take that first step, and again and again that first step.... This is not a mere act of faith; it is an entering into the life that has to be lived on that day with all the active fullness of a created person. This activity is within man's capacity: uncurtailed and not to be curtailed, the capacity is present through all the generations. God concedes the might to abridge this central property of decision to no primordial "fall," however far-reaching in its effects, for the intention of God the Creator is mightier than the sin of man. The Jew knows from his knowledge of creation and of creatureliness that there may be burdens inherited from prehistoric and historic times but that there is no overpowering original sin that can prevent the latecomer from deciding as freely as did Adam; as freely as Adam let God's hand go the latecomer can clasp it. We are dependent on grace; but we do not do God's will when we take it upon ourselves to begin with grace instead of beginning with ourselves. Only our beginning, our having begun, poor as it is, leads us to grace. God made no tools for Himself; He needs none; He created for Himself a partner in the dialogue of time [*Weltzeit-Gespräch*] and one who is capable of holding converse.

In this dialogue God speaks to every man through the life that He gives him again and again. Therefore, man can only answer God with the whole of life—with the way in which he lives this given life. The Jewish teaching of the wholeness of life is the other side of the Jewish teaching of the unity of God. Because God bestows not only spirit on man, but the whole of His existence, from its "lowest" to its "highest" levels as well, man can fulfill the obligations of his partnership with God by no spiritual attitude, by no worship, on no sacred upper story; the whole of life is required, every one of its areas and every one of its circumstances. There is no true human share of holiness without the hallowing of the everyday. As Judaism unfolds itself through the history of its faith—and as long as it does unfold itself through that history—it holds out against that "religion" that is an attempt to assign a circumscribed part to God, to satisfy him who bespeaks and lays claim to the whole. But this unfolding of Judaism is really an unfolding and not a metamorphosis....

The "Holy" strives to include within itself the whole of life. The "Law" differentiates between the holy and the profane, but the "Law" desires to lead the way toward the messianic removal of the differentiation to the all-sanctification. Hasidic piety no longer recognizes anything as simply and irreparably profane: "the profane" is for Hasidism only a designation for the not yet sanctified, for that which is to be sanctified.[5] Everything physical—all drives and urges and desires—everything creaturely, is material for sanctification. From the very same passionate powers that, undirected, give rise to evil, when they are turned toward God, give rise to good. One does not serve God with the spirit only but with the whole of his nature, without any subtractions. There is not one realm of the spirit and another of nature; there is only the growing realm of God. God is not spirit, but what we call spirit and what we call nature hail equally from the God who is beyond and equally conditioned by both, and whose kingdom reaches its fullness in the complete unity of spirit and nature.

The second focus of the Jewish soul is the basic consciousness that God's redeeming power is at work everywhere and at all times but that a state of redemption exists nowhere and never. The Jew experiences as a person what every openhearted human being experiences as a person: the experience, in the hour when he is most utterly forsaken, of a breath from above, the nearness, the touch, the mysterious intimacy of light out of darkness. And the Jew, as part of the world, experiences, perhaps more intensely than any other part, the world's lack of redemption. He feels this lack of redemption against his skin, he tastes it on his tongue; the burden of the unredeemed world lies on him. Because of this almost physical knowledge of his, he *cannot* concede that the redemption has taken place; he knows that it has not. It is true that he can discover prefigurations of redemption in past history, but he always discovers only that mysterious intimacy of light out of darkness that is at work everywhere and at all times; no redemption that is different in kind, none that by its nature would be unique, that would be conclusive for future ages, and that had but to be consummated. Most of all, only through a denial of his own meaning and his own mission would it be possible for him to acknowledge that in a world that still remains unredeemed an anticipation of the redemption had been effected by which the human soul—or rather merely the souls of men who in a specific sense are believers—had been redeemed.

With a strength that original grace has given him and that none of his historic trials has ever wrested from him, the Jew resists the radical division of soul and world that forms the basis of this conception; he resists the conception of a divine splitting of existence; he resists most passionately the awful notion of a *massa perditionis*.[6] The God in whom he believes has not created the totality to let it split apart into one blessed and one damned half. God's eternity is not to be conceived by man; but—and this we Jews know until the moment of our death—there can be no eternity in which not *everything* would be accepted into God's atonement, when God has drawn time back into eternity. Should there be a stage, however, in the redemption of the world in which redemption is first fulfilled in one *part* of the world, we would derive no claim to redemption from our faith, much less from any other source. "If You do not yet wish to redeem Israel, then at least redeem the *goyim*," the Rabbi of Koznitz used to pray.

It is possible to argue with me that there has been eschatology in Judaism other than that which I have indicated, that the apocalyptic stands beside the prophetic eschatology. It is actually important to make clear to oneself where the difference between the two lies. The prophetic belief about the end of time is essentially autochthonous; the apocalyptic belief is essentially built up of elements from Iranian dualism. Accordingly, the prophetic promises a consummation of creation, the apocalyptic its abrogation and supersession by another world, completely different in nature; the prophetic allows "the evil" to find the direction that leads toward God and to enter into the good; the apocalyptic sees good and evil severed forever at "the end of days"—the good redeemed, the evil unredeemable for all eternity; the prophetic believes that the earth shall be hallowed, the apocalyptic despairs of an earth that it considers to be hopelessly doomed; the prophetic allows God's creative original will to be fulfilled completely; the apocalyptic allows the unfaithful creature power over the Creator, in that the creatures' actions force God to abandon nature....

Still another important difference separates the two forms of Jewish belief about "the end of days." The apocalyptists wished to predict an unalterable immovable future event; they were following Iranian conceptions in this point as well. For, according to the Iranians, history is divided into equal cycles of thousands of years, and the end of the world, the final victory of good over evil, can be predetermined with mathematical accuracy.

Not so the prophets of Israel: They prophesy "for the sake of those who turn [*Umkehrende*]" (Berakhot 34b). That is, they do not warn against something that will happen in any case but against that which will happen if those who are called upon to turn do not.

The Book of Jonah is a clear example of what is meant by prophecy. After Jonah has tried in vain to flee from the task God has given him, he is sent to Nineveh to prophesy its downfall. But Nineveh turns [*kehrt um*], and God changes its destiny. Jonah is vexed that the word for whose sake the Lord had broken his resistance had been rendered void; if one is forced to prophesy, one's prophecy must stand. But God is of a different opinion; He will employ no soothsayers, but messengers to the souls of men—the souls that are able to decide which way to go and whose decision is allowed to contribute to the forging of the world's fate. Those who turn cooperate in the redemption of the world....

The extent and nature of the participation assigned to the creature remains secret. "Does that mean that God cannot redeem his world without the help of his creatures?" "It means that God does not *will* to be able to do it." "Has God need of man for his work?" "He wills to have need of man."...

The mystery of the act, of the human part in preparing the redemption, passes through the darkness of the ages as a mystery of concealment, as a concealment within the person's relation to himself as well, until one day it will come into the open. To the question why according to tradition the Messiah was born on the anniversary of the day of the destruction of Jerusalem, a Hasidic rabbi answered, "The power cannot rise, unless it has dwelt in the great concealment.... In the shell of oblivion grows the power of remembrance. That is the power of redemption. On the day of the Destruction the power will be lying at the bottom of the depths and growing. That is why on this day we sit on the ground; that is why on this day we visit the graves; that is why on this day was born the Messiah."

Though robbed of their real names, these two foci of the Jewish soul continue to exist for the "secularized" Jew as well, insofar as he has not lost his soul. They are, first, the immediate relationship to the Existent One, and second, the power of atonement at work in an unatoned world. That is, first, the *non-incarnation* of God who reveals himself to the "flesh" and is present to it in a mutual relationship, and second, the unbroken continuity of human history, which turns toward fulfillment and decision. These two centers constitute the ultimate division between Judaism and Christianity.

We "unify" God when, living and dying, we profess His unity; we do not unite ourselves with Him. The God in whom we believe, to whom we are pledged, does not unite with human substance on earth. But the very fact that we do not imagine that we can unite with Him enables us the more ardently to demand, "that the world shall be perfected under the kingship of the Mighty One."

We feel salvation happening, and we feel the unsaved world. No savior with whom a new redeemed history began has appeared to us at any definite point in history. Because we have not been stilled by anything that has happened, we are wholly directed toward the coming of that which is to come.

Thus, though divided from you, we have been attached to you. As Franz Rosenzweig wrote in the letter that I have already quoted, "You who live in an *ecclesia triumphans* need a silent servant to cry to you whenever you believe you *have partaken* of God in bread and wine—'Lord, remember the last things.' "[7]

What have you and we in common? If we take the question literally, a book and an expectation.

To you the book is an antechamber; to us it is the sanctuary. But in this place we can dwell together and together listen to the voice that speaks here. That means that we can work together to evoke the buried speech of that voice; together we can redeem the imprisoned living word.

Your expectation is directed toward a second coming; ours to a coming that has not been anticipated by a first. To you the phrasing of world history is determined by one absolute midpoint, the year nought; to us it is an unbroken flow of tones following each other without a pause from their origin to their consummation. But we can wait for the advent of the One together, and there are moments when we may prepare the way before Him together.

Premessianically our destinies are divided. Now to the Christian, the Jew is the incomprehensibly obdurate man, who declines to see what has happened; and to the Jew, the Christian is the incomprehensibly daring man, who affirms in an unredeemed world that its redemption has been accomplished. This is a gulf that no human power can bridge. But it does not prevent the common watch for a unity to come to us from God, which, soaring above all of your imagination and all of ours, affirms and denies, denies and affirms what you hold and what we hold, and that replaces all the creedal truths of earth by the ontological truth of heaven, which is one.

It behooves both you and us to hold inviolably fast to our own true faith, that is, to our own deepest relationship to truth. It behooves both of us to show a religious respect for the true faith of the other. This is not what is called "tolerance;" our task is not to tolerate each other's waywardness but to acknowledge the real relationship in which both stand to the truth. Whenever we both, Christian and Jew, care more for God himself than for our images of God, we are united in the feeling that our Father's house is differently constructed than our human models take it to be.

Notes

Source: "Die Brennpunkte der jüdischen Seele," first in *Der Morgen* 8, no. 5 (December 1932). Greta Hort, trans., in *Mamre: Essays in Religion* (Melbourne: Melbourne University Press, 1946), pp. 18–31; also in *Israel and the World: Essays in a Time of Crisis* (New York: Schocken, 1948), pp. 28–40.

Editor's note: The address was delivered at a convention of the four German Protestant Judenmissionsgesellschaften (societies for the mission of the Jews) in Stuttgart in March 1930. The mission societies date back to the Old Testament scholar and orientalist Franz Julius von Delitzsch (1813–1890), a Lutheran of Jewish descent, who, in 1886, founded the Institutum Judaicum (later Institutum Delitzschianum) in Leipzig to promote a Christian–Jewish understanding, albeit with the goal of mission (with the same goal in mind Delitzsch also translated the New Testament into Hebrew [1877]). The main audience, therefore, was one of active Protestant theologians who were genuinely interested in Judaism and in Jewish–Christian conversation, in the hope for mission; hence, the opening passage in Buber's lecture and its apologetic tone, underscored by the correspondence between Franz Rosenzweig (who returned to Judaism) and Eugen Rosenstock-Huessy (who embraced Calvinism).

1. See Editor's note above.
2. Franz Rosenzweig (1886–1929), German–Jewish philosopher and close associate of Martin Buber, authored the *Star of Redemption* (1921). The letter Buber is referring to is, in fact, from 7 November, 1916. The recipient was the philosopher of language, Eugen Rosenstock-Huessy (1888–1973), a Calvinist of Jewish descent. The exchange appeared as an addendum to Rosenzweig's published letters ("Judentum und Christentum," in Franz Rosenzweig, *Briefe* [Berlin: Schocken 1935], p. 688 for the quoted letter; English: *Judaism Despite Christianity*, ed. Eugen Rosenstock-Huessy [Tuscaloosa: University of Alabama Press, 1969], p. 133).
3. On Buber's distinction between *pistis* and *emunah*, see his short treatise of 1950, *Two Types of Faith*, trans. Norman Goldhawk (London: Routledge & Paul, 1951).
4. Franz Baader (1765–1841), philosopher and theologian, authored *Beiträge zur dynamischen Philosophie im Gegensatz zur mechanischen* (1809). Buber encountered his work probably during research for his dissertation on Jakob Böhme.
5. See The Life of the Hasidim (1908) (p. 79 in this volume).
6. Latin, literally, lost masses or doomed masses. Buber refers to the theory of double predestination by the church father Augustine (354–430); cf. Augustine, *Epistolae,* 217 v. 16.
7. F. Rosenzweig to E. Rosenstock-Huessy, in *Judaism Despite Christianity*, p. 133.

Jewish Religiosity (1923)*

Jewish religiosity is not, as many people think, a matter of an admittedly special dignity but an otherwise negligible moment for the so-called "solution of the Jewish question." It is, rather, now as always, the only matter of unconditional moment for Judaism—motive power of its fate, guidepost to its destiny, a force whose upsurging blaze would restore it to new life and whose total extinction would deliver it to death. Renewal of Judaism means in reality renewal of Jewish religiosity....

I say and mean religiosity, not religion. Religiosity is man's sense of wonder and adoration, an ever new becoming, an ever-new articulation and formulation of his feeling that, transcending his conditioned being yet bursting from its very core, there is something that is unconditioned. Religiosity is his longing to establish a living communion with the unconditioned, his will to realize the unconditioned through his action, transposing it into the world of man. Religion is the sum total of the customs and teachings articulated and formulated by the religiosity of a certain epoch in the life of a people; its prescriptions and dogmas are rigidly determined and handed down as unalterably binding to all future generations, without regard for their newly developed religiosity, which seeks new forms. Religion is true as long as it is creative; but it is creative only as long as religiosity, accepting the yoke of the laws and doctrines, is able (often without even noticing it) to imbue them with new and incandescent meaning, so that they will seem to have been revealed to every generation anew, revealed today, thus answering men's very own needs—needs alien to their fathers. But once religious rites and dogmas have become so rigid that religiosity cannot move them or no longer wants to comply with them, religion becomes uncreative and therefore untrue. Thus, religiosity is the creative, and religion, the organizing, principle. Religiosity

---

* From *On Judaism* by Martin Buber, ed. Nahum Glatzer, trans. Eva Jospe, copyright © 1967 by Schocken Books, a division of Random House, Inc. Used by permission of Schocken Books, a division of Random House, Inc.

starts anew with every young person, shaken to his very core by the mystery; religion wants to force him into a system stabilized for all time. Religiosity means activity—the elemental entering into relation with the absolute; religion means passivity—an acceptance of the handed-down command. Religiosity has only one goal; religion has several. Religiosity induces sons who want to find their own God, to rebel against their fathers; religion induces fathers to reject their sons who will not let their fathers' God be forced upon them. Religion means preservation; religiosity means renewal. But whatever the way another people may find its salvation, to the Jewish people it will be disclosed only in the living force to which its peoplehood was ever bound, and through which it had its existence: not in its religion but in its religiosity. The Baal-Shem[1] says, "We say 'God of Abraham, God of Isaac and God of Jacob;' we do not say 'God of Abraham, Isaac and Jacob,' so that you may be told: Isaac and Jacob did not rely on Abraham's tradition, but they themselves searched for the Divine."[2]

I shall try to extricate the unique character of Jewish religiosity from the rubble with which rabbinism and rationalism have covered it.

The act that Judaism has always considered the essence and foundation of all religiosity is the act of decision as realization of divine freedom and unconditionality on earth. The late Jewish saying, "The world was created for the sake of the choice of him who chooses," is only the mature formulation of an idea that, although still unformulated, already existed and was basic in biblical times. Just as the sequence of Sinaitic laws opens with the call to an exclusive and unconditional decision for the One, so do Moses's greatest words serve to support the same demand: "You shall be whole-hearted with the Lord your God" (Deut. 18:13) and "... serve the Lord your God with all your heart and with all your soul" (Deut. 11.13). The prophets proclaim the same, beginning with Elijah, who speaks to the people: "How long will you continue to hobble along on two tree-limbs?" (1 Kings 18:21). The idea is developed with increased poignancy in postbiblical literature. The Mishnah (oral Torah) interprets the phrase, "Thou shalt love God with all thy heart" to mean, with both your inclinations, the "good" as well as the "evil"[3]; that is, with and by your decision,[4] so that the ardor of passion is converted and enters into the unified deed with all its strength. For no inclination is evil in itself; it is made evil by man when he surrenders to it instead of controlling it. The Midrash has God say to man, "You turned passion which was given into your hand into evil...."[5]

And it is stated with still greater emphasis, "Only when you are undivided" (i.e., when you have overcome your inner dualism by your decision) "will you have a share in the Lord your God."[6] On the other hand, inertia and indecisiveness are called the root of all evil; sin is basically nothing more than inertia. The man who has fallen prey to it but later, by a wrenching decision, extricates himself from it; who has sunk into the abyss of duality but later hews his way out of it to unity; and who, taking himself into his own hands, like an inert earthen clod, kneads that self into a human being—that man above all is dearest to God. Or, in the words of the Gemara (Rabbinic commentary), "Even the perfectly righteous may not stand in the place where those who have returned [*Umkehrende*] are standing."[7] The great decision is the supreme moment in the life of man, indeed, in the life of the entire world. "One hour of return in this world," it is stated in the Sayings of the Fathers, "is better than the entire life in the world to come."[8] For the latter is merely being, whereas the former is the great becoming. Sin means to live not in freedom, that is, decision making, but in bondage, that is, being acted upon, conditioned. The man who "returns" rises to freedom; he rises from conditionality into unconditionality; he is, as the Zohar (Kabbalistic text) calls it, "alive all around, at one with the tree of life."

No man knows the abyss of inner dualism as well as the Jew, but neither does anyone know as well the miracle of unification, which cannot be accepted on faith but must be experienced. Therefore, nothing already realized can ever suffice, but only the act that starts anew with every human being: realization [*Verwirklichung*]. This is the intent of the teaching of return: that everyone, alone and from his own depth, must strive for divine freedom and unconditionality; no mediator can help him, nothing already accomplished by another can facilitate his own deed, for all depends on the shattering force of his own action, which can only be weakened by any kind of help from outside. That is why the early Christian movement became barren for the Jew when it converted Jesus's truly Jewish proclamation that every man could become a son of God by living unconditionally into the doctrine that nothing except belief in the only begotten son of God could win eternity for man. And that is why Hasidism had to lose its renewing effect upon the people when it replaced with the mediation of the *zaddik* its former wondrous self-liberation—that immediate relationship to God in which man "reaches the root of all teaching and all commandment, God's I, the simple unity and boundlessness in which commandments and laws fold their wings," because He has risen above all of them through His unconditionality. To say of this basic view of religiosity that it is an outpouring of the Holy Spirit into the man who purifies and sanctifies himself[9] is no exaggeration but only the strongest way of expressing it.

The meaning of the act of decision in Judaism is falsified if it is viewed as merely an ethical act. It is a religious act, or, rather, it is *the* religious act; for it is God's realization through man.

Three distinct strata underlie this concept of realization in Jewish religiosity. Their sequence reveals the development of the subterranean Judaism that, secret and suppressed, remains authentic and bears witness, in contradistinction to an official, sham Judaism whose power and public representation have neither authority nor legitimacy.

On the first, earliest, stratum, the act of decision is conceived as meaning God's realization through imitation, an *imitatio Dei*. God is man's goal, the primal being whose image he ought to strive to become, "for God created man to be His image" (Gen. 1:27), that is, so that he may *become* His image. Fundamental to this concept is the text from Leviticus, "Ye shall be holy, for I, your God, am holy" (Lev. 19:2; 20:26). This is interpreted to mean, "As I am set apart," that is, determined by nothing, removed from all conditionality, "so you, too, shall be set apart."[10] And further, "As God is one and only, so your service be one." God is one; therefore man shall overcome his duality and become one. God is unconditioned; therefore, man shall extricate himself from the shackles of his conditionality and become unconditional.... That there is no other way to this goal but the way of decision and unconditionality is shown by the myth of the "fall:" Man had the audacity to "be like God" (Gen. 3:5) and thus to frustrate life's meaning that lies in *becoming* like God; therefore, he obtained nothing more than an awareness of the dualism of the Divine and the human—the "knowledge of good and evil."

On the second stratum, the act of decision is conceived as meaning God's realization through an intensification of His reality. The more man realizes [*verwirklichen*] God in the world, the greater His reality. This seemingly paradoxical formulation of the idea is instantly grasped when the words, "'Ye are My witnesses,' saith the Lord" (Isa. 43:10) are complemented by the interpretation given them by Rabbi Simeon bar Yohai, "If you are my witnesses, I am the Lord, and if you are not my witnesses, I am not the Lord."[11] God is man's goal; therefore, the force of all human decision flows into the sea of divine power. In the same spirit, the words of the psalm, "Ascribe ye strength unto God" (Ps. 68:35), are explained by the statement that the righteous increase the power of the upper dominion. Later writings, especially Kabbalistic literature, greatly enlarged the idea that the man who acts unconditionally is God's partner and helper in the eternal work of creation. Thus, a pillar rises for the righteous, reaching from earth to heaven, supporting the universe. In the same vein, the Zohar explains the words of the psalm, "The works of His hands...are faithfulness and justice" (Ps. 111:7), as meaning that man who acts faithfully and justly influences the becoming of the world;[12] and the passage "God had not yet caused it to rain upon the earth and there was no man to till the ground" (Gen. 2:5) is interpreted to mean that no action emanated from above because no deed emanated from below. Then, however, "there went up a mist from the earth and watered the whole face of the ground" (Gen. 2:6), which means that action below effected action above.

Finally, on the third stratum, which first appears in the Kabbalah, the concept of God's realization through man is expanded by the notion that man's deed affects God's destiny on earth. His *shekhinah* has fallen into the world of the conditioned; it is, like Israel, in dispersion, in *galut;* like Israel, it wanders and strays, tossed into the realm of things; like Israel, it wants to be redeemed, to be reunited with the divine being. But this consummation can be effected only through him who, within himself, lifts the conditioned to the unconditioned: thereby the world, that is, the *shekhinah,* will be lifted. That is why a Hasidic adage declares that those who return redeem God. And just as, with the entrance of the soul into the human body, the king, God, is lovingly inclined toward the queen, the *shekhinah*, so the queen, in the overcoming of the conditioned by means of the returning soul, lovingly raises herself up to the king. By such loving union, being is eternally renewed. "Thus life grows from above and from below, the primal source fills eternally, eternally fills the sea, and there is sustenance for all."

All three strata have in common a concept that is innate in Jewish religiosity: the concept of the absolute value of man's deed, a value that cannot be judged by our meager knowledge of the causes and effects of this world. Something infinite flows into a deed of a man; something infinite flows from it. The doer cannot perceive who the powers are whose emissary and acting agent he is; he must nevertheless be aware that the fullness of the world's destiny, namelessly interwoven, passes through his hands. It is said in the Gemara, "Every man shall say, 'It is for me that the world was created.' "[13] And again, "Every man shall say, 'The world rests on me,' " which is corroborated by the Hasidic text: "Yes, he is the only one in the world, and its continued existence depends on his deed."

In the unconditionality of his deed man experiences his communion with God.... Whether God is "transcendent" or "immanent" does not depend on Him; it depends on man. The Zohar remarks, in connection with the tale in Genesis of the three men who came to Abraham "in the heat of the day" (Gen. 18:1); "When the world below is ablaze with desire for the world above, the upper world will descend to the lower, and both will unite and permeate each other in man." A similar interpretation may be given to the words of the psalm, "The Lord is close unto all them that call upon Him, to all that call upon Him in truth" (Ps. 145:18), which means, in the truth they *do*.

In the truth they do. This truth is not a "what" but a "how." The matter of a deed does not determine its truth but the manner in which it is carried out: in human conditionality, or in divine unconditionality. Whether a deed will peter out in the outer courtyard, in the realm of things, or whether it will penetrate into the Holy of Holies is determined not by its content but by the power of decision that brought it about and by the sanctity of intent that dwells in it. Every deed, even one numbered among the most profane, is holy when it is performed in holiness, in unconditionality.

Unconditionality is the specific religious content of Judaism. Jewish religiosity is built neither on doctrine nor on an ethical prescription, but on a fundamental perception that gives meaning to man: that one thing above all is needed. This perception is transformed into a demand [*Forderung*] wherever religiosity is community-forming and religion-founding—wherever it moves from the life of individual man into the life of the community. The founding of the Jewish religion and all its essential revolts are marked by this demand and the struggle for it.

The founding of the Jewish religion was consummated in demand and struggle. When Moses, his eyes ablaze with the fire of the Burning Bush, steps before the elders of Israel, one can anticipate all that is going to happen. I know of no greater, more awful event in world history or world myth. The people had broken away from the One whom they could not yet grasp, and the sons of Levi, at Moses's command, walked through the camp, slaying three thousand of their brothers (cf. Exod. 32:26). The Exodus generation cannot withstand the tribulations of the desert; it must die out in the desert. In the annihilation of everything that is halfhearted and inadequate, the proclaimed God reveals Himself as the consuming fire of unconditionality.

Here the two dominant human types who wage the struggle of Judaism's internal history are already juxtaposed to each other: the prophet and the priest. Moses is the man of demand who listens only to the voice—acknowledges only the deed. Aaron is the mediator, as accessible to the voices as to the voice, who destroys the people's discipline by his directionless and subservient formalism. The prophet wants truth; the priest, power. They are eternal types in the history of Judaism.

In the struggle, Jewish religiosity turned from the spirit of Moses to religion. Still struggling, it must repeatedly renew itself from within religion, whose formalism threatens to choke it; must endeavor, again and again, to recast, by its fervid demand, the solidified mass. It never succeeds in wresting dominance from official Judaism; but, overtly or covertly, it always has a profound effect on the development of the people's spirit. At times religion rises to a new, higher life. At other times it breaks out of the communal structure. And occasionally, after a brief flowering, it decays. The history of Judaism furnishes representative examples of all these possibilities.

Israel's sacrificial cult may have originated in the primitive need for a living communion with God through some sacramental act, such as a communal meal; undoubtedly, this was soon complemented by a quite different feeling: the need for a sacrificial offering that could symbolize, as well as proffer, the intrinsically desired and intended self-sacrifice. Under the leadership of the priest, however, the symbol became a substitute. The sacrificial cult was so elaborated and codified that in every phase of his life, at every moment of his destiny, man had at his disposal a prescribed sacrifice for establishing a communion with God; but this communion no longer consisted of anything but the sacrifice.... With imperious passion, Amos and Micah, Isaiah and Jeremiah repudiated the "abomination" of the sacrificial cult, demanding true service of God: "justice," that is, living unconditionally with God and with men. The prophetic message shares its substance and its ethical norms with the teachings of other nations; what is unique in it and specifically Jewish is the breath of unconditionality that pulsates in it from beginning to end, the postulate of decision that resounds in all its words and in the very rhythm of its demands: its religiosity. Every construct of a "pure ethics" of Judaism misses this basic point. Wherever the unconditioned deed reveals the hidden divine countenance, there is the core of Judaism.

The prophets wanted to demolish a sacrificial cult devoid of intention. They were unable to lessen its dominion; leadership remained in the hands of the priest. Nevertheless, they renewed Jewish religiosity, and the people's soul; thus, imperceptibly, are victories of the spirit consummated.

In the Second Commonwealth a new religious institution became central: the Scriptures. These were gradually canonized as the fixed expression of the state religion. Corps of compilers, subordinate to the priesthood, sifted from the wealth of material whatever seemed to them mythical or suspect. Thus came into being the one book that encompassed all the writings henceforth considered valid. This book became so all-embracing that all writings not included in the canon disappeared. But it triumphed not only over all other writings; it triumphed also over life. Henceforth, Scripture was truth; one could reach God only by adhering to it in every detail. But it was not viewed, either by the priest or later by the originally more liberal-minded scholar, as a proclamation to be meaningfully adapted to life and given new significance for life. It was viewed as a statute, a sum of prescriptions, formalistically circumscribed by the priest, dialectically spun out by the scholar, and always directed toward the narrow, the rigid, the unfree—thwarting instead of promoting living religiosity.

This tendency of official Judaism engendered two counteractions: One was the more moderate counteraction, developed within its own camp, whose late literary deposit we find in the Aggadah (Rabbinic narrative); the other, the more radical, counteraction developed within the self-segregating Essene community and in the movement surging around it that eventually flowed into early Christianity.... But none of these movements succeeded in renewing Jewish religion. The Aggadah did not succeed because its influence had been only fragmentary and because it did not consolidate its forces. Essenism did not succeed because it succumbed to a sterile separation and did not reach out to the people. And early Christianity was lost as a source of renewal for Judaism when it became untrue to itself, narrowing the great idea that had carried it aloft, the idea of the God-winning "turning," to a communion by grace with the Christ; at that point it won the nations and abandoned Judaism by sundering the structure of its community. From then on Christianity rose to dominion over the nations, and Judaism sank into rigidity, humiliation, and degradation; but its core unshakably maintained its claim to be the true *ecclesia,* the ever faithful community of divine immediacy.

Ever since the destruction of the Temple, tradition has been at the center of Judaism's religious life. A fence was thrown around the law to keep at a distance everything alien or dangerous; but often it kept living religiosity at a distance as well. Surely, to manifest itself in a community of men, to establish and maintain a community—indeed, to exist as a religion—religiosity needs forms; a continuous religious community, perpetuated from generation to generation, is possible only when a common way of life is maintained. But when, instead of uniting them for freedom in God, religion keeps men tied to an immutable law and damns their demand for freedom; when, instead of viewing its forms as an obligation upon whose foundation genuine freedom can build, it views them as an obligation to exclude all freedom; when, instead of keeping its elemental sweep inviolate, it transforms the law into a heap of petty formulas and allows man's decision for right or wrong action to degenerate into hairsplitting casuistry; then religion no longer shapes but enslaves religiosity.

This process characterizes the history of Jewish tradition. Religiosity's counteraction assumes a twofold shape. One is the sporadic flare-ups of the heretical rebellions, often tied to powerful messianic movements, which arouse all of the people. The other is the steady, constructive activity of Jewish mysticism, which strives to revive the ossified rites through the notion of *kavanah*[14] (intention) and to endow every religious act with a hidden significance directed toward God's destiny and the redemption of the world. In the older Kabbalah this tendency was still imbued with an inherently theologically allegorizing element that prevented it from becoming popular. It is only in the later Lurianic Kabbalah[15] that this tendency acquired a dimension of intuitiveness and immediacy. In Hasidism it developed into a great folk movement. Hasidism had no desire to diminish the law; it wanted to restore it to life, to raise it once again from the conditioned to the unconditioned: every man, by living authentically, shall himself become a Torah, a law. Out of Hasidism a renewal of Jewish religiosity could have come, as never before. But, charged with heresy, slandered, denounced by official Judaism, and degenerating because of the weakness of the people, which was not yet equal to the decisiveness of its teachings, Hasidism deteriorated before it had done its work.

All three movements—the prophetic, the Essenic-early Christian, and the Kabbalistic-Hasidic—share a resolve to make man's life not easier but more difficult while at the same time enspiriting and exalting it. All have in common the impetus to restore decision as the determining motive power of all religiosity. Through ossification of the sacrificial cult, of Scripture and tradition, man's free decision has been suppressed. It is no longer the deed, born of decision and drawing breath in unconditionality, that is viewed as the way to God, but compliance with rules and regulations. Prophecy, early Christianity, and Hasidism, on the other hand, call for decision, remembering that this is the soul of Jewish religiosity. The timeless meaning these movements have for Judaism and their importance for us in the work of renewal is to be found not in how they ended but from whence they came; not in their forms but in their forces. These are the forces that never assumed adequate form, never won dominion in Judaism, and have always been suppressed by official Judaism, that is, by its ever-dominant dearth of vitality. They are not the forces that belong to specific periods in the people's life or to specific segments of the people, nor are they the forces of insurrection and sectarianism. They are the forces that fight living Judaism's spiritual battle against bondage; they are the eternal forces. Only from them can come the religious inner shock without which no renewal of Jewish peoplehood can succeed.

Religiosity is, as I have said, man's urge to establish a living communion with the unconditioned; it is man's desire to realize the unconditioned through his deed and to establish it in his world. Genuine religiosity, therefore, has nothing in common with the fancies of romantic hearts, or with the self-pleasure of aestheticizing souls, or with the clever mental exercises of a practiced intellectuality. Genuine religiosity is *doing*. It wants to sculpt the unconditioned out of the matter of this world. The countenance of God reposes, invisible, in an earthen block; it must be wrought—carved—out of it. To engage in this work means to be religious—nothing else.

Social life, open to our influence as is no other thing in this world, is the task apportioned to us in its most inward immediacy. Here, as nowhere else, multiplicity is given into our hands, to be transformed into unity; a vast, formless mass, to be "in-formed" (given form to) by us with the Divine. The community of men is as yet only a projected opus that is waiting for us, a chaos that we must put in order, a Diaspora that we must gather in, a conflict to which we must bring reconciliation. But this we can accomplish only if, in the natural context of a life shared with others, every one of us, each in his own place, will perform the just, the unifying, the "in-forming" deed. For God does not want to be believed in, to be debated and defended by us, but simply to be realized through us.

Notes

Source: "Jüdische Religiosität" (lecture), first in *Vom Geist des Judentums. Reden und Geleitworte* (Leipzig: Kurt Wolff, 1916). Eva Jospe, trans., in *On Judaism* (New York: Schocken, 1967).

Editor's note: The lecture was one of three delivered between 1912 and 1914 at the Prague Jewish student organization, Bar Kochba. Invited by the young Prague philosopher (Shmuel) Hugo Bergmann (1883–1975), Buber gave three cycles of a total of eight lectures before the Bar Kochba group (1909–11, 1912–14, and 1918–19), which then appeared as *Reden über das Judentum* (Frankfurt/M.: Rütten & Loening, 1923). It should be noted that the Bar Kochba organization (named after the second-century Jewish revolutionary and messianic pretender) remained under strong influence by Buber's speeches and became one of the intellectual centers of cultural and spiritual Zionism. The present speech is built upon the distinction of "religion" and "religiosity" that was made, among others, by Buber's former teacher Georg Simmel (1858–1918).

1. Israel Ben-Eliezer (Baal-Shem Tov, 1700–1760) founder of the Hasidic movement.
2. Cf. Martin Buber: *Tales of the Hasidim: The Early Masters* (New York: Schocken, 1947), p. 48 (N. Glatzer).
3. Berakhot 9, 5 (M.B.).
4. Buber uses the term decision [*Entscheidung*] mostly in the literal sense of decision, the overcoming of inner division.
5. Tanhumna on Gen. 3:22 (N. Glatzer).
6. Sifra on Deut. 33:5 (N. Glatzer).
7. Berakhot 34b (N. Glatzer).
8. Sayings of the Fathers 4, 17 (M.B.).

9. Avodah Zarah 20b (N. Glatzer).
10. Sifra on Lev. 20:26 (N. Glatzer).
11. Sifra on Deut. 33:5 (N. Glatzer).
12. Zohar 2, 32b.
13. Sanhedrin 4, 5 (M.B.).
14. See also The Life of the Hasidim (1908) (p. 78 in this volume).
15. Isaac Luria (1534–1572), prominent mystic of Safed whose (oral) teachings were propagated by his student Hayyim Vital and the Italian Kabbalist Israel Sarug.

Heruth: On Youth and Religion (1919)*

> "God's writing engraved on the tablets" read not *haruth* (engraved) but *heruth* (freedom).
> —Sayings of the Fathers 6, 2

Among all the problems of present-day Jewish life, that of youth's attitude toward religion is probably most in need of elucidation. But, one may ask, does youth really have a special religious problem? Is youth, as such, concerned with religion at all?

Is youth concerned with religion? This means, individually, young people may be religious or irreligious, depending on their personal disposition, upbringing, or environmental influences; but in what way does youth, as youth, have a definite attitude toward religion? Are we justified in demanding that it have one? Youth is the time of total openness. With senses totally open, youth absorbs the world's variegated abundance; with a will that is totally open, it gives itself to life's boundlessness. It has not yet sworn allegiance to any one truth for whose sake it would have to close its eyes to all other perspectives; it has not yet obligated itself to abide by any one norm that would silence all of its other aspirations. Youth's quest for knowledge knows no limits other than those set by its own experience; its vitality, no responsibility other than the one to the totality of its own life. Sooner or later it will have to subordinate its own power of perception and volition to the restrictive power of natural and moral laws, thus losing its boundlessness. The decision of whether to submit to religious or other theorems, to religious or other rules, should therefore be left to youth itself. Whoever imposes religion upon it closes all but one of the thousand windows of the circular building in which youth dwells—all but one of the thousand roads leading into the world.

---

* From *On Judaism* by Martin Buber, ed. Nahum Glatzer, trans. Eva Jospe, copyright © 1967 by Schocken Books, a division of Random House, Inc. Used by permission of Schocken Books, a division of Random House, Inc.

This admonition would be justified if religion were really, by nature, the dispenser of fixed orientations and norms, or a sum of dogmas and rules. By nature, however, it is neither. Dogmas and rules are merely the result, subject to change, of the human mind's endeavor to make comprehensible, by a symbolic order of the knowable and doable, the working of the unconditional it experiences within itself. Primary reality is constituted by the unconditional's effect upon the human mind, which, sustained by the force of its own vision, unflinchingly faces the Supreme Power. Man's mind thus experiences the unconditional as that great something that is counterposed against it, as the Thou as such [*Du an sich*]. By creating symbols, the mind comprehends what is in itself incomprehensible; thus, in symbol and adage, the illimitable God reveals Himself to the human mind....

It is not God who changes, only theophany—the manifestation of the Divine in man's symbol-creating mind—until no symbol is adequate any longer, and none is needed; and life itself, in the miracle of man's being with man, becomes a symbol—until God is truly present when one man clasps the hand of another.

But such is the mysterious interconnection of the mind that in this most essential of all human concerns, every human being comprises, potentially, all of mankind, and every human destiny—all of history. At some time or other, be it ever so fleeting and dim, every man is affected by the power of the unconditional. The time of life when this happens to all, we call youth. At that time, every man experiences the hour in which the infinite beckons him, testing whether, sustained by the power of his vision and the creation of symbols, by his dedication and response, he can confront it unflinchingly. In this most inward sense, every man is destined to be religious. Indeed, what the total openness of youth signifies is that its mind is open not merely to all, but to the All. But most men fail to fulfill their destiny. Whether they remain close to their ancestral religion or become alienated from it, whether they continue to believe in and to practice this religion and its symbolism or refuse to adhere to its command, they are unable to withstand the impact of the unconditional and therefore evade it. They do not approach it with the power of their vision and their work, with their dedicated and responsive deed; they turn away from it and toward the conditional....

We are not concerned, then, with imposing religion upon youth, or with forcing it into a system of the knowable and doable, but with awakening youth's own latent religion, that is, its willingness to confront, unwaveringly, the impact of the unconditional. We must not preach to youth that God's revelation becomes manifest in only one, and in no other, way; rather, we must show it that nothing is incapable of becoming a receptacle of revelation. We must not proclaim to youth that God can be served by only one, and by no other, act, but we must make it clear that every deed is hallowed if it radiates the spirit of unity. We must not ask young people to avow as exclusively binding in their lives only that which emanated at some hour of the past, but we must affirm for them that "every man has his hour,"[1] when the gate opens for him and the word becomes audible to him. We who stand in awe of that which is unknowable do not want to transmit to youth a knowledge of God's nature and work. We who consider life as more divine than laws and rules do not want to regulate the life of youth by laws and rules attributed to God. We want to help youth not to bypass its destiny, not to miss its metaphysical self-discovery by being asleep, and to respond when it senses within itself the power of the unconditional. By so doing, we do not diminish the openness of youth but promote and affirm it; we do not curtain any of its windows but let it absorb the all-encompassing view; we do not shut off any road but make it easier for youth to see that all roads, if walked in truth and consecration, lead to the threshold of the Divine.

But one may ask, "If religion's basic significance lies not in the mores or institutions of a community united by precept and cult but rather in acts derived from an innate awareness common to all men, that is in 'universally human' acts, how then is it possible to speak of a specific kinship between Jewish youth and religion? Or, to put it more generally, how is it possible to speak of a specific kinship between the youth of any people and religion?"

For an answer, we must first look at the general aspect of this question and then investigate whether some special elements, nonexistent in any other people, are not at work in Judaism and in its youth.

I have pointed out the error that threatens all young people and to which many fall prey: Unable to withstand the impact of the unconditional, they evade it. But there exists still another, more serious, error: the *pretense* of withstanding—a deception not only of others but of oneself. The unconditional affects a person when he lets his whole being be gripped by it, be utterly shaken and transformed by it, and when he responds to it with his whole being: with his mind, by perceiving the symbols of the Divine; with his soul, by his love of the All; with his will, by his standing the test of active life.

But it is possible, by some odd perversity, that an individual entertains the illusion that he has surrendered himself to the unconditional whereas in fact he has evaded it: He interprets the fact of having been affected by the unconditional, as having had an "experience" [*Erlebnis*].[2] His being remains wholly unperturbed and unchanged, but he has savored his hour of exaltation. He does not know the response; he knows only a "mood" [*Stimmung*]. He has psychologized God.

The first of these errors, evasion, was especially characteristic of an earlier generation, which inclined toward superficial rationalism; the second, a quasi-acceptance, is common to the new generation, which is given to no less superficial emotionalism. This latter error is by far the more serious one, for a quasi-affirmation is always more questionable than a negation. In some way, religiosity may possibly penetrate the evaders but never the pretenders. One can be a rationalist, a freethinker, or an atheist in a religious sense, but one cannot, in a religious sense, be a collector of "experiences," a boaster of moods, or a prattler about God. When the teeming swarms of the marketplace have scattered into the night, the stars shine over the new stiffness, as over a mountain's silence; but no eternal light can penetrate the fumes of the chatter-filled public house.

But how can youth be saved from this error? Or, rather, how can youth save itself from it? It has a great helper by its side: the living community of the people.... The man who is truly bound to his people cannot go wrong, not because he has at his disposal the symbols and forms that millennia of his people's existence have created for envisioning as well as for serving the unconditional, but because the faculty to create images and forms flows into him from this bond to his people....

When bound to his people, man is aware that the living community of this people is composed of three elements. Preceding him, there is the people's sacred work, expressed in literature and history—the scroll of words and deeds whose letters tell the chronicle of this people's relation to its God. Around him, there is the present national body in which, no matter how degenerate it may be, the divine Presence continues to live, immured in the tragic darkness of the everyday, yet shedding upon it the radiance of its primordial fire. And within him, in his soul's innermost recesses, there is a silent, age-old memory from which, if he can but unlock it, knowledge pours forth for him, truer than that from the shallow wavelets of his private experiences. But this deep wellspring can be unlocked only by him who has made his wholehearted decision for such a bond.

Three elements, then, compose his people's living community—a threefold source of strength for the young, a threefold anchorage for his relation to the unconditional!...

What I said about the young person's relation to the religious life of his people is especially relevant to Judaism, for two reasons. The first is the autonomy of Judaism's religious development, an autonomy not experienced by Western people. Among them, the natural growth of religious tendencies and forms was circumscribed and transformed by a spiritual principle imposed from the outside, Christianity; and despite all the artful attempts of the Christian Church to incorporate into its doctrine and its service the primal forces that had been at work in pagan myth and magic and had stirred the people's emotions, no perfect unity was achieved. Hence, in Christianity, the young person who wishes to derive sustenance and support for his personal relation to the unconditional from his association with his people must turn not so much to religion proper as to the primal forces that live on, covertly, in the faithful images of a people's life: its customs and tales; its songs and sayings. In Judaism, however, other influences notwithstanding, all religious development sprang exclusively from forces inherent in the people's own soul, and foreign elements had no part in the conflicts that accompanied this development. Here, therefore, the young person faces a unified realm, and when the official outward forms of his religion do not provide him with the help he needs, he need not turn away from them to another sphere of his people's existence; he has only to descend into their own depths, to those ramifications of Jewish religiosity that not having become dominant, still continue to live beneath the surface.

But an even more essential reason is the fact that he *cannot* turn to any other sphere of his people's existence, for in the life of the Jewish people no sphere is unconnected with the religious one. Not only is Judaism's specific productivity bound up with its relationship to the unconditional, but so too is its specific vitality. Any distinction between different fields of endeavor, characteristic of most other peoples, is alien to the nature of Judaism; its extrareligious elements are either so peripheral as to have no part in its creative expression or they are, in one way or another, determined by and dependent upon religious factors. It is characteristic that even the people's original defection from the God of biblical religion assumed a religious form: The defecting masses were not content with surrendering themselves to their newly freed instincts; they expressed their driving passion by gathering together their valuables for the casting of an idol.[3] The case of the modern Hebrew poet who, not content with forswearing allegiance to the old God, worshiped instead Apollo's statue, exemplifies the same characteristic.[4] No matter what form religious creativity may assume in Judaism, it never loses its basic character. The greatest philosophical genius Judaism has given to the world, Spinoza, is the only one of the great philosophers for whom, in reality, God is the sole subject of thought; and ancient messianic dreams live on in the ideologies of Jewish socialists.

I am well aware that ever since the demand for Jewish regeneration in our time became more insistent, there have been men who deplore the predominance of the religious element in Judaism, though they are far from holding any shallow enlightenment theories. They see in this predominance a narrowing of the people's life, a weakening of its vitality, and a divergence of its energies from their natural tasks. These men demand a secularization of Judaism, and, given the vegetating *galut* life in which religious demands in their narrowest sense have so frequently stifled the people's vitality, I recognize that there is justification for such a view. Nevertheless, it is based on a fundamental error that mistakes the historical outward forms of its religion for Judaism's great religious creativity. Religion is detrimental to an unfolding of the people's energies only when it concentrates—as it has indeed done to an ever-increasing degree in the Diaspora—on the enlargement of the *thou shalt not,* on the minute differentiation between the permitted and the forbidden. When this is the case, it neglects its true task, which is and remains man's response to the Divine, the response of the total human being; hence, the unity of the spiritual and the worldly, the realization of the spirit, and the spiritualization of the worldly; the sanctification of the relationship to all things; that is, freedom in God. But Hasidism, though still closely tied to the tradition of the *thou shalt not,* already presents a great, though unsuccessful, attempt at a synthesis between the spiritual and the worldly order—a fusion of fundamental religious consciousness with the unaffectedness and fullness of natural life. And the future of creative Judaism lies not in a weeding out of religiosity but in the direction of this synthesis. The growing striving for this synthesis is youth's guarantee that it will not find decomposing rocks but the waters of genuine life when it descends into the depths of Jewish religion in search of help for its soul.

Intellectualization, in the making for centuries and accomplished within recent generations, has brought a depressing loneliness to the youth of present-day Europe. By intellectualization I mean the hypertrophy of intellect that has broken out of the context of organic life and become parasitic, in contradistinction to organic spirituality, into which life's totality is translated. Because the bridge of immediate community, whether its name be love, friendship, companionship, or fellowship, connects only man with man and, hence spirit with spirit, but not thinking apparatus with thinking apparatus, this intellectualization begets loneliness.... However, owing to the anomaly of *galut* life, intellectualization has progressed still further, and the loneliness of Jewish youth has been intensified. In addition, a large segment of Jewish youth, especially in the Western world, is cut off from its natural national existence and gradually loses the illusion that it has organic ties to another one. And this too intensifies its longing for community.

Only a genuine bond with the religiously creative life of its people can still this longing of Jewish youth and overcome the loneliness of its intellectualization.

I have already indicated why youth needs this bond for the building of its inner religious life: to enable it to confront the unconditional not with the arbitrary mood of the dreamer who has had an "experience" but with the readiness of the fighter and worker who, despite all personal freedom, binds himself to his people's creativity and pursues it in his own life. But youth needs this bond no less for its inner national life. It must no longer permit itself the illusion that it can establish a decisive link to its people merely by reading Bialik's[5] poems or by singing Yiddish folksongs; or by the addition of a few quasi-religious sentiments and lyricisms. It must realize that something bigger is at stake: that one must join, earnestly and ready for much struggle and work, in Judaism's intense creative process, with all its conflicts and subsequent reconciliations; that one must recreate this process from within, with reverence of soul and awareness of mind; that one must participate in it not only with his inwardness but with his total life, by affirming and translating into reality all one finds along the way; that what needs to be done is to get ready for renewal.... Renewal is in the making when Judaism's spiritual process, which is a process of religious struggle and religious creativity, is restored to life in word and deed by a generation earnestly resolved in translating its idea into reality.

But restoration demands something more creative than mere joining in, though it cannot be achieved without it. And here the basic question comes to the fore, What should the nature and the object of this joining in be?

Depending on whether the essence of Jewish religion is viewed as lying in its teaching [*Lehre*] or in its law [*Gesetz*], two ways are advocated for today's youth to follow: to commit itself either to Jewish teaching or to Jewish law.

I shall begin with the first of these views. Its leading proponents sublimate the many-faceted and vital fullness of religion into a system of abstract concepts. But in the process, the nurturing, creative, inexplicable element of religion, the awareness of its suprarationality, is lost. Dogmas, primarily the dogma of God's oneness, and moral commandments, primarily the commandment to love one's neighbor, are singled out and summarized in formulations that as a rule are shaped to fit a certain dominant philosophical school. Consequently, to anyone unfamiliar with the suprarational wealth of Jewish religiosity, Judaism appears to be a curious, awkward detour to some modern philosophical theorems, as, for instance, the idea of God as a postulate of practical reason, or the categorical imperative—a detour that historically was probably unavoidable, but that has now become wholly superfluous.

The originators of such theories overlook the fact that religious truth is not a conceptual abstraction but has existential relevance, that is, that words can only point the way and that religious truth can be made adequately manifest only in the individual's or the community's life of religious actualization [*Bewährung*]. Indeed, they overlook the fact that a master's teachings lose their religious character as soon as they are taken out of the context of his own life and the life of his followers and transformed into a wholly nonpersonal, autonomous maxim, recognizable and acknowledgeable as such. Frozen into a declaration of what is or into a precept of what ought to be, the words of religious teaching represent a more enspirited, but also a more primitive, variation of a metaphysical or ethical ideology. But viewed as part of the utterances of a great life to which conceptualization cannot do justice, they are beyond the sphere of all ideologies and not subject to their criteria; they are truth *sui generis*, contingent upon no other: religious truth. Here, not the words themselves are truth, but life as it has been, and will be, lived; and the words are truth only by virtue of this life. In Judaism, therefore, the truth of God's oneness encompasses not only the "I shall be there"[6] but also all of Moses's life; not only the "Hear, O Israel"[7] but also the death of the martyrs.

Furthermore, the authors of the aforementioned theories overlook the fact that religious truth is not static but dynamic, that is, it neither belongs to nor is finished with any single historical moment in time. Nor can it be taken out of the context of such a single moment. Instead, every moment of the past, no matter how rich in revelation, is one phase of this truth, as is in fact every religiously creative period. Thus, in Judaism, conjoined to the truth of God's oneness is its entire development and all its transformations: the multiplicity of God's biblical names in their gradation from a natural plurality to a spiritual singularity; and equally the separation of the *shekhinah,* in correspondence with the growing awareness of the empirical world's imperfection....

Religious truth, in contradistinction to philosophical truth, is not a maxim but a way; it is not a thesis but a process. That God is merciful is an abstract statement; to penetrate the religious truth that lies beyond it, we must not shrink from opening the Bible to one of its most awful passages, the one where God rejects Saul, His anointed (upon whom, at election, He bestowed a new spirit), because he spared the life of Agag, the conquered king of the Amalekites.[8] Let us not resist the shudder that seizes us, but let us follow where it leads as the soul of the people struggled for an understanding of God. We shall then come to that wondrous passage in the Talmud where, according to an old biblical interpretation, God rejoices in Goliath's soul and answers the angels who remind Him of David: "It is incumbent upon Me to turn them into friends."[9] Here we see a religious truth.

Purity of soul is an ethical concept. Nevertheless, let us not recoil from reading, in the third Book of Moses, the paragraphs that describe purification by the blood of sheep and doves as well as the great purification through the scapegoat. And when our hearts tremble under the impact of the great, ancient, but also alien, symbol, let us follow the way of the people's soul as it struggled for its purity, a way leading beyond prophets and psalmists to Akiba's liberating cry, "God is the purifying bath of Israel!"[10] Only then will we become fully aware of the religious element in this concept of purity.

A bond between virtue and reward has become unacceptable to our own sensibility toward life and the world. But we must not read this attitude into the records of the ancient Jewish religion in which, from God's covenant with the patriarchs, through Moses's blessing and curse, to the promises and threats of the prophets, the belief in reward and punishment constitutes a self-evident basis for the moral postulate—a belief perpetuated even in the abstraction of the Maimonidean articles of faith.[11] At the same time we must not close our eyes to the struggle in which men of sacred will turned, with ever increasing determination, away from this belief....

We must therefore reject commitment to a claim that Jewish teaching is something finished and unequivocal. For us, it is neither. It is, rather, an enormous process, still uncompleted, of spiritual creativity and creative response to the unconditional. It is in this process that we want to participate with our conscious, active life, in the hope that we, too, may not be denied a creative spark. But to achieve this participation, we must fully discern this process—discern not merely some of its isolated aspects or effects, not only maxims or theses, but, in earnest awareness, its whole development up to the present, recreating it in its entirety from within.

Yet this is not enough. We must truly *will* this process, all of it, from its beginnings, through all of its ups and downs, conflicts and reconciliations, up to ourselves—the lowly but God-inspired sons of a transitional generation, doing their share to the best of their abilities—and beyond our time.

The second of the two views I spoke of renders the word Torah not as "teaching" but as "law;" its proponents bid Jewish youth to commit itself to Jewish law. By the term "law" they mean the sum of all the statutes, preserved at first in unwritten form but later committed to writing, that God, according to tradition, gave to Moses on Mount Sinai, within the hearing of the assembled people of Israel. The tradition of this giving of the law, reinforced by the life and death of a long chain of generations, is so powerful and venerable that some of its power and venerability is imparted to every man who truly dwells within it, that is, to the man who with his total being adheres to its commandments and prohibitions, not because he was taught and conditioned to do so by his parents or teachers, but because he feels certain in his very soul that these 613 commandments[12] and prohibitions are the core and substance of God's word to Israel....

Genuine affirmation of the law must be anchored in this certitude of the fact of revelation, as well as in the affirmation that its content has been faithfully preserved in the 613 *mitzvot* (commandments) and their framework. Indeed, such affirmation has religious value only insofar as it is supported by this certitude. The legitimacy of the life of the man whose observance of the law is grounded on this basis is unassailable, the legitimacy of what, to him, is truth, is irrefutable. He deserves our esteem and approbation, especially when, for the sake of observing the law, he gladly assumes the burden of overcoming the countless difficulties and temptations presented by our society. But if he lacks this certitude, his sacrificial spirit, whether a result of piety or of habit, loses its religious import and hence its special sanctity.

Observance of commandments because one knows or feels that this is the only way in which to live in the name of God has a legitimacy all its own, essentially inaccessible to all outside criticism, whose criteria it can reject. But observance without this basic attitude means exposure of oneself, as well as the commandments, to a test by criteria of a wholly different ethos. For relationship to the unconditional is a commitment of the total man, whose mind and soul are undivided; to divorce the actions indicative of this commitment from the yea-saying of man's undivided soul, to sever them from their accord with man's undivided mind, is to profane them. But it is such profanation that is perpetrated by those blind followers of the law who demand that it be accepted not out of certitude of its divine origin but out of obedience to the authority of the collective Jewish will. They declare that first and foremost, the law must be observed; everything else will then follow. The law, they say, restrains the will but leaves the personality free.

We reject this dialectic completely. In the image of man to which we aspire, conviction and volition, personality and performance, are one and indivisible. And though it may yet take lengthy, indescribably difficult battles against the enormous resistance of external and internal forces before this unity is realized in all other areas, there is one particular area in which there must be no further delay: the area of religiosity. For this is the true realm of unity—the realm where man, in every other respect still divided, split apart, and torn by conflict, may at any moment become whole and one....

For those who have not been granted the certitude I spoke of, this insight charts a course that is incompatible with the acceptance of traditional law. And no one familiar with the new religious consciousness of a new youth...no one who has ever been close to the secret of this becoming will think it could contain the belief in a one-time revelation, transmitted in its entirety and binding for all time.

It would seem, however, that the passionate will for community that I spoke of is motivating Jewish youth to commit itself to traditional teaching and law after all. It feels an ever-growing urge to truly find its way back to its people—not merely to this people's recorded past and dreamed-about future but also to its actual present—and to become an organic part of the people; to merge with it. And it seems to some of them that such a merging can be achieved only by acceptance of the special teachings and customs of the Jewish people, which constitute the teachings and customs of Jewish tradition. They are supported in this view by exhorters and zealots who, dissatisfied with their experience of Jewish nationalism—dissatisfied because, in their opinion, it is not Jewish enough; dissatisfied, in truth, because it is not human enough—now proclaim, as the last and redeeming word, a commitment to the law of their common tradition. But those who clutch at this belief are blind to the signs appearing, at this hour, on the firmament of our destiny and the destiny of the world. There is greatness in the national body, and its faithful adherence to the law is awe inspiring. Yet greater still is the working of the national spirit, and he who, in sensitive awareness, has opened his soul to it knows that something new will rise out of it.

But neither will this new element rise out of nothingness. It, too, will develop and transform already existing material; it, too, will be a discovery and raising of an ancient treasure, an unveiling and freeing of something that has grown beneath the surface. It behooves us, therefore, to grasp the old, with our hearts and minds, but not lose our hearts and minds to it. We want to remain faithful to the intent of that great spiritual movement that we call the Jewish movement—a movement that is not romanticism but a renaissance. For, even though the admonishers and zealots may not concede it, it is always romanticism when the spirit, in its search for a people, submits and surrenders to the forms developed in that people's past and transmitted, in word and custom, from that past. And it is always a renaissance when the spirit brings to life the primal forces encapsuled in those forms, calling them forth to new creation—when it encounters a people and makes it creative.

In the light of this perception we shall try to find an answer to the question that occupies our minds....

As we have seen, we cannot commit ourselves to an acceptance of Jewish teaching if this teaching is conceived as something finished and unequivocal; nor can we commit ourselves to Jewish law if this law is taken to mean something closed and immutable. We can commit ourselves only to the primal forces, to the living religious forces that, though active and manifest in all of Jewish religion, in its teaching and its law, have not been fully expressed by either.... They are the eternal forces that do not permit one's relationship to the unconditional ever to wholly congeal into something merely accepted and executed on faith—the forces that, from the totality of doctrines and regulations, consistently appeal for freedom in God. Though religious teaching may assign to the Divine a Beyond from where our world is enjoined, rewarded, and punished, the primal forces point beyond this division (apparently without violating religious teaching) by permitting the birth of unity in the free deed of the complete human being. And though the law may proclaim a differentiation between the holy and the profane, these primal forces overcome this differentiation (apparently without violating the law) by permitting the hallowing of the profane in the free deed of the complete human being. Their task is to call forth man's response to the Divine—the response of the *complete* human being, and, hence, the unification of the spiritual and the worldly: the realization of the spirit and the hallowing of the worldly, the sanctification of the relationship to all things, that is, freedom in God. God's writing on the tablets constitutes freedom; the religious forces persistently strive to rediscover those symbols of divine freedom again. God's original tablets are broken. The religious forces of eternal renewal persistently strive to restore the blurred outlines of divine freedom on the second tablets, the tablets of the teaching and the law. The eternally renewed effort of these forces denotes the endeavor to fuse, once again, fundamental religious consciousness with the unbiasedness and fullness of natural life, as they had been fused on God's original tablets. There are intimations of a new endeavor. We believe it will succeed; we have faith in the new element trying to emerge from the people's spirit. To help prepare this emergence of the new, a generation willing to put its ideals into practice and to restore Judaism's spiritual process to life, in word and deed, must commit itself to the primal forces. This generation is the treasure that must be uncovered and raised, the subterranean growth that must be brought to light and freed. We need its help to withstand the impact of the unconditional in this hour of death and birth.

Mankind's religious longing, awakening at this hour, is akin to Judaism's primal forces. Today, thinking men can at last no longer tolerate the dualism of spirit and "world"—the antithesis between the soul's hypothetical independence from the world's deadening hustle and bustle and life's dependence on it. They no longer want to bear the yoke of this conflict sanctioned by the churches; they want to grasp the unity of spirit and world, realize it, and thus bring about true freedom, that is, freedom in God. Divided man is, of necessity, unfree; only unified man becomes free. Divided man can never effect anything but division; only unified man can establish unity. Unified, or unifying, total man who is free in God, is the goal of mankind's longing that is awakening at this hour, just as he is the meaning of Judaism's religious forces. Herein resides the power that alone can raise Judaism above degeneracy and torpidity, and by doing so, this power will enable it to once again write its message into the history of the world....

But we cannot participate in this spiritual process nor walk inwardly along the path of the primal forces solely with our emotions. It must be done in reverent and unbiased knowledge—a knowledge that though it will always owe to intuition its access to the heart of things, cannot dispense with the reliable tools of assembling, sifting, and examining the facts before it can ever find this access. Only the fusing of all that has been found will be the business of our freely creative emotions.

I say reverent and unbiased knowledge, for it is a painful failing of our youth to approach matters of Jewish religion partly without reverence and partly without freedom from bias....

Our religious literature must become the object of reverent and unbiased knowledge. The reader of the Bible must attempt to understand the spirit of its original language, the Hebrew—an understanding that is service [*dienendes Wissen*]. He will approach it not as a work of literature but as the basic documentation of the unconditional's effect on the spirit of the Jewish people; whatever his knowledge of old as well as new exegesis, he will search beyond it for the original meaning of each passage. No matter how familiar he is with modern biblical criticism's distinction between sources, he will penetrate beyond this criticism to more profound distinctions and connections. Though unafraid of bringing to light the mythical element, no matter how initially alien it may be to him, he will not advance a mythical interpretation where there exists an adequate historical one. He will read the Bible with an appreciation of its poetic form, but also with an intuitive grasp of the suprapoetic element that transcends all form. To such a reader the Bible will reveal a hidden treasure and the operation of primal forces from which the seed of new religiosity can derive sustenance and substance. Such reading of the Bible should be followed by earnest study of later literature, without omitting the unwieldy and seemingly unpromising material.

Similarly, the Jewish masses and all their beliefs and customs must also become an object of reverent and unbiased understanding. We must come close to their inner life, submerging ourselves in its inwardness and ardor, which have not been diminished, and indeed cannot be diminished, by any misery; we must perceive how the Jewish people's old religious fervor still endures among them, though in distorted and occasionally degraded form, and how there burns within it the desire, as yet unstilled, to hallow the earthly and to affirm the covenant with God in everyday life. We must discern, simultaneously, two things: that this people is in need of regeneration and that it is capable of achieving it, for, along with those of decadence, it carries within itself the elements of purification and of redemption.

Together, these two undertakings, exploring the people's literature and probing the depths of its life, will enable a generation that possesses reverent and unbiased understanding to go step by step along the course of the primal forces as it leads up to its own time....

Walking along the pathway of the primal forces, the generation at the turning encounters its own self; it can encounter it solely along this pathway. But only when it finds that the forces it has discerned dwell also within its own self can it make a choice and give direction to its own innermost powers.

When the primal forces become truly alive within a new Jewish generation and desirous of being reactivated, then, in close linkage to them, this new generation must allow the forces to work again; must begin to prepare a new work site for them within its own community, on the soil where, under cinders and ashes, still glimmer sparks of the old forge.

We must create a community, cemented by joint labor and joint sacrifice—a community of men who, in the name of the nameless God, will journey to the Zion of His realization. The mystery within their hearts is swelling, beyond all confines of teaching and law, toward the still inexpressible, the still formless. Discernment of the primal forces has disclosed to them the power whereby the inexpressible and formless can undergo a new incarnation: the human response to the Divine; the unification of spirit and world. There is only one road that will deliver us from the doom of our time: the road leading to freedom in God. If we know this, not through concepts or "moods" but through genuine awareness of a life of decision, then, no matter how far removed from all tradition we may seem to an insensible glance, we will have committed ourselves to the great course of Judaism.

Notes

Source: Cheruth—Eine Rede über Jugend und Religion (Vienna: R. Löwit, 1919). Eva Jospe, trans., in *On Judaism* (New York: Schocken, 1967), pp. 149–74.

Editor's note: "Heruth" was the last of the Jewish addresses that Buber delivered at the Bar Kokhba student organization (see editor's note on Jewish Religiosity [1923] [p. 123 in this volume]). When, in 1923, Buber's collected addresses on Judaism appeared, the philosopher Franz Rosenzweig took to task Buber's "Heruth" and what he perceived as a rejection of Jewish law in a famous letter ("Builders"), which Buber published in his journal *Der Jude* in 1924. The Buber-Rosenzweig correspondence on Jewish law is now available in Franz Rosenzweig, *On Jewish Learning,* ed. N. Glatzer (New York: Schocken, 1965).

1. Sayings of the Fathers 4, 3.
2. See Buber's critique of the term *Erlebnis* in Religion as Presence (1922) (p. 169f, in this volume).
3. See Exod. 32.3f.
4. Buber is referring to the poem "Before the Statue of Apollo" by the Hebrew poet Saul Tchernechovsky (1875–1943) (N. Glatzer).

5. Hayyim Nahman Bialik (1873–1934), outstanding poet of the Hebrew renaissance and editor of Midrashic literature. Buber's following discussion of "Law" and "Teaching" might well be influenced by Bialik's famous essay "Halakha and Aggadah" *of 1917*.
6. Exod. 3:14. See also *The Election of Israel: A Biblical Inquiry* (1938) (p. 25 in this volume) and *The Faith of Judaism* (1929) (p. 103 in this volume).
7. Deut. 6:4.
8. 1 Sam. 15:9–23.
9. Sanhedrin 105a.
10. Mishnah Yoma 8, 9.
11. Moses Maimonides (1135–1204), preeminent medieval Jewish philosopher and authority on Jewish law (*Halakha*), listed thirteen articles of faith in his commentary on Sanhedrin 10. Buber refers to article 11: "I believe with complete faith that the Creator, blessed be His Name, rewards with good those who observe His commandments, and punishes those who violate His commandments." It is customary to recite the thirteen articles after the morning prayers (*Shacharit*).
12. The number 613 is the traditional number of commandments (*mitzvot*) given in the Torah. They are commonly divided into 248 positive and 365 negative commandments.

On the [Jewish] Renaissance (1903)

We are speaking of the Jewish Renaissance. By this we understand the peculiar and basically inexplicable phenomenon of the progressive rejuvenation of the Jewish people in language, customs, and art. We justifiably call it "renaissance" because it resembles—in the transfer of human fate to national fate—the great period that we call Renaissance above all others, because it is a rebirth, a renewal of the entire human being like this Renaissance, and not a return to old ideas and life forms; [it is] the path from semi-being to being, from vegetation to productivity, from the dialectical petrification of scholasticism to a broad and soulful perception of nature, from medieval asceticism to a warm, flowing feeling of life, from the constraints of narrow-minded communities to the freedom of the personality, the way from a volcanic, formless cultural potential to a harmonious, beautifully formed cultural product.

To understand this beautiful and joyous phenomenon we must comprehend it as of one piece, trace it back to its origin, into the period during the late eighteenth century when two powerful influences penetrated the ossified existence of Judaism from within and from without—Hasidism and *Haskalah*—creating a new, incredible, and previously unimagined life.

Until the mid-eighteenth century the energy of Judaism was restrained not only from outside..., not only by the suppression of the "host nations" but also from within, by the tyranny [*Zwingherrschaft*] of the "Law," that is, a misunderstood, ornate, distorted, and perverted religious tradition. [It was restrained] by the ban of a hard, rigid imperative that was removed from reality, which turned everything into heresy and destroyed what was intuitively bright and joyous, everything that thirsted for beauty and all flights of fancy. Feeling was wrenched and thought was put in shackles.[1] And the "Law" achieved a power as no law in any other people or period. The education of the generations occurred exclusively in the service of Jewish law. There was no personal action born of feeling; only action based on the "Law" could survive. There was no personal creative thought; only the shared brooding over books on the "Law" and the hundreds of books of commentary on the "Law" and the thousands of books of commentary on the commentary. To be sure, heretics emerged again and again but what could the heretic achieve vis-à-vis Jewish law? Dogma, which one is to believe may be shaken by heretics who appeal to reason rather than faith. But a law for life that governs action can only be repealed through the development of human beings to self-determination or be overcome through the development of human beings to a higher law. Then, finally, both happened. For centuries it surely struggled beneath the surface, and those heresies that appeared daily anew and only to be stifled were surely manifestations of this struggle that undermined Jewish law. Then it announced itself in a double rush against the philosophy and the doctrine of the "Law." First, the progression to a higher law for life found expression in Jewish mysticism, namely Hasidism, the liberation of feeling; then the progression to self-determination, in the *Haskalah,* or Jewish Enlightenment—the liberation of thought. Both led to spiritual and physical struggles filled by the most moving tragedy and the most grandiose comedy. Both brought about the Jewish Renaissance without wanting it and without knowing it.

To be a Hasid means to be pious, and one could almost interpret Hasidism to mean pietism. If we take this word in its usual sense, however, that would be wrong. The Hasidic worldview lacks all sentimentality; it is mysticism full of power and emotion, which definitely brings the Beyond to the Here and Now and allows this [life] to be formed by the Beyond as the body [is formed] by the soul—an absolutely original, popular, and living renewal of Neoplatonism, a simultaneously most divine and most realistic direction to ecstasy. It is a teaching of the active feeling as a bond between the human being and God. Creating [*Schaffen*] is an everlasting process; creation continues today and always, and the human being participates in the creation process through energy and love. Everything that is done with a pure heart is worship. It is the goal of Jewish law that the human being becomes a law unto himself. This shatters the forced rule. But the founders of Hasidism were no nay-sayers. They did not abrogate the traditional forms but infused them with new meaning and thereby liberated them. Hasidism, or rather the deep spiritual stream that created and sustained it, created the emotionally regenerated Jew.

The *Haskalah* followed another path; it fought Hasidism as well as Rabbinics because both were based on "faith" and not on "knowledge." The *Haskalah* emerged in the name of knowledge, civilization, and Europe. It wanted to enlighten and was as superficial as all enlightenment must be if its premise is knowledge as a certain and unproblematic thing; it wanted to popularize, and it was just as dull and useless as all so-called popular philosophy that lives off the blood of others like all true parasites. What distinguishes the *Haskalah,* however, from all other enlightenment[2] is, first, its enemy, the most rigid and most established of all orthodoxies;

[then] its fresh youthful aggression [*Losgehen*] and the fact that it was at all times involved with the feeling of a holy war for self-determination, for the determination of action through our own thinking, not through the traditions. But it also contained positively Jewish, futuristic elements, as much as it believed that it was negating the tradition. The *Haskalah* wanted to Europeanize the Jews, but it did not intend their denationalization. It treated the language of the Bible with intense cultic reverence. It turned a lifeless language that was alienated from reality—Hebrew—into the tool of a living struggle and thereby enriched and strengthened it. And what has been done for language has also been done for the ideas. In this way the *Haskalah* served as a means for the [intellectual][3] regeneration of the Jewish people.[4]

From these inner revolutions, whose expressions and, at the same time, tools, were Hasidism and the *Haskalah,* the Jewish Renaissance was born. It is noteworthy that here the same elements interacted as in the great time of the 1300s and 1400s: the mystical-emotional [elements] that appeared then partly as Divine wisdom and partly as poetics and the ideal of language that then was called humanism. And just as in that time—I would like to emphasize this again—the Jewish Renaissance does not mean a return, but a rebirth of the whole human being: a rebirth that evolved very slowly, very gradually, from the days of the *Haskalah* and of Hasidim to our time and will continue to evolve. Slowly and gradually a new type of Jew will develop.

The Talmudic Jew was a passive hero. He suffered all stages of martyrdom without complaint and without pride, with silent lips and a silent heart—motionless. His refusal of the world was his only resistance, and nothing could break it down. This passivity, however, was not only greatness but also misery and pity. The Jew did not only struggle passively; he also acted and thought passively. One individual, Spinoza,[5] possessed enough *natura naturans*[6] to step from the ghetto into the cosmos actively and peacefully and to take hold in the Infinite as no one else before him. But how much of the most delicious temporality did he have to sacrifice—how much of the most irreplaceable emotional connection with past and future generations of his tribe? Which new and unspeakable martyrdom did he have to take upon himself and with him into his great peace? What barely intimated mystery of an incredible separateness did this liberated Talmudic Jew leave for posterity! The new Jew, the Jew of the Emancipation era, strolls in the paths of Spinoza, without genius but with a demonic daring. He is no longer passive, but acts freely; he no longer acts according to the Jewish law, but according to his own thought and feeling; and thus he strives for the creative. But creativity was denied to him for a long time and even to this day has not revealed itself to him in its ultimate secrets: self-unburdening, self-purification, self-redemption.... The rebirth of the Jew begins with a tragic episode, which today still has not ended and which did not even mean an emancipation of the people from ignoble elements. Even some of the best could not stand up against it; in fact, it was precisely those who were most aglow by the daring who drifted the farthest apart. Actually, some original individuals at the beginning of the nineteenth century achieved a peculiar cosmopolitanism, a being at home in the universe, but it could only prevail in all its beauty as long as the spirit of these Jews had to conquer their freedom, thereby gaining a fascinating greatness. When spiritual freedom [*Geistesfreiheit*] had become an accomplished fact also for Jews, this cosmopolitanism too turned into assimilation. European civilization had descended on the Jews too quickly and too directly for the *maskilim*[7] to digest it in peace. This way a portion of the people were misled to fall from their unspoken ideals of autonomy and to accept, at the expense of their own souls, the new ready-made from the hands of the cultivated nations instead of acquiring it and incorporating it gradually. This pathological manifestation was encouraged by two factors: the geographical dispersion and the abnormal acceleration of the emancipation process as a result of the great revolution.[8]

The fact that assimilation did not manage to reverse the Renaissance, in spite of all this, but became merely a slowing factor, is based on a major reality of the Jewish problem—the fundamental difference in essence and destiny of Eastern and Western Jewry. Eastern Jewry had always been less dispersed than Western Jewry; its charter resembled more a great and self-contained community and, thus, also possessed more Jewish cultural components. To this we can add that civilization crept east ever so slowly and that the emancipation process had almost no validity there. Therefore, the *Haskalah,* which had its true place in the East (as is the case with all other factors of the Renaissance), was able to incorporate the elements of civilization gradually and naturally. Also, a more large-scale assimilation was not thinkable because the host nation was not culturally stronger, but weaker. Additionally, the Jews of the East were socially healthier because they were less affected by the evil of an unproductive money economy. If Western Jews had to succumb to their environment because they had no language [of their own] and adopted not only foreign words but also foreign ideas and thoughts, Eastern Jews achieved stabilization in a strange, absolutely abnormal and yet thoroughly healing linguistic development. On the one hand, a rich Hebrew literature and commentary developed, and the language of the Bible became more and more a perfect instrument of modern science and of modern ideas while, at the same time, it became the coarse yet full-sounding tool of an original type of literature: Next to it and simultaneously, the idiom of the people, Yiddish, which was wrongfully called "jargon," developed. Yiddish is by no means a dialect (as is usually assumed), but a *res sui generis,* a completely equal language, less abstract but warmer than Hebrew amended with Yiddish, without the purely spiritual pathos [of Hebrew] but full of incomparably gentle and coarse, tender and malicious nuances. In Yiddish the popular itself became language, and this much-despised language has created the beginnings of charming poetry, melancholically dreamy lyrics, and strong novellas based on sound observation. This dualism is the strongest symptom of the Jewish Renaissance in its rich attempts, yet pathological forms, at expression.

Now we can understand why piece after piece broke off in the West while the Renaissance was able to take hold and create positive values in the East. Its strongest expression became the Jewish movement, which is sometimes also mistakenly called the national Jewish movement. It [the Jewish movement] is conceived more broadly and more deeply than national movements generally are; it is more authentic and more tragic. Its content is national—the striving for national freedom and autonomy—but its form is supranational. The complex of ideas that it brings forth belongs to the thought process of all humanity. And the liberation for which it stands approximates the great symbol of redemption.

In the final analysis the Jewish movement is striving for free and total activity of the newly awakened energies of the nation. If we wish to conceive the people of the Renaissance in the form of an organism (not considering all the contrary or undeveloped elements), the national idea is its self-consciousness, and the national movement its will power. And just as will power occurs initially reflex-like, and spontaneously, then becomes more and more differentiated and intellectual because of the influence of the developing consciousness, so the Jewish movement under the influence of the Renaissance idea develops from a drive for survival to an ideal.

If the Jewish movement sees the most favorable conditions or the necessary precondition for the accomplishment of its goal in the creation of a new Jewish community in Eretz Israel (Land of Israel), and if it endeavors to create such, we call it Zionism.... On the other hand, we will have to consider all views and actions that reject the regeneration of Judaism and wish to find a home for Jews merely to alleviate their plight, not as Zionists, but as a humanitarian undertaking, guided by more or less high-minded ideals, which may well meet the Jewish movement here but ultimately has nothing in common with it.

But also within Zionism we can discern two basic concepts: a logical and an illogical one. For the latter, the notion of territory displaces all other thoughts and allows it to negate, fully or partly, openly or covertly, all cultural work, that is, the current and direct emotion of the people's energies. The logical person includes cultural activity in his agenda, for he feels that the Renaissance has become will and sees in it his natural range of action. Some people claim that such a view creates a diffusion of energy. But they are wrong, for true cultural activity is also the most significant means to reach territorial goals—to win the land....

Notes

Source: "Das jüdische Kulturproblem und der Zionismus," first in *Die Stimme der Wahrheit—Jahrbuch für wissenschaftlichen Zionismus,* ed. Lazar Schön (Würzburg: N. Philippi, 1905). Gilya Gerda Schmidt, trans., in *The First Buber: Youthful Zionist Writings of Martin Buber* (New York: Syracuse University Press, 1999), pp. 176–95. The section in this volume was written in 1903 and published as a slightly different version in 1916 as "Renaissance und Bewegung" in *Die Jüdische Bewegung—Gesammelte Aufsätze und Ansprachen 1900–1915* (Berlin: Jüdischer Verlag, 1916). Schmidt's translation follows the version published in 1905 and has been revised slightly for this volume.

Editor's note: "On the Renaissance" is the first of a three-part essay entitled "The Jewish Cultural Problem and Zionism," published in 1905. The other parts were entitled "On Politics" and "On Cultural Activity." Buber wrote the first part in 1903 in connection with his participation in the Democratic Faction and its program of cultural Zionism (see also Introduction, p. xxx). But the essay is, in fact, a substantial rewrite of Buber's earlier essay, "Jewish Renaissance" that appeared in the pilot volume of the Berlin journal *Ost und West* 1, no. 1, January 1901. Both essays are indebted to the Swiss cultural historian Jakob Burckhardt (1818–1897), whose interpretation of the Italian Renaissance as creative rebirth rather than mere revival of antiquity contributed to the popularization of the Renaissance at the turn of the century (headed by the Burckhardt student Friedrich Nietzsche, as well as Joseph Arthur Gobineau, Stefan George, and many others). Also common to both essays is Buber's emphasis on Hasidism and *Haskalah* as liberating undercurrents in Judaism.

1. Not in G. Schmidt's translation.
2. This is a rather free rendering of the German original, which is unclear in the version of 1905 and was revised by Buber in 1916 to the effect of the present translation. G. Schmidt follows the version of 1905.
3. Not in the version of 1905.
4. G. Schmidt: . . . regeneration of Jewish thought.
5. Baruch de Spinoza (1632–1677), born to a Portuguese–Jewish family in Amsterdam, soon became a prominent rationalist thinker and forerunner of the European Enlightenment and modernization. On 27 July 1656, he was excommunicated from the Jewish community of Amsterdam for what was perceived as his heretical writings. In 1670, Spinoza published his *Theological-Political Treatise* anonymously, as a major critique of (Jewish) tradition and religion. It was Spinoza's personal fate and his rebellious, freethinking attitude toward tradition more than his philosophy that made him attractive to Buber and the young Zionist movement.
6. Latin, literally "naturing Nature," refers to the active system of nature that, according to Spinoza, cannot be different in essence from God. Allusion to Spinoza's major philosophical work, *Ethics* (1660).
7. Hebrew: enlightened person; follower of the *Haskalah*.
8. The Revolution of 1848.

*The Renewal of Judaism (1911)**

When I speak of renewal I am well aware that this is a bold, indeed almost daring, term, which, being at variance with the current outlook upon life and the world, is unacceptable to it. All activities of the typical man of today are governed by the concept of evolution, that is, the concept of gradual change—or, as it is also called, progress—emerging from the collective effect of many small causes. This concept, which, as one begins to realize, can claim only a relative validity even in the realm of natural processes, has, to be sure, greatly stimulated and advanced the natural sciences, but its effect upon the realm of the mind and the will has been highly deleterious. Man's spirit has been as greatly depressed by a sense of inescapable evolution as it had once been depressed by the sense of inescapable predestination, induced by Calvinism. The extinction of heroic, unconditional living in our time must be ascribed, to a great extent, to this sense. Once the great doer expected to alter the face of the world with his deed and to inform all becoming with his own will. He did not feel that he was subject to the conditions of the world, for he was grounded in the unconditionality [*Unbedingtheit*] of God, whose Word he sensed in the decisions he made as clearly as he felt the blood in his veins. This confidence in the suprahuman has been undermined; man's consciousness of God and deed had already been stifled in his cradle; all one could hope for was to become the exponent of some small "progress." And whoever can no longer desire the impossible will be able to achieve nothing more than the all too possible. Thus, the power of the spirit was replaced by "busyness," and the might of sacrifice by bargaining skill. And even the longing for a new heroic life was corrupted by this tendency of the time. The most tragic example of this corruption

---

* From *On Judaism*, by Martin Buber, ed. by Nahum Glatzer, trans. by Eva Jospe, copyright © 1967 by Schocken Books, a division of Random House, Inc. Used by permission of Schocken Books, a division of Random House, Inc.

is probably the man who, though he longed for such a life more intensely than any other man, could not free himself from the dogma of evolution: Friedrich Nietzsche.

I am aware that when I speak of renewal [*Erneuerung*], I am leaving the domain of our time and entering that of a new time—a time to come. For by renewal I do not in any way mean something gradual—a sum total of minor changes. I mean something sudden and immense—by no means a continuation or an improvement, but a return [*Umkehr*], and a complete transformation [*Umwandlung*].[1] Indeed, just as I believe that in the life of individual man there may occur a moment of elemental reversal, a crisis and a shock, a becoming new that starts down at the roots and branches out into all of existence, so do I believe that it is possible for such an upheaval to take place in the life of Judaism as well.

The last part of Isaiah has God say, "I create new heavens and a new earth" (Isa. 65:17); and the author of the Apocalypse claims, "I saw a new heaven and a new earth" (Rev. 21:1). This is not a metaphor, but a direct experience. It is the experience of a man whose essence has been renewed and, with it, the essence of the world. His body is the same mind-endowed body it has always been, and no faculty that was not already there has entered it. But in his shattering experience, all of his capacities have been welded into one, and no other power equals the primal power of unity.

Precisely this is what I believe will take place in Judaism: not merely a rejuvenation or revival but a genuine and total renewal.

Even though the concept of renewal in this absolute sense has, in our time, remained largely alien to the minds of those who are concerned with the survival of Judaism, they nevertheless recognize that ours is a moment of the highest tension and of final decision—a moment that has two faces, one looking toward death, the other toward life. They also recognize that Judaism can no longer be preserved by mere continuation but that there is need for intervention and transformation [*Umbildung*], for healing and liberation. However, true to the spirit of our time, they hold that what is needed, and is possible, is a relative, that is, a gradual and partial, renewal. I can best describe the meaning the term renewal has for me by discussing how it is understood by these men and by the intellectual movements that they represent.

Essentially, there are two basic concepts of renewal. They differ in their view of the nature of renewal because they differ in their view of the nature of Judaism. One regards Judaism as a religious community; the other, as a national one. I shall discuss both concepts not as they are viewed by their average followers but as they are seen by their most prominent representatives. In the case of the first, this is not easy, for I have not found a truly independent and superior mind among its adherents. However, I shall choose one of the best: Moritz Lazarus.[2] The second concept, on the other hand, proffers a representative personality: the modern Hebrew thinker, Ahad Ha'am.[3]

Lazarus, a clever and amiable popular philosopher, is of special interest to us because of the recent, posthumous publication of his small volume, *Renewal of Judaism*.[4] With singular expectation I read on the title page the words that had for many years reposed in my mind as a dark and still unopened sanctuary. And at first it seemed that expectation would not be disappointed. A sentence on one of the first pages went straight to my heart: It stated that our goal should be "the revival, the true re-establishment of prophetic Judaism."[5]

The magnitude of this goal made me tremble. "The true re-establishment of prophetic Judaism"! What had prophetic Judaism been if not a command to live unconditionally? An injunction not to pay lip service to God by a declaration of faith while serving the utilitarian ends of a petty life by one's deeds; not to go all the way in one's thinking, yet stop at the halfway mark in one's actions; but to be whole at all hours and in all things, and to realize the consciousness of God [*Gottgefühl*] at all times, so that, as Amos says, we let "righteousness well up as a mighty stream" (Amos 5:24).

Never in the history of mankind had the watchword "All or nothing" been proclaimed with so powerful a voice. And this was now to be fulfilled. At last there would be Jews of the kind enjoined by the prophets, namely, unconditional men. We would free ourselves from the designing hustle and bustle of modern society and begin to transform our existence into true life. Though the halfhearted, the indolent, the greedy might continue to call themselves Jews, only those men who labored earnestly for the reestablishment of prophetic Judaism would really be Jews. Yes, no doubt, this had to lead to a renewal of Judaism, and to a renewal of mankind.

But I read on, and my dreams dissolved. For, alas, what was predicated further on was an altogether different matter. This "revival of prophetic Judaism" was basically nothing more than a Jewish variant of what Luther had meant when he spoke of a revival of evangelical Christianity. Rationalization of faith, simplification of dogma, modification of the ritual law—that was all. Negation, nothing but negation! No, it was wrong to drag in Luther's name by way of comparison; Luther's concept of evangelical life had been infinitely more creative. What was preached here was not reformation, only reform; not transformation, only facilitation; not a renewal of Judaism, but its perpetuation in an easier, more elegant, Westernized, more socially acceptable form. Truly, I prefer a thousandfold the gauche dullards who, in their simplemindedness, observe day after day and without any shortcuts every detail of what they believe to be the command of their God, of their fathers' God. How could this feeble program dare to call itself a revival of prophetic Judaism? The prophets, it is true, spoke of the futility of rituals; not, however, to facilitate religious life, but to proclaim the holiness of the deed. Only when we demand something other than this so-called "purified religion," only when we demand the wholly unconditioned deed, only then may we invoke the prophets of Israel.

A totally different, incomparably more profound and more authentic world is made known to us in the thinking of Ahad Ha'am. Something of the spirit of prophetic Judaism does truly reside in this world. It lacks, however, this spirit's original fire and ecstatic power and is steeped, instead, in Talmudic problematics and Maimonidean abstractions. But in the trueness of its inner vision and in the relentlessness of its demand, it is reminiscent of our prophetic heritage. Still, the idea of an absolute renewal is not to he found here either.

Ahad Ha'am anticipates a renewal with the establishment of a spiritual center of Judaism in Palestine.... Whatever its emergent form, a central Jewish settlement in Palestine would undoubtedly have great significance—a significance unparalleled in history: the possible development of a nucleus of a healthy Jewish people that, in the course of generations, would undoubtedly beget cultural values as well. In all probability such a settlement would also have an invigorating and cohesive influence on Jewish life in the Diaspora. But it could not guarantee a renewal of Judaism in the absolute meaning of the term; moreover, the center of the Jewish people would become the center of Judaism as well only if it were created not for the sake of renewal but out of and through renewal. An intellectual center can promote scholarly work; it can even disseminate and propagate ideas, though it cannot create them. Indeed, it can perhaps even become a social model. But it cannot beget the only things from which I expect the absolute to emerge—return and transformation, and a change [*Umschwung*] in all elements of life. In fact, it seems to me that the great ambivalence, the boundless despair, the infinite longing, and pathetic inner chaos of many Jews of today provide more propitious ground for the radical shake-up that must precede such a total renewal than does the normal and confident existence of a settler in his own land.

But to comprehend the one thing that could bring about the change of which I am speaking, we must recall what this Judaism is whose renewal we desire. When we view it as a religion, we touch only the most obvious fact of its organizational form; we arrive at a deeper truth when we call it a nationality, but we must look still deeper to perceive its essence. Judaism is a spiritual process, documented in the internal history of the Jewish people, as well as in the works of the great Jews. We have too limited a notion of this process if we identify it either with the Jewish precept of unity or with prophetic Judaism, as do Lazarus and Ahad Ha'am, each in his own language. The Jewish precept of unity is only one element, and prophetic Judaism only one phase, of the great spiritual process called Judaism. Only by grasping this process in its total magnitude—in the wealth of its elements and the manifold transmutations of its historical revelation—can we understand the meaning of what I call here renewal.

The spiritual process of Judaism manifests itself in history as the striving for an ever more perfect realization of three interconnected ideas: the idea of unity, the idea of the deed, and the idea of the future. When

I speak of ideas I do not, of course, mean abstract concepts; I mean innate predispositions of a people's ethos that manifest themselves with such great force and so enduringly that they produce a complex of spiritual deeds and values that can be called that people's absolute life. Every greatly and singularly gifted people possesses such unique predispositions and, in turn, a world of unique deeds and values created by them. It therefore lives, as it were, two lives: one transitory and relative, lived in the sequence of earthly days, of generations that come and go; the other (lived simultaneously) permanent and absolute, a life lived in the world of the wandering and searching human spirit. Whereas in the first, the relative life, all seems chance and often terrifyingly meaningless; in the other, the absolute life, great, luminous outlines of meaning and exigency are revealed, step by step. The relative life remains the possession of the unconsciousness of the people; the absolute life becomes, directly or indirectly, part of the consciousness of mankind....

In the relative life of the Jewish people, in what is commonly called its history, as well as in the everyday aspect of its present, there is a superabundance of cross-purposes, of haste, obsession, torment; but out of all this emerge, radiant and taller than life, the goals, writing their indestructible signs on the firmament of eternity. And to the vision that penetrates the relative life and perceives the absolute, it is revealed that the profusion of the first exists solely for the second to arise from it, and that, fundamentally, the second is reality and the first is merely variegated, manifold appearance. This becomes manifest in Judaism more clearly and unequivocally than anywhere else, and this precisely is why I am justified in calling Judaism a spiritual process.

This process, as I have already said, is evidenced in the striving for the realization of three ideas or tendencies.... The spiritual process of Judaism assumes the form of an ideological struggle [*Geisteskampf*]—an eternally renewed inner struggle for the pure realization of these national tendencies. The struggle stems from the fact that the determining virtues in the life of individual man are nothing more than his reformed, redirected passions, elevated to ideality; by the same token, the determining ideas in the life of a people are nothing more than its inherent tendencies, elevated to the spiritual and the creative. And just as in the life of individual man his passions, breaking into the realm of virtue and disturbing its pure realization, resist a reforming and redirecting, so do a people's tendencies resist spiritualization, tarnishing the purity of their realization, that is, their elevation to the absolute life of the people. Thus, the ideas actually struggle for their own selves, for their liberation from the narrowness of the people's tendencies, for their independence, and for their realization. I shall try to demonstrate this by outlining, though only sketchily, the three ideas of Judaism—unity, deed, and future—but I can single out only a few especially memorable phases of this ideological battle.

The idea of unity and the tendency toward it inherent in the nature of the people originate in the fact that the Jew has at all times perceived more keenly the context in which phenomena appear than the individual phenomena as such. He sees the forest more truly than the trees, the sea more truly than the wave, the community more truly than the individual. He is therefore more inclined to pensiveness than to imagery and, for the same reason, is also impelled to conceptualize the fullness of things even before he has wholly experienced them.[6] But he does not stop with a concept; he is driven to press on to higher higher forms of unity— to the highest idea of unity that sustains, as well as crowns all concepts and binds them into one, just as the phenomena had been bound into a single concept.

But there is a second, deeper source for the Jew's unitary tendency, the one I have already mentioned: the longing to rescue himself from his inner duality and raise himself to absolute unity. Both sources converge in the God-idea of the prophets. The idea of a transcendent unity springs into being: the, world-creating, world-ruling, world-loving God. The whole pathos of the prophets, the most powerful pathos in the history of mankind, serves this idea; but it is a peak of the spiritual process. Gradually, the outer source grows stronger than the inner—the penchant for conceptualization stronger than the faithfulness to one's yearning. The idea becomes diluted, and fades, until the living God is transmuted into the lifeless schema characteristic of the later period of priestly rule and of the beginning of rabbinism.

The unitary tendency, however, would not be dragged down. The battle between schema and longing raged unceasingly.... For a moment, the active unitary tendency rose once again, in Hasidism. Then the movement weakened, and the battle grew limp. The sterile period—our period— begins. What happened to the battle-sustaining forces? Desert sands are about our feet; as a desert generation we wander about, not knowing whereto. But our longing is not dead. It raises its head, calling its desire into the desert. It cries out in the desert as John the Baptist once did, at a time like ours: for renewal.

Judaism's second idea is that of the deed. This tendency, inherent in the ethos of the people, stems from the fact that the Jew is endowed with greater motor than sensory faculties; his motor system works more intensely than his sensory system.[7] He displays more substance and greater personality in action than in apperception, and he considers what he accomplishes in life more important than what happens to him. It is for this reason, to give an example, that the Jew's art is so rich in gesture, and that its expression is more specifically his own than its meaning or content.[8] For this reason, too, he considers *doing* more essential than *experiencing*. Hence, even in antiquity, not faith but the deed was central to Jewish religiosity. This conception may in fact be viewed as the fundamental difference between Orient and Occident: For the Oriental, the decisive bond between man and God is the deed; for the Occidental, it is faith. The difference is especially pronounced and emphasized in the Jew. All the books of the Bible speak very little of faith, but so much more of deeds. It should not, however, be assumed that this means a soulless glorification of works or rituals devoid of inner significance; on the contrary, every deed, even the smallest and seemingly most negligible, is in some way oriented toward the Divine, and the words of a later period, "Let all your acts be done for the sake of God" (Sayings of the Fathers 2, 17), are already applicable here, and in an especially poignant sense. At the time of the most naive relationship to God, the prescribed acts stood for a mysterious, magic union with Him. Thus, animal sacrifice was a symbolic substitute for the offering of one's own life; the flame of the altar was perceived as the soul's emissary to heaven.

But the acts lost their meaning; and yet the injunction still demanded continued observance of what had become meaningless, because, as Yohanan Ben-Zakkai[9] explains, God has "set up a statute, and has issued a decree."[10] Thus, out of the religiosity of the deed arose the ritual law. The deed tendency rebelled against this inflexibility. In self-segregation, it founded life communities, which, instead of observing a law that had lost its meaning, wanted to practice, once again, the living deed that binds man to God. The earliest known community of this kind must have been that of the Rehabites, mentioned in the Book of Jeremiah. Their ideas and organization were, apparently, misinterpreted, probably not unintentionally, by the law-observing redactors of the canon. In all likelihood an unbroken chain of tradition links the Rehabites to the Essenes, the antiquity of whose traditions are attested by historians. Along the way, the deed tendency grew; the idea of the deed became ever purer, the concept of a bond with God ever greater and holier.

At the same time, however, the ritual law [*Zeremonialgesetz*][11] became more rigid and alienated from life, whereupon the movement spread from the self-segregated communities to the very core of the people and set ablaze the revolution of ideas [*Geistesrevolution*] that today, erroneously and misleadingly, is called early, original Christianity. With greater justification, it could be called original Judaism—though in a different sense than that of the historical term—for it is much more closely related to Judaism than to what is today called Christianity. It is a peculiar phenomenon of *galut* psychology that we not only tolerate the fact that this significant chapter was torn out of our history of ideas but that we ourselves aided and abetted the tearing. We did all this only because syncretist elements attached themselves, though purely superficially, to this movement, so that not much was left of the original substance. Whatever was not eclectic, whatever was creative in the beginnings of Christianity, was nothing but Judaism. This revolution of ideas had burst into flame in a Jewish land; it had first stirred in the womb of ancient Jewish communal societies; it had been spread by Jewish men; the people they addressed were, as is repeatedly proclaimed, the Jewish people and no other; and what they proclaimed was nothing other than the renewal, in Judaism, of the religiosity of the deed.

It was only in the syncretistic Christianity of the West that faith, as it is known to the Occidental, assumed primary importance; to earliest

Christianity, the deed was central. As for the meaning or content of this striving toward the deed, it is clearly attested in one of the most original parts of the Gospels, which points most indubitably to a creative personality. In the first chapter of the Sermon on the Mount, it is stated, "Do not think that I have come to abolish the law or the prophets; I have not come to abolish but to fulfill" (Matt. 5:17). The meaning of this statement emerges from the subsequent comparison between the old and new teaching: It is not at all the intention of the new teaching to be new; it wants to remain the old teaching but a teaching grasped in its absolute sense. It wants to restore to the deed the freedom and sanctity with which it was originally endowed, a freedom and sanctity diminished and dimmed by the stem rule of the ritual law, and to release it from the straits of prescriptions that became meaningless, to free it for the holiness of an active relationship with God, for a religiosity of the deed. And to rule out any misunderstanding, Matthew adds, "For I say to you truly: Until heaven and earth vanish, neither the smallest letter nor a tittle of the law shall vanish, until all of this be done." This means, until the teachings of unconditionality [*Unbedingtheit*] are fulfilled in all their purity, and with all the power of one's soul; until the world is sanctified, is God informed, through the absolute deed.

Early Christianity teaches what the prophets taught: the unconditionality of the deed....

However, this movement, which has had so great a significance for the absolute life of the Jewish people, has, in its relative life, remained an episode, unable to put a stop to the increasing ossification of the law. But the battle for the deed idea did not let up. In ever new forms it filled the millennia. It was dialectical as well as inward, public as well as hidden. In the places of learning it spoke the language of keen intellects; in the homes, the language of women. It assumed large proportions in the rejected heretics, and small ones in the small audacities of the ghetto. And thus it flickered and burned around the becrowned corpse of the law, until another great movement arrived, a movement that cut to the very core of truth and stirred the very core of the people: Hasidism.

Original Hasidism—which has almost as little in common with the Hasidism of today as early Christianity has with the [present-day] Church, can be understood only if one is aware that it is a renewal of the deed idea.[12] To Hasidism, the true meaning of life is revealed in the deed. Here, even more distinctly and profoundly than in early Christianity, what matters is not what is being done, but the fact that every act carried out in sanctity, that is, with God-oriented intent, is a road to the heart of the world. There is nothing that is evil in itself; every passion can become a virtue; every inclination "a vehicle of God." It is not the matter of the act that is decisive but its sanctification. Every act is hallowed, if it is directed toward salvation [*Heil*]. The soul of the doer alone determines the character of his deed. With this, the deed does in truth become the life center of religiosity. Simultaneously, the fate of the world is placed in the hands of the doer. The fallen divine sparks; the erring souls dispersed in things and beings are liberated through the deed that is sanctified by its intention. By his acts man works for the redemption of the world. Indeed, he works for the redemption of God Himself, for, through the supreme concentration and tension of his deed and for an unfathomable instant's period of grace, he can cause the exiled glory of God to draw closer to its source....

Now the free deed can confront the law as, to use a term employed by early Christianity, the perfect law of freedom. For Hasidism, therefore, man's final objective is this: to become, himself, a law—a Torah. And just as early Christianity had not wanted to abolish the law, so Hasidism too did not want to abolish it—only to fulfill it; that means, it wanted to raise it from the conditioned to the unconditioned and at the same time to transform it from the rigidity of a formula into the fluidity of the immediate.

It did not succeed, because, having flourished, it soon began to disintegrate and to degenerate, for reasons not to be discussed here. In the absolute life of the Jewish people, it betokens the greatest triumph of the deed idea achieved so far; in their relative life, Hasidism, too, remained only an episode. It was followed by a decline in which the struggle between law and deed reached its lowest level. I am referring to the bickering, devoid of ideas and spirit, between the Orthodox and the Reformers. It may well be the most bitter irony of our fate that the Reformers of this era are allowed to pose as the proponents of the deed idea of prophetic Judaism. We must restore the greatness to the struggle for the deed idea if we want Judaism to be great once again. If there are once more men who experience all the pride and all the magnificence of Judaism, they must demand that the striving of the people's spirit for the deed be renewed and that it be given new form, in accord with our own new attitude toward the world.

The third tendency in Judaism is the idea of the future. This national trait stems from the fact that the Jew's sense of time is much more strongly developed than his sense of space: The descriptive epithets of the Bible speak, in contrast, for instance, to those of Homer, not of form or color but of sound and movement. The artistic form of expression most satisfying to the Jew is the art whose specific element is time: music. And the interrelatedness of the generations is a stronger life principle for him than the enjoyment of the present. His consciousness of peoplehood and of God is, essentially, nourished by his historical memory and his historical hope, the hope being the intrinsically positive and constructive element. And just as each of the three tendencies has its vulgar as well as its sublime aspect, just as the unity idea produced the conceptual constructs of rabbinism as well as the people's great yearning for God, and the deed tendency led to a soulless panritualism as well as to a holy will to unconditionality, so is it also with the future tendency.

On the one hand, it drives the Jew into a bustling activity with diverse objectives and spurs on his urge for action; this urge is, however, directed not toward his own comfort but toward the happiness of the next generation. The next generation, even before it becomes conscious of itself, is in turn charged with the task of taking care of still another generation, so that all reality of existence is dissolved in the care for the future. On the other hand, this tendency awakens messianism in the Jew—the idea of an absolute future that transcends all reality of past and present as the true and perfect life.

Messianism is Judaism's most profoundly original idea. Think about it: In the future, in the eternally remote, eternally imminent sphere, as receding yet stationary as the horizon, in the realm of the future into which as a rule only playful, wavering, substanceless dreams venture, the Jew dared to build a house for mankind—the house of true life. Whatever yearning, hope, and desire for a future crept into the consciousness of other peoples was wholly relative; its advent, either imminent or remote, might manifest itself in such and such a manner, but also in another manner. One wished for and dreamed about its coming, but who knew whether it would indeed come? Who dared to believe in it when the cold, clear light of day shone through one's window? But here, in messianism, something fundamentally different was at work. Here, it was not a question of whether the future might come; it had to come. Every moment guaranteed it; one's blood guaranteed it, and so did God. Nor was the coming to take place either imminently or at some remote time; it was to take place at the end of time, in the fullness of time, at the end of days; in the absolute future. And though very often what was expected to come was something relative—the liberation of a tortured people and its ingathering around God's sanctuary—on the summit it was the absolute—the redemption of the human spirit and the salvation of the world—where the relative was considered the means toward this absolute. Here, for the first time and with full force, the absolute was proclaimed as the goal—a goal to be realized in and through mankind.

At the same time, messianism prepared, as it were, the ground for the final and complete realization of Judaism's two other tendencies, the unity idea and the deed idea. But just as an incessant battle had been waged around those ideas, so here, too, a battle raged; and we frequently find, at one and the same time, the most exalted concept of the messianic ideal next to the vulgar notions of future comforts. Hence, the messianic movements are a mixture of the most holy and most profane, of a future-oriented purpose and lack of restraint, of love of God and avid curiosity. Here, too, the people's bents resist spiritualization and tarnish the purity of fulfillment.

It should be noted that early Christianity also was distinguished by the idea of an absolute future, "the end of days"—a redemption of the world not yet accomplished but still to come. Here, a conflict flared up as well, the conflict between the messianic ideal and the transference of messianic concepts to the person of the leader and master.

Still another significant phenomenon calls for a closer look. As is true of Spinoza's philosophy in the realm of the unity idea, this phenomenon, though part of the absolute life of Judaism, transcends its relative life and has therefore not entered the people's consciousness. I am speaking of socialism. Modern socialism has two psychological wellsprings: (1) critical insight into the nature of man's coexistence with man, into the nature of the community and of society; and (2) longing for a purer, truer, more beautiful life—for a pure, a true coexistence of man with man, for a human community built on love, mutual understanding, and mutual help.

The first wellspring, though it probably did not originate there, has nevertheless received its strength from the wisdom of the West. Plato is the master whose image hovers over the first swelling of its waters. The second spring originated in Judaism and steadily received a new influx from it. The prophets were the first to proclaim its message; the Essenes, the first community to attempt to live accordingly, in unconditionality. Clear at one time, dim at another, the longing was never wholly extinguished. And when the Jews left the ghetto and entered the life of the nations, both springs flowed in them, to become the tenet and the apostolate of modern socialism. This modern socialism is a diminution, a narrowing, a "finitizing" [*Verendlichung*] of the messianic ideal, though sustained and nurtured by the same force, the future idea. But the future idea will rise above socialism, to enter once again the infinite, the absolute. We can only sense its future shape, but our sensing it is in itself a sign that this idea of Judaism, too, lives on—a mute, underground life, awaiting its day, the day of renewal.

It is only now that we can see what renewal of Judaism means. The great spiritual process whose outlines I have depicted has come to a standstill. If Judaism is not to continue its sham existence, if it is to be resurrected to true life, its spirit must be renewed and its spiritual process started anew. The true life of Judaism, like the true life of any creative people, is that which I have called its absolute life. Only such a life can create not merely an aggressive or defensive, but a positive consciousness of peoplehood—the consciousness of the people's immortal substance. At the present time, the Jewish people knows only a relative life; it must regain its absolute life—living Judaism....

This is the danger threatening the Jewish people: that it may lose the life of the spirit. We cannot comfort ourselves in believing that the danger has passed by pointing to the flourishing of a new literature or to any other values that we are accustomed to calling "Jewish Renaisssance,"[13] an expression of hope rather than reality. I have pointed out these beginnings so often that I need not fear to be misunderstood when I say that all this still does not in any way signify a renewal of Judaism. A renewal must originate in deeper regions of the people's spirit, where the great tendencies of Judaism were once born. The battle for fulfillment must begin anew.

But this alone is not enough. For now we know the innermost sickness of the uprooted people and their abysmal fate. We know that their absolute and their relative life are sundered; that what constitutes the summit and the eternal for the absolute life is wholly, or almost wholly, unperceived by the relative life, or is at best looked upon as a quickly to be forgotten episode. Hence, renewal must also mean this: that the battle for fulfillment encompasses the entire people; that the ideas penetrate the day's reality; that the spirit enters life. Only when Judaism once again reaches out, like a hand, grasping each Jew by the hair of his head and carrying him, in the tempest raging between heaven and earth, toward Jerusalem, as the hand of the Lord once grasped and carried Ezekiel, the priest, in the land of the Chaldeans[14]—only then will the Jewish people be ready to build a new destiny for itself, where the old one once broke into fragments. The bricks may be, indeed must be, assembled now; but the house can be built only when the people have once more become builders.

Nor is it enough for only single ideas to be renewed, whether it be one or another, or even the one and the other. For Judaism cannot be renewed in bits and pieces. Renewal must be all of one piece. And since we who have undertaken to discern the meaning of past times and the meaning of our time know all this, we should be allowed to state what we sense will be the substance of the renewal of Judaism: a creative synthesis of Judaism's three ideas, in accord with the attitude toward the world of men yet to come....

... In a new attitude toward the world. I mean the attitude that is beginning to germinate in us, in the men of today, in the men who lead the way and pass on, and that will sprout in the men of some future generation. This human attitude is still unexpressed today. The molding of it and the renewal of Judaism are two sides of one process. "For salvation comes from the Jews"[15]; Judaism's basic tendencies constitute the elements out of which, recurrently, a new universal conception of the world is created. Thus, the most deep-seated humanity of our soul and its most deep-seated Judaism mean and desire the same thing.

But what the nature of this future synthesis will be, how it will be born, of this no word can be said. We know that it will come; we do not know how it will come. We can only be prepared.

To be prepared, however, does not mean to wait immovably. It means to educate oneself and others to the consciousness of Judaism, the consciousness in which the spiritual process of Judaism becomes manifest in all its magnitude, in the fullness of its substance, in the manifold transmutations of its historical revelation, and in the nameless mystery of its latent forces.

To be prepared means even more. It means to realize Judaism's great tendencies in our personal lives: the tendency toward unity, by molding our souls into a single entity, to enable them to conceive unity; the tendency toward the deed, by filling our souls with unconditionality, to enable them to realize the deed; the tendency toward the future, by unbinding our soul from the utilitarian bustle and directing them toward the goal, in order to enable them to serve the future.

We read in Isaiah, "The voice cries: In the wilderness prepare the path of the Lord!" (Isa. 40:3). To be prepared means to prepare.

Notes

Source: "Die Erneuerung des Judentums," in *Drei Reden über das Judentum* (Frankfurt/M.: Rütten & Loening, 1911). Eva Jospe, trans., and Nahum Glatzer, ed., *On Judaism* (New York: Schocken, 1967), pp. 34–55.

Editor's note: "Renewal of Judaism" was the third speech delivered at the Bar Kochba student group between 1909 and 1911 (see Jewish Religiosity [1923], Editor's note, p. 123 in this volume). The lecture is not only a concise representation of Buber's project of "renewal" that resonated already in his earlier essays on the Jewish Renaissance, but it is also one of the few instances of Buber engaging in an open critique of the ideas of liberal or Reform Judaism.

1. Jospe translates "*Umwandlung*" simply as "transformation," which is not quite strong enough.
2. Moritz Lazarus (1824–1903), leading figure in the German–Jewish liberal movement, author of *Die Ethik des Judentums* (1898).
3. Ahad Ha'am (pen name of Asher Zvi Ginsberg, 1856–1927), Hebrew essayist, philosopher, and advocate of spiritual Zionism; editor of the Odessa-based Hebrew monthly *Hashiloach* (1896–1927). Buber corresponded with Ahad Ha'am on several occasions and sent him a copy of *Der große Maggid* (see Ahad Ha'am's letter to Buber of 20 July 1923, in Grete Schaeder, ed., *Martin Buber. Briefwechsel aus sieben Jahrzehnten* [Heidelberg: Lambert Schneider, 1973], vol. 2, p. 167).
4. Moritz Lazarus, *Die Erneuerung des Judentums: Ein Aufruf* (The Renewal of Judaism: A Call) (Berlin: Georg Reimer, 1909) (published posthumously).
5. Ibid., p. 10.
6. Buber follows the well-established dichotomization of Hebraism and Hellenism as expounded, most prominently, by Mathew Arnold (see, for instance, his essay "Hebraism and Hellenism," 1898). See also Buber's essay, "The Spirit of the Orient and Judaism" (1916), in *On Judaism* (New York: Schocken, 1967).
7. Cf. Martin Buber: "The spirit of the Orient and Judaism," in *On Judaism* (New York: Schocken, 1967), p. 57: "I would define the Oriental type of human being...as a man of pronounced motor faculties, in contrast to the Occidental type...whose sensory faculties are greater than his motor [faculties]."
8. On the subject of art see, Buber's essays, "On Jewish Art" (1901) and "Jewish Artists" (1903), in *The First Buber: Youthful Writings of Martin Buber,* ed. and trans. Gilya G. Schmidt (New York: Syracuse University Press, 1999).
9. Yohanan Ben-Zakkai (first century C.E.): Leading teacher of the Tannaitic period after the destruction of the second temple (70 C.E.) who is credited with moving the rabbinic Academy from Jerusalem to Javneh.
10. Pesikta de Rav Kahana 40a–b (M.B.).
11. The term became fashionable in the writings of Baruch Spinoza (1632–1677) and Moses Mendelssohn (1729–1786), the leading philosopher of the Jewish Enlightenment (*Haskalah*). Because of its connotation of mere "ceremonial" actions, it was often adopted by liberal Judaism to legitimize the rejection of ritualistic elements in Jewish tradition. On a critique of the term see Samson R. Hirsch's essay "Die jüdische Ceremonialgesetze" (1857). It is likely that Buber uses the term "Zeremonialgesetz" here precisely for its (unwanted) connotation of rigidity and remoteness from life.
12. See also The Life of the Hasidim (1908) (p. 74 in this volume).
13. See On the [Jewish] Renaissance (1903) (p. 139 in this volume).
14. Cf. Ezek. 1:3; 3:14 (N. Glatzer).
15. John 4:22 (N. Glatzer).

Hebrew Humanism (1941)

Humanitas[1]

At the beginning of the century, when a circle of young people to which I belonged began to direct the attention of Jews in German-speaking countries to a rebirth of the Jewish people[2] and of the Jew as an individual,[3] we defined the goal of our efforts as a Jewish Renaissance. It was not by mere chance that we chose a historical concept that was not purely national. It is true that the beginnings of the Italian Renaissance were inspired by the idea of renewing the *populus Romanus,* of regenerating Italy. But there was something else behind the Renaissance. The nature of this "something" was demonstrated at the time by my teacher, the philosopher Wilhelm Dilthey,[4] and with particular clarity ten years later by Konrad Burdach,[5] the distinguished German philologist who followed our work with warm sympathy. They showed us that behind the Renaissance was the idea of affirming man and the community of man, and the belief that peoples as well as individuals could be reborn. We felt this to be the truth, and it was in this sense that I used the term Renaissance in my first essay on the subject.[6] But its full meaning dawned on us only gradually in the course of the last four decades, when our own work brought us to realize the basic consequences deriving from our choice of this term. When in 1913 a group of my friends discussed the founding of a Jewish school of advanced studies[7]—a project frustrated by World War I—it was this realization that led me to define the spirit required to direct a program of this kind as Hebrew humanism. And in 1929, when I spoke at the Zionist Congress and tried to summarize in one concept what I felt was lacking in our Palestinian system of education, I again used the term Hebrew humanism to express what I thought we needed. However, fearing that this might be interpreted as a plea for what, in Europe, is called a "humanistic Gymnasium," merely substituting Hebrew for Latin and Greek, I added, "Hebrew humanism in the most real sense of the term."[8] These words were also intended to indicate that what I had in mind was not merely a pedagogical enterprise but that whatever pedagogical elements it contained were inherent in the very goal of the movement for a Jewish rebirth, as I had, in the meantime, come to realize very clearly. I wished to point out the nature of this goal by saying humanism instead of "renaissance" and Hebrew instead of "Jewish." When Adolf Hitler stepped into power in Germany, and I was faced with the task of strengthening the spirituality of our youth to bear up against his nonspirituality, I called the speech in which I developed my program, "Biblical Humanism,"[9] to make the first half of my concept still clearer. The title indicated that in this task of ours, the Bible—the great document of our own antiquity—must be assigned the decisive role that in European humanism was played by the writings of classical antiquity. Now that we Jews from Germany must contribute to the education of our people in Palestine who are striving for regeneration [*Erneuerung*], now that we are called on to communicate what we envision such regeneration to be, I should like to define the second half of the concept, and so I shall not speak of humanism, but of humanity—*humanitas*—Hebrew *humanitas*. The adjective "Hebrew" is inserted to prevent the misunderstanding that I am concerned with some sort of vague humanity at large. By *humanitas* I mean the content of true humanism. I am using the word to imply that we are not merely striving for an intellectual movement but for one that will encompass all of life's reality.

If we investigate the origin of the concept of *humanitas* on which humanism is based, we discover that it is primarily the belief in man as such, the belief that man is not merely a zoological species, but a unique creature, this is true, however, only if he really is human, that is, if he translates into the reality of his life the one characteristic element that cannot be found anywhere else in the universe.... But what if the human element threatens to pale and even disintegrate not only in the individual but in an entire epoch of world history? Then we must turn for help to an age when it existed in its full strength and purity, even though it had to struggle against inhumanity a thousand times—provided the existence of that age became manifest and that this manifestation was transmitted. I consider that to have been an important mainspring of early European humanism. There is, of course, another factor: We connect the individual instances of a new and freer humanity that we find in certain eras with the type of humanity that has been transmitted from antiquity and regard it as an existential renewal of antiquity. Only both taken together: both the pattern in the writings of antiquity and the pattern of new life—lend us the power to struggle against the threatened downfall of humanity. The individual instances are not regarded as something new but as a renewal of the old, as the living proof of the eternity of the old, even though it is obvious that here, other conditions have produced another form.

In investigating certain roots of humanism, we must not, of course, lose sight of the fact that the human pattern of antiquity was transmitted in a special sense through language. We do not have merely reports or merely descriptions of the ideal man of antiquity. Human beings who strove toward this ideal preserved something of the essence of this humanity in the way in which they expressed themselves, and to receive and absorb their utterances with the right understanding gives one more direct access to that pattern of humanity than all the reports and descriptions.... This means that, as far as true humanistic understanding is concerned, literary tradition is not essentially a matter of aesthetic appreciation, or of historical learning, or of patriotic pride, although all of these enter into it side by side with still other elements. Humanistic understanding sees literary tradition as the authority and the standard, for it shows us how to distinguish between what is human and what is inhuman; it bears witness to man and reveals him.

I will give one more observation about the humanistic relationship to the human pattern of antiquity. We must at this point ask a question that is essential even though it is specifically modern. We must ask whether a human pattern that was evolved under an entirely different set of historical conditions can be valid for our own times—whether it can help realize humanity in an era that is utterly different in character. The answer is in the affirmative, provided we can separate the timeless elements in this pattern, the elements that are valid for all time, from those that were conditioned by its epoch. Thus, true humanism involves a twofold task with regard to the linguistic tradition of the antique ideal of man—the task of reception and of criticism. Neither has meaning nor can persist without the other.

In the first place, then, Hebrew humanism means the return to the linguistic tradition of our own classical antiquity—the return to the Bible. In the second place, it means reception of the Bible, not because of its literary, historical, and national values, important though these may be, but because of the normative value of the human patterns demonstrated in the Bible. Third, it means distinguishing between what is conditioned by the times and what is timeless, to make that reception achieve its purpose. And fourth, it means setting the living human patterns thus obtained before the eyes of our time with its special conditions, tasks, and possibilities, for only in terms of special conditions can we translate the content we have received into reality.

Zionism and Humanism

In his essay on the origin of humanism, Konrad Burdach elucidates his subject by quoting from Dante's *Convivio*: "The greatest desire Nature has implanted in every thing from its beginning is the desire to return to its origin."[10] Burdach accordingly believes that the goal of humanism is "to return to the human origin, not by way of speculative thought, but by way of a *concrete transformation* of the whole of inner life."[11] The Zionist movement was also moved by the drive to return to the origin of our nature through the concrete transformation of our life. By "return," neither Burdach nor the Zionist movement meant the restoration of bygone forms of life. So romantic an ideal is as alien to our humanism as it was to the earlier [concept of humanism]. In this connotation, return means reestablishing the original foundation to which we want to return with the material of a fundamentally different world of man, under set conditions of our contemporary existence as a people, with reference to the tasks the present situation imposes on us, and in accordance with the possibilities we are given here and now. As we consider these points, we may well speak of a similarity between European and Hebrew humanism. But on another point, we must reach for a farther goal than European humanism. The concrete transformation of our whole inner life is not sufficient for us. We must strive for nothing less than the concrete transformation of our life as a whole. The process of transforming our inner lives must be expressed in the transformation of our outer life—of the life of the individual as well as that of the community. And the effect must be reciprocal: The change in the external arrangements of our life must be reflected in and renew our inner life time and again....

Zionist thinking in its current forms has failed to grasp the principle that the transformation of life must spring from the return to the origin of our nature. It is true that every thoughtful Zionist realizes that our character is distorted in many ways, that we are out of joint and expect the new life in our own land, the bond to the soil and to work, to set us straight and make us whole once more. But what a great many overlook is that the powers released by this renewed bond to the soil do not suffice to accomplish a true and complete transformation. Another factor, the factor of spiritual power—that same return to our origin—must accompany the material factor. But it cannot be achieved by any spiritual power save the primordial spirit of Israel, the spirit that made us such as we are and to which we must continually account for the extent to which our character has remained steadfast in the face of our destiny. This spirit has not vanished. The way to it is still open; it is still possible for us to encounter it. The "Book" still lies before us, and the voice speaks forth from it as on the first day. But we must not dictate what it should and should not tell us. If we require it to confine itself to instructing us about our great literary productions, our glorious history, and our national pride, we shall only succeed in silencing it. For that is not what it has to tell us. What it does have to tell us, and what no other voice in the world can teach us with such simple power, is that there is truth and there are lies and that human life cannot persist or have meaning save in the decision on behalf of truth and against lies; that there is right and wrong and that the salvation of man depends on choosing what is right and rejecting what is wrong; and that it spells the destruction of our existence to divide our life up into areas in which the discrimination between truth and lies and right and wrong holds, and others in which it does not hold, so that in private life, for example, we feel obligated to be truthful but can permit ourselves lies in public, or that we act justly in man-to-man relationships but can and even should practice injustice in national relationships. The *humanitas* that speaks from this "Book" today, as it has always spoken, is the unity of human life under one divine direction that divides right from wrong and truth from lies as unconditionally as the words of the Creator divided light from darkness. It is true that we are not able to live in perfect justice, and to preserve the community of man, we are often compelled to accept wrongs in decisions concerning the community. But what matters is that in every hour of decision we are aware of our responsibility and summon our conscience to weigh exactly how much is necessary to preserve the community, and accept just so much and no more; that we do not interpret the demands of a will to power as a demand made by life itself; that we do not make a practice of setting aside a certain sphere in which God's command does not hold but regard those actions as against His command, forced on us by the exigencies of the hour as painful sacrifices; that we do not salve, or let others salve, our conscience when we make decisions concerning public life but struggle with destiny in fear and trembling lest it burden us with greater guilt than we are compelled to assume. This trembling of the magnetic needle that points the direction notwithstanding—this is biblical *humanitas*. The men in the Bible are sinners, like ourselves, but there is one sin they do not commit—our arch-sin: They do not dare confine God to a circumscribed space or division of life, to "religion." . . . He who has been reared in our Hebrew biblical humanism goes as far as he must in the hour of gravest responsibility and not a step farther. He resists patriotic bombast that clouds the gulf between the demand of life and the desire of the will to power. He resists the whisperings of false popularity, which is the opposite of true service to the people. He is not taken in by the hoax of modern national egoism, according to which everything that can be of benefit to one's people must be true and right. He knows that a primordial decision [*Vorentscheidung*] has been made concerning right and wrong, between truth and lies, and that it confronts the existence of the people. He knows that in the final analysis, the only thing that can help his people is what is true and right in the light of that age-old decision. But if, in an emergency, he cannot obey this recognition of "the final analysis," but responds to the nation's cry for help, he sins like the men in the Bible and, like them, prostrates himself before his Judge. That is the meaning in contemporary language of the return to the origins of our being. Let us hope that the language of tomorrow will be different, that to the best of our ability it will be the language of a positive realization of truth and right, in both the internal and external aspects of the structure of our entire community life.

National Humanism

I am setting up Hebrew humanism in opposition to the Jewish nationalism that regards Israel as a nation like unto other nations and recognizes no task for Israel save that of preserving and asserting itself. But no nation in the world has this as its only task, for just as an individual who wishes merely to preserve and assert himself leads an unjustified and meaningless existence, so a nation with no other aim deserves to pass away.

By opposing Hebrew humanism to a nationalism that is nothing but empty self-assertion, I wish to indicate that at this juncture, the Zionist movement must decide either for national egoism or national humanism. If it decides in favor of national egoism, it too will suffer the fate that will soon befall all shallow nationalism, that is, nationalism that does not set the nation a true supernational task. If it decides in favor of Hebrew humanism, it will be strong and effective long after shallow nationalism has lost all meaning and justification, for it will have something to say and to bring to mankind.

Israel is not a nation like other nations, no matter how much its representatives have wished it during certain eras. Israel is a people like no other, for it is the only people in the world which, from its earliest beginnings, has been both a nation and a religious community. In the historical hour in which its tribes grew together to form a people, Israel became the carrier of a revelation. The covenant that the tribes made with one another and through which they became "Israel" takes the form of a common covenant with the God of Israel.... Israel was and is a people and a religious community in one, and it is this unity that enabled it to survive in an exile no other nation had to suffer—an exile that lasted much longer than the period of its independence. He who severs this bond severs the life of Israel.

One defense against this recognition is to call it a "theological interpretation" and, in this way, debase it into a private affair concerning only such persons as have interest in a subject as unfruitful as theology. But this is nothing but shrewd polemics. For we are, in reality, dealing with a fundamental historical recognition without which Israel as a historical factor and fact could not be understood....

There is still another popular device for evading the recognition of Israel's uniqueness. It is asserted that every great people regard themselves as the chosen people, that is, awareness of peculiarity is interpreted as a function of nationalism in general. Did not the National Socialists believe that destiny had elected the German people to rule the entire world? According to this view, the very fact that we say, "Thou hast chosen us," would prove that we are like other nations. But the weak arguments that venture to put, "It shall be said unto them: Ye are the Children of the living God" (cf. Hos. 2:1) on a par with "The German essence will make the whole world well," are in opposition to the basic recognition that we glean from history. The point is not whether we feel or do not feel that we are chosen. The point is that our role in history is actually unique. There is even more to it. The nature of our doctrine of election is entirely different from that of the theories of election of the other nations, even though they frequently depend on our doctrine. What they took over was never the essential part. Our doctrine is distinguished from their theories, in that our election is completely a demand [*fordernde Erwählung*]. This is not the mythical shapes of a people's wishful dreams. This is not an unconditional promise of magnitude and might to a people. This is a stern demand, and the entire future existence of the people is made dependent on whether or not this demand is met. This is not a God speaking whom the people created in their own image, as their sublimation. He confronts the people and opposes them. He demands and judges. And He does so not only in the age of the prophets at a later stage of historical development, but from time immemorial; and no hypothesis of Bible criticism can ever deny this. What He demands He calls "truth" and "righteousness," and He does not demand these for certain isolated spheres of life but for the whole life of man, for the whole life of the people. He wants the individual and the people to be "whole hearted" with Him. Israel is chosen to enable it to ascend from the biological law of power, which the nations glorify in their wishful thinking, to the sphere of truth and righteousness. God wishes man whom He has created to become man in the truest sense of the word and wishes this to happen not only in sporadic instances, as it happens among other nations, but in the life of an entire people, thus providing an order of life for a future mankind—for all the peoples combined into one people. Israel was chosen to become a true people, and that means God's people.

Biblical man is man facing and recognizing such election and such a demand. He accepts it or rejects it. He fulfills it as best he can or he rebels against it. He violates it and then repents. He fends it off and surrenders. But there is one thing he does not do: He does not pretend that it does not exist or that its claim is limited. And classical biblical man absorbs this demand for righteousness so wholly with his flesh and blood that, from Abraham to Job, he dares to remind God of it. And God, who knows that human mind and spirit cannot grasp the ways of His justice, takes delight in the man who calls Him to account, because that man has absorbed the demand for righteousness with his very flesh and blood. He calls Job His servant and Abraham His beloved. He tempted both; both called Him to account, and both resisted temptation. That is Hebrew humanity.

Renewal

It remained for our time to separate the Jewish people and the Jewish religious community, which were fused from earliest beginnings, and to establish each as an independent unit, a nation like unto other nations and a religion like unto other religions. Thanks to the unparalleled work in Palestine, the nation is on the rise. The religion, however, is on a steep downward decline, for it is no longer a power that determines all of life; it has been confined to the special sphere of ritual or sermons. But a Jewish nation cannot exist without religion any more than a Jewish religious community can exist without nationality. Our only salvation is to become Israel again; to become a whole, the unique whole of a people and a religious community—a renewed people, a renewed religion, and the renewed unity of both.

According to the ideas current among Zionists today, all that is needed is to establish the conditions for a normal national life, and everything will come of itself. This is a fatal error. We do, of course, need the conditions of normal national life, but these are not enough—not enough for us, at any rate. We cannot enthrone "normalcy" in place of the eternal premise of our survival. If we want to be nothing but normal, we shall soon cease to be at all.

The great values we have produced issued from the marriage of a people and a faith. We cannot substitute a technical association of nation and religion for this original marriage, without incurring barrenness. The values of Israel cannot be reborn outside the sphere of this union and its uniqueness....

Notes

Source: "Humaniut 'Ivrit," first in *Ha-Poel ha-zair* 30, no. 5 (1941). Also in *Ha-Ruah veha-Metziut* (Tel Aviv: Mahbarot le-Siftrut, 1942). Olga Marx, trans., in *Israel and the World: Essays in a Time of Crisis* (New York: Schocken, 1948).

Editor's note: Together with Biblical Humanism (1933) (see p. 46 in this volume) and On the [Jewish] Renaissance (1903) (see p. 139 in this volume), Hebrew Humanism forms a unit in Buber's thought that connects his earlier and later work. Buber's interest in the (Italian) Renaissance dates back to his doctoral research in the early 1900s, and his later use of renaissance and humanism is much indebted to Jakob Burckhardt's seminal book of 1860, *Die Kultur der Renaissance in Italien: Ein Versuch* (An Essay in the Culture of the Renaissance in Italy) whose Hebrew edition (1949) includes a preface by Buber. Note that Hebrew Humanism was written in response to the Holocaust in Europe and to the increasing outbreaks of violence between Arabs and Jews in Palestine.

1. Subheadings are not in the original.
2. The Hebrew version states, "people of Israel."
3. The Hebrew version states, "Israeli individual."
4. Wilhelm Dilthey (1833–1911), German philosopher best known for his foundational theory of the human sciences and hermeneutical approach of understanding (*Verstehen*). Buber took courses from Dilthey in general history of philosophy at the Friedrich Wilhelm University, Berlin, between 1899 and 1901.
5. Konrad Burdach (1859–1936), German historian and philologist. The reference is to Burdach's book of 1918 *Reformation, Renaissance, Humanismus* (Darmstadt: Wissenschaftliche Buchgesellschaft, 1963). Buber apparently met Burdach at least once in Berlin and was "very impressed" (cf. letter to Ernst Simon, 9 January 1928; Grete Schaeder, ed., *Martin Buber. Briefwechsel aus sieben Jahrzehnten* [Heidelberg: Lambert Schneider, 1973], no. 259).
6. "Jüdische Renaissance," in *Ost und West* 1, no. 1 (January 1901); Gilya Gerda Schmidt, trans., *The First Buber: Youthful Zionist Writings of Martin Buber* (New York: Syracuse University Press, 1999). See also On the [Jewish] Renaissance (1903) (p. 139 in this volume).
7. The group was organized by Martin Buber, Erich Kahler, and Arthur Salz and met on 30 March at the Hotel Savoy in Berlin (see also Hans Kohn, *Martin Buber—Sein Werk und seine Zeit* (Cologne: J. Melzer 1961, p. 150).
8. Cf. Zionism and Nationalism (1929) (p. 279 in this volume).
9. See Biblical Humanism (1933) (p. 46 in this volume).
10. Konrad Burdach: *Reformation, Renaissance, Humanismus*, p. 157
11. Ibid., p. 158.

PART IV

Dialogue and Anthropology

From Religion as Presence *(1922)*

It Experiences*

[N]ow that we have examined the various attempts to make religion a function of some spiritual domain—now that we have examined these attempts and rejected them[1]—we shall, so to speak, begin at the beginning. Now that we have established the "No," we can begin at the beginning to inquire about the "Yes," as if we had not even spoken of all that. And, in an ultimate sense, if it were not for this very specific moment in time, we would not have had to speak of it. But on this new stretch of the way that we want to walk together, some of you will, I suspect, find the going hard or less comfortable—not because the things that we now have to discuss are getting more complicated but, rather, precisely because they are simpler. So simple are they, in fact, that a certain conceptuality, a certain philosophical terminology that has become firmly set in most people's heads, conflicts with them, and if I proceed one step at a time I fear that many of you will ask, out of this conceptuality, how what I am going to say relates to this or that. I should therefore like to request that insofar as possible, you refrain from juxtaposing what I have to say to ready-made, traditional formulations and, instead, that you juxtapose it only to your self-experience, to what you know from yourself about these things, and forget other formulations as much as possible. Do not start out by assuming that a particular philosophical formulation is right, but suspend judgment on it completely for the time being and ask yourself, starting from the very beginning, what these things actually mean, as if there were no terminology and no formulation at all.

Once, in a book, I stumbled upon a sentence that went something like this: "And since our conscious life consists of experiences [*Erfahrungen*], ..." and it went on from there. This sentence seemed a little strange to me. What does it really mean, that our conscious life consists of experiences?

---

* From Lecture 4 (12 February 1922).

Either it is a tautology and means nothing more than that our conscious life consists of conscious events—but then the sentence says nothing at all—or it is more than that; for then it means that our conscious life consists of events in which we experience something. Experiences would then be events in which something, "some thing," an object, is experienced. Here is how this word, this remarkable word,[2] *erfahren* (to experience), arose. *Erfahrungen* (experiences) is a very recent plural. Originally, the word existed only in the singular, *Erfahrung,* meaning that which one acquires when one travels [*fährt*], when one goes over the surface [*befährt*] of the world, or, I would almost like to say, when one goes over the surface of things. One experiences [*erfährt*] things, and, in so doing, extracts experience [*Erfahrung*] from them; one extracts a knowledge of things, so to speak, out of things, and this knowledge then has things as its object. One experiences what things are; what there is to things.[3] Thus, it is always a matter of something that is experienced. One comes to know the condition of things; one grasps something knowable and assertable.

Thus, if the statement that our conscious life consists of experiences is to mean anything, it would be this: Our conscious life consists of events in which we experience something knowable and assertable about the condition of things, that is, of outer and inner things. For, of course, inner experiences also belong to the region of experiences. The things we experience by no means have to be things of the outer world; they can also be things of the inner world. And this statement would merely be displaced if it were true that we also have some experiences that exceed the limits of the senses and the narrower [ ].[4] If what people usually call occult experiences, or whatever the term, were true (I should like to suspend judgment on this), they would still only be events in which we experience something from some domain—something knowable and assertable. And so, the basic question with which we will start is this: Does our conscious life indeed consist of such events? Do such events, such experiences, indeed constitute our conscious life? . . . If you reflect on yourselves, not under the influence of any conceptuality but in a completely unbiased manner, does your memory indeed reflect your conscious life back to you as a series of experiences and nothing more? Or are there things, moments, or events in your life that you cannot designate as experience? Are there events in your life in which what is brought to you is not something, the condition of something, something knowable and sayable, but in which you confront something or other, a so-called inner or outer thing, differently from the way you would confront an experienceable object, an object about whose condition I can know and say something, about which it is given to me to know and say something? Is my question clear to all of you? For we cannot go on unless it is.

Question: Is there also a distinction to be made between lived experiences (*Erlebnissen*) and experiences (*Erfahrungen*)?[5]

Answer: Yes. I have already discussed the concept of experience once. This concept seems to me very indefinite and inadequate because it refers to something psychic that occurs in me and not to an event in which I participate; and second, because "experience" does not say anything definite, comprehensible. I can call experiences "lived experiences" if I wish. "Lived experience" means merely that I ascribe a certain piece of my life, so to speak, to myself as a subject; I relate it to myself. But this does not convey what it actually is, so I avoid this expression because of its fluctuating, vague character.

But I believe there is a much simpler and more accurate word to designate what occurs besides experiences in our conscious life. Before I go into this, I would like to approach the matter from another angle. It would gratify me if you, yourselves, could arrive at the point I mean. What is meant by experience, in the sense that I am speaking, could perhaps be designated somewhat more definitively as It experiences. I always experience something—a content, an object, something that is situate—as an It in the world of things, outer and inner. In this sense I can perhaps say that these experiences are It experiences. And if we want to hold onto the word "experiences" a moment longer before giving it up, we could perhaps start by asking, Is there perhaps another kind of experience? Are there only It experiences? Are there only such events in which things are brought to us as an It, as a something in the world of things? Or are there events in which a thing or being of the outer or inner world confronts us in a different manner?

Question: Feeling, perception through feeling [*Erfühlen*]?

Answer: Feeling is also a kind of experience, one in which we still have an It, although a psychic kind, whether it is a feeling of tension or relaxation, of pleasure or pain.[6] We do not locate it in an external world, but still it is a definite content that we experience in this manner. We can describe this feeling somehow; it is a feeling among other feelings, so that we can say of it: Such and such is the case.

Question: I think, though, that all experiences are It experiences. Whether It experiences are sayable is the second question. The thought has occurred to me that It experiences may be connected with assertable experiences.

Answer: By "assertable," we of course do not mean assertable by this individual at this moment but, assertable in general.

Question: Yes. Then there would still be the question whether this It is assertable in its entirety or whether some final remnant is left over, whereas experience is of course always It experience.

Answer: That is quite true. Now the question would be whether this remnant is actually experienced as an It. I admit that really there are only It experiences, but apparently one would like to say that there are still other experiences.

Question: They are not experiences; rather, they are original knowledge, a knowledge of, a becoming manifest (*Offenbartwerden*).[7]

Answer: I mean something quite simple.

Question: Is there only object experience or is there experience from the subject as such without an object?

Answer: That would be a psychic experience. I experience something, a psychic fact.

Question: From the inside of the thing outward, not passing beyond the outer world.

Answer: You mean then it would be limited to something that occurs in the subject itself.

Question: No, then this word no longer applies.

Answer: I mean something simpler; not some very special compartment that is entered only in particular moments of grace but something that each of you has lived and lives again and again.

Question: Of I and Thou?

Answer: Quite right, that's it. This is indeed a perfectly simple matter that is different in kind from an experience, that we can at first, just for a moment, call Thou experience. That is the simple fact of being confronted by a Thou. Perhaps you can make present to yourselves, from your own self-knowledge—your memory—how these things stand.

Four Examples of Encounter

1. The Human

I confront a human being—to give the clearest example—whom I love. What does that mean? What kind of event is it when I actually confront this person as a Thou? Does it mean that I am experiencing something about this person's condition, that this person is now given to me somehow as a He or a She in the world of things and that I now perceive this person as an aggregate of qualities that I can know and express?[8]

Whoever is acquainted with this very simple fact of relation (I think every human being is acquainted with it) knows this. It is something that is totally separate from It experiences. Or, in other, more accurate words, these are not experiences at all or anything that we can designate subjectively—experience still sounds subjective—but something we can designate only objectively as an event in which we participate; in a word, these are relationships.

Our conscious life, to take up the statement again, consists not only of experiences but of relationships. And if you go one step further in this introspection, which I invite you to explore, you will note that these relationships, the relations to a Thou—to the Thou—are the primal, essential occurrences of life. I should like to clarify this by a few more examples.

We began with the relation to a beloved human being. This person can of course also become an object of experience for me. I can put him into the world of things and thus come to know, to experience, to assert something of him, of his qualities. He can become for me a complex of qualities, a thing among things, an experience. But in this moment, or to put it more accurately, for this moment, I have lost the decisive relation to him. And I can only recapture it when it once again confronts me as a Thou, as something to which I stand in relation and that I do not experience.[9]

2. Nature

Now let us proceed to an example that is perhaps not quite so self-evident. How is it with nature? What are our decisive relations to nature? What do they look like? What are the decisive moments in which we take something of nature into our lives? Are they the moments in which we take component parts of nature, if I may use the expression, into our experience? Or are they the moments in which we confront nature as a Thou that confronts us and to which we have this unique, unprecedented, incomparable relationship, which in its essence can only be lived, whose essence cannot be converted to experience, and which we can of course step out of, time and again, to enter the domain of experience to know, experience, and assert something about that to which we stood in relation. But this, obviously is after we have turned; turned away; after we have turned back.

Question: Could one then apply the adjective "nonconscious" to the word "relationships?"

Answer: I should not like to say that. When you say "nonconscious," it sounds as if you were talking about the unconscious life.

Question: That isn't really what I mean.

Answer: Of course not, but it sounds a little that way. Nonconscious, yes, not conscious—to the extent that we mean consciousness as knowing, in the sense of knowing something. But we should not say "nonconscious." I avoid the expression because it sounds like unconscious. We want to fix this in our minds at this point: It is something that belongs very much to our conscious life, and I might say, to put it paradoxically, we know it but not as an It. We know the beloved person and nature to which we stand in relation, but not as an It that we experience.[10]

3. The Creative Conception of a Work of Art

Another example concerns the act of the artist; I mean the actual creative conception. The work—what the artist calls with a very primal, very accurate word the idea of the work—in the sense of the primal form of the work, appears to the artist. The work appears to the artist not as an It in the world of things, for example, of inner things—not at all—but as a Thou pure and simple: just like the beloved person, just like nature, as something exclusive. As in the relation to the beloved human being, it is not that there are all sorts of things around this person, among which he stands as one of them. Rather, in the exclusivity of the relationship—I shall come back to this—he is, as it were, the world, the Thou pure and simple, to which one stands in an exclusive relationship. As we have actual relationships with nature, only insofar as we relate to nature and to nothing else, actual artistic conception exists only when "the idea of the work"—or I would prefer to say "the work"—is encountered as a Thou in the exclusivity of relationship, which has eliminated everything experienceable. Here, you can see that it would be wrong to grasp the Thou from the point of view of the It. That is, the Thou is an object with which we enter into relation.

For this work, if grasped from the objective point of view, is, so to speak, not yet there at all. From the point of view of the experienceable world, I still have to create it. And yet I stand in relation to it. It is present to me in the relationship. Thus, you see that the whole level of the experienceable world is no longer adequate here. For from the point of view of the experienceable world, one would have to designate this conception of the work as fiction, as something fictive, which is merely given to me in imagination. But in the world of Thou, this contemplated work to which I stand in relation as to a Thou has a thoroughly immediate and unconditional reality. That is, the creation of which we are speaking here, the creation of this work that confronts me as a Thou, means nothing other than a discovery, an uncovering of this Thou, a bringing over of this Thou—though a bringing over that as we have seen, necessarily makes this Thou also into an It. We shall yet come to speak of this process—the process of the Thou becoming It.[11]

4. Decision

...Here is one more example, which will perhaps make still clearer at what level we are dealing. We have spoken of the decision of the person who acts. Decision, the moment in which a human being decides to do something, is also an event of relationship. For just as in the artistic, creative conception, the work approached the artist as a Thou with the exclusivity that causes everything else to sink from sight, so the person who decides is confronted by his deed, the deed that he chooses. The deed becomes present for him as a Thou in an exclusivity that causes all other possibility of action to fade, just as in the artistic conception all other possibilities of the artistic act sank from sight. Everything else is, as it were, rejected by the exclusivity of this relation, and this one thing is chosen. Even though here, even more than in the artistic event, it looks, from the viewpoint of the world of objects—of experience—like something fictive, something that is not yet apparent. In actuality, seen from the viewpoint of the Thou itself, it is definitely something that has being and to which I stand in relation and that I now must actualize.

For this is something that all of these relations have in common: The Thou that encounters me is not something I must experience, it is something I must realize. By entering into a relationship with it, I do not make it an experience; rather, I make it an actuality, a presence, or, to put it more correctly, it becomes a presence for me, through me, in confrontation with me. This is what all relationships have in common....

The Thou*

...I mean, however, the pure, truthful relationship in which one confronts this person, truthfully, as his Thou. In this relationship one does not

---

* From Lecture 5 (19 February 1922).

experience anything about this person. One confronts this person truly as his Thou. Here, this person appears not as an aggregate of experienceable qualities; he is not an object that I can come to know, of which I then know something, about which I could now probably assert something. Rather, he is nothing more or less than my Thou, and in this exclusivity of the Thou—the Thou, unlike the He and She and It, is never juxtaposed to others but is always exclusive—the essence of the relationship is a world in itself. The same is true in a relationship with some confrontation, some piece of nature. If I do not place nature, or what I can grasp of nature in this moment, in a temporal—spatial world that is a certain condition and takes a certain course, but, rather, if I confront [nature] in this thing or being as a Thou and actually say "Thou" to it in an unmediated way, then this thing is for me not a content of experience. But it is something exclusive, unique, unfolded only in this relationship, present only in this relationship. And it cannot, it need not, however, by any means, belong to the sphere that can be immediately translated into experience....

What, then, does one experience of the Thou? One experiences nothing. It is not an aggregate of qualities; it is not an object; it is not anything that I—not that either—not something that I know but cannot assert because my language is too weak, too inadequate. It is not an object at all. I experience nothing of it. What, then, does one know of the Thou? Only everything. That is, nothing, no particulars, nothing objectifiable, only everything.[12]

Can one then fulfill the Thou relation, the relationship, through knowledge? No. Only through actualization. If you have followed me to this point, then in this moment you understand what I meant by calling these lectures "Religion as Presence." Now, at last, we have arrived at the first meaning of the word ["presence"]. There is presence in life to the extent and only to the extent that there is relation, that there is Thou, that there is relation to a Thou. From such a relation, and from such a relation alone, presence arises. When something confronts us and becomes our confronter—our exclusive confronter—by the fact that something becomes present to us, presence arises; and only on the strength of this is there presence.

To put it still more plainly, all things that we spoke of—everything that confronts us as a Thou—can, and even must, become an It. The very person we love—who in the Thou relation was not an aggregate of qualities for us, who did not have a certain character but who was thoroughly unique and devoid of characteristics—was only present, exclusively present, not to be known but only to be lived, to be actualized. This very person must necessarily—because of the finiteness of the Thou of which we have spoken, the finiteness of all things—cross over into the It world. He becomes a He or a She, of whom one can indeed know many things, many characteristics, of whom one can and must state all sorts of qualities.

The very part of nature that in the Thou relation did not border on any other parts becomes a content that can be experienced, that is subject to the so-called natural laws and can be considered under their aspect, observed and ascertained.

The next example enters perhaps even more deeply into the particular, perhaps one may say tragic, connection and entanglement of these things, into which the work of the artist enters by its very actualization, by the very fact that he creates it. That is, he makes it from a presence into an objective reality; by this very fact it enters into the actuality of things, becomes a thing among things that one now, indeed, cannot help knowing. Even the artist cannot help knowing all kinds of things. But now, of course, it is something that he can describe, of which he knows something, that is composed of qualities.

And the deed done by a person who decides has entered, by the very fact that it is done, into the world of It, of the experienceable. It has become objective.

Thus, presence becomes object, and I ask that you confront yourselves with these words in a very immediate way. Then you will find that the one, which designates something, which one usually uses for something that is apparently quite transient, which only exists in the moment and passes away with the moment—that the word presence in truth designates that which is lasting, that which, one might well say, leads one across, that which waits in truth, that which lastingly confronts me, that which is eternal.

The word "object" (*Gegenstand*) is the stopping point, the breaking off, the becoming fixed, dense, flowing away to something that is now squeezed, forced into the It world. Objects exist only in the past. The past is object. By becoming object, presence becomes past.

Three Layers of the World

We can also express it in this way: Beings live in the present; objects exist in the past. I have pointed out, and I should like to repeat briefly that this duality corresponds to the development of the human being and probably also to the development of the human race, and that it [shows] itself in the life, in the immediate life, of the individual. And, I repeat, this is what we are talking about. We are not talking about something conceptual but only about life, about the actual life of each one of us, just as in immediate life it shows itself in the development of life. If, for instance, we look at the development of the I in the child, we see that the development of the I is the same as the development of the consciousness of I, so the two cannot be separated at all. The development of the I occurs in two different ways. The I comes into being only by being set off. In the beginning, there is no I. The primal, undifferentiated life, the natural life out of which the human being grows—in which he grows up—this life knows no I and, of course, no Thou and no He either. It is merely undifferentiated life; it is creation. Out of this undifferentiatedness of the world of creation, when the human being is born, the I forms itself in two ways: [in one way] by setting itself off from a world of He, She, It, as one usually assumes. Indeed, one usually considers this setting off as the only way; one usually says: "I come to consciousness." This is again the false attitude, in which one believes that he can separate consciousness from the coming into being of the I by saying: Thus, the I comes to consciousness by setting itself off from other things. But precisely this attitude, which I regard as the decisive one, is merely secondary; the primary and decisive formation of the I, the setting off of the I, occurs not as a setting off against an It but as a setting off against a Thou.

The primary act of the child, who reaches over the undifferentiated creation and, so to speak, out of and away from it, is the reaching for a Thou, and not only for a certain Thou that is experienced, such as the mother or an object, but for the Thou, for the still nameless, still unknown, undetermined Thou, pure and simple. The more strongly this Thou confronts the child, the more strongly it learns to set itself off against it as an I, that is, as the one who reaches for it and who is not this "Thou being" as the one who stands in relation to it. Even in this early stage, these two worlds are inherent: the world of Thou, which tends toward pure connection, connection not union, for relation is connection; and the world of It, which tends toward pure separation, of severance.

Objectively formulated, there are three layers of the world: the world of nondifferentiation—the world of creation; the world of It—that is, the experiential world, or, as one usually says, the world of perception [*Wahrnehmungswelt*] (one takes [*nimmt*] something to be true [*wahr*]); and the Thou world, the world of realization. And this Thou is not something that approaches the human being after the fact—that is merely superimposed; it is not an empirical fact that is presented to man. Rather, it is something that is already inherent in man. There is an innate Thou. This innate Thou unfolds by confronting the child; and therefore it is already clear at this point that all of this cannot be grasped from the experience of particular objects, but it is something that exists in itself and merely presents itself in the so-called objects.

And I should like to illustrate what can be inferred insofar in the case of the primitive man as well as in the child—all the elemental events of the life of the child and of the primitive human being—that is valid to the extent that the human being is still close to the Undifferentiated—to all of the elemental processes. Then all of the elemental convulsions of this life are based on the relation to a Thou, on the tremendous thing that thus happens to the child, to the primitive human being when this innate Thou confronts him bodily. And it may even be a dream, or what one must call a dream; that is, localized in the world of experience, it can be a dream, an image.

For in the world of the child and the primitive human being, the corporeal is simply not determined from the standpoint of experience. And, therefore, an image is as corporeal for him as anything that we have established as corporeal by experiential criteria.

The Thou and the Absolute Thou

Are Thou relations only isolated moments? I think that since every Thou, because of its finiteness as a thing or its being delimited as a thing (I remind you of the work and the deed), must change from a Thou to an It. Therefore, the relations are necessarily moments of life that come and go—lightning flashes in the sky of life that disappear, among which there is no continuity. If this were true, and it seems to be, then a Thou world would be impossible. Only an infinity of Thou moments, world moments, would be possible, and the continuous world would remain the world of It, the world of orientation, the world in which there are things, qualities, and objects. What could this reality of the innate Thou then mean? Could this be merely something that is inherent in us, that has been placed in us, suggesting a task that we are unable to perform? For how is a world of Thou, a world of immediate truth, to be built up if nothing of it enters our life except moments without continuity—transitory moments? If we juxtapose the two elemental basic attitudes of which I have spoken, then we may well feel first of all that the construction of an It world means somehow a betrayal, a falling away, a distancing of ourselves from the task that is inherent in us. This is the task of constructing the world from the Thou—a distancing that is of course necessary and that is ordained by our human nature but that nevertheless remains a distancing, a falling away, a betrayal. But if in actuality the Thou relationships were isolated moments, then this falling away would be not only inevitable but eternally insuperable. Then we could never raise ourselves from the world of orientation to a true world, at least as long as we were beings—human beings.

There are always attempts to make the world, as a whole, the It world, independent, to detach it from relation, to know it as that which is, to fathom its secret. And from the standpoint of the Thou, from the knowledge of the Thou, we grasp that all these attempts are in vain, that all this so-called world is nothing other than a creation that has run away from God. But if the Thou relation consists of isolated moments, then our fate would be insuperable, then this flight from the Thou would be the only possibility of remaining in life. If all Thou, by the nature of each of these Thous, becomes objective, becomes It, then there is apparently no continuity of the Thou world, that is, no present that does not become past. And there is no presence that lasts and fulfills life. This is the basic issue in light of which we can, I believe, alone grasp what may rightfully be called religion. It is the question of the continuity of the Thou, of the unconditionality of the Thou.

God is the absolute Thou, which by its nature can no longer become It. When we address as Thou not any limitable thing that by its nature must become an object but the unconditional—Being itself—then the continuity of the Thou world is opened up. The human being's sense of Thou, of every innate Thou that is latent in him and unfolds in the relationship, which must again and again experience the disappointment of the Thou becoming It, strives through and beyond all of them toward its adequate Thou. There is in truth no God-seeking; rather, one discovers something, beyond all obstacles, that was with one from the very beginning.

It is not a seeking but a finding. It is a finding without seeking: It is a discovery of that which is the most primal and most immediate. The human being's Thou sense, which is insatiable until it finds the Thou as such, has this Thou present in itself from the beginning and needs only to bring out this presence and make it wholly actual.

It is not that this Thou must be inferred from something else, for instance, from nature as its cause, from history as that which reigns in it and over it, or from the subject as its final subjectivity and I quality, which can be inferred from pure thought. It is not that something else is primary and this Thou is then inferred from it, but even what is immediate and first for us and present before all and in confrontation with everything, which is assertion, means necessarily a limitation, an overstraining, an attempt at falling away.

The pure relation, which is the truth of life, finds here its fulfillment and also its continuity. Here lies the guarantee of the construction of a world from the Thou....

Notes

Source: Religion als Gegenwart (eight lectures delivered at the Frankfurt Lehrhaus between 15 January and 12 March 1922), stenograph. First in Rivka Horwitz, *Buber's Way to "I and Thou": An historical Analysis and the First Publication of Buber's Lectures "Religion als Gegenwart"* (Heidelberg: Lambert Schneider, 1978). Esther Cameron, trans., in Rivka Horwitz, *Buber's Way to "I and Thou": The Development of Martin Buber's Thought and His "Religion as Presence" Lectures* (Philadelphia, New York, Jerusalem: Jewish Publication Society, 1988), pp. 55–59; 61–65; 74; 77–84.

Editor's note: The Frankfurt Free Jewish School (Freies jüdisches Lehrhaus) was founded in 1920 by the Orthodox Rabbi Nehemia Anton Nobel (1871–1922) and headed by Franz Rosenzweig after Nobel's unexpected death. Modeled after the German *Volkshochschule,* the Lehrhaus presented itself as a modern, unconventional *Beit Midrash* for a diverse group of observant and nonobservant Jewish adults who, in Rosenzweig's words, sought a way "from life ... back to the Torah." Among the prominent teachers at the Lehrhaus between 1920 and 1926 were the scholar on Jewish mysticism, Gershom Scholem (1899–1982), the political philosopher, Leo Strauss (1899–1973), and the writer, Shmuel Yosef Agnon (1888–1970). In 1933, the Lehrhaus was revived by Buber and continued to operate until 1938. In his lectures, "Religion as Presence," Buber developed his dialogical philosophy for the first time systematically. It is evident from the many parallels to *I and Thou,* which was published less than a year later, that Buber made extensive use of the existing stenograph of his lectures, even including comments and questions by his students.

1. Lectures 1, 2, and 3 are concerned with the history of defining religion as a spiritual phenomenon distinct from everyday life. Buber takes issue with Georg Simmel, Dostoyevsky, Nietzsche, Kant, Schleiermacher, Rudolf Otto, Max Scheler, and others.
2. R. Horwitz: Misprinted as "world."
3. Cf. From *I and Thou* (p. 182 in this volume).
4. The stenographer may have left a space for a missing word (R. Horwitz).
5. Buber's rather positive attitude toward *Erlebnis* (lived experience) that can be found, for instance, in his early work of 1913, *Daniel* (*Daniel: Dialogues on Realization,* trans. Maurice Friedman [New York: Holt, Rinehart & Winston, 1964]), did indeed change. As Rivka Horvitz points out, Buber distanced himself from the term *Erlebnis* in his essays, "The Holy Way" (1918) and "Heruth" (1919); see also Heruth: On Youth and Religion (1919) (p. 127 in this volume).

6. Cf. From *I and Thou* (1923) (p. 182 in this volume).
7. Cf. ibid., p. 182.
8. Cf. ibid., p. 183.
9. Cf. ibid., p. 184.
10. On Buber's conception of knowledge as relation, see also *Philosophical and Religious World View* (1928) (p. 219 in this volume).
11. See Lecture 5, p. 178, cf. From *I and Thou* (1923) (p. 186 in this volume).
12. Cf. ibid., p. 184.

From I and Thou*

The First Part

The world is twofold for man in accordance with his twofold attitude.

The attitude of man is twofold in accordance with the two basic words he can speak.

The basic words are not single words but word pairs.

One basic word is the word pair I–You.

The other basic word is the word pair I–It; but this basic word is not changed when He or She takes the place of It.

Thus, the I of man is also twofold.

For the I of the basic word I–You is different from that in the basic word I–It.[1]

★

Basic words do not state something that might exist outside them; by being spoken, they establish a mode of existence [*Bestand*].

Basic words are spoken with one's being [*Wesen*].

When one says You, the I of the word pair I–You is said too.

When one says It, the I of the word pair I–It is said, too. The basic word I–You can only be spoken with one's whole being.

The basic word I–It can never be spoken with one's whole being.

★

There is no I as such but only the I of the basic word I–You and the I of the basic word I–It.

When a man says I, he means one or the other. The I he means is present when he says I. And when he says You or It, the I of one or the other basic words is also present.

---

* Reprinted with the permission of Scribner, a division of Simon & Schuster from I and Thou, by Martin Buber, trans. Walter Kaufmann. Translation copyright © 1970 by Charles Scribner.

Being I and saying I are the same. Saying I and saying one of the two basic words are the same.

Whoever speaks one of the basic words enters into the word and stands in it.

★

The life of a human being does not exist merely in the sphere of goal-directed verbs. It does not consist merely of activities that have something for their object.

I perceive something. I feel something. I imagine something. I want something. I sense something. I think something. The life of a human being does not consist merely of all this and its like.

All this and its like is the basis of the realm of It.

But the realm of You has another basis.

★

Whoever says You does not have something for his object. For wherever there is something, there is also another something; every It borders on other Its; It is only by virtue of bordering on others. But when You is said, there is no something. You has no borders.

Whoever says You does not have something; he has nothing. But he stands in relation.

★

We are told that man experiences his world. What does this mean?

Man goes over the surfaces of things and experiences them.[2] He brings back from them some knowledge of their condition—an experience. He experiences what there is to things.

But experiences alone do not bring the world to man.

For what they bring to him is only a world that consists of It and It and It, of He and He and She and She and It.

I experience something.

All this is not changed by adding "inner" experiences to the "external" ones, in line with the noneternal distinction that is born of mankind's craving to take the edge off the mystery of death. Inner things like external things—things among things!

I experience something.

And all this is not changed by one adding "mysterious" experiences to "manifest" ones, being self-confident in the wisdom that recognizes a secret compartment in things, reserved for the initiated, and holds the key. Oh, mysteriousness without mystery, Oh, piling up of information! It, it, it!

★

Those who experience do not participate in the world. For the experience is "in them" and not between them and the world.

The world does not participate in experience. It allows itself to be experienced, but it is not concerned, for it contributes nothing, and nothing happens to it.

★

The world as experience belongs to the basic word I–It.
The basic word I–You establishes the world of relation.

★

Three are the spheres in which the world of relation arises.

The first is life with nature. Here, the relation vibrates in the dark and remains below language. The creatures stir across from us, but they are unable to come to us, and the You we say to them sticks to the threshold of language.

The second is life with men. Here, the relation is manifest and enters language. We can give and receive the You.

The third is life with spiritual beings. Here, the relation is wrapped in a cloud but reveals itself; it lacks but creates language. We hear no You and yet feel addressed; we answer, creating, thinking, acting. With our being, we speak the basic word, unable to say You with our mouth.

But how can we incorporate into the world of the basic word what lies outside language?

In every sphere, through everything that becomes present to us, we gaze toward the train[3] of the eternal You; in each, we perceive a breath of it; in every You, we address the eternal You, in every sphere according to its manner....

★

When I confront a human being as my You and speak the basic word I–You to him, then he is no thing among things nor does he consist of things.

He is no longer He or She, limited by other Hes and Shes—a dot in the world grid of space and time—nor a condition that can be experienced and described, a loose bundle of named qualities.[4] Neighborless and seamless, he is You and fills the firmament. Not as if there were nothing but he; but everything else lives in *his* light.

Even as a melody is not composed of tones, nor a verse of words, nor a statue of lines—one must pull and tear to turn a unity into a multiplicity—so it is with the human being to whom I say You. I can abstract from him the color of his hair, or the color of his speech, or the color of his graciousness; I have to do this again and again; but immediately he is no longer You.

And even as prayer is not in time but time in prayer, the sacrifice not in space but space in the sacrifice—and whoever reverses the relation annuls the reality—I do not find the human being to whom I say You in any Sometime and Somewhere. I can place him there and have to do this again and again, but immediately he becomes a He or a She, an It, and no longer remains my You.

As long as the firmament of the You is spread over me, the tempests of causality cower at my heels, and the whirl of doom congeals.

The human being to whom I say You I do not experience. But I stand in relation to him, in the sacred basic word.[5] Only when I step out of this do I experience him again. Experience is remoteness from You.

The relation can obtain even if the human being to whom I say You does not hear it in his experience. For You is more than It knows. You does more, and more happens to it, than It knows. No deception reaches this far: Here is the cradle of actual life....

★

What, then, does one experience of the You?
Nothing at all. For one does not experience it.
What, then, does one know of the You?
Only everything. For one no longer knows particulars.[6]...

★

The You encounters me by grace—it cannot be found by seeking. But that I speak the basic word to it is a deed of my whole being; it is my essential deed.

The You encounters me. But I enter into a direct relationship to it. Thus, the relationship is election and electing, passive and active at once: An action of the whole being must approach passivity, for it does away with all partial actions and thus with any sense of action, which always depends on limited exertions.

The basic word I–You can be spoken only with one's whole being. The concentration and fusion into a whole being can never be accomplished by me; can never be accomplished without me. I require a You to become; becoming I, I say You.

All actual life is encounter....

★

This, however, is the sublime melancholy of our lot that every You must become an It in our world.[7] However exclusively present it may have been in the direct relationship, as soon as the relationship has run its course or is permeated by *means*,[8] the You becomes an Object among objects, possibly the noblest one and yet one of them, assigned its measure and boundary. The actualization of the work involves a loss of actuality. Genuine contemplation never lasts long; the natural being that only now revealed itself to me in the mystery of reciprocity has again become describable, analyzable, classifiable—the point at which manifold systems of laws intersect. And even love cannot persist in direct relation; it endures but only in the alternation of actuality and latency. The human being who but now was unique and devoid of qualities, not at hand but only present, not experienceable, only touchable,[9] has again become a He or She, an aggregate of qualities, a quantum with a shape. Now I can again abstract from him the color of his hair, his speech, his graciousness; but as long as I can do that he is my You no longer and not yet again.

Every You in the world is doomed by its nature to become a thing or at least to enter into thinghood again and again. In the language of objects, every thing in the world can—either before or after it becomes a thing—appear to some I as its You. But the language of objects catches only one corner of actual life.

The It is the chrysalis; the You, the butterfly.[10] Only not always do these states take turns so neatly; often it is an intricately entangled series of events that is tortuously dual. . . .

★

The world is twofold for man in accordance with his twofold attitude.

He perceives the being that surrounds him, plain things and beings as things; he perceives what happens around him, plain processes and actions as processes, things that consist of qualities and processes that consist of moments, things recorded in terms of spatial coordinates and processes recorded in terms of temporal coordinates, things and processes that are bounded by other things and processes and that are capable of being measured against and compared with those others—an ordered world, a detached world. This world is somewhat reliable; it has density and duration; its articulation can be surveyed; one can get it out again and again; one recounts it with one's eyes closed and then checks with one's eyes open. There it stands, right next to your skin if you think of it that way, or nestled in your soul if you prefer that: It is your object and remains that, according to your pleasure, and it remains primally alien both outside and inside you. You perceive it and take it for your "truth;"[11] it permits itself to be taken by you, but it does not give itself to you. It is only about it that you can come to an understanding with others; although it takes a somewhat different form for everybody, it is prepared to be a common object for you, but you cannot encounter others in it. Without it you cannot remain alive; its reliability preserves you. But if you were to die into it, then you would be buried in nothingness.

Or man encounters being and becoming as what confronts him—always only *one* being and everything only as a being. What is there reveals itself to him in the occurrence, and what occurs there happens to him as being. Nothing else is present but this one—but this one cosmically [*welthaft*]. Measure and comparison have fled. It is up to you how much of the immeasurable becomes reality for you. The encounters do not order themselves to become a world, but each is for you a sign of the world order. They have no association with each other, but every one guarantees your association with the world. The world that appears to you in this way is unreliable, for it appears always new to you, and you cannot take it by its word. It lacks density, for everything in it permeates everything else. It lacks duration, for it comes even when not called and vanishes even when you cling to it. It cannot be surveyed: If you try to make it surveyable, you lose it. It comes—comes to fetch you—and if it does not reach you or encounter you it vanishes; but it comes again, transformed. It does not stand outside you; it touches your ground. And if you say "soul of my soul" you have not said too much. But beware of trying to transpose it into your soul; that way you destroy it. It is your present. You have a present only insofar as you have it, and you can make it into an object for yourself and experience and use it—you must do that again and again—and then you have no present any more. Between you and it there is a reciprocity of giving: You say You to it and give yourself to it; it says You to you and gives itself to you. You cannot come to an understanding about it with others; you are lonely with it, but it teaches you to encounter others and to stand your ground in such encounters. And through the grace of its advents and the melancholy of its departures it leads you to that You in which the lines of relation, though parallel, intersect. It does not help you to survive; it only helps you to have intimations of eternity.

The It world hangs together in space and time.
The You world does not hang together in space and time.
The individual You *must* become an It when the event of relation has run its course.
The individual It *can* become a You by entering into the event of relation.

These are the two basic privileges of the It world. They induce man to consider the It world as the world in which one has to live and also can live comfortably; and that world offers us all sorts of stimulations and excitements, activities and knowledge. In this firm and wholesome chronicle, the You moments appear as queer lyric-dramatic episodes. Their spell may be seductive, but they pull us dangerously to extremes, loosening the well-tried structure, leaving behind more doubt than satisfaction, shaking up our security—altogether uncanny, altogether indispensable.[12] Since one must eventually return into "the world," why not stay in it in the first place? Why not call to order that which confronts us and send it home into objectivity? And when one cannot get around saying You, perhaps to one's father, wife, or companion, why not say You and mean It? After all, producing the sound "You" with one's vocal cords does not by any means entail speaking the uncanny basic word. Even whispering an amorous You with one's soul is hardly dangerous as long as in all seriousness one means nothing but experiencing and using.

One cannot live in the pure present: It would consume us if care were not taken that it is overcome quickly and thoroughly. But one can live in pure past; in fact, only there can a life be arranged. One only has to fill every moment with experiencing and using, and it ceases to burn.

And in all the seriousness of truth, listen[13]: Without It a human being cannot live. But whoever lives only with that is not human.[14]

The Second Part

... The basic word I–It does not come from evil, any more than matter comes from evil.[15] It comes from evil-like matter that presumes to be that which has being.[16] When man lets it have its way, the relentlessly growing It world grows over him like weeds, his own I loses its actuality, until the incubus over him and the phantom inside him exchange the whispered confession of their need for redemption.

The Third Part

Extended, the lines of relationships intersect in the eternal You.

Every single You is a glimpse of that. Through every single You the basic word addresses the eternal You. The mediatorship of the You of all beings accounts for the fullness of our relationships to them—and for the lack of fulfillment. The innate You is actualized each time without ever being perfected. It attains perfection solely in the immediate relationship to the You that in accordance with its nature cannot become an It.

Men have addressed their eternal You by many names. When they sang of what they had thus named, they still meant You: The first myths were hymns of praise. Then the names entered into the It language; men felt impelled more and more to think of and to talk about their eternal You as an It. But all names of God remain hallowed because they have been used not only to speak *of* God but also to speak *to* him.

Some would deny any legitimate use of the word God because it has been misused so much. Certainly it is the most burdened of all human words. Precisely for that reason it is the most imperishable and unavoidable.[17] And how much weight has all erroneous talk about God's nature and works (although there never has been nor can be any such talk that is not erroneous) compared with the one truth that all men who have addressed God really meant Him? For whoever pronounces the word God and really means You, addresses, no matter what his delusion, the true You of his life that cannot be restricted by any other and to whom he stands in a relationship that includes all others.

But whoever abhors the name and fancies[18] that he is godless, when he addresses with his whole devoted being the You of his life that cannot be restricted by any other, he addresses God.

Notes

Source: Ich und Du (Leipzig: Insel Verlag, 1923). Translated first by Ronald Gregor Smith, *I and Thou* (Edinburgh: T. & T. Clark, 1937). The present selection follows the translation by Walter Kaufmann, *I and Thou* (New York: Scribner, 1970; now: New York: Simon & Schuster/Touchstone Books, 1996), pp. 53–57; 59–60; 61; 62; 68–69; 82–85; 95–96; 123–24.

Editor's note: Undoubtedly, *I and Thou* is Martin Buber's best-known work. It appeared in December 1922, but was conceived, by Buber's own account, in 1916 (see also Introduction, p. 8, n. 40). Initially, *I and Thou* was to become what Buber called in 1919, the "Prolegomena to a Philosophy of Religion." But after 1922, the larger project itself was abandoned, possibly because

Buber became aware of the overall significance of the dialogical conception. Whether Buber had indeed read the manuscript of Franz Rosenzweig's *Star of Redemption* (1921) or merely "glanced" at it (as he suggests) is still subject to a scholarly debate (see, in particular, Rivka Horwitz: *Buber's Way to "I and Thou:" The Development of Martin Buber's Thought and His "Religion as Presence" Lectures* [Philadelphia, New York, Jerusalem: Jewish Publication Society, 1988], pp. 161–74). A similar question remains open concerning Ferdinand Ebner's *Das Wort und die geistigen Realitäten* (1921). What is certain is that Buber sent Rosenzweig the galleys of *I and Thou* in September 1922 and received a letter of rather frank criticisms that is published in Grete Schaeder, ed., *Martin Buber. Briefwechsel aus sieben Jahrzehnten* (Heidelberg: Lambert Schneider, 1973), vol. 2, no. 103 and subsequent letters. Rosenzweig, as well as Florens Christian Rang (1864–1924), who too read the proofs, was particularly critical of what he considered Buber's simplistic dichotomization of "You" and "It," which left the "It" a "cripple" compared to the "You." For Buber, however, the "It" was filled with the intrinsic value of a "You" potential, that is, *potentially* a "You" and, therefore, not bound to a strictly dualistic conception. It should be noted that Kaufmann's translation of 1970 employs the much more personal "You" for the German "Du," whereas Ronald Gregor Smith (1937) uses the more formal "Thou."

1. In the first edition the next section began: "Basic words do not signify things but relations [*Verhältnisse*]." This sentence was omitted by Buber in 1957 and in all subsequent editions. (W. Kaufmann).
2. Cf. Religion as Presence (1922) (p. 170 in this volume). In linking the German *erfahren* (experience) to *befahren* (go/drive on the surface of something), Buber manages to intimate a superficiality inherent in experiences. (See also W. Kaufmann, trans., *I and Thou* [New York: Simon & Schuster/Touchstone Books, 1996], p. 55, n. 4.)
3. W. Kaufmann suspects an allusion to Isa. 6:1 here ("...and his train filled the temple.") The German is *Saum* (hem, edge).
4. Cf. Religion as Presence (1922) (p. 172 in this volume).
5. Cf. Ibid., p. 172.
6. Cf. Ibid., p. 175.
7. Cf. Ibid., p. 175.
8. Buber sets up a contrast between "direct" [*unmittelbar*] in the previous sentence and "means" [*Mittel*] in this sentence. Kaufmann translates "*unmittelbar*" both as "unmediated" and "direct" and explains his choice in *I and Thou* (New York: Simon & Schuster/Touchstone Books, 1996), p. 62, n. 7 and p. 68, n. 1.
9. Before 1957: "*erfüllbar*" (fulfillable) (W. Kaufmann).
10. Before 1957: eternal chrysalis...eternal butterfly (W. Kaufmann).
11. Buber renders the German "*wahrnehmen*" literally. Cf. Dialogue (1932) (Wahrnahme; p. 198 in this volume).
12. "*Unentbehrlich;*" before 1957, "*entbehrlich*" (dispensable). R. Smith translates from the first version "...moments we can well dispense with." W. Kaufmann points out the consistency of "dispensable" with the ironic character of the first version and considers the second a change "for the worse." (W. Kaufmann, trans., *I and Thou* [New York: Simon & Schuster/Touchstone Books, 1996] p. 85, n. 4.)
13. The German says "*du,*" not "listen;" an expression of intimacy that cannot be reproduced in English. R. Smith translates: "hear this."
14. The wording resonates Hillel's saying in Sayings of the Fathers 1:14 (W. Kaufmann).
15. W. Kaufmann suspects an allusion to Matt. 5:37.
16. *das Seinde zu sein.*
17. Buber uses a word play here: *das unvergänglichste und unumgänglichste.*
18. *wähnt;* before 1957, *glaubt* (believes). Buber might have changed the word for its relatedness to *Wahn* (madness).

From Dialogue (1932)

Part 1. Description

Silence that is Communication

Just as the most eager speaking at one another does not make a conversation (this is most clearly shown in the curious sport, aptly termed discussion, that is, "breaking apart," which is indulged in by men who are, to some extent, gifted with the ability to think); so no sound is necessary for a conversation, not even a gesture. Speech can renounce all the medium of sense, and it is still speech.

Of course I am not thinking of lovers' tender silence, resting in one another, the expression and discernment of which can be satisfied by a glance—indeed, by the mere sharing of a gaze that is rich in inward relations. Nor am I thinking of the mystical shared silence, such as is reported of the Franciscan Aegidius and Louis of France (or, almost identically, of two rabbis of the Hasidim) who, meeting once, did not utter a word but "taking their stand in the reflection of the divine Face," experienced one another. For here, too, there is still the expression of a gesture, of the physical attitude of the one to the other.

What I am thinking of I will make clear by an example.

Imagine two men sitting beside one another in any type of solitude of the world. They do not speak with one another; they do not look at one another; not once have they turned to one another. They are not in one another's confidence; the one knows nothing of the other's career; early that morning they got to know one another in the course of their travels. In this moment neither is thinking of the other; we do not need to know what their thoughts are. The one is sitting on the common seat, obviously in his usual manner—calm and hospitably disposed to everything that may come. His being seems to say it is not enough to be ready; one must also be really *there*. The other, whose attitude does not betray him, is a man who holds himself in reserve—withholds himself. But if we know about him, we know that a childhood spell has been laid on him, that his withholding of himself is something other than an attitude; behind all attitude is entrenched the impenetrable inability to communicate himself. And now—let us imagine that this is one of the hours that succeed in bursting asunder the seven iron bands about our heart—imperceptibly, the spell is lifted. But even now the man does not speak a word; he does not stir a finger. Yet he does something. The spell has been lifted from him—no matter from where—without his doing. But this is what he does now: He releases in himself a reserve over which only he, himself, has power. Unreservedly, communication streams from him, and the silence bears it to his neighbor. Indeed, it was intended for him, and he receives it unreservedly as he receives all genuine destiny that meets him. He will be able to tell no one, not even himself, what he has experienced. What does he now "know" of the other? No more knowing is needed. For where unreserve has ruled, even wordlessly, between men, the word of dialogue has happened sacramentally.

Opinions and the Factual

Therefore, although it has its distinctive life in the sign, that is in sound and gesture (the letters of language have their place here only in special instances, as when, between friends in a meeting, notes describing the atmosphere skim back and forth across the table), human dialogue can exist without the sign, but admittedly not in an objectively comprehensible form. On the other hand, an element of communication, however inward, seems to belong to its essence. But in its highest moments, dialogue reaches out even beyond these boundaries. It is completed outside contents, even the most personal, which are or can be communicated. Moreover, it is completed not in some "mystical" event but in one that is in the precise sense factual, thoroughly dovetailed into the common human world and the concrete time sequence....

Disputations in Religion

... Two believers in conflict about their doctrines are concerned with the execution of the divine will, not with a fleeting personal agreement. For the man who is so related to his faith that he is able to die or to slay for it, there can be no realm where the law of the faith ceases to hold. It is laid on him to help truth to victory; he does not let himself be misled by sentiments. The man holding a different, that is, a false, belief must be converted, or at least instructed. Direct contact with him can be achieved only outside the advocacy of the faith; it cannot proceed from it. The thesis of religious disputation cannot be allowed to "go."...

...Luther and Calvin believe that the Word of God has so descended among men that it can be clearly known and must therefore be exclusively advocated. I do not believe that; the Word of God crosses my vision like a falling star to whose fire the meteorite will bear witness without making it light up for me, and I myself can only bear witness to the light but not produce the stone and say, "This is it." However, by no means should this difference of faith be understood merely as a subjective one. It is not based on the fact that we who live today are weak in faith, and it will remain even if our faith is ever so much strengthened. The situation of the world, itself, in the most serious sense—more precisely, the relation between God and man—has changed. And this change is certainly not comprehended in its essence by our thinking only of the darkening of the supreme light, only of the night of our being, empty of revelation, which is so familiar to us. It is the night of an expectation, not of a vague hope, but of an expectation. We expect a theophany of which we know nothing but the place, and the place is called community. In the public catacombs of this expectation there is no single God's Word that can be clearly known and advocated, but the words delivered are clarified for us in our human situation of being turned to one another. There is no obedience to the coming one without loyalty to his creature. To have experienced this is our way.

A time of genuine religious conversations is beginning, not those so-called fictitious conversations where none regard and address his partner in reality, but genuine dialogues, speech from certainty to certainty but also from one openhearted person to another openhearted person. Only then will genuine common life appear; not that of an identical content of faith that is alleged to be found in all religions, but that of the situation, of anguish, and of expectation.

Setting of the Question

The life of dialogue is not limited to men's traffic with one another; it is—it has shown itself to be—a relation of men to one another that is only represented in their interaction.

Accordingly, even if speech and communication may be dispensed with, the life of dialogue seems, from what we may perceive, to have inextricably joined to it as its minimum constitution one thing, the mutuality of the inner action. Two men bound together in dialogue must obviously be turned to one another; they must therefore—no matter with what measure of activity or indeed of consciousness of activity—have turned to one another.

It is good to put this forward so crudely and formally. For behind the formulating question about the limits of a category under discussion is hidden a question that bursts all formulas asunder.

Observing, Looking On, Becoming Aware

We may distinguish three ways in which we are able to perceive a man who is living before our eyes. (I am not thinking of an object of scientific knowledge, of which I do not speak here.) The object of our perception does not need to know of us, of our being there. It does not matter at this point whether he stands in a relation or has a standpoint toward the perceiver.

The *observer* is wholly intent on fixing the observed man in his mind, on "noting" him. He probes him and writes him up. That is, he is diligent to write up as many "traits" as possible. He lies in wait for them, that none may escape him. The object consists of traits, and it is known what lies behind each of them. Knowledge of the human system of expression constantly incorporates in the instant the newly appearing individual variations and remains applicable. A face is nothing but physiognomy; movements, nothing but gestures of expression.

The *onlooker* is not at all intent. He takes up the position that lets him see the object freely and awaits, undisturbed, what will be presented to him. Only at the beginning may he be ruled by purpose; everything beyond that is involuntary. He does not go around taking notes indiscriminately; he lets himself go; he is not in the least afraid of forgetting something ("Forgetting is good," he says). He gives his memory no tasks; he trusts its organic work, which preserves what is worth preserving. He does not lead in the grass as green fodder, as the observer does; he turns it and lets the sun shine on it. He pays no attention to traits ("Traits lead astray," he says). What stands out for him from the object is what is not "character" and not "expression" ("The interesting is not important," he says). All great artists have been onlookers.

But there is a perception of a decisively different kind.

The onlooker and the observer are similarly orientated, in that they have a position; namely, the very desire to perceive the man who is living before our eyes. Moreover, this man is for them an object separated from themselves and their personal life, who can in fact for this sole reason be "properly" perceived. Consequently what they experience in this way, whether it is a sum of traits, as with the observer, or, an existence, as with the onlooker, neither demands action from them nor inflicts destiny on them. But, rather, the whole is given over to the aloof fields of esthesis.

It is a different matter when in a receptive hour of my personal life I meet a man about whom there is something, which I cannot grasp in any objective way at all, that "says something" to me. This does not mean, "says something to me" about what manner of man this is, what is going on in him, and the like. It means, "says something to me," addresses something to me, speaks something that enters my own life. It can be something about this man, for instance, that he needs me. But it can also be something about myself. The man, himself, in his relation to me has nothing to do with what is said, because he has no relation to me; he has indeed not noticed me at all. It is not he who says it to me, as that solitary man silently confessed his secret to his neighbor on the seat; but *it* says it.

To understand "say" as a metaphor is not to understand. The phrase "that doesn't say a thing to me" is an outworn metaphor, but the saying I am referring to is real speech. In the house of speech are many mansions, and this is one of the inner [mansions].

The effect of having this said to me is completely different from that of looking on and observing. I cannot depict, or denote, or describe the man in whom, through whom, something has been said to me. Were I to attempt it, that would be the end of saying. This man is not my object; I "have got to do with" him. Perhaps I have to accomplish something about him; but perhaps I have only to learn something, and it is only a matter of my "accepting." It may be that I have to answer at once to this very man before me; it may be that the saying has a long and manifold transmission before it, and that I am to answer some other person at some other time and place, in who knows what kind of speech, and that it is now only a matter of taking the answering on myself. But in each instance, a word demanding an answer has happened to me.

We may term this way of perception, becoming aware [*Innewerden*].[1]

It by no means needs to be a man of whom I become aware. It can be an animal, a plant, or a stone. No kind of appearance or event is fundamentally excluded from the series of the things through which, from time to time, something is said to me. Nothing can refuse to be the vessel for the Word. The limits of the possibility of dialogue are the limits of awareness. . . .

A Conversion

In my earlier years, the "religious" was for me the exception. There were hours that were taken out of the course of things. From somewhere or other the firm crust of everyday was pierced. Then the reliable permanence of appearances broke down; the attack that took place burst its law asunder. "Religious experience" was the experience of an otherness that did not fit into the context of life.[2] . . .

Since then I have given up the "religious," which is nothing but the exception, extraction, exaltation, ecstasy; or it has given me up. I possess nothing but the everyday, out of which I am never taken. The mystery is no longer disclosed; it has escaped or it has made its dwelling here where everything happens as it happens. I know no fullness but each mortal hour's fullness of claim and responsibility. Though far from being equal to it, I know that in the claim I am claimed and may respond in responsibility, and know who speaks and demands a response.

I do not know much more. If that is religion then it is just *everything*, simply all that is lived in its possibility of dialogue. Here is space also for religion's highest forms. As when you pray you do not thereby remove yourself from this life of yours but in your praying refer your thought to it, even though it may be to yield it; so, too, in the unprecedented and surprising, when you are called upon from above—required, chosen, empowered, sent, you with this your mortal bit of life are referred to— this moment is not extracted from it, but it rests on what has been and beckons to the remainder that still has to be lived; you are not swallowed up in a fullness without obligation, but you are willed for the life of communion....

Above and Below

Above and below are bound to one another. The word of he who wishes to speak with men without speaking with God is not fulfilled; but the word of he who wishes to speak with God without speaking with men goes astray.

There is a tale that a man inspired by God once went out from the creaturely realms into the vast waste. There he wandered until he came to the gates of the mystery. He knocked. From within came the cry, "What do you want here?" He said, "I have proclaimed your praise in the ears of mortals, but they were deaf to me. So I come to you that you yourself may hear me and reply." "Turn back," came the cry from within. "Here is no ear for you. I have sunk my hearing in the deafness of mortals."

True address from God directs man into the place of lived speech, where the voices of the creatures grope past one another and, in their very missing of one another, succeed in reaching the eternal partner.

Responsibility

The idea of responsibility is to be brought back from the province of specialized ethics, of an "ought" that swings free in the air, into that of lived life. Genuine responsibility exists only where there is real responding.[3]

Responding to what?

To what happens to one, to what is to be seen, and heard, and felt. Each concrete hour allotted to the person, with its content drawn from the world and from destiny, is speech for the man who is attentive. Attentive, for no more than that is needed to make a beginning with the reading of the signs that are given to you. For that very reason, as I have already indicated, the whole apparatus of our civilization is necessary to preserve men from this attentiveness and its consequences. For the attentive man would no longer, as his custom is, "master" the situation the very moment after it stepped up to him: It would be laid upon him to go up to and into it. Moreover, nothing that he believed was always available to him would help him—no knowledge and no technique, no system and no program—for now he "would have to do with" what cannot be classified, with concretion itself. This speech has no alphabet, each of its sounds is a new creation and can only be grasped as such.

It will, then, be expected of the attentive man that he faces creation as it happens. It happens not as speech; as speech rushing out over his head but as speech directed precisely at him. And if one were to ask another if he too heard and he said that he did, they would have agreed only about an experiencing and not about something experienced.

But the sounds of which the speech consists—I repeat it to eliminate the misunderstanding, which is perhaps still possible, that I referred to something extraordinary and larger than life—are the events of the personal everyday life. In them, as they now are, "great" or "small," we are addressed, and those that count as great yield no greater signs than the others.

Our attitude, however, is not yet decided through our becoming aware of the signs. We can still wrap silence about us—a reply characteristic of a significant type of the age—or we can step aside into the accustomed way; although in either act we carry away any productivity or any narcosis. Yet it is possible that we venture to respond, stammering perhaps—the soul is but rarely able to attain to surer articulation—but it is an honest stammering, as when sense and throat are united about what is to be said, but the throat is too horrified at it to utter purely the already composed sense. The words of our response are spoken in the speech, untranslatable like the address, of doing and letting, whereby the doing may behave like a letting and the letting like a doing. What we say in this way with the being is our entering upon the situation, into the situation, which has at this moment stepped up to us, whose appearance we did not and could not know, for its like has not yet been.

Nor are we now finished with it; we have to give up that expectation. A situation of which we have become aware is never finished with, but we subdue it into the substance of lived life. Only then, true to the moment, do we experience a life that is something other than a sum of moments. We respond to the moment, but at the same time we respond on its behalf; we answer for it. A newly created concrete reality has been laid in our arms; we answer for it. A dog has looked at you, and you answer for its glance; a child has clutched your hand, and you answer for its touch; a host of men moves about you, and you answer for their need.

Morality and Religion

Responsibility that does not respond to a word is a metaphor of morality. Factually, responsibility only exists when the court is there to which I am responsible, and "self-responsibility" has reality only when the "self" to which I am responsible becomes transparent into the absolute. But he who practices real responsibility in the life of dialogue does not need to name the speaker of the word to which he is responding; he knows him in the word's substance that presses on and in, assuming the cadence of an inwardness, and stirs him in his heart of hearts. With all his strength, a man can ward off the belief that "God" is there; and he tastes Him in the strict sacrament of dialogue.

Yet let it not be supposed that I make morality questionable to glorify religion. Religion, certainly, has the advantage over morality that it is a phenomenon and not a postulate and, further, that it is able to include composure as well as determination. The reality of morality—the demand of the demander—has a place in religion, but the reality of religion—the unconditioned being of the demander—has no place in morality. Nevertheless, when religion does itself justice and asserts itself, it is much more dubious than morality, just because it is more actual and inclusive. Religion as risk, which is ready to give itself up, is the nourishing stream of the arteries; as system, possessing, assured, and assuring, religion that believes in religion is the veins' blood, which ceases to circulate. And if there is nothing that can so hide the face of our fellow man as morality can, religion can hide from us, as nothing else can, the face of God. Principle there, dogma here; I appreciate the "objective" compactness of dogma, but behind both, the war—profane or holy—lies in wait against the situation's power of dialogue; the "once-and-for-all" lies in wait, which resists the unforeseeable moment. Dogma, even when its claim of origin remains uncontested, has become the most exalted form of invulnerability against revelation. Revelation will tolerate no perfect tense, but man with the arts of his craze for security props it up to perfection.

Part 2. Limitation

The Realms

The realms of the *life* of dialogue and the *life* of monologue do not coincide with the realms of dialogue and monologue even when forms without sound and gesture are included. There are not merely great spheres of the life of dialogue that in appearance are not dialogue; there is also dialogue that is not the dialogue of life, that is, it has the appearance but not the essence of dialogue. At times, indeed, it seems as though there were only this kind of dialogue.

I know three kinds. There is genuine dialogue—no matter whether spoken or silent—in which each of the participants really has in mind the other or others in their present and particular being and turns to them with the intention of establishing a living mutual relation between himself and them. There is technical dialogue, which is prompted solely by the need of objective understanding. And there is monologue disguised as dialogue, in which two or more men, meeting in space, speak each with himself in strangely tortuous and circuitous ways and yet imagine they have escaped the torment of being thrown back on their own resources. The first kind, genuine dialogue, as I have said, has become rare; where it arises, in no matter how "unspiritual" a form, witness is borne on behalf of the continuance of the organic substance of the human spirit. The second—technical dialogue—belongs to the inalienable sterling quality of "modern existence." But real dialogue, here, is continually hidden in all kinds of odd corners and, occasionally in an unseemly way, breaks surface surprisingly and inopportunely—certainly it is arrogantly tolerated more often than downright scandalizing—as in the tone of a railway guard's voice, in the glance of an old newspaper vendor, or in the smile of the chimney sweeper. And the third, monologue disguised as dialogue, ...

... a *debate,* in which thoughts are not expressed in the way in which they existed in the mind but in speaking are so pointed that they may strike home in the sharpest way, and moreover without the men that are spoken to being regarded in any way present as persons; a *conversation,* characterized by the need neither to communicate something, nor to learn something, nor to influence someone, nor to come into connection with someone but solely by the desire to have one's own self-reliance confirmed by marking the impression that is made, or if it has become unsteady to have it strengthened; a *friendly chat,* in which each regards himself as absolute and legitimate and the other as relativized and questionable; a *lovers' talk,* in which both partners alike enjoy their own glorious soul and their precious experience—what an underworld of faceless specters of dialogue!

The life of dialogue is not one in which you have much to do with men, but one in which you really have to do with those with whom you "have to do." It is not the solitary man who lives the life of monologue, but he who is incapable of making real [*verwirklichen*] the community in which he moves by virtue of his destiny....

Being—lived in dialogue—receives even in extreme dereliction a harsh and strengthening sense of reciprocity; being—lived in monologue—will not, even in the most tender intimacy, grope out over the outlines of the self. This must not be confused with the contrast between "egoism" and "altruism," conceived by some moralists....

Nor is dialogic to be identified with love. I know no one in any time who has succeeded in loving every man he has met. Of "sinners," even Jesus obviously loved only the loose, lovable sinners; sinners against the "law"—not those who were settled and loyal to their inheritance and sinned against him and his message. Yet to the latter, as to the former, he stood in a direct relation. Dialogic is not to be identified with love. But love, without dialogic, without real outgoing to the other, reaching to the other, and companying with the other, the love remaining with itself—is called Lucifer....

The Basic Movements

I term basic movement an essential action [*Wesenshandlung*] of man (it may be understood as an "inner" action, but it is not there unless it is there to the very tension of the eyes' muscles and the very action of the foot as it walks), around which an essential attitude [*Wesenshaltung*] is built up. I do not think of this happening in time, as though the single action preceded the lasting attitude; the latter, rather, has its truth in the accomplishment, over and over again, of the basic movement, without forethought but also without habit....

The basic movement of the life of dialogue is the turning toward the other [*Hinwendung*]. That, indeed, seems to happen every hour and quite trivially. If you look at someone and address him, you turn to him, of course with the body, but also in requisite measure with the soul, in that you direct your attention to him. But what of all this is an essential action, done with the essential being—in such a way, that out of the incomprehensibility of what lies at hand, this one person steps forth and becomes a presence? Now to our perception [*Wahrnahme*], the world ceases to be an insignificant multiplicity of points to one of which we pay momentary attention. Rather it is a limitless tumult around a narrow breakwater, brightly outlined and able to bear heavy loads—limitless, but limited by the breakwater, so that, though not engirdled, it has become finite in itself, been given form, released from its own indifference. And yet none of the contacts of each hour is unworthy to take up from our essential being as much as it may. For no man is without strength for expression, and our turning toward him brings about a reply, however imperceptible, however quickly smothered, in a looking and sounding forth of the soul that are perhaps dissipating in mere inwardness and yet do exist. The notion of modern man that this turning to the other is sentimental and does not correspond to the compression of life today is a grotesque error, just as his affirmation that turning to the other is impractical in the bustle of this life today is only the masked confession of his weakness of initiative when confronted with the state of the time. He lets it dictate to him what is possible or permissible, instead of stipulating, as an unruffled partner, what is to be stipulated to the state of *every* time, namely, what space and what form it is bound to concede to creaturely existence.

The basic movement of the life of monologue is not turning away as opposed to turning toward; it is "bending back" [*Rückbiegung*].[4] . . .

Bending back is something different from egoism and even from "egotism." It is not that a man is concerned with himself, considers himself, fingers himself, or enjoys, idolizes, and bemoans himself; all that can be added, but it is not integral to bending back. (Similarly, to the turning toward the other, completing it, there can be added the realizing of the other in his particular existence, even the encompassing of him, so that the situations common to him and oneself are experienced also from his, the other's, end.) I term it bending back when a man withdraws from accepting with his essential being another person in his particularity—a particularity that is by no means to be circumscribed by the circle of his own self and, though it substantially touches and moves his soul is in no way immanent in it—and lets the other exist only as his own experience, only as a "part of myself." For then, dialogue becomes a fiction, the mysterious intercourse between two human worlds, only a game; and in the rejection of the real life confronting him the essence of all reality begins to disintegrate.

The Wordless Depths

Sometimes I hear it said that every *I and Thou* is only superficial, deep down word and response cease to exist, and there is only the one primal being unconfronted by another. We should plunge into the silent unity, but for the rest leave its relativity to the life to be lived, instead of imposing on it this absolutized *I* and absolutized *Thou* with their dialogue.

Now from my own unforgettable experience I know well that there is a state in which the bonds of the personal nature of life seem to have fallen away from us and we experience an undivided unity. But I do not know—what the soul willingly imagines and indeed is bound to imagine (mine too once did it)—that in this I had attained to a union with the primal being or the godhead. That is an exaggeration no longer permitted to responsible understanding. Responsibly, that is, as a man holding his ground before reality—I can elicit from those experiences only that in them, I reached an undifferentiable unity of myself without form or content....

The unity of his own self is not distinguishable in the man's feeling from unity in general. For he who in the act or event of absorption is sunk beneath the realm of all multiplicity that holds sway in the soul cannot experience the cessation of multiplicity except as unity itself. That is, he experiences the cessation of his own multiplicity as the cessation of mutuality, as revealed or fulfilled absence of otherness. The being that has become one can no longer understand itself on this side of individuation nor indeed on this side of *I and Thou*. For to the border experience of the soul, "one" must apparently mean the same as "the One."

But in the actuality of lived life, the man in such a moment is not above, but beneath, the creaturely situation, which is mightier and truer than all ecstasies. He is not above, but beneath, dialogue. He is not nearer the God who is hidden above *I and Thou,* and he is farther from the God who is turned to men and who gives himself as the *I* to a *Thou* and the *Thou* to an *I,* than that other who in prayer, and service, and life does not step out of the position of confrontation and awaits no wordless unity, except that which perhaps bodily death discloses....

Of Thinking

To all unprejudiced reflection it is clear that all *art* is from its origin essentially of the nature of dialogue. All music calls to an ear that is not the musician's own, all sculpture to an eye not the sculptor's; architecture, in addition, calls to the step as it walks in the building. They all say, to him who receives them, something (not a "feeling" but a perceived mystery) that can be said only in this one language. But there seems to cling to *thought* something of the life of monologue to which communication takes a second, secondary place. Thought seems to arise in monologue. Is it so? Is there—where, as the philosophers say, pure subject separates itself from the concrete person to establish and stabilize a world for itself—a citadel that rises towering over the life of dialogue, inaccessible to it, in which man with himself—the single one—suffers and triumphs in glorious solitude?

Plato repeatedly called thinking a voiceless colloquy of the soul with itself. Everyone who has really thought knows that within this remarkable process there is a stage at which an "inner" court is questioned and replies. But this is not the arising of the thought but the first trying and testing of what has arisen. The arising of the thought does not take place in colloquy with oneself. The character of monologue does not belong to the insight into a basic relation with which cognitive thought begins; nor to the grasping, limiting, and compressing of the insight; nor to its moulding into the independent conceptual form; nor to the reception of this form, with the bestowal of relations, the dovetailing and soldering, into an order of conceptual forms; nor, finally, to the expression and clarification in language (which until now had only a technical and reserved symbolic function). Rather, elements of dialogue are to be discovered here. It is not himself that the thinker addresses in the stages of the thought's growth—in their answerings—but, as it were, the basic relation in the face of which he has to answer for his insight, or the order in the face of which he has to answer for the newly arrived conceptual form. And it is a misunderstanding of the dynamic of the event of thought to suppose that these apostrophizings of a being existing in nature or in ideas are "really" colloquies with the self....

If we are serious about thinking between *I* and *Thou,* it is not enough to cast our thoughts toward the other subject of thought framed by thought. We should also, with the thinking—precisely with the thinking—live toward the other man, who is not framed by thought but bodily present before us; we should live toward his concrete life. We should live not toward another thinker of whom we wish to know nothing beyond his thinking but, even if the other is a thinker, toward his bodily life over and above his thinking—rather, toward his person, to which, to be sure, the activity of thinking also belongs....

Community

In the view customary today, which is defined by politics, the only important thing in groups, in the present as in history, is what they aim at and what they accomplish. Significance is ascribed to what goes on within them only insofar as it influences the group's action with regard to its aim. Thus, it is conceded to a band conspiring to conquer the state power that the comradeship that fills it is of value, just because it strengthens the band's reliable assault power. Precise obedience will do as well, if enthusiastic drill makes up for the associates remaining strangers to one another; there are indeed good grounds for preferring the rigid system. If the group is striving even to reach a higher form of society, then it can seem dangerous if, in the life of the group itself, something of this higher form begins to be realized in embryo. For from such a premature seriousness a suppression of the "effective" impetus is feared. The opinion apparently is that the man who whiles away his time as a guest in an oasis may be accounted lost for the project of irrigating the Sahara.

By this simplified mode of valuation, the real and individual worth of a group remains as uncomprehended as when we judge a person by his effect alone and not by his qualities. The perversion of thought grows when chatter is added about sacrifice of being, about renunciation of self-realization.... Happiness, possession, power, authority, and life can be renounced, but sacrifice of being is a sublime absurdity. And no moment, if it has to vouch for its relation to reality, can call upon any kind of later, future moments for whose sake, to make them fat, it has remained so lean....

The feeling of community does not reign where the desired change of institutions is wrested in common, but without community, from a resisting world. It reigns where the fight that is fought takes place from the position of a community struggling for its own reality as a community. But the future too is decided here at the same time; all political "achievements" are at best auxiliary troops to the effect that changes the very core and that is wrought on the inscrutable ways of secret history by the moment of realization. No way leads to any other goal but to that which is like it.

But who in all these massed, mingled, marching collectivities still perceives what it is for which he supposes he is striving—what community is? They have all surrendered to its counterpart. Collectivity is not a binding but a bundling together: individuals packed together, armed and equipped in common, with only as much life from man to man as will inflame the marching step. But community, growing community (which is all we have known so far) is the being no longer side by side but with one another of a multitude of persons; and this multitude, though it also moves toward one goal, yet experiences everywhere a turning to, a dynamic facing of, the other, a flowing from *I* to *Thou*. Community is where community happens. Collectivity is based on an organized atrophy of personal existence; community, on its increase and confirmation in life lived toward one other. The modern zeal for collectivity is a flight from community's testing and consecration of the person—a flight from the vital dialogic, demanding the staking of the self, which is in the heart of the world.

The men of the "collective" look down superciliously on the "sentimentality" of the generation before them, of the age of the "youth movement." Then, the concern, wide-ranging and deeply pondered, was with the problem of all life's relations; "community" was aimed at and made a problem at the same time. One went around in circles and never left the mark. But now there is commanding and marching, for now there is the "cause." The false paths of subjectivity have been left behind, and the road of objectivism, going straight for its goal, has been reached. However, although a pseudosubjectivity existed with the former, since the elementary force of being a subject was lacking, so a pseudo-objectivism exists with the latter, since here one is fitted not into a world but into a worldless faction. As in the former, all songs in praise of freedom were sung into the void, because only freeing from bonds was known but not freeing to responsibility, so in the latter even the noblest hymns on authority are a misunderstanding. For, in fact, they strengthen only the semblance of authority that has been won by speeches and cries; behind this authority is hidden an absence of consistency draped in the mighty folds of the attitude. But genuine authority, celebrated in those hymns—the authority of the genuine charismatic in his steady response to the lord of Charis[5]—has remained unknown to the political sphere of the present. Superficially the two generations are different in kind to the extent of contradiction; in truth they are stuck in the same chaotic condition. The man of the youth movement, pondering his problems, was concerned (whatever the particular matter at different times) with his very own share in it; he "experienced" his *I* without pledging a self, not to have to pledge a self in response and responsibility. The man of the collective undertaking, striding to action, succeeded beforehand in getting rid of himself and thus radically escaping the question of pledging a self. Progress is nevertheless to be recorded. With the former, monologue presented itself as dialogue. With the latter, it is considerably simpler, for the life of monologue is by their desire driven out from most men, or they are broken of the habit; and the others, who give the orders, have at least no need to feign any dialogic.

Dialogue and monologue are silenced. Bundled together, men march without *Thou* and without *I*—those of the left who want to abolish memory, and those of the right who want to regulate it: hostile and separated hosts, they march into the common abyss.

Part 3. Confirmation

Conversation with the Opponent

I hope for two kinds of readers for these thoughts: For the *amicus,* who knows about the reality to which I am pointing with a finger, I should like to be able to stretch out like Grünewald's Baptist;[6] and for the *hostis* or *adversarius,* who denies this reality and therefore contends with me, because I point to it (in his view misleadingly) as to a reality. Thus, he takes what is said here just as seriously as I myself do, after long waiting, writing what is to be written—just as seriously, only with the negative sign. The mere *inimicus,* with which I regard everyone who wishes to relegate me to the realm of ideology and there let my thoughts count, I would gladly dispense with.

I need say nothing at this point to the *amicus.* The hour of common mortality and the common way strikes in his and in my ears as though we stood even in the same place with one another and knew one another.

But it is not enough to tell the *adversarius* here what I am pointing at—the hiddenness of his personal life, his secret—and that, stepping over a carefully avoided threshold, he will discover what he denies. It is not enough. I dare not turn aside his gravest objection. I must accept it, as and where it is raised, and must answer.

So now the *adversarius* sits, facing me in his actual form as he appears in accordance with the spirit of the time, and speaks, more above and beyond me than toward and to me, in accents and attitude customary in the universal duel, free of personal relation.

"In all this the actuality of our present life, the conditioned nature of life as a whole, is not taken into account. All that you speak of takes place in the never-never land, not in the social context of the world in which we spend our days, and by which if by anything our reality is defined. Your 'two men' sit on a solitary seat, obviously during a holiday journey. In a big city office you would not be able to let them sit; they would not reach the 'sacramental' there. Your 'interrupted conversation' takes place between intellectuals who have leisure a couple of months before the huge mass event to spin fantasies of its prevention through a spiritual influence. That may be quite interesting for people who are not taken up with any duty. But is the business employee to 'communicate himself without reserve' to his colleagues? Is the worker at the conveyor belt to 'feel himself addressed in what he experiences'? Is the leader of a gigantic technical undertaking to 'practice the responsibility of dialogue'? You demand that we enter into the situation that approaches us, and you neglect the enduring situation in which everyone of us, so far as we share in the life of community, is elementally placed. In spite of all references to concreteness, all that is prewar individualism in a revised edition."

And I, out of a deep consciousness of how almost impossible it is to think in common, if only in opposition, where there is no common experience, reply.

Before all, dear opponent, if we are to converse with one another and not at and past one another, I beg you to notice that I do not demand. I have no call to that and no authority for it. I try only to say that there is something and to indicate how it is made: I simply record. And how could the life of dialogue be demanded? There is no ordering of dialogue. It is not that you *are* to answer but that you *are able*.

You are really able. The life of dialogue is no privilege of intellectual activity like dialectic. It does not begin in the upper story of humanity. It begins no higher than where humanity begins. There are no gifted and ungifted here, only those who give themselves and those who withhold themselves. And he who gives himself tomorrow is not noted today; even he himself does not know that he has it in himself, that we have it in ourselves—he will just find it, "and finding, be amazed."

You put before me the man taken up with duty and business. Yes, it is precisely him that I mean: him in the factory, in the shop, in the office, in the mine, on the tractor, at the printing press—man. I do not look for men. I do not seek men out for myself; I accept those who are there. I have them—I have him—in mind; the yoked, the wheel-treading, the conditioned. Dialogue is not an affair of spiritual luxury and spiritual luxuriousness; it is a matter of creation, of the creature, and he is that, the man of whom I speak. He is a creature, trivial and irreplaceable....

It is not sufficient, dear opponent, first of all to ascribe to me the pathos of "all or nothing" and then to prove the impossibility of my alleged demand. I know neither what "all" nor what "nothing" is; the one appears to me to be as inhuman and contrived as the other. What I mean is the simple *quantum satis,*[7] of that which this man in this hour of his life is able to fulfill and to receive, if he gives himself. That is, if he does not let himself be deceived by the compact plausibility that there are places excluded from creation; that he works in such a place and is able to return to creation when his shift is over. Or that creation is outstripped, that it once was but is irrevocably over. Now there is business, and now it is a case of stripping off all romanticism, gritting the teeth, and getting through with what is recognized as necessary. I say, if he does not let himself be deceived.

No factory and no office is so abandoned by creation that a creative glance could not fly up from one working place to another, from desk to desk, a sober and brotherly glance that guarantees the reality of creation that is happening *quantum satis.* And nothing is so valuable a service of dialogue between God and man as such an unsentimental and unreserved exchange of glances between two men in an alien place....

You ask, with a laugh, can the leader of a great technical undertaking practice the responsibility of dialogue? He can. For he practices it when he makes present to himself in its concreteness, as far as he can, *quantum satis,* the business that he leads. He practices it when he experiences it, instead of as a structure of mechanical centers of force and their organic servants (among which there is for him no differentiation but the functional one), as an association of persons with faces and names and biographies, bound together by a work that is represented by, but does not consist of, the achievements of a complicated mechanism. He practices it when he is inwardly aware, with a latent and disciplined fantasy, of the multitude of these persons, whom naturally he cannot separately know and remember as such; so that now, when one of them, for one reason or another, actually steps into the circle of his vision and the realm of his decision as an individual, he is aware of him without strain, not as a number with a human mask, but as a person. He practices it when he comprehends and handles these persons as persons—for the most part necessarily indirectly, by means of a system of mediation that varies according to the extent, nature, and structure of the undertaking, but also directly, in the parts that concern him by way of organization. Naturally at first, both camps—that of capital and that of the proletariat—will decry his masterly attitude of fantasy as fantastic nonsense and his practical attitude to persons as amateurish; but just as naturally, only until his increased figures of production accredit him in their eyes. (By this, of course, it is not to be implied that those increases necessarily come to pass: between truth and success there is no prestabilized harmony.) Then, to be sure, something worse will follow. He will be pragmatically irritated, that is, people will try to use his "procedure" without his way of thinking and imagining. But this demoniac element inherent in spiritual history (think only of all the making magic of religion) will, I think, shipwreck here on the power of discrimination in men's souls. And meanwhile, it is to be hoped that a new generation will arise, learning from what is alive, and will take all this in real seriousness [as in the example of the leader of the great technical undertaking].

Unmistakably men are more and more determined by "circumstances." Not only the absolute mass but also the relative might of social objectives is growing. As one determined partially by them, the individual stands in each moment before concrete reality that wishes to reach out to him and receive an answer from him; laden with the situation, he meets new situations. And yet, in all the multiplicity and complexity, he has remained Adam. Even now, a real decision is made in him—whether he faces the speech of God articulated to him in things and events or whether he escapes. And a creative glance toward his fellow creature can, at times, suffice for response.

Man is, in growing measure, sociologically determined. But this growing is the maturing of a task not in the "ought" but in the "may" and in "need," in longing and in grace. It is a matter of renouncing the pan-technical mania or habit with its easy "mastery" of every situation; of taking everything up into the might of dialogue of the genuine life, from the trivial mysteries of everyday to the majesty of destructive destiny.

The task becomes more and more difficult and more and more essential; the fulfillment, more and more impeded and more and more rich in decision. All the regulated chaos of the age waits for the breakthrough, and wherever a man perceives and responds, he is working to that end.

Notes

Source: "Zwiesprache," first in *Die Kreatur* 3, no. 3 (1929). Revised and expanded as independent edition (Berlin: Schocken, 1932 and 1934). Ronald Gregor Smith, trans., in *Between Man and Man* (London: Routledge & K. Paul, 1947), pp. 1–39.

Editor's note: In an afterword to *Dialogue* that was included in the editions of 1932 and 1934, but does not appear in the English editions, Buber called his book a "supplement to *I and Thou* of 1923," emphasizing the fact that he still intended to write an actual "sequel" ("Nachwort" to *Zwiesprache* [Berlin: Schocken, 1932, p. 103]). The sequel never appeared, nor did the collection "On Community," which Buber announced in the same "Nachwort" (ibid., p. 103). Unlike the book *I and Thou* (for an excerpt see I and Thou [1923] [pp. 181 in this volume], which remained on a primarily theoretical level, *Dialogue* was conceived as a situational exemplification and application of the dialogical principle, rendering it more personal and accessible than the former.

1. The term connotes both becoming aware and internalization.
2. Cf. From Religion as Presence (1922) (p. 170 in this volume).
3. Buber takes responsibility [*Verantwortung*] literally, as responding [*antworten*], or being answerable.
4. R. Smith uses the word "reflexion," noting, however, that it is "by no means a perfect rendering" (*Between Man and Man,* translator's note 4). W. Kaufmann, in his translation of *I and Thou,* uses "bending back" instead, which I have adopted here (Cf. *I and Thou,* trans. Walter Kaufmann [New York: Simon & Schuster, 1996], p. 165).
5. Greek, benevolence, charity; in Homer, goddess of good deeds. Buber's etymological explanation of the "genuine charismatic" has to be seen as a thinly veiled commentary on the political climate in Germany at the time.
6. Matthias Grünewald (1475–1518). The reference is to the Isenheim altar, created between 1512 and 1516. See also Buber's essay "Der Altar," in *Hinweise: Gesammelte Essays* (Zurich: Manesse Verlag, 1953), pp. 25–29.
7. Latin, literally, as much as is enough. Here, best as "to the extent of one's ability."

Distance and Relation (1950)

The Principle of Human Life[1]

The question I wish to raise is that of the principle of human life [*Menschsein*], that is, its beginning.

This cannot be thought of here as a beginning in time. It is not sensible to try to discover when and how a certain species of life, instead of being content like the rest with the perception of things and conditions, began to perceive its own perceiving as well. The only way is to consider, in all its paradox and actuality, the category of being characterized by the name of man, to experience its ground and its beginning.

It would be quite wrong to make the reality of the spirit the starting point of the question. The one way to expose the principle of a being is first to contrast its reality with that of other known beings. But the reality of the spirit is not given to us apart from man: All the spiritual life that is given to us has its reality in him. Nature alone presents itself to us for this act of contrasting—nature, which certainly includes man, but which, as soon as we penetrate to his essentiality, is compelled to loosen its grasp and even to relinquish for our separate consideration this child that is an aberration, from its standpoint. This separate consideration takes place thereafter not within nature but starts from nature.

Starting from nature, that is, in this case, starting from the association of "living beings" to which man, as far as he is a part of nature, must be reckoned as belonging, does not mean noting those characteristics that distinguish him from the others, but it means examining the ground of being of those characteristics as a whole. Only in this way shall we learn both the fact and the reason for the fact that those distinguishing characteristics as a whole constitute not only a special group of beings but a special way of being, and thus constitute a special category of being. The act of contrasting, carried out properly and adequately, leads to the grasp of the principle.

In this way, we reach the insight that the principle of human life is not simple but twofold, being built up in a twofold movement that is as such, one movement as the presupposition of the other. I propose to call the first movement "the primal setting at a distance" [*Urdistanz*], and the second "entering into relation" [*In-Beziehungtreten*].² That the first movement is the presupposition of the other is plain from the fact that one can enter into relation only with a being that has been set at a distance or, more precisely, has become an independent opposite. And it is only for man that an independent opposite exists.... An animal's "image of the world," or, rather, its image of a realm, is nothing more than the dynamic of the presences bound up with one another by bodily memory to the extent required by the functions of life that are to be carried out. This image depends on—it clings to—the animal's activities.

It is only man who replaces this unsteady conglomeration, whose constitution is suited to the lifetime of the individual organism, by a unity that can be imagined or thought by him as existing for itself. With soaring power he reaches out beyond what is given him, flies beyond the horizon and the familiar stars, and grasps a totality. With him—with his human life—a world exists. The meeting of natural being with the living creature produces those more or less changing masses of usable sense data that constitute the animal's realm of life. But only from the meeting of natural being with man does the new and enduring arise, that which comprehends and infinitely transcends the realm. An animal in the realm of its perceptions is like a fruit in its skin; man is, or can be, in the world as a dweller in an enormous building that is always being added to, and to whose limits he can never penetrate, but that he can nevertheless know as one knows a house in which one lives; for he is capable of grasping the wholeness of the building as such. Man is like this because he is the creature [*Wesen*] through whose being [*Sein*] "what is" [*das Seiende*] becomes detached from him and recognized for itself. It is only the realm that is removed, lifted out from sheer presence, withdrawn from the operation of needs and wants, set at a distance and thereby given over to itself, that is more and other than a realm. Only when a living being [*Seiendes*] faces³ an independent structure of being [*Seinszusammenhang*]—as an independent opposite—does a world exist....

Now the second movement has been added to the first: Man turns to the withdrawn structure of being and enters into relation with it. "First" and "second" are not to be taken in the sense of a temporal succession; it is not possible to think of an existence facing a world [*Einer-Welt-Gegenübersein*] that is not also an attitude to it as a world [*Zu-ihr-als-Welt-sich-Verhalten*], and that means the outline of an attitude of relation [*Beziehungsverhalten*]; that is, no more than that an animal does not know the state of relation because one cannot stand in a relation to something that is not perceived as contrasted and existing for itself. The rainmaker who deals with the cloud that is sailing up beyond the orbit of his sight acts within the same category as the physicist who has worked out the existence of the still unseen planet and communicates with it at his desk.

We may characterize the act and the work of entering into relation with the world as such—and, therefore, not with parts of it, and not with the sum of its parts, but with it as the world—as synthesizing apperception, by which we establish that this pregnant use of the concept involves the function of unity: By synthesizing apperception I mean the apperception of a being as a whole and as a unity. Such a view is won, and won again and again, only by looking upon the world as a world. The conception of wholeness and unity is, in its origin, identical with the conception of the world to which man is turned. He who turns to the realm that he has removed from himself and that has been completed and transformed into a world—he who turns to the world and looking upon it steps into relation with it—becomes aware of wholeness and unity in such a way that from then on he is able to grasp being as a wholeness and a unity; the single being has received the character of the unity that is perceived in it from the wholeness and unity perceived in the world. But a man does not obtain this view simply from the "setting at a distance" and "making independent." These would offer him the world only as an object, as only an aggregate of qualities that can be added to at will—not a genuine wholeness and unity. Only the view of what I face in the world in its full presence, with which I have set myself, present in my whole person, in relation—only this view gives me the world truly as whole and one. For only in such an opposition are the realm of man and what completes it in spirit finally one. So it has always been, and so it is in this hour.

What has been indicated here must not be misunderstood as meaning that the I "establishes" [*setzten*] the world,[4] or the like. Man's act of setting at a distance is no more to be understood as primary than his act of relation that is bound up with it. Rather, it is the peculiarity of human life that here and here alone a being [*Wesen*] has arisen from the whole, endowed and entitled to detach the whole as a world from himself and to make it an opposite to himself, instead of cutting out with his senses the part he needs from it, as all other beings do, and being content with that. This endowment and this entitlement of man produce, out of the whole, the being of the world [*Weltsein*], and this being can only mean that it is there for man as something that is for itself, with which he is able to enter into relation.

We must now look afresh at the twofold nature of the principle. Though the two movements are bound together in it very closely and with many strands, they are not to be understood as just two aspects of the same event or process. There is no kind of parallelism here—nothing that would make the carrying out of the one movement bring about the carrying out of the other. Rather, it must be firmly maintained that the first creates the presupposition for the second—not its source, but its presupposition. With the appearance of the first, therefore, nothing more than room for the second is given; if, when, and how the second manifests itself can no longer be determined by looking at the first.[5] It is only at this point that the real history of the spirit begins, and this history takes its eternal rise in the extent to which the second movement shares in the intimations of the first—to the extent of their mutual interaction [*Aufeinander-zu-Wirken*], reaction [*Gegeneinanderwirken*], and cooperation [*Zusammenwirken*]. Man can set at a distance without coming into real relation with what has been set at a distance. He can fill the act of setting at a distance with the will to relation—relation having been made possible only by that act; he can accomplish the act of relation in the acknowledgment of the fundamental actuality of the distance. But the two movements can also contend with one another, each seeing in the other the obstacle to its own realization. And, finally, in moments and forms of grace, unity can arise from the extreme tension of the contradiction as the overcoming of it, which is granted only now and in this way.

Things

He who, with his eyes on the twofold principle of human life, attempts to trace the spirit's course in history, must note that the great phenomena on the side of acts of distance are preponderantly universal, and those on the side of acts of relation preponderantly personal, as indeed corresponds to their connection with one another. The facts of the movement of distance yield the essential answer to the question, How is man possible? The facts of the movement of relation yield the essential answer to the question, How is human life realized? The first question is strictly one about category; the second is one of category and history. Distance provides the human situation; relation provides man's becoming in that situation.

This difference can be seen in two spheres, within the connection with things and within the connection with one's fellow men. . . .

Only man, as man, gives distance to things that he comes upon in his realm; he sets them in their independence as things that, from now on, continue to exist ready for a function and that he can make wait for him so that on each occasion he may master them again and bring them into action. . . . Every change made in the stuff of things that is intended to make them more suitable for fulfilling a purpose—every strengthening and refining, every differentiation and combination, every technique is built on this elementary basis—that a person sets aside something that he finds and makes it into something for itself, in which state, however, having become a tool, it can always be found again and always as this same tool ready to carry out this same work. . . .

But now something new and essentially different can enter the situation.

Let us think of a tribe that is close to nature and that already knows the ax, a simple but reliable stone ax. Then it occurs to a lad to scratch a curved line on his ax with the aid of a sharper stone. This is a picture of something and of nothing: it may be a sign, but even its author does not know of what. What was in his mind? . . . We have to turn to the principle of human life in its twofold character to establish what has happened. Man sets things that he uses at a distance; he gives them into an independence in which function gains duration; he reduces and empowers them to be the bearers of the function. In this way, the first movement of the principle is satisfied, but the second is not. Man has a great desire to enter into personal relation with things and to imprint on them his relation to them. To use them, even to possess them, is not enough; they must become his in another way, by imparting to them in the picture-sign [*Bildzeichen*] his relation to them.

But the picture-sign grows to be a picture; it ceases to be accessory to a tool and becomes an independent structure. The form indicated by even the clumsiest ornament is now fulfilled in an autonomous region as the sediment of man's relation to things. Art is neither the impression of natural objectivity nor the expression of spiritual subjectivity, but it is the work and witness of the relation between the *substantia humana* and the *substantia rerum*;[6] it is the realm of "the between" that has become a form.

Human Beings

The twofold principle of human life can be clarified still more fully in men's relation to one another....

Man has always stood opposed to natural powers as the creature equipped with the tool that awaits him in independence, who forms his associations of independent single lives. An animal never succeeds in unraveling its companions from the knot of their common life, just as it never succeeds in ascribing to the enemy an existence beyond its hostility, that is, beyond its own realm. Man, as man, sets man at a distance and makes him independent; he lets the lives of men like himself go on about him, and so he, and he alone, is able to enter into relation, in his own individual status, with those like himself. The basis of man's life with man is twofold and yet one: The wish of every man to be confirmed as what he is, even as what he can become, by men; and the innate capacity in man to confirm his fellow men in this way. That this capacity lies so immeasurably fallow constitutes the real weakness and questionableness of the human race: Actual humanity exists only where this capacity unfolds. On the other hand, of course, an empty claim for confirmation, without devotion for being and becoming, again and again mars the truth of the life between man and man.

The great characteristic of men's lives with one another, speech, is doubly significant as a witness to the principle of human life. Men express themselves to men in a way that is different, not in kind or degree but essentially, from the way animals express themselves to their companions. Man and many animals have this is common, that they call out to others [*Anrufen*]; to speak to others [*Anreden*] is something essentially human[7] and is based on the establishment and acknowledgment of the independent otherness of the other with whom one fosters relation, addressing and being addressed on this very basis. The oldest form of word, along with and perhaps even before the "holophrastic" characterization of situations by means of words in the form of sentences, which signified the situations for those who had to be informed, may have been the individual's name: when the name let the companion and helper at a distance know that his presence, his and no other, was needed in a given situation. Both the holophrase and the name are still signals, yet also words; for—and this is the second part of the witness of speech to the principle of human life—man also sets his calls at a distance and gives them independence; he stores them, like a tool he has prepared, as objects that are ready for use; he makes them into words that exist by themselves. Here in speech, the addressing of another, as it were, cancels out—it is neutralized—but to come to life again and again, not in those popular discussions that misuse the reality of speech, but in genuine conversation. If we ever reach the stage of making ourselves understood only by means of the dictating machine, that is, without contact with one another, the chance of human growth would be lost indefinitely.

Genuine conversation, and therefore every actual fulfillment of relations between men, means acceptance of otherness. When two men inform one another of their basically different views about an object, each aiming to convince the other of the rightness of his own way of looking at the matter, everything depends, as far as human life is concerned, on whether each thinks of the other as the one he is, whether each, that is, with all his desire to influence the other, nevertheless unreservedly accepts and confirms him in his being this man [*Dieser-Mensch-sein*] and in his being made in this particular way [*So-beschaffen-sein*]....

Human life and humanity come into being in genuine meetings. There, man learns not merely that he is limited by man, cast upon his own finitude, partialness, need of completion, but his own relation to truth is heightened by the other's different relation to the same truth—different in accordance with his individuation and destined to take seed and grow differently. Men need, and it is granted to them, to confirm one another in their individual being by means of genuine meetings. But beyond this, they need—and it is granted to them—to see the truth, which the soul gains by its struggle, light up to the others, the brothers, in a different way, and even so be confirmed.

Making Present

The realization of the principle in the sphere between men reaches its height in an event that may be called "making present" [*Vergegenwärtigung*].[8] As a partial happening, something of this is to be found wherever men come together; but in its essential formation, I should say it appears only rarely. It rests on a capacity possessed to some extent by everyone, which may be described as "imagining" the real: I mean the capacity to hold before one's soul a reality arising at this moment but not able to be directly experienced. Applied to intercourse between men, "imagining" the real means that I imagine to myself what another man is at this very moment wishing, feeling, perceiving, thinking, and not as a detached content but in his very reality, that is, as a living process in this man. The full "making present" surpasses this in one decisive way: Something of the character of what is imagined is joined to the act of imagining, that is, something of the character of an act of the will is added to my imagining of the other's act of will, and so on....

The principle of human life that we have recognized suggests "how making" present may be understood in its ontological significance. Within the setting of the world at a distance and making it independent, yet also essentially reaching beyond this and in the proper sense not able to be included in it, is the fact of man himself being set at a distance and made independent as "the others." Our fellow men, it is true, live around us as components of the independent world facing us, but insofar as we grasp each one as a human being he ceases to be a component and is there in his self-being as I am; his being at a distance does not exist merely for me, but it cannot be separated from the fact of my being at a distance for him. The first movement of human life puts men into mutual existence that is fundamental and even. But the second movement puts them into mutual relation with me, which happens from time to time and by no means in an even way, but depends on our carrying it out. Relation is fulfilled in a full "making present" when I think of the other not merely as this very one, but experience, in the particular approximation of the given moment, the experience belonging to him as this very one. Here and now for the first time does the other become a self for me, and the making independent of his being that was carried out in the first movement of distancing is shown in a new highly pregnant sense as a presupposition—a presupposition of this "becoming a self for me," which is, however, to be understood not in a psychological but in a strictly ontological sense, and should therefore be called "becoming a self with me." But it is ontologically complete only when the other knows that he is "made present" by me in his self and when this knowledge induces the process of his inmost self-becoming. For the inmost growth of the self is not accomplished, as people like to suppose today, in man's relation to himself but in the relation between the one and the other, between men, that is, preeminently in the mutuality of the making present—in the making present of another self and in the knowledge that one is made present in his own self by the other—together with the mutuality of acceptance, of affirmation and confirmation.

Man wishes to be confirmed in his being by man and wishes to have a presence in the being of the other. The human person needs confirmation because man, as man, needs it. An animal does not need to be confirmed, for it is what it is unquestionably. It is different with man: Sent forth from the natural domain of species into the hazard of the solitary category, surrounded by the air of a chaos that came into being with him, secretly and bashfully he watches for a "Yes" that allows him to be and can come to him only from one human person to another. It is from one man to another that the heavenly bread of self-being is passed.

Distance and Relation (1950)

Notes

Source: "Urdistanz und Beziehung," first in *Studia Philosophica—Jahrbuch der Schweizerischen Philosophischen Gesellschaft,* Separatum Vol. 10 (Basel: Verlag für Recht und Gesellschaft, 1950). Ronald Gregor Smith, trans., in *The Hibbert Journal* 49 (January 1951). Also in *The Knowledge of Man—Selected Essays,* ed. M. Friedman (New York: Harper & Row, 1965), pp. 59–71.

Editor's note: In the 1940s, already in Jerusalem, Buber became increasingly interested in anthropology. His *Ba'ayat ha'adam* (*Between Man and Man* [London: Routledge & K. Paul, 1947]) of 1943 was conceived as an intellectual–historical introduction to a later "foundation" of his anthropology, the first part of which was "Distance and Relation" (see Buber's preface to the first German edition, Heidelberg, 1948). That Buber saw his anthropology as a continuation of *I and Thou* is clearly expressed in the preface to the first independent edition of "Distance and Relation" (*Urdistanz und Beziehung* [Heidelberg: Lambert Schneider, 1951]).

1. The subheadings were not included in the first German and English editions but were added by Buber in 1951.
2. This basic action must not be, of course, confused with a mere relation of any kind that exists between things. (M.B.)
3. R. Smith translates the German "*gegenüber*" consistently as "over against." However, Buber uses "*gegenüber sein*" as an active term that is best expressed in the verbal form "to face."
4. R. Smith: ...that I "establish" the world...
5. Not in R. Smith.
6. Latin, literally, substance of things.
7. The animal, especially if domesticated, is indeed capable of looking at man in a "speaking" manner; it can mean to express itself to man, but it cannot grasp man as an independent being outside this act of speech [*Anspruch*].... (M.B.)
8. Buber uses the term in its literal meaning as "making present," rather than in the more common meaning of bringing to mind, visualizing, or realizing. Note that the German *Gegenwart* has both a temporal and spatial/ontological dimension that can be rendered "present" and "presence" in English.

Genuine Dialogue (1954)

We must now summarize and clarify the marks of genuine dialogue. In genuine dialogue the turning [*Hinwendung*][1] to the partner takes place in all truth, that is, it is a turning of the being. Every speaker "means" the partner or partners to whom he turns as this personal existence. To "mean" someone in this connection is at the same time to exercise that degree of making present which is possible to the speaker at that moment. The experiencing senses and the imagining of the real [*Realphantasie*] that completes the findings of the senses work together to make the other present as a whole and as a unique being, as the person that he is. But the speaker does not merely perceive the one who is present to him in this way; he receives him as his partner, and that means that he confirms this other being, so far as it is for him to confirm. The true turning of his person to the other includes this confirmation, this acceptance. Of course, such a confirmation does not mean approval; but no matter in what I am against the other, by accepting him as my partner in genuine dialogue I have affirmed him as a person.

Further, if genuine dialogue is to arise, everyone who takes part in it must bring himself into it. And that also means that he must be willing on each occasion to say what is really in his mind about the subject of the conversation. And that means further that on each occasion he makes the contribution of his spirit without reduction and without shifting his ground. Even men of great integrity are under the illusion that they are not bound to say everything "they have to say." But in the great faithfulness that is the climate of genuine dialogue, what I have to say at any one time already has in me the character of something that wishes to be uttered, and I must not keep it back, keep it in myself. It bears for me the unmistakable sign that indicates that it belongs to the common life of the word. Where the dialogical word genuinely exists, it must be given its right by keeping nothing back [*Rückhaltung*]. To keep nothing back is the exact opposite of unreserved speech. Everything depends on the legitimacy of "what I have to say." And of course I must also be intent to raise into an inner word and then into a spoken word what I have to say at this moment but do not yet possess as speech. To speak is both nature and work, something that grows and something that is made, and where it appears dialogically, in the climate of great faithfulness, it has to fulfill ever anew the unity of the two.

Associated with this is that overcoming of semblance to which I have referred. In the atmosphere of genuine dialogue, he who is ruled by the thought of his own effect as the speaker of what he has to speak, has a destructive effect. If instead of what has to be said, I try to bring attention to my I, I have irrevocably miscarried what I had to say; it enters the dialogue as a failure, and the dialogue is a failure. Because genuine dialogue is an ontological sphere which is constituted by the authenticity of being, every invasion of semblance must damage it.

But where the dialogue is fulfilled in its being, between partners who have turned to one another in truth, who express themselves without reserve and are free of the desire for semblance, there is brought into being a memorable common fruitfulness which is to be found nowhere else. At such times, at each such time, the word arises in a substantial way between men who have been seized in their depths and opened out by the dynamic of an elemental togetherness. The interhuman opens out [*erschließt*][2] what otherwise remains unopened [*unerschlossen*].

This phenomenon is indeed well known in dialogue between two persons; but I have also sometimes experienced it in a dialogue in which several have taken part....

One more point must be noted. Of course it is not necessary for all who are joined in a genuine dialogue actually to speak; those who keep silent can on occasion be especially important. But each must be determined not to withdraw when the course of the conversation makes it proper for him to say what he has to say. No one, of course, can know in advance what it is that he has to say; genuine dialogue cannot be arranged beforehand. It has indeed its basic order in itself from the beginning, but nothing can be determined, the course is of the spirit, and some discover what they have to say only when they catch the call of the spirit....

Notes

Source: From "Elemente des Zwischenmenschlichen," first in *Die Schriften über das dialogische Prinzip* (Heidelberg: Lambert Schneider, 1954). Ronald G. Smith, trans., first in *Psychiatry* 20, no. 2 (May 1957). Also in *The Knowledge of Man* (London: George Allen & Unwin, 1965), pp. 72–88.

1. Cf. From Dialogue (1932) (p. 197 in this volume).
2. The term has to be understood from Buber's distinction between "imposing" [*Auferlegung*] and "unfolding," or "opening up" [*Erschließung*], the former being characteristic of political language, the latter being a fundamental attitude in dialogical action and genuine education.

PART V

Philosophy and Religion

Philosophical and Religious World View (1928)

The verb "to know" is used in a twofold sense: First, according to the customary manner of speaking, "to know" means, in effect, "to regard a thing as an object." At the bottom of it lies the relation of subject and object (philosophical worldview). Second, the verb "to know" has another sense in the biblical sentence, "Adam *knew* his wife Eve." Here, the relationship of being to being is meant in which the real *knowing of I and Thou* takes place, but not of subject to object. This knowing lays the foundation for the religious worldview.

The first kind of knowing, the philosophical, is, of course, an indispensable necessity and duty of human existence. It guarantees the continuity of thought through which man has acquired his special position in nature; it lays the foundation for the cohesion of the experience and the thought of mankind. But it is purchased at the price of renouncing the lasting I–Thou relationship; in particular, it can found no community. Subject and object are necessary artifacts of the act of thought. The living "to each other" does not know this division. The man who knows in the subject–object relation and, hence, before all the philosophical man, begins therefore by looking away from his *concrete situation*. Philosophy is the application of this subject–object relation to the total connection of being. It is grounded in the belief in the all powerfulness of thinking; it totalizes the partial—thinking's function as a part. It was Kant's pathfinding discovery that in subject–object knowing and, hence, in philosophical–scientific knowing, we only know that which has been formed beforehand in our categories of thought.[1] Phenomenology, too, regards the contents of thought in its determination as content of thought; it is the praxis to Kant's theory of knowledge.

But the great systems are not therefore fictitious: They are announcements of *real* thought relationships to existing being. But they can only become possible through the reestablishment of the object–subject relation and, hence, through entering into the mortal duty of knowledge. Being, insofar as it metes itself out to the human thought contents, is *also* in the thinking of man, and the knowing spirit is a spark of the *pneuma*,[2] even though a detached spark—spirit in the attitude of self-contemplation. For all our duty to this thinking, it remains the case: In the act of looking away, *all* scientific and philosophical thinking tears asunder not merely the wholeness of the concrete person but also God and man from each other.

The science of history, for example, is driven by necessity as though there were no working of God. When the acknowledgment of God's working in history is taken seriously, the science of history is not possible, namely, in the situation of being taken seriously. There is a knowledge of faith about the working of God in history but not within philosophy and scholarship: No faith exists within the attitude of scholarship. The history of religion does not have to do with the working of God but with religion as a *human* expression of life; not with the divine side of history but with the material of religious experience. The legitimacy of scholarship is based on the fact that it includes nothing from beyond systematic knowledge in the scholarly observation. But the scholar is allowed and charged with the glimpse of the limit—the looking out to the concrete situation and to the concrete divine working. If science has this genuine glimpse as its limit, if it thus knows what it does, and does not overstep its limit, then it does not, of course, lose the problematic nature of the subject–object relation. But it still remains installed within an integral part of the relationship of I and Thou and avoids the particular fall into sin of the thinker of our time: the false autonomy, the hardening before God.

Beyond this limit of philosophy and scholarship, there arises, single and underivable, the unique reality of the world *concretum* presented me by God: the continual creation in each moment. This religious situation that accosts me is not foreseeable and foreknowable and, hence, cannot be caught in any religious world continuity or in any religious worldview. I must *enter* into the religious situation, must *hold my ground* in the face of the world *concretum* presented to me. If philosophy, even every philosophy of religion is directed to and reflects on the object–subject relationship as Being, then religion, is not directed to the relationship but to the Thou; it *practices* the living relationship of I–Thou.

How, then, do scientific–philosophical statements differ from religious ones?

Every scientific–philosophical statement stands under the law of contradiction: "A" is not equal to "non-A." The religious statement simply does not stand under the law of contradiction. When theologians believe that they can make statements about God under the law of contradiction, they are not acting from the standpoint of religion. This holds even for the negative theology of Karl Barth: It is not permissible to say God is the Wholly Other without God also being recognized, at the same time, as the Wholly Near, the intimate.[3] The religious situation is simply the abode of the lived *complexio oppositorum*.[4] In the religious situation it is not permissible to say, "God is transcendent and not immanent," or the reverse; he is both. Every religious statement is a risk that may be risked when it takes place in the living *complexio oppositorum,* as a pointing to the situation in which God only shows himself biographically. Even faith is not faith that something is; not knowledge with a content but factual event, lived life in dialogue: being addressed by word and sign, answering by doing and not doing, by holding one's ground and being responsible in the lived everyday. The religious statement is the witness of this dialogue.

If the philosophical–scientific man speaks of the unknown mystery, then he always does so only as of the mystery knowable "in itself." The religious man knows only the mystery to whose nature the inscrutability belongs and to which only standing firm and involvement open access.

This immediate relationship means for the person, the becoming whole of the soul. For only with a whole soul can one enter into the concrete. What characterizes our present condition of stress are the various forces of the soul becoming autonomous. But this immediate relationship to the mystery also means the becoming whole of the spiritual life: The individual spiritual spheres that have become independent *unite* when a genuine religious communal life again exists. The separation of the spiritual spheres has led to the many modern idols. But the dreadfulness of our situation lies in the fact that religion is regarded as *one* aspect of the spiritual world. Any martyrdom is more conducive to religion than this freedom to operate as one of the spiritual spheres next to others. Much less still, of course, is religion a synthesis of the spiritual spheres.

Concretely seen, the contemporary so-called "worldviews" ["*Weltanschauungen*"] present themselves to us as systems of flight, as securities against the duty of really beholding the world. But genuine religious *grasping* of the world [*Welt-Erfassung*][5] includes proceeding from the present concrete being and situation of the person; entering into the present world situation as the speech of God to me; beholding all that is presented to me and its origination—its being created together with me ("We see the things in God"); and the responsible answer of man, the loving hallowing of the things in the everyday. *To this real relation, however, one can be educated.*

From the Discussion

The religions speak to one another of a common *abstractum* (congress of religions); but I believe in the common *concretum* (the coming together), the kingdom of God. From the common *concretum* one can, one may, one must speak. And that is, then, the genuine speech. Its criterion is that it does not stream out of *one* independent province of the inner life but out of the totality: It does not *withhold* itself. That is, one can only speak on the foundation of *confessing,* not confessing religion, but confessing *oneself!* Philosophical thinking is the self-contemplation of the human spirit. It assures the connection of thought of man and assures that men understand one another in conceptual speech. But in conceptual speech lies the tension of falling away from one another: We do not mean the same things by our concepts and so, basically, we do not understand one another. Therefore, philosophy too is incapable of forming community. But it is inexorably necessary as a phenomenon belonging to the way of redemption.

The "vision" is the first disengagement from the I–Thou relationship. The man in I–Thou "beholds" nothing but what he sees with his senses: the world in God, not the face of God. Because he is taken into the duty of knowing, he passes through a condition in which the relationship of I–Thou is still illuminated; but at the same time the detachment begins— no longer I–Thou knowing; *not yet* subject–object knowing.

The false autonomy is the absolute life of man in self-enjoyment, in concerning himself with himself. The consequence of this is the becoming independent of the spiritual spheres. It is then held, for example, that aesthetics has nothing to do with ethics; politics, nothing to do with religion. The politician can be a pious man and yet engage in immoral politics, and so forth. But there also exists a genuine, God-willed autonomy: the life in all seriousness of man, from the human, to God; an act that works in the sense of obedience and proves itself obedient.

In revelation, something happens to man from a side that is not man, not soul, not world. Revelation does not take place in man and is not to be explained through any psychologism. He who speaks of "the God in his breast" stands on the outermost rim of being: One cannot, one may not, live from there. Revelation does not gush forth from the unconscious; it is mastery over the unconscious. Revelation comes as a might from without, but not in such a way that man is a vessel that is filled or a mere mouthpiece. Rather, the revelation seizes the human elements that are at hand and recasts them: It is the pure shape of the meeting.

Notes

Source: "Philosophische und religiöse Weltanschauung" (speech at the Hohenrodter Bund), first in *Rhein-Mainische Volkszeitung,* Kulturbeilage (15 June 1928). Maurice Friedman, trans., in *A Believing Humanism: My Testament 1902–1965* (New York: Simon & Schuster, 1967), pp. 130–5.

Editor's note: Beginning in 1923, the Hohenrodter Bund convened on a yearly basis to discuss a comprehensive educational reform in Germany. Buber was introduced to the Bund by the social pedagogue, Theodor Bäuerle (1882–1956), later minister of culture in Württemberg-Baden. The sixth convention (May 1928) was devoted to the theme "World View and Adult Education."

1. Immanuel Kant (1724–1804), leading philosopher of the European Enlightenment. Kant's theory of the categories of thought was developed most thoroughly in his *Critique of Pure Reason* (1781). In his "Autobiographical Fragments," Buber names Plato and Kant as the first two authors who introduced him to philosophy (see *The Philosophy of Martin Buber* [Library of Living Philosophers, vol. 12], eds. Paul A. Schilpp and Maurice Friedman [La Salle, Ill.: Open Court, 1967], p. 11).
2. Greek: spirit, breath, life. The Septuagint translates the Hebrew *ruah* as *pneuma;* also "Holy Spirit."
3. Karl Barth (1886–1968), Protestant theologian and philosopher. Barth's basic idea of distance and nearness was developed in his *Commentary on the Romans* (*Römerbrief*) of 1918.
4. Latin, literally, interwovenness of opposites.
5. M. Friedman: "comprehending of the world."

Religion and Philosophy (1951)

★

The difficulty in making a radical distinction between the spheres of philosophy and religion, and, at the same time, the correct way of overcoming this difficulty, appear most clearly to us when we contrast two figures who are representative of the two spheres—Epicurus[1] and Buddha.

Not only does Epicurus teach that there are gods, that is, immortal and perfect beings who live in the spaces between the worlds and yet are without power over the world or interest in it, but he also holds that one should worship these gods through pious representations of them and through the traditional rites, especially devout and fitting sacrifices. He says that he himself worships and sacrifices but then cites the words of a character from a comedy: "I have sacrificed to gods who take no notice of me." Here is a kind of dogma and also a cultic practice and yet, clearly, a philosophical rather than a religious attitude.

Buddha treats the gods of popular belief, as far as he deigns to mention them at all, with calm and considered goodwill, not unmixed with irony. These gods are, to be sure, powerful and, unlike the gods of Epicurus, concerned with the human world. But they are bound like men by the chain of desire; heavenly figures entangled, even as men, in the "wheel of births." One may worship them, but the legends consistently picture them as paying homage to him, the Buddha, the "Awakened One," freed and freeing from the wheel of births. On the other hand, Buddha knows a genuinely divine, an "Unborn, Unoriginated, Uncreated." He knows it only in this wholly negative designation, and he refuses to make any assertions about it. Yet he stands related to it with his whole being. Here is neither proclamation nor worship of a deity, yet unmistakable religious reality.

★

Thus, the personal manifestation of the Divine is not decisive for the genuineness of religion. What is decisive is that I relate myself to the Divine as to Being, which faces me, though *not* me *alone.* Complete inclusion of the Divine in the sphere of the human self abolishes its divinity. It is not necessary to know something about God really to believe in Him: Many true believers know how to talk *to* God but not *about* Him. If one dares to turn toward the unknown God, to go to meet Him, to call to Him, Reality is present. He who refuses to limit God to the transcendent has a fuller conception of Him than he who does so limit Him. But he who confines God within the immanent means something other than Him....

Protagoras[2] once remarked that he could ascertain neither that gods exist nor that they do not, for the discovery is hindered by the mysteriousness of the subject and the brevity of human life. This famous saying translates the situation into the language of philosophical consciousness, but it is a consciousness that is strongly conditioned by the time in which Protagoras lived. For this particular consciousness, which caught up and absorbed all that was absolute in the mirror of a universal relativism, the question about the gods had become merely the question whether it was possible to ascertain their existence. To the great thinkers of the preceding age this question would have appeared meaningless. In Heraclitus's saying, "Here also are gods,"[3] the word "also" is a strong indication of the existence of immediately present divine being. And when he explains that the One that alone is wise wishes and does not wish to be called by the name of Zeus,[4] he has given philosophical expression to an original relation between religion and philosophy as that between the meeting with the Divine and its objectification in thought. The dissolution of this relation is proclaimed by the Sophist, to whom the myths and cults of popular tradition are no longer witness and symbol of a transcendent presence but, rather, only something in the nature of imagination or play. To the man who is no longer able to meet, yet is as able as ever to think, the only possible religious question is whether man can ascertain the existence of the gods. In the absence of any experience, this question must be answered in the negative. With the complete separation of philosophy from religion, however—with religion being of interest to philosophy only from the standpoint of the history of the human spirit—the possibility and the task of a radical distinction between the two spheres come into existence for the first time. This possibility and this task certainly encompass not only the epochs of separation but also those early periods in which each philosophy is still connected with a religion yet cogitative truth and reality of faith are already sharply distinguished. Indeed, it is just when we examine those early periods that many important distinguishing marks come to light most clearly.

★

All great religiousness shows us that reality of faith means living in relationship to Being "believed in," that is, unconditionally affirmed, absolute Being. All great philosophy, on the other hand, shows us that cogitative truth means making the absolute into an object from which all other objects must be derived. Even if the believer has in mind an unlimited and nameless absolute that cannot be conceived in a personal form, if he really thinks of it as existing Being that faces him, his belief has existential reality. Conversely, even if he thinks of the absolute as limited within personal form—if he reflects on it as on an object—he is philosophizing. Even when the "Unoriginated" is not addressed with voice or soul, religion is still founded on the duality of I and Thou. Even when the philosophical act culminates in a vision of unity, philosophy is founded on the duality of subject and object. The duality of I and Thou finds its fulfillment in the religious relationship; the duality of subject and object sustains philosophy while it is carried on. The first arises out of the original situation of the individual, his living before the face of Being, turned toward him as he is turned toward it. The second springs from the splitting apart of this togetherness into two entirely distinct modes of existence: one that is able to do nothing but observe and reflect; and one that is able to do nothing but be observed and reflected upon. I and Thou exist in, and by means of, lived concreteness; and subject and object, products of abstraction, last only as long as that power is at work. The religious relationship, no matter what different forms and constellations it takes, is in its essence nothing other than the unfolding of the existence that is lent to us. The philosophical attitude is the product of a consciousness that conceives of itself as autonomous and strives to become so. In philosophy the spirit of man gathers itself by virtue of the spiritual work. Indeed, one might say that here, on the peak of consummated thought, spirituality, which has been disseminated throughout the person, first becomes spiritual substance. But in religion, when this [relationship] is nothing other than simple existence that has unfolded as a whole person facing eternal Being, spirituality too becomes a part of personal wholeness.

Philosophy errs in the presumption of religion being founded in a noetic act, even if an inadequate one, and in therefore regarding the essence of religion as the knowledge of an object that is indifferent to being known. As a result, philosophy understands faith as an affirmation of truth lying somewhere between clear knowledge and confused opinion. Religion, on the other hand, insofar as it speaks of knowledge at all, does not understand it as a noetic relation of a thinking subject to a neutral object of thought but, rather, as mutual contact, as the genuinely reciprocal meeting in the fullness of life between one active existence and another. Similarly, it understands faith as the entrance into this reciprocity, as binding oneself in relationship with an undemonstrable and unprovable, yet—even in relationship—knowable Being, from whom all meaning comes.

*

Another attempt at demarcation, the mature attempt of modern philosophy, distinguishes between the intention of each. According to this conception, philosophy is directed toward the investigation of essence;

religion, toward inquiry about salvation. Now salvation is, to be sure, a genuine and proper religious category, but the inquiry into salvation differs from the investigation of essence only in the way in which it is considered. The principal tendency of religion is, rather, to show the essential unity of the two. This is illustrated by the Old Testament phrase, the "way of God," which is also preserved in the language of the Gospels.[5] The "way of God" is by no means to be understood as a sum of prescriptions for human conduct but, rather, primarily as the way of God in and through the world. It is the true sphere of the knowledge of God since it means God's becoming visible in His action. But it is at the same time the way of salvation of men since it is the prototype for the imitation of God. Similarly, the Chinese Tao, the "path" in which the world moves, is the cosmic primal meaning. But because man conforms this, his life, to it and practices "imitation of the Tao," it is, at the same time, the perfection of the soul.

Something further, however, is to be noted in that regard, namely, that as high as religion may place the inquiry into salvation, it does not regard it as the highest and the essential intention. What is really intended in the search for salvation is the attainment of a condition freed from intention—from arbitrariness. The search for salvation is concerned with the *effect* of salvation, but the "way" itself is the unarbitrary. Philosophy really means philosophizing; the more real religion is, the more it means its own overcoming. It wills to cease to be the special domain "religion" and wills to become life. It is concerned in the end not with specific religious acts but with redemption from all that is specific. Historically and biographically, it strives toward the pure "everyday." Religion is, in the religious view, the exile of man; his homeland is unarbitrary life "in the face of God." . . .

★

When we look at the history of a historical religion, we see the reoccurrence, in different periods and phases, of an inner battle that remains essentially the same. It is the struggle of the religious element against the nonreligious elements that invade it from all sides—metaphysics, gnosis, magic, politics, and so forth. This medley seeks to take the place of the flowing life of faith that is renewed in the flux. It finds helpers in myth and cult, both of which originally served only as expression of the religious relationship. To preserve its purity the religious element must combat the tendency of this conglomerate to become autonomous and to make itself independent of the religious life of the person. This battle is consummated in prophetic protest, heretical revolt, reformational retrenchment, and a new founding that arises through the desire to return to the original religious element. It is a struggle for the protection of lived concreteness as the meeting place between the human and the divine. The actually lived concrete is the "moment" in its unforeseeability and its irrecoverableness, in its undivertible character of happening but once, in its decisiveness, in its secret dialogue between that which happens and that which is willed, between fate and action, address and answer. This lived concreteness is threatened by the invasion of the extrareligious elements, and it is protected on all fronts by the religious in its unavoidable aloneness.

The religious essence in every religion can be found in its highest certainty, that is the certainty that the meaning of existence is open and accessible in the actual lived concrete, not above the struggle with reality but in it.

That meaning is open and accessible in the actual lived concrete does not mean it is to be won and possessed through any type of analytical or synthetic investigation or through any type of reflection upon the lived concrete. Meaning is to be experienced in living action; and suffering itself, in the unreduced immediacy of the moment. Of course, he who aims at the experiencing of experience will necessarily miss the meaning, for he destroys the spontaneity of the mystery. Only he who stands firm reaches the meaning, without holding back or reservation, before the whole might of reality and answers it in a living way. He is ready to confirm with his life the meaning that he has attained.

Every religious utterance is a vain attempt to do justice to the meaning that has been attained. All religious expression is only an intimation of its attainment. The reply of the people of Israel on Sinai, "We will do it, we will hear it," expresses the decisive with naive and unsurpassable pregnancy. The meaning is found through the engagement of one's own person; it only reveals itself as one takes part in its revelation.

★

All religious reality begins with what biblical religion calls the "fear of God."[6] It comes when our existence between birth and death becomes incomprehensible and uncanny, when all security is shattered through the mystery. This is not the relative mystery of that which is inaccessible only to the present state of human knowledge and is hence in principle discoverable. It is the essential mystery, the inscrutableness of which belongs to its very nature; it is the unknowable. Through this dark gate (which is only a gate and not, as some theologians believe, a dwelling) the believing man steps forth into the everyday that is henceforth hallowed as the place in which he has to live with the mystery. He steps forth, directed and assigned to the concrete, contextual situations of his existence. That he henceforth accepts the situation as given him by the Giver is what biblical religion calls the "fear of God."...

That one accepts the concrete situation as given to him does not, in any way, mean that he must be ready to accept that which meets him as "God-given" in its pure factuality. He may, rather, declare the most extreme enmity toward this happening and treat its "givenness" as only intended to draw forth his own opposing force. But he will not remove himself from the concrete situation as it actually is; he will, instead, enter into it, even if in the form of fighting against it. Whether field of work or field of battle, he accepts the place in which he is placed. He knows no floating of the spirit above concrete reality; to him, even the most sublime spirituality is an illusion if it is not bound to the situation. Only the spirit that is bound to the situation is prized by him as bound to the *pneuma*,[7] the spirit of God.

As an objection to the definition of religion that I have suggested, one might adduce the ascetic tendencies of some religions. However, insofar as they do not weaken the religious itself, these tendencies do not mean any turning away from the lived concrete. The disposition of life and the choice of life elements to be affirmed has changed here. But this change is not in the direction of slackening the relation to the moment, which one is rather seeking to intensify. One desires to rescue the relation to the moment by means of asceticism because one despairs of being able to subjugate the nonascetic elements and, hence, the fullness of life, to the religious. The meaning no longer appears to him as open and attainable in the fullness of life.

The ascetic "elevation" is something entirely different from the philosophical. It is also a form of concretion, though one that is attained through reduction.

★

Philosophizing and philosophy, in contrast, begin ever anew with one definitely looking away from his concrete situation and, hence, with the primary act of abstraction.

What is meant here by abstraction is simple, anthropological matter of fact and not the "radical abstraction" with which Hegel demands that the philosopher begin.[8] Hegel can call the creation of the world an abstraction from nothing, whereas for us it involves precisely the establishment of that concrete reality from which the philosophizing man does and must look away. Hegel can describe "the highest being" as "pure abstraction," whereas the religious man, on the contrary, is certain that in the course of this, his, mortality he can meet God in God's very giving and in his, man's, receiving of the concrete situation. By primary abstraction we mean the inner action in which man lifts himself above the concrete situation into the sphere of precise conceptualization. In this sphere the concepts no longer serve as a means of apprehending reality but, instead, represent being as the object of thought freed from the limitations of the actual.

The decisiveness of this abstraction, of this turning away, is sometimes hidden from sight when a philosopher acts as if he would and could philosophize within his concrete situation. Descartes[9] offers us the clearest example. When we hear him talk in the first person, we feel as if we were hearing the voice of direct personal experience. But it is not so. The I in the Cartesian *ego cogito*[10] is not the living, body–soul person whose corporality had just been disregarded by Descartes as being a matter of doubt. It is the subject of consciousness, supposedly the only function that belongs entirely to our nature. In lived concreteness, in which consciousness is the first violin but not the conductor, *this* ego is not present at all. *Ego cogito* means to Descartes, not simply, "I have consciousness," but "It is I who have consciousness." *Ego cogito* is, therefore, the product of a triply abstracting reflection. Reflection, the "bending back" [*Zurückbiegung*][11] of a person on himself, begins by extracting from what is experienced in the concrete situation "consciousness" (*cogitatio*), which is not as such experienced there at all. It then ascertains that a subject must belong to a consciousness and calls this subject "I." In the end, it identifies the person, this living body–soul person, with that "I," that is, with the abstract and abstractly produced subject of consciousness. Out of the "that" of the concrete situation, which embraces perceiving and that which is perceived, conceiving and that which is conceived, thinking and that which is thought, arises, to begin with, an "I think that." A subject thinks this object. Then the really indispensable "that" (or Something or It) is omitted. Now we reach the statement of the person about himself: Therefore, I (no longer the subject, but the living person who speaks to us) have real existence; for this existence is involved in that *ego*.

In this way Descartes sought, through the method of abstraction, to capture the concrete starting point as knowledge, but in vain. Not through such a deduction but only through genuine intercourse with a Thou can the I of the living person be experienced as existing. The concrete, from which all philosophizing starts, cannot again be reached by way of philosophical abstraction; it is irrecoverable.

Philosophy is entitled, however, to proclaim and to promise as the highest reward of this necessary abstraction a looking upward—no longer a looking here—at the objects of true vision, the "ideas." This conception, prepared for by the Indian teaching of the freeing of the knower from the world of experience, was first fully developed by the Greeks. The Greeks established the hegemony of the sense of sight over the other senses, thus making the optical world into *the* world, into which the data of the other senses are now to be entered. Correspondingly, they also gave to philosophizing, which for the Indian was still only a bold attempt to catch hold of one's own self, an optical character, that is, the character of the contemplation of particular objects. The history of Greek philosophy is that of a visualizing of thought, fully clarified in Plato and perfected in Plotinus.[12] The object of this visual thought is the universal existence or as a reality higher than existence. Philosophy is grounded on the presupposition that one sees the absolute in universals.

In opposition to this, religion, when it has to define itself philosophically, says that it means the covenant of the absolute with the particular, with the concrete. For this reason, the central event of Christian philosophy, the scholastic dispute over the reality or unreality of universals, was in essence a philosophical struggle between religion and philosophy, and that is its lasting significance. In religious-sounding formulas such as

Malebranche's[13] "we see things in God," it is also philosophical abstraction that speaks; for these "things" are not those of the concrete situation but are as general as Platonic ideas ("*les idées intelligibles*"). When, on the contrary, the religious man (or Malebranche no longer as philosophical systematizer but as the religious man that he was) speaks the same sentence, he transforms it. "Things" now do not mean to him archetypes or "perfect essences," but the actual exemplars, the beings and objects with which he, this bodily person, spends his life. When he ventures to say that he sees them in God, he does not speak of looking upward but of looking here. He acknowledges that meaning is open and attainable in the lived concreteness of every moment....

★

Religion, however, is not allowed, even in the face of the most self-confident pride of philosophy, to remain blind to philosophy's great engagement. To this engagement necessarily belongs the actual, ever-recurring renunciation of the original relational bond, of the reality that takes place between I and Thou, of the spontaneity of the moment. Religion must know knowledge not only as a need but also as a duty of man. It must know that history moves along the way of this need and duty—that, Biblically speaking, the eating of the tree of knowledge leads out of Paradise but into the world.

The world—the world as objective and self-contained connection of all being—natural and spiritual, would not exist for us if our thinking, which develops in philosophizing, did not melt together the world *concreta* that are presented to us. It would not exist if our thinking did not merge these world *concreta* with one another and with all that man has ever experienced and comprehended as experienceable. And spirit all the more would not genuinely exist for us as objective connection if thought did not objectify it, if spirit itself as philosophy did not objectify and unite itself. Only through the fact that philosophy radically abandoned the relation with the concrete did that amazing construction of an objective thought continuum become possible, with a static system of concepts and a dynamic one of problems. Every man who can "think" may enter this continuum through the simple use of this ability—through a thinking comprehension of thought. Only through this is there an "objective" mutual understanding, that is, one that does not, like the religious, entail two men, each recognizing the other by the personal involvement in life that he has achieved. Instead, both fulfill a function of thought that demands no involvement in life and bears in fruitful dialectic the tension between the reciprocal ideas and problems.

The religious communication of a content of being takes place in paradox. It is not a demonstrable assertion (theology that pretends to be this is rather a questionable type of philosophy) but a pointing toward the hidden realm of existence of the hearing man himself and that which is to be experienced there and there alone. Artistic communication, which ought not remain unmentioned here, takes place in the *Gestalt*,[14] from which a communicated content cannot be detached and given independent existence. A content of being is objectively communicable and translatable only in and through philosophy and, consequently, only through the objectifying elaboration of the situation.

A skeptical verdict about the ability of philosophy to lead to and contain truth is in no way implied here. The possibility of cogitative truth does not, indeed, mean a cogitative possession of being but a cogitative real relation to being. Systems of thought are manifestations of genuine thought relations to being made possible through abstraction. They are not mere "aspects" but, rather, valid documents of these cogitative voyages of discovery.

A similarity and a difference between the ways in which religion and philosophy affect the person remain to be mentioned.

In religious reality the person has concentrated himself into a whole, for it is only as a unified being that he is able to live religiously. In this wholeness, thought is naturally also included as an autonomous province but one that no longer strives to absolutize its autonomy. A totalization also takes place in genuine philosophers but no unification. Instead, thinking overruns and overwhelms all the faculties and provinces of the person. In a great act of philosophizing, even the fingertips think, but they no longer feel.

★

For man, the existent is either face-to-face being or passive object. The essence of man arises from this twofold relation to the existent. These are not two external phenomena but the two basic modes of existing with being. The child that calls to his mother and the child that watches his mother or—to give a more exact example—the child that silently speaks to his mother by simply looking into her eyes and the same child that looks at something on the mother as at any other object, show the twofoldness in which man stands and remains standing. Something of the sort is sometimes even noticed in those near death. What is apparent here is the double structure of human existence itself. Because these are the two basic modes of our existence with being, they are the two basic modes of our existence in general—I–Thou and I–It. I–Thou finds its highest intensity and transfiguration in religious reality, in which unlimited Being becomes, as absolute person, my partner. I–It finds its highest concentration and illumination in philosophical knowledge. In this knowledge the extraction of the subject from the I of the immediate lived togetherness of I and It and the transformation of the It into the object detached in its essence produce the exact thinking of contemplated existing beings; yes, of contemplated Being itself.

According to Franz Rosenzweig, divine truth, wishes to be implored "with both hands"—that of philosophy and that of theology. "He who prays with the double prayer of the believer and the unbeliever," he continues, "to him it will not deny itself."[15] . . .

The religious reality of the meeting with the Meeter, who shines through all forms and is Himself formless, knows no image of Him, nothing comprehensible as object. It knows only the presence of the Present One. Symbols of Him, whether images or ideas, always exist first when and insofar as Thou becomes He, and that means It. But the ground of human existence in which it gathers and becomes whole is also the deep abyss out of which images arise. Symbols of God come into being, some that allow themselves to be fixed in lasting visibility even in earthly material and some that tolerate no other sanctuary than that of the soul. Symbols supplement one another; they merge; they are set before the community of believers in plastic or theological forms. And God, we may surmise, does not despise all these similarly and necessarily untrue images but, rather, suffers that one look at Him through them. Yet they always quickly desire to be more than they are—more than signs and pointers toward Him. Finally, time and again they swell themselves up and obstruct the way to Him, and He removes Himself from them. Then comes round the hour of the philosopher, who rejects both the image and the God that it symbolizes, and opposes to it the pure idea, which he even at times understands as the negation of all metaphysical ideas. This critical "atheism" (*Atheoi* is the name that the Greeks gave to those who denied the traditional gods) is the prayer that is spoken in the third person in the form of speech about an idea. It is the prayer of the philosopher to the again unknown God. It is well suited to arouse religious men and to impel them to set forth right across the God-deprived reality to a new meeting. On their way they destroy the images that manifestly no longer do justice to God. The spirit that moved the philosopher also moves them.

Notes

Source: "Religion and Philosophy" (lecture, 1951). Maurice Friedman, trans., first in *Eclipse of God: Studies in the Relation between Religion and Philosophy* (New York: Harper, 1952), pp. 25–46. The German version appeared first in *Gottesfinsternis: Betrachtungen zur Beziehung zwischen Religion und Philosophie* (Zurich: Manesse, 1953).

Editor's note: On his first trip to America (1951–52), Buber was invited to lecture at a number of institutions, including the Jewish Theological Seminary in New York, the School of Judaism in Los Angeles, the College of Jewish Studies in Chicago, as well as at the University of Chicago, Stanford, Princeton, Yale, and Columbia. "Religion and Philosophy" was one of the lectures delivered during this trip. Buber had already given an earlier version of it, however, at the Frankfurt Schopenhauer Society in 1929 (published in the 16. Jahrbuch der Schopenhauer–Gesellschaft für das Jahr 1929, Heidelberg, 1929).

1. Epicurus of Samos (approx. 341–271 B.C.E.), radical exponent of philosophical skepticism and hedonism. In Rabbinic literature, often synonymous with heretic ("*apikores*").
2. Protagoras (approx. 490–430 B.C.E.), first Sophist.
3. Heraclitus of Ephesus (approx. 540–480 B.C.E.), pre-Socratic philosopher best known for his cryptic style and radical relativism. The quote is from the famous passage "Heraclitus at the Kitchener," fragment DK 22 A 9 in the Diels/Kranz edition (Jaap Mansfeld, trans. and ed., *Die Vorsokratiker* [Stuttgart: Philipp Reclam, 1983], p. 283).
4. Ibid., Fragment DK 22 B 32.
5. Cf. The Faith of Judaism (1929) (p. 102 in this volume).
6. Buber echoes one of the morning stanzas of the Siddur: "The beginning of wisdom is the fear of God" (Ps. 111:10).

7. Greek: spirit; in the Septuagint also Holy Spirit.
 8. Georg W. F. Hegel (1770–1871): Last major exponent of German idealism, author of *Phenomenology of Spirit* (1807). The "abstractness" of his philosophical system was criticized especially by Søren Kierkegaard and the philosophical existentialists of the twentieth century (including Franz Rosenzweig).
 9. René Descartes (1596–1650), French-born philosopher associated with rationalism and often called the father of modern philosophy, lived and worked mostly in Holland. Buber is referring to Descartes's *Meditationes de Prima Philosophia* (1641).
10. Latin: I am thinking. Founding principle of Descartes's philosophy.
11. Cf. Dialogue (1932) (p. 198 in this volume).
12. Plotinus (204–270 C.E.), founder of neo-Platonism and author of the *Enneads*. Buber is taking issue with Plotin's concept of *theoria* (on-looking) as developed especially in his third Ennead.
13. Nicolas Malebranche (1638–1715), French Catholic theologian and Cartesian philosopher. Author of *De la Recherche de la Verité* (1674), later expanded by the *Ecclairissements*, in which he developed the idea of a vision in God.
14. German: form, figure, shape. The term is to be understood in the context of *Gestalttheorie*.
15. Franz Rosenzweig (1886–1929), German-Jewish philosopher, author of *The Star of Redemption* (1921). The passage is from *The Star of Redemption*, trans. William Hallo (New York: Holt, Rinehart and Winston, 1970), p. 104. For a further discussion of this passage see Paul Mendes-Flohr, "Franz Rosenzweig's Concept of Philosophical Faith," in *Leo Baeck Institute Yearbook* 34 (1989), pp. 257–369. My thanks to Paul Mendes-Flohr for pointing me to the source.

Teaching and Deed (1934)*

Among all peoples, two kinds and lines of propagation exist side by side; for quite as continuous as the biological line and parallel to it, in the words of the philosopher Rudolf Pannwitz,[1] is the line of "the propagation of values." Just as organic life is transmitted from parents to children and guarantees the survival of the community, so the transmission and reception—the new begetting and new birth of the spirit—goes on uninterruptedly. The life of the spirit of a people is renewed whenever a teaching generation transmits it to a learning generation which, in turn—as learners grow into teachers—transmits the spirit through the lips of new teachers to the ears of new pupils; yet this process of education involves the person as a whole, just as in physical propagation.

In Judaism, this cycle of propagation involves another peculiar factor. In Israel of old, the propagation of values itself assumed an organic character and penetrated the natural life of the people. It is true that it does not imitate biological reproduction in guaranteeing the survival of the community as such; it only guarantees its survival as Israel. But can we drown out the voice that tells us that if our life as Israel were to come to an end we could not go on living as one of the nations? We, and we alone, once received both life and the teachings at once, and the selfsame hour became a nation and a religious community. Since then, the transmission of life and the teachings have been bound together, and we consider the spiritual transmission as vital as bodily propagation.

The Talmudic sages say, "He who teaches the tradition to his fellow man is regarded as though he had formed and made him, and brought him into the world. As it is said (Jer. 15:19), 'And if thou bring forth the precious out of the vile, thou shalt be as My mouth.'" In this quotation from the Bible, God summons the prophet, who has just begged for help to wreak vengeance on his foes, to the turning, to the conquest of his

---

* Address delivered at the Frankfurt Lehrhaus in 1934.

own hatred and repugnance, and promises him that if he turns he shall be allowed adequately to fulfill a divine action. And the "forming" [*Bilden*] and the "making" of the child in the womb (Jer. 1:5; Ps. 139:15) are counted among such divine action. The influence of the teacher upon the pupil—of the right teacher upon the right pupil—is not merely compared to, but even set on a par with, divine works that are linked with the human, maternal act of giving birth. The inner turning of the prophet is an actual rebirth, and the educator, who brings the precious ore in the soul of his pupil to light and frees it from dross, affords him a second birth—birth into a loftier life. Spirit begets and gives birth; spirit is begotten and born; spirit becomes body.

Even today, in spite of all deterioration [*Entartung*], the spiritual life of Jewry is not merely a superstructure, a nonobligatory transfiguration, or an object of pride that imposes no duties. Rather, it is a binding and obligatory power, but one that attains to earthly, bodily reality only through that which it binds to the obligations of Jewish spiritual life. So profoundly is the spirit here merged with the physical life that even the survival of the community in time can be guaranteed only by both operating together.

But if we are serious about the simile of generation, we must realize that in spiritual as well as in physical propagation it is not the same thing that is passed on, but something that acquires newness in the very act of transmission. For tradition does not consist in letting contents and forms pass on, finished and inflexible, from generation to generation. The values live on in the host who receives them by letting them become part of his very flesh, for they choose and assume his body as the new form that suits the function of the new generation. A child does not represent the sum total of his parents; the child is something that has never been before, something quite unpredictable. Similarly, a generation can only receive the teachings in the sense that it renews them. We do not take unless we also give. In the living tradition it is not possible to draw a line between preserving and producing. The work of embodiment takes place spontaneously; and the person is honest and faithful who utters words he has never heard as though they had come to him; for it is thus—and not as if he had "created" them—that such words live within him. Everyone is convinced that he is doing no more than further advancing that which has advanced him to this point, and he may, nonetheless, be the originator of a new movement.

... What matters is that time and again an older generation, staking its entire existence on that act, comes to a younger one with the desire to teach, waken, and shape it; then the holy spark leaps across the gap. Transmitted content and form are subordinate to the tradition of existence as such [*Seins-Tradition*] and become valid only because of it....

We have already indicated that in our case[2] teaching is inseparably bound up with doing. Here, if anywhere, it is impossible to teach or to learn without living. The teachings must not be treated as a collection of knowable material; they resist such treatment. Either the teachings live in the life of a responsible human being, or they are not alive at all. The teachings do not center in themselves; they do not exist for their own sake. They refer to, they are directed toward, the deed. In this connection the concept of "deed" does not, of course, connote "activism," but life that realizes the teachings in the changing potentialities of every hour.

Among all the nations in the world, Israel is probably the only one in which wisdom that does not lead directly to the unity of knowledge and deed is meaningless. This becomes most evident when we compare the biblical concept of *hokhmah* with the Greek concept of *sophia*. The latter specifies a closed realm of thought—knowledge for its own sake. It is totally alien to the *hokhmah,* which regards such a delimitation of an independent spiritual sphere, governed by its own laws, as the misconstruction of meaning, the violation of continuity, the severance of thought from reality.

The supreme command of *hokhmah* is the unity of teaching and life, for only through this unity can we recognize and avow the all-embracing unity of God. In the light of our doctrine, He who gives life and gives that life meaning is wronged by a teaching that is satisfied with and delights in itself, which rears structures, however monumental, above life, and yet does not succeed in wresting even a shred of realization out of all the outer and inner obstacles we must struggle with in every precarious hour of our lives. For our God makes only one demand upon us. He does not expect a humanly unattainable completeness and perfection, but only the willingness to do as much as we possibly can "with all your heart" [Deut. 6:6] at every single instant.

Therefore, to the instruction [*Weisung*] to "study" the laws and judgments, the task is added to "do" them as well (Deut. 5:1). To know the laws and judgments is only of value if, and to the extent as the impulse to action [*Tatantrieb*] is grounded in reality. It is said in the Talmud (Jevamot 109), "He who always says only the teaching counts... his teaching will not count." One cannot legitimately *have* spirit but only live it.[3]

Man is a creature able to make spirit independent of physical life, and the great danger is that he may tolerate and even sanction existence on two different levels: (1) up above and fervently adored, the habitation of the spirit; and (2) down below, the dwelling of urges and petty concerns, equipped with a fairly good conscience acquired in hours of meditation in the upper story.

The teachings do not rely on the hope that he who knows them will also observe them. Socratic man believes that all virtue is cognition, and that all that is needed to do what is right is to know what is right. This does not hold for Mosaic man, who is informed with the profound experience that cognition is never enough, that the deepest part of him must be seized by the teachings, that for realization to take place his elemental totality must submit to the spirit as clay to the potter.

Here dualism is fought with the utmost vigor. "One who studies with a different intent than to act," says the Talmud, "it would have been more fitting for him never to have been created."[4] It is bad to have teaching without the deed, and worse when the teaching is one of action. Living in the detached spirit is evil, and worse when the spirit is one of ethos. Again and again, from the Sayings of the Fathers down to the definitive formulation of Hasidism, the simple man who acts is given preference over the scholar whose knowledge is not expressed in deeds. "He whose deeds exceed his wisdom, his wisdom shall endure; but he whose wisdom exceeds his deeds, his wisdom shall not endure."[5] And in the same vein: "He whose wisdom exceeds his deeds—what does he resemble? A tree with many boughs and few roots. A wind, springing up, uproots it, and overturns it. But he whose deeds exceed his wisdom—what does he resemble? A tree with few boughs but many roots. Though all the winds in the world come and blow at it, it cannot be budged."[6] What counts is not the extent of spiritual possessions, not the thoroughness of knowledge nor the keenness of thought, but to know what one knows and to believe what one believes so directly that it can be translated into the life one lives.

I repeat that in Judaism the true value of the deed has nothing to do with "activism." Nothing is more remote from Judaism than the glorification of self-confident virtue. But Judaism knows that *true* autonomy is one with true theonomy: God wants man to fulfill his commands as a human being and with the quality peculiar to human beings. The law is not thrust upon man; it rests deep within him, to waken when the call comes.... In Jewry, the way that leads to that promised time—the way of man's contribution to ultimate fulfillment—is trodden whenever one generation encounters the next—whenever the generation that has reached its full development transmits the teachings to the generation that is still in the process of developing—so that the teachings spontaneously waken to new life in the new generation.

We live in an age when deeds tend to assert their superiority over the teachings. The present generation universally believes more and more unreservedly that it can get along without the teachings and rely on a mode of action that—in its own opinion—is correct.... But I know that we, who believe that there can be no teaching apart from doing, will be destroyed when our doing becomes independent of the teachings.

A Jewish house of study—that is a declaration of war upon all those who imagine they can be Jews and live a Jewish life outside of the teachings, who think by cutting off the propagation of values to accomplish something salutary for Jewry. A truly Jewish communal life cannot develop in Palestine if the continuity of Judaism is interrupted. Let me reiterate that such continuity does not imply the preservation of the old, but the ceaseless begetting and giving birth to the same single spirit and its continuous integration into life. Do not let us delude ourselves: Once we are content to perpetuate biological substance and a "civilization" springing from it, we shall not be able to maintain even such a civilization. For the land and the language in themselves will not support our body and soul on earth—only land and language when linked to the holy origin and the holy destination. Moreover, in this crisis of humanity in which we stand at the most exposed point, the Diaspora cannot preserve its vital connection, which has so long defied history's attempt at severance, without recognizing and renewing the power that the teachings possess, a power strong enough to overcome all corroding forces. For all that which is merely social, merely national, merely religious, and therefore lacking the fiery breath of the teachings, is involved in the abysmal problem of the hour and does not suffice to ward off decay. Only the teachings truly rejuvenated can liberate us from limitations and bind us to the unconditional, so that spiritualized and spirited, united within the circle of the eternal union, we may recognize one another and ourselves and, empowered by the fathomless laws of history, hold out against the powers moving on the surface of history.

Concerning the words of Isaac, the patriarch, "The voice is the voice of Jacob, but the hands are the hands of Esau" (Gen. 27:22), the *Midrash* tells this story: Delegates of the other nations were once dispatched to a Greek sage to ask him how the Jews could be subjugated. This is what he said to them: "Go and walk past their houses of prayer and of study... So long as the voice of Jacob rings from their houses of prayer and study, they will not be surrendered into the hands of Esau. But if not, the hands are Esau's and you will overcome them."[7]

The teachings cannot be severed from the deed, but neither can the deeds be severed from the teachings! Our tradition assigned quite as much importance to the one danger as to the other. The Talmud tells us that at a gathering of sages the question arose as to which was greater, deeds or teachings. And one of them, who seemed to share our point of view, said that deeds were greater. But Rabbi Akiba said, "The teachings are greater!" And all agreed, saying, "The teachings are greater, for the teachings beget the deed."[8] This sounds like a contradiction of the assertions of the importance of action. But after we have pondered these assertions more deeply, we comprehend that the teachings are central and that they are the gate through which we must pass to enter life. It is true that simple souls can live the true life without learning, provided they are linked to God. But this is possible only because the teachings that represent just such a link to God have, although [these souls] are unaware of it, become the very foundation of their existence. To do the right thing in the right way, the deed must spring from the bond with Him who commands us. Our link with Him is the beginning, and the function of the teachings is to make us aware of our bond and make it fruitful.

Again, we are confronted with the concepts of continuity and spontaneity, the bond of transmission and begetting. The teachings themselves are the way. Their full content is not comprehended in any book, in any code, or in any formulation. Nothing that has ever existed is broad enough to show what they are. That they may live and bring forth life, generations must continue to meet, and the teachings assume the form of a human link, awakening and activating our common bond with our Father. The spark that leaps from him who teaches to him who learns rekindles a spark of the fire that lifted the mountain of revelation "to the very heart of heaven."

Notes

Source: "Die Lehre und die Tat" (address delivered at the Frankfurt Lehrhaus in 1934), first in *Jüdische Rundschau* 39, no. 6 (19 January 1934). Olga Marx, trans., in *Israel and the World: Essays in a Time of Crisis* (New York: Schocken, 1948), pp. 137–45.

Editor's note: In 1933, the Frankfurt Jewish Lehrhaus resumed its program under Buber's leadership in an effort to sustain Jewish life under the mounting duress of the National Socialist regime (see Introduction, p. 10f). Given the historical context and the specifically Jewish concern, "Teaching and Deed" seems to be set apart from Buber's discussion on philosophy and religion. The distinction between *sophia* and *hokhmah,* however, is essential to Buber's understanding of the relationship between philosophical and religious thinking.

1. Rudolf Pannwitz (1881–1969), German philosopher of culture, strongly influenced by Nietzsche. Author of *Dionysische Tragödien* (1913) and *Die Krisis der Europäischen Kultur* (1917). Buber is referring to the volume, *On Education* (1909), that Pannwitz contributed to Buber's series, *Die Gesellschaft*.
2. In the case of Jewish learning and adult education.
3. This paragraph is not in O. Marx.
4. Palestinian Talmud, Shabbat 3b (M.B.).
5. Pirkei Avot (Sayings of the Fathers) 3:12.
6. Pirkei Avot 3:22.
7. Bereshit Rabbah (Midrashic commentary) on Gen. 27:22 (M.B.).
8. Kiddushin 40b (M.B.).

PART VI
Community

Comments on the Idea of Community (1931)

The ambiguity of the concept that is employed is greater here than anywhere else. One says, for example, that socialism is the passing of the control over the means of production from the hands of the entrepreneur into that of the collective; but everything depends on what one means by collective. If it is what we are accustomed to calling the state, that is, an institution in which an essentially unstructured mass lets its business be conducted by a so-called representation, then in a socialist society essentially this will have changed—that the workers will feel themselves to be represented by the possessors of the power of the disposal of the means of production. But what is representation? Is it not in the all too far-reaching "allowing oneself to be represented" that the worst defect of modern society lies? And in a socialist society will not the economic "letting oneself be represented" be added to the political so that only then for the first time the almost unlimited being represented and thereby the almost unlimited central accumulation of power will predominate? But the more a human group lets itself be represented in the determination of its common affairs and the more from outside, so much less does community life exist in it, and so much poorer in community does it become. For community—not the primitive but that which is possible and suitable for men of today—proclaims itself above all in the common active handling of the common and cannot endure without it.

The primal hope of all history depends upon a genuine and, hence, thoroughly communally disposed [*gemeinschaftshaltig*] community of the human race. Fictitious, counterfeit, a planet-size lie would be the unity that was not established out of real communal living of smaller and larger groups that dwell or work together and out of their reciprocal relationships. Everything depends, therefore, upon the collective, into whose hands the control over the means of production will pass, making possible and demanding by its structure and its institutions real communal living of manifold groups—indeed that these groups themselves become the true subjects of the process of production; thus, that the mass be as articulated and, in its articulations (the various communes), be as powerful as the common economy of mankind affords; thus, that the centralistic "letting oneself be represented" only extend as far as the new order absolutely demands. The inner question of destiny does not take the form of a fundamental "either/or:" It is the question of the legitimating, ever newly drawn demarcation line—the thousandfold system of demarcation lines between the realms that it is necessary to centralize and those that it is necessary to liberate—between the law of unity and the claim of community....

For the sake of this, its life meaning, all sentimentality, all exaggeration, and overenthusiasm must be kept far from our thinking about community. Community is never mood, and even where it is feeling, it is always the feeling of a state of existence [*Verfassung*]. Community is the inner constitution of a common life that knows and embraces the parsimonious "account," the opposing "accident," the suddenly invading "care." It is commonness of need and only from this commonness of spirit; commonness of trouble and only from this commonness of salvation. Even the community that calls the spirit its master and salvation its promise, the "religious," is only community when it serves its master in the unselective, unexalted simple reality that it has not chosen for itself, that rather, just thus, has been sent; only when it prepares the way for its promise through the brambles of this pathless hour. Certainly, "works" are not required, but the work of faith is required. It is only truly a community of faith when it is a community of work.

The real essence of community is undoubtedly to be found in the fact—manifest or hidden—that it has a center. The real origin of community is undoubtedly only to be understood by the fact that its members have a common relationship to the center, superior to all other relations: The circle is drawn from the radii, not from the points of the periphery. And undoubtedly, the primal reality of the center cannot be known if it is not known as transparent into the divine. But the more earthly, the more creaturely, the more bound a character the circle takes, so much the truer and the more transparent it is. The "social" belongs to it; not as a subdivision but as the world of authentication, in which the truth of the center proves itself. The early Christians were not satisfied with the communes that were next to or above the world, and they went into the desert so as to have no community except that with God and no more disturbing world. But it was shown to them that God does not will that man be alone with Him, and above the holy impotence of solitude grew the brotherly order. Finally, overstepping the realm of Benedict, Francis established the bond with the creatures.

Yet a community does not need to be founded. When historical destiny put a human band in a common nature and life space, there was space for the development of a genuine commune; and no altar of a city god was necessary in the center if the inhabitants knew themselves to be united for the sake of and through the unnameable. A living and ever-renewed togetherness was given and needed only to be developed in the immediacy of all relationships. The common concerns were deliberated and decided in common—in the most favorable cases not through representatives but in the gathering in the marketplace, and the unification experienced in public radiated out into each personal contact....

But, objectors tell me, that is now quite irrecoverable. The modern city has no agora,[1] and modern man has no time for the transactions of which he can be relieved by his chosen representatives. A concrete togetherness is already destroyed by the compulsion of quantity and the form of organization. Work joins one person to another more than leisure does; sport does so more than politics do. Day and soul are tidily divided. But the ties are just factual; people pursue common interests and tendencies and have no use for "immediacy." Collectivity is no intimate crouching down together but a great economic or political union of forces, unproductive for romantic play of the imagination but comprehensible as numbers, expressing itself in actions and effects to which the individual may belong without intimacies but in consciousness of his energetic contribution. Those "bonds" that resist the inevitable development must dissolve. There is still the family, to be sure, which as a "house community" appears to demand and guarantee a measure of living life together; but it too will emerge out of the crisis into which it has entered as a union for a purpose, or it will disappear.

In opposition to this mixture of correct evidence and distorted conclusions, I espouse the rebirth of the commune. Rebirth, not restoration. It cannot be restored, in fact, although it seems to me that each breath of neighborliness in the apartment building, each wave of a warmer comradeship during the rest period in the highly rationalized factory, means a growth of communal-mindedness of the world, and although at times an upright village commune pleases me more than a parliament. It cannot be restored. But whether a rebirth of the commune takes place out of the waters and the spirit of the approaching transformation of society— by this, it seems to me, the lot of the human species will be determined. An organic communal being—and only such is suitable for a formed and articulated mankind—will never be erected out of individuals, only out of small and the smallest communities: A people is community to the extent that it is communally disposed.

If the family does not emerge from the crisis, which today appears like ruin, purified and renewed, then the form of statehood will end up being only a furnace that will be fueled with the bodies of the generations. The commune that can be renewed in such a manner exists only as a residue. If I speak of a rebirth, I do not think of a continuing, but of a changed world situation. By the new communes—one could also call them new fellowships—I mean the subject of the transformed economy, the collective into whose hands the control over the means of production shall pass. Once again, everything depends upon whether they will be made ready—whether they will *be* ready.

... The relation of centralism and decentralization is a problem that, as has been said, is to be dealt with not fundamentally but, like everything that concerns the traffic of the idea, with reality, with the great tact of the spirit, with the untiring weighing of the legitimate "how much." Centralization, yes, but only as much as must be centralized according to the conditions of the time and the place; if the high court that is summoned to the drawing and redrawing of the line of demarcation remains awake in its conscience, then the division between base and apex of the power pyramid will be entirely different from today's, even in states that call themselves communist, which certainly still means striving for community. A system of representation must also exist in the form of society that I have in mind; but it will not present itself, like those of today, in the seeming representation of amorphous masses of voters but in the work-tested representatives of economic communities. The represented will not be bound with their representatives in empty abstractions—through the phraseology of a party program, as today—but concretely, through common activity and common experience.

But the most essential must be that the process of the formation of community must continue into the relations of the communities to each other. Only a community of communities may be called a communal being.

The picture that I have hastily sketched will be put on the shelf of "utopian socialism" until the storm turns over the leaves again. Just as I do not believe in Marx's "gestation" of the new form of society, so I do not believe in Bakunin's[2] virgin birth out of the womb of the revolution. But I believe in the meeting of image and destiny in the plastic hour.

Notes

Source: "Bemerkungen zur Gemeinschaftsidee" (from an address at the Arbeitswoche on the Comburg), first in *Kommende Gemeinde* 3, no. 2 [July 1931]. Maurice Friedman, trans., in *A Believing Humanism: My Testament 1902–1965* [New York: Simon & Schuster, 1967], pp. 87–92.

1. Marketplace and center of ancient Greek and Roman cities.
2. Mikhail Aleksandrovitch Bakunin (1814–1876), Principal ideologue of Russian populism and communism. A revolutionary thinker, influenced by Fichte, Feuerbach, and Comte, Bakunin advocated the total destruction of the "positive" order by forces of negation. His essay "Die Reaktion in Deutschland," which appeared in Arnold Ruge's *Deutsche Jahrbücher* (1942), became standard reference for German anarchists. Radical communist Zionists, too, referred to Bakunin as a model (e.g., Yitzhak Tabenkin, 1887–1971).

Community (1919)

It is the most mature insight of recent sociology as a genetic self-discovery of contemporary mankind that the modern culture of the West has moved from community toward society, that a mechanical way of living together has infiltrated and disintegrated the organic way.[1] Community is the expression and manifestation of an original, naturally homogeneous, relation-bearing will that represents the totality of mankind; society [is the expression and manifestation] of a differentiated, profit-seeking [will] that is generated by detached thought and removed from the totality [of mankind].... Community is grown relatedness [*Verbundenheit*], welded together by common possession (predominantly soil), common work, common customs, common belief; society means regulated segregation, held together externally by force, contract, convention, or public opinion.... The medieval city represents the first in its basic form; the modern mega city, the second. The first is the monumental, dome-like grown attempt "to organize a close-knit association of mutual help and support for consumption and production, and for the entire social life, without, however, binding the individual with the shackles of the state but, rather, under complete protection of the creative expressions of a particular group of individuals."[2] The second is but a structured unity in a mechanical light; in truth, a mass of "numerous free individuals who repeatedly come in contact with each other during interaction, who exchange and cooperate without, however, any community and communal will arising in their midst other than a sporadic remnant of an earlier, still lingering condition."[3] ...

At this point, modern socialism in its dominant form enters the scene. It aims at overcoming the atomization and amorphization of contemporary life by granting the state an all-encompassing power that regulates work and [social] interaction in a uniform fashion. This kind of socialism views itself as bearer and fulfiller of an evolution. But the evolution it tries to promote and complete is only the course leading from community into society. For what is left from the *autonomy of organic will* is bound to be consumed by the effects of this movement.... This is not to be considered error or failure; rather, it is the immanent logic of a historical ideology. To be sure, socialism wants to rebuild society from the blueprints of justice, but if the laws of spirit were to become all-controlling statutes of an all-powerful state, then, as an inevitable result of their rule, the rare flower of free, soul-filled justice would become extinct. The state of common irrationality that we have lived in until now was a feverish tyrant whose cramps and suffering caused the destruction of millions,[4] but in whose midst, removed from its power and unnoticed, the holy child of community survived in hidden unions and comradeships. Once it reached unlimited sovereignty, however, a socialist state would be like a dim-eyed, indifferent master in whose territories, to be sure, no exploitation of man by man, no humiliation of those born to be means to themselves would be tolerated, but in whose territories, at the same time, there would also no longer be room and refuge for community....

Is the decline of community, then, an inescapable evolution? Or is there a way of return?...

It is a fact that we who have gone through the age of individualism, that is, the separation of the person from its natural social connex, can no longer find our way back to the original life of community. For [this original life] was not a union of separate individuals, but a whole that presented itself as binding together the manifoldness of individuals with strong and untouchable holy bonds, just as in great poems the verse is not a stringing together of words, but the other way round: The words are an untangling of the original unity of the verse. To such elementary wholeness we cannot return. But we can advance to a different, creative unity that, though it is not *grown* like the first, can still be *created* from true soul material and is, therefore, no less authentic....

Both community and society are expressions and formulations of willpower. We no longer possess the will for totality [*Totalwille*] in its natural form, for we have irrecoverably lost its vegetative unity. But is it not true that in the purest hours of our life we feel the buried energies breaking forth to create a unity born from spirit, to gather behind a new, vitally conscious will for totality?...

Looking at an evolution of doom only helps strengthen our determination—as paradoxical as it might seem to the historical worldview—to contribute to the making of an inner turning, of a true revolution. Against the socialism that strives to advance and fulfill this [historical] evolution, we pit a different socialism that wants to resolve and overcome it. If the first socialism is the product of the ideological climax in a great social process, then the second shall be the preparation and announcement of a great religious process. It is not the first time for religious forces to proffer renewal and redemption in a social crisis.

For it is not *one* movement that rises against the present intoxication and obsession with power, but two very different ones: The first is a movement aboveground [*oberirdisch*], visible and effective, clearly stating its goal, and based upon the primacy of an economy that can orderly satisfy human needs.... The other is a movement underground [*unterirdisch*], apparent only to the probing eye, still unfelt in the material world, stammering a miraculous dream, and based upon the primacy of a spirit that bespeaks a creative human longing for God, a longing that is grounded in the striving of all authentic mankind for true community as the revelation of a once more unknown God.... The first [movement] will seize control of the state and replace its institutions with new ones, thinking that this will transform human relations at their core. The second knows that new public institutions can only be effective if they can promote, clarify, and generally enable the transformation of real life between man and man. Real life between man and man, however, does not occur in the abstractness of the state but, in essence, only where a vitality of spiritual togetherness exists in space, function, and feeling: in the community; in the village and city, at work and in cooperatives, in comradeship, and in religious unification. Today, this real life is suppressed and pushed aside. A homonculus called state has sucked the communities dry.... The communities of the village and the city have shrunk into an apparatus of administration, the cooperative into the tool of an economic party; comradeship has become a club, and religious unification the parish of a church. To all of them we have to restore blood, power, and valid reality. It is necessary to liberate the real life between man and man. Society, today, is an organism of dying cells, a ghostly fact that is obscured by the reliable functionality of the highly sophisticated parts in a pseudo-organic mechanism—the state.... Only from within, through the revival of cell tissue, can healing and renewal begin. Community in all its manifestations must be replenished with reality, with the reality of immediate, pure, and just relations between man and man, between men and men, so that true communal existence can develop from the coexistence of true communities while the rusty wheelwork [of society] is falling apart, piece by piece....

What is needed is the liberation of real life between men and men. What is needed is the rebirth of community.... Only there can the inner bonds of pristine community, namely, common land, common work, common custom, common belief—the four principles of bonding that represent the four types of community—be tied together in a new form. Not state, but only community can be the legitimate subject of common land; not state, but only cooperative can be the subject of common production; not in society, but only in comradeship can new custom grow; not in the church, but only in brotherhoods can new faith ripen.

This requires a free space for the communities and an unchallenged validity of their will within the natural environment. It requires unlimited freedom of action within the limits of its natural duties: true autonomy that is only limited between the communities and above the communities, that has boundaries only where the matter is common to more than one community and requires deliberation, decision, and administration—to be carried out best in a system of equated representation.

In the present state, however, this free space and autonomy of communities—which in its innermost sense equals an autonomy of organic spheres of will—would never have been recognized; even less so in a socialist state, which is a strictly centralized, perfect mechanism that would not dare to pronounce its own decentralization for the sake of an organic [community]. Only the state that is in the process of becoming a socialist state... will have to pay heed to the strong demands of socialist communities—communities of people who are willing to live and work commonly. But to be heard, these communities first will have to be truly willing.

Autonomy cannot be decreed. It cannot be erected in any other way than by a growing and self-assertive communal existence, elevating itself from fictitious to real being....

For all this to be achieved, however, men and groups of men will have to renounce many a private advantage and privilege for the sake of community, and to offer their entire working capacity to a communal economy. What is necessary, therefore, is the unheard of: that men and groups of men *want* the community from the depths of their souls....

This, however, is the problem of our time, where community dissolves into society: That man, if he participates in public life, in the *res publica*, does so fictitiously, without being in relation.... When, for instance, a circle of intellectuals explains and defends the transformation of human relations with dialectical passion while, at the same time, its members converse only indirectly and without real knowledge of each other, as is so common among intellectuals today, then this circle will not be able to influence social reality any more than its own reality [as a group]. The truthfulness of one's political beliefs is established only in one's natural, "unpolitical" sphere. There, the seeds of true communal power are to be found. To the illuminating Hasidic teaching that every man is in charge of his immediate environment, to redeem it, should be added that no shorter way than this leads to the redemption of the world....

Regardless of how passionately modern men long for community—they do not seem to have the power to reach it.... There is only one who can do it: the eternal spirit of turning, who overcomes evolution; the One, who alone gives perplexed man what he needs in the hour of darkest plight—human longing for God [*Gottwollen*].

And it is this spirit that is meant by the immortal, once more subterraneous movement, apparent only to the probing eye, unfelt still in the material world, stammering a miraculous dream. Again, it means longing for God—the spirit of turning.

Human will can turn what appears as human fate, but only if it is directed toward the fact that God is. For only then is God's will with it....

Human longing for God and divine longing for man cannot be separated. If human will proclaims the freedom to will God in a world of determination, then divine freedom is with man. Turning has a double countenance; and one of the two is the countenance of willing mankind.

Theophanies resemble each other in the mystery of their becoming; but in the mystery of their being, they are different. Here it becomes obvious to the highest extent that history is still a process of truth and purpose. For the Divine wants to ripen within mankind.... We feel its presence sprout whenever man truly reaches out for the hand of man, but we sense that it can grow from experience [*Erlebnis*] to life only in true community.

Men who long for community long for God. All craving for real relationship points to God; and all craving for God points to real community. But craving God is not the same as willing God. Men search for God but cannot find Him, for He is "not there." Men want to possess God, but God does not give Himself to them, for He does not wish to be possessed but to be realized. Only when men want God to be will they practice community.

The ultimate plight calls for a will for God; for the spirit of turning.

Notes

Source: "Gemeinschaft," first in *Worte an die Zeit. Eine Schriftenreihe von Martin Buber,* Volume 2 (Munich: Dreiländerverlag, 1919). Trans., Asher Biemann, for this volume.

Editor's note: In the aftermath of World War I and the assassination of his longtime friend Gustav Landauer (1870–1919) during the Bavarian Revolution, Buber turned to the publisher, Kurt Wolff, with the idea of a series, *Worte an die Zeit,* devoted to the conception of a new society (or community). In 1919, two short volumes of the series appeared; the first entitled *Grundsätze* (Foundations), and the second, *Gemeinschaft* (Community), both written by Buber himself. Gemeinschaft is the first essay that Buber devoted explicitly to this subject since his speech, "Alte und neue Gemeinschaft" of 1901.

1. The distinction was made by the German sociologist Ferdinand Tönnies (1855–1936) in his work *Gemeinschaft und Gesellschaft* (Leipzig, 1887; Charles Loomis, trans., *Community and Society* [New Brunswick: Transaction Books, 1988]). In the original version of "Gemeinschaft" Buber uses Tönnies as motto: "And now that all of culture has turned into social and governmental civilization, the transformed culture itself comes to an end..." (cf. Tönnies, *Community and Society,* p. 231).
2. Buber is referring to Pyotr Alekseyevitch Kropotkin (1842–1921), the founder of anarchist communism, influenced by the work of Mikhail Bakunin (1814–1876).
3. Cf. Tönnies, *Community and Society,* pp. 64f.; 76.
4. Buber is writing still under the impression of World War I.

How Can Community Happen? (1930)*

Delegates of the Jewish youth in Germany! You have called on me to attempt an answer to your question of how community can happen. You have not called on me to give you a nice sermon; and I shall appeal to Rabbi Baruch, the grandson of the Baal-Shem, who, when a guest heard him speak and said, "Rabbi, you speak so beautifully," replied, "I should rather be mute than speak beautifully." ...

Your question may have emerged from a present crisis in your membership group; but it also touches upon a question that concerns the world—upon a deep yearning of the world. The world yearns to become a community.... World and humankind are predisposed by creation alone to become a community.

If we try to grasp the great religious term—perhaps the greatest religious term pointing toward the world, "*malkhut shamayim*[1]—the kingdom of the heavens," from below, that is, from the perspective of our lives, then its meaning is that the world, humankind, is destined to become a true, lasting, and all-embracing community. Thus, it is promised to the world and humankind, and thus the world and humankind feel the promise of their own souls in their natural tendency. But, at the same time, the world and humankind experience again and again, generation after generation, hour after hour, that they cannot become community....

A great German sociologist, Max Weber,[2] distinguished between society and community, or as he put it, socialization [*Vergesellschaftung*] and communization [*Vergemeinschaftung*], between the becoming of a society and the rise of a community, in the following way: Socialization is based on shared interests, and interest commonality; communization is based on the commonality of feelings. I am not sure this is a sufficient definition.... Feeling alone cannot be the foundation of a community.... I would like to suggest a distinction between an association of interests [*Interessensverband*] and an

---

* Speech at the Convention of Jewish Youth Organizations in Germany, Munich, June 1930.

association of life [*Lebensverband*], rather than between an association of interests and an association of feeling. The association of interests I would call society; the association of life, community. If people feel that they are more likely to see their interests carried out if they combine interests that they share, then they have formed an association of interests. But if people group together nothing short of their lives—please do not substitute the word life with a concept of feeling or something that only exists in a holy hour, for life is an everyday occurrence, which happens day after day, hour after hour, in lofty as well as in humble situations, a demand of heavens and earth; all this together and nothing less I mean when I say life—if people, then, group together their lives, are willing to live together, and if their will is not a mere agreement that has emerged from the mind and remains in the mind, but a will that grows in the real soil of life, then community can happen as destiny and calling among men....

I shall illustrate what I mean with an example that today seems critical, the example of the family. The family is an example of special importance. I do not believe that true communal existence can happen without the association of communal cells [*Gemeinschaftszellen*]. I believe that communal existence emerges not from individuals but from communities.... I cannot believe in a future communal existence, in the rebirth of community without the rebirth of the communal cell, of the family whose members are related by blood and destiny and who live in close togetherness.... In its very essence, the family is a true association of life; but this association of life has entered a state of decay in which its own members have stopped believing in [the family] and have failed to live up to it.... And this brings us to the question, How can community happen? Does it depend on us?

Can community be established; can it be made? Can one really want community in the same way one makes plans, sets goals, and contemplates the means of how to reach these goals by the quickest path and with the least amount of effort? Can such a will of community really be successful? I am afraid I must tell you that it cannot. Imagine if a person resolves to develop a personality. He wakes up one day and says to himself, "It can't go on like this, I must develop a personality."... There are different ways to develop a personality, but one certain way to fail to develop a personality is to want it. Unfortunately, it is no different with community. Like personality, community cannot be "made." High values like this can only come into existence as by-products....

When people really engage with each other, experience [*erfahren*] each other and respond to this experience with their own lives, when people have a "living middle" [*lebendige Mitte*] at their center, then community can arise among them. If they do not intend for community to arise, if they are not under the delusion that they only have to reach for a human hand to their right and to their left for the global circle to be closed, but, rather, if they feel and know that something is in their midst, whether they cannot name it or whether it is without name, and if they feel and know that they can serve this "middle" and do what it demands by virtue of their being or coming together, then community will happen.

Let us, in this context, consider the great historical forms of community.... The first form is the national community [*Volksgemeinschaft*]; it is the community of fate [*Schickslasgemeinschaft*] par excellence. A people comes into existence when men come together in a certain area and under a certain fate, and if a bonding occurs among them that they did not know before.... They have experienced common historical time in a common historical space and have become closer to each other, after a process of resembling each other in blood or in a mixture of blood, through their conjunction in the common historical space in the common historical time, that is, in the home and fate of the people. And this commonality, this being brought together, the people will not experience as something they have done, but only as something that was done for them by forces, by primeval forces, by forces of creation, and finally, by forces of the "living middle." In this secret genesis of a people, generation after generation can participate in an immediate way; and if they reflect upon what it is that has brought them together to such an almost physical bonding, then they will experience and live through, always in awe and always anew, the primeval mystery of becoming a people.

A smaller and less perfected type of a community of fate is the community of work [*Werkgemeinschaft*]. We can see it in the historical example of the village community as a primitive community of ownership, as well as in the sense of close bonding in the German Christian city of medieval times....

The second manifestation of community in history is the community of faith [*Glaubensgemeinschaft*]. What distinguishes it from the community of fate is primarily the fact that the "living middle" that presented itself as the mystery of a community in progress is now, as it were, visible, and given a name; that the "living middle" is addressed and believed in; that people enter a believing relationship with it, a relationship of vows. Faith means to promise [*geloben*], to make a vow [*angeloben*];[3] not merely to believe that something is true, that something is, but to submit oneself to a being, to a "living middle." In this way, the "living middle" that ties together all individual members of a community organically and vitally, becomes visible. It now can be spoken to, and we can experience it speaking to us, not only as individuals: Rather, the entire community of faith experiences being spoken to, and the entire community responds. This primeval bonding—to be sure, new people join from time to time, but their addition is constantly absorbed by the mainstream, bonded since the beginning of time—this unintentional, instinctive bonding and being woven together as equal participation in the "middle," in God; this primeval bonding, I say, is what defines the great teaching of a community of faith also for our time....

We have to keep in mind, however, that with the growth of the great historical communities, their alienation [*Verfremdung*] grew as well.... One has tried to stop alienation through artificial scaffolding, through the jointed scaffolds of state and church. But whatever the benefits of these imposing scaffolds might be, they have not succeeded in renewing community. Nation-states and church religions may be respectable institutions, but they have not been able to raise the content of community [*Gemeinschaftsgehalt*]....

With this, I have touched upon Judaism. Perhaps unique among all communities, Judaism was both a community of fate and faith at the same time, both joined together inseparably: a people by virtue of revelation and a revelation carried by the people.... The forms [of Judaism] still continue in the *minyan:* Ten men facing God, addressing God together, and each other with the word of God; but you yourself feel how little of true life has remained in these forms....

For the past years, we have advocated a renewal of Judaism, though, more and more hesitantly, given the increasingly dire circumstances in recent times. What we had in mind was exactly the renewal of both a community of fate and a community of faith together—a renewal of Judaism as an association of life. These attempts at renewal, however, must be viewed with the same critical eye as our past, if we do not want to deceive ourselves.... All romantic, illusory attempts at renewal are worthless as long as the involved do not realize with their entire being that only those who are capable of community [*Gemeinschaftsfähige*] and who totally devote their lives to the community can experience community with each other, that is, only if they turn toward the nameless or named "middle" around which this community has gathered or has been gathered.... People who have not been transformed, who are not capable of community, who do not know of the "middle," can neither establish nor renew community. Good intentions alone cannot make community happen but create only a communal illusion....

At this point, many of you may quietly express an objection: All this [you might say] applies to the society of today; ... however, we, think that there is no other community today than the realization of a new social order. But, dear friends, I must tell you that this, too, is an illusion. Not the new social order as such is an illusion, for I am wholeheartedly on the side of those who work with their lives toward a new social order. But do not think that it suffices to establish a new social order for community to happen.... The capability of community ... can prove itself in a society of rebellion and opposition no less than in a society of order. Not long ago, there was a community in Russia, and this was the Russian Revolution in its early stages. There were individuals who gave up all their personal enterprises and riches to live among the people and to help prepare revolution; there, community happened. These people knew [community] in the comradeship of their illegal cooperation, to an extent that is no longer known in Russia today.

This example, however, teaches us that there is a third [type of community] in addition to the great historical and pristine communities—the happening community; the community in progress.

This third [type of community] has always been and will always be in history—and I believe, indeed, that it can also be in the present: It is there when a group of people, whether it has emerged from one historical community, a single community of fate and faith, or from various [such communities], experiences a communal moment together in a catastrophically and transforming way, in the way of a most unsettling and serious decision, and responds to this moment with a communal attitude and communal action....

Let us think of such a group that is stirred, as a group, by the gravity of a moment and responds as a group, reacts and refrains—acts, therefore, also by not acting, but acts together. Jewish youth—and this is the origin and destination of our question—cannot be satisfied with a romantic renewal of Judaism without recognizing that such a renewal can only grow from the renewal of the whole life....

But if you asked me, "What is to be done?" I would have to tell you that I do not have a prescription in my pocket, and I have nothing that resembles a prescription. For this call of the moment that all of you ought to hear cannot be translated into a formula. What is necessary is that ear and heart open themselves up, and that our entire energy makes itself available to what is calling us, each one in his own power and place where he can act concretely. If each one is serious about community with his innermost, sacred heart, he can realize it only in his own environment; he can realize community only to the extent of his own capabilities; he can realize it only if he does not seek to experience community, if he does not seek "community" at all, but lives up to it as being capable of community, by truly living together with others.

From the Conclusion

... Some of the questions you have asked me deal with an apparent misunderstanding. To clarify these issues is of the highest importance to me.... I believe in an evolving mankind. I believe that all of mankind, that all of creation, by virtue of being creation, is destined to become community, and that this entire world, without exception, can become a place of the realization of God. And I believe that this goal of creation is inextricably linked with the decisions we make in this or that moment. What we are destined to know is that there is no extraordinary moment in our ordinary everyday lives where world and creation are not linked.... Community can only be realized in the givenness of everyday life, at its lowest level....

Social struggle is not enough.... Social struggle is not only insufficient, it is also misleading, in that it aims at reducing work hours and believes this to be sufficient.... But can we sanction the division of work [*Hölle*] and freedom from work [*Höllenfreiheit*] only because our lives are torn in two? Can we sanction this inhumanely rationalized philosophy of work whose principle is the exploitation of physical human power without regard for the humaneness of work? A social movement that does not take issue with these [conditions] is barred from the path toward community....

The social movement of our time demands too little; does too little to humanize the entire social life. The rationalization of economy and technology is accomplished by human reason. But today, human reason rationalizes behind the backs of humaneness. What I mean here is not the romantic notion of returning to a prerational state, but the giving of humane tasks to reason. A life in community will become possible in human history only when those who administer reason rationally put technology and inventors to new tasks that do not reduce but perhaps even increase productivity; a productivity, however, that truly incorporates the living, personal human being....

This objective demand, however, is complemented by a subjective, personal demand: that as long as the social goals mentioned above have not yet been reached, the individual person, wherever he stands, practices and protects humaneness to the best of his abilities.... What is essential for man in the relation between man and God is what man does at this very hour, his responsibility for the moment, the response that he can give at any time to what God speaks to him at any time. God speaks to us hour after hour in everyday life, in the treadmill of work, and we can answer him by how we live in the treadmill of work, in the possibilities of space and time, and of this moment. There we can hallow and approach God. If not there, then nowhere.

Notes

Source: "Wie kann Gemeinschaft werden?" (speech at the Convention of Jewish Youth Organizations in Germany, Munich, June 1930), first in *Der Jugendbund* (Düsseldorf, July–August 1930). Trans., Asher Biemann, for this volume.

1. Hebrew, literally, Kingdom of heavens (Kingdom of God).
2. Max Weber (1864–1920), leading German sociologist and exponent of the "verstehende Soziologie."
3. Cf. Two Foci of the Jewish Soul (1932) (p. 108 in this volume).

Three Theses of a Religious Socialism (1928)

> Any socialism whose limits are narrower than God and man is too narrow for us.
>
> —Leonhard Ragaz[1]

Thesis 1

Religious socialism cannot mean the joining of religion and socialism in such a manner that each of the constituents could achieve, apart from the other, independence if not fulfillment; it cannot mean merely that the two have concluded an agreement to unite their autonomies in a common being and working. Religious socialism can only mean that religion and socialism are essentially directed to each other—that each of them needs the covenant with the other for the fulfillment of its own essence. *Religio,* that is, the human person's binding of himself to God, can only attain its full reality in the will for a community of the human race, out of which God, alone, can prepare His kingdom. *Socialitas,* that is, mankind's becoming a fellowship—man's becoming a fellow to man—cannot develop other than out of a common relation to the divine center, even if this be again and still nameless. Unity with God and community among the creatures belong together. Religion without socialism is disembodied spirit and, therefore, not genuine spirit; socialism without religion is body emptied of spirit and, hence, also not genuine body. But—socialism without religion does not hear the divine address; it does not aim at a response. Still it happens that it responds; religion without socialism hears the call but does not respond.

Thesis 2

All "religious" forms, institutions, and societies are real or fictitious according to whether they serve as expression, as shape and bearer of real *religio*—a real self-binding of the human person to God—or merely exist alongside it or even conceal the flight from actual *religio,* which comprises the concrete response and responsibility of the human person in the here and now. So, too, all "socialist" tendencies, programs, and parties are real or fictitious according to whether they serve as strength, direction, and instrument of real *socialitas*—mankind's really becoming a fellowship—or only exist alongside its development or even conceal the flight from real *socialitas,* which comprises the immediate living with and for one another of men in the here and now. At present, the prevailing religious forms, institutions, and societies have entered into the realm of the fictitious; the prevailing socialist tendencies, programs, and parties have not yet emerged from the fictitious. Today, appearance is currently opposed to appearance. But the meeting has begun to take place within the hidden sphere of the future.

Thesis 3

The point where religion and socialism can meet each other in the truth is the concrete personal life. As the truth of religion consists not of dogma or prescribed ritual but means standing and withstanding in the abyss of the real reciprocal relation with the mystery of God, so socialism in its truth is not doctrine and tactics but standing and withstanding in the abyss of the real reciprocal relation with the mystery of man. As it is presumption to "believe" in something without—however inadequately—living that in which one believes, so it is presumption to wish to "accomplish" something without—however inadequately—living what one wants to accomplish. As the "there" refuses to give itself to us when the "here" is not devoted to it, so the "then" must refuse when the "now" does not authenticate it. Religion must know that it is the everyday that sanctifies or desecrates devotion. And socialism must know that the decision as to how similar or dissimilar the end that is attained will be to the end that was previously cherished is dependent upon how similar or dissimilar to the set goal are the means whereby it is pursued. Religious socialism means that man in the concreteness of his personal life takes seriously the fundamentals of this life; the fact that God is, that the world is, and that he, this human person, stands before God and in the world.

Notes

Source: "Drei Sätze eines religiösen Sozialismus," first in *Neue Wege* 22, no. 7/8 (July–August 1928). Maurice Friedman, trans., in *Pointing the Way: Collected Essays* (New York: Harper & Brothers, 1957), pp. 112–14.

Editor's note: In April 1928, the Swiss Protestant theologian Leonhard Ragaz (1868–1945) and Martin Buber organized a convention in Heppenheim on the subject of religious socialism (see *Sozialismus aus dem Glauben—Verhandlungen der Sozialistischen Tagung in Heppenheim* [Zurich: Rotapfel Verlag, 1929]). Buber and Ragaz, who was also the editor of *Neue Wege. Blätter für religiöse Arbeit* (1906–1945), shared a common interest in the formulation of a "religious socialism" based on the teachings of the Hebrew prophets and early Christianity. Ragaz expressed his feeling of this commonality in a letter of 1916 (cf. Grete Schaeder, ed., *Martin Buber. Briefwechsel aus sieben Jahrzehnten,* vol. I, no. 328 [Heidelberg: Lambert Schneider, 1973]). In April 1923, Buber reviewed Ragaz's book, *Weltreich, Religion und Gottesherrschaft* (Erlenbach-Zurich: Rotapfel Verlag, 1923) for the literary section of the *Frankfurter Zeitung* (Maurice Friedman, trans., in *A Believing Humanism: My Testament 1902–1965* [New York: Simon & Schuster, 1967], pp. 109–12). Buber's own plan to establish a group of "Jewish religious socialists" (in response to similar Christian groups) with the help of the Marxist pedagogue, Hermann Gerson, however, was never realized (see Buber's letter to H. Gerson, in Schaeder, ed., *Briefwechsel,* vol. II, no. 364).

1. See Editor's note, above.

PART VII
Zionism and Nationalism

Concepts and Reality (1916)*

Very esteemed Professor [*Geheimrat*],[1] you published a pamphlet entitled *Zionism and Religion,* which in many respects seems remarkable to me in its claims as well as in its challenges....

In an unusually journalistic–polemic tone, you express your fear that the danger Zionism represents, in your opinion, will only grow and become more real as a result of international tensions. The rise of anti-Semitism, you say, makes assimilation seem futile and makes Zionism seem a last resort. On the other hand, you say it is precisely Zionism that heightens a sensitivity for national difference, which drives many to send their children to the baptismal font, thinking that they cannot overcome [this difference] in any other way. The liberal Jew, however, equally devoid of religion and fatherland, is "derided and despised by Zionism," called a "coward and hypocrite." [He is called] a hypocrite even regarding his religion, for Zionists, you claim, deny all those who do not have a national feeling, religiosity as well. The Zionists, on the other hand, enter an unnatural alliance with Orthodoxy while professing pantheism and sanctifying the Jewish race.... Nationality, you declare, is the "natural condition and foundation for religious continuity." But nationality, you say, is completely different from nation. Nationality is a fact of nature; nation, a creation by the state....

Nationalism[2]

You state that you view the same nationality that we are used to understanding as a historical category only as a "fact of nature." And, indeed, in all of your writings, the terms "nationality," "ethnic stock" [*Stamm*], and "descent" [*Abstammung*] are used synonymously. But how could you, from your traditionally Jewish [*altjüdisch*] viewpoint of strict monotheism, treat

---

* From a response to Hermann Cohen.

descent as a mere "fact of nature?" The primeval Jewish concept of "seed" is never absent when God enters and renews his covenant with Abraham and Abraham's descendents, ... and you claim that this principle of covenant is not God's will and purpose in history but a fact of nature? ...

No, nationality cannot be defined through the concept of fact of nature. Nationality is a historical reality and moral task. To be sure, its roots lie also in the natural; but our humanity, too, has its roots in the natural. Yet, it is not within the limits of the natural that the essence of humanity is revealed but in the spiritual struggle of mankind and in the infinite striving to *fulfill the idea of man*. ... Nationality is a reality of spirit and ethos in a twofold sense: a reality of spirit and ethos in history ... and, with all this transplanted into our personal lives ... a call to become what we are—a test and a purification, and a selection. ...

Never has Zionism, as you claim, equated religion with nationality; nor will it ever allow nationhood [*Volkstum*] to be relegated to an anthropological means for the propagation of religion. Rather, every Zionist for whom, as for me, religiosity is in the center of Judaism will know and acknowledge, as I do, that Jewish religiosity—remember that I do not mean a phenomenon and an interpretation of religion but the entire infinite religiosity of Judaism that floats, undefinable and unlimitable, above doctrines and laws ... —that this Jewish religiosity is a function, the highest function of the mighty Jewish nationhood. It is a function that is not only unable to propagate itself without its bearer, as you think, but one that could not *exist* without its bearer. It is a function that thrives on the blood [of the nation], is nourished by its forces, and operates on its will. Without the vitality of the nation, without its ardent and suffering power, religiosity would have no place on earth. What applies to history applies to the life of the individual as well: The idea cannot be realized without realizing nationhood first. Realization is what truly matters. Nationality, as a mere fact of nature, is a fiction, in the same way humanity, as a mere fact of nature, is a fiction. Only when we view nationality as a reality of spirit and ethos can we also turn it into a reality in our own lives.

If nationality, then, is not a natural fact but a spiritual reality in history and personal calling, it can differ from the nation at most in its degree, ... not in its kind. ... For you, nation and state are downright identical terms. ... The nationalities, you say, are parts of the nation. But what about nationalities that believe or know themselves to be oppressed by the leading nations of their states? Well, all those questions about nationalities are resolved most easily—disposed of through your terminological method. A particular nationality complaining about its fate—is it not part of the ruling nation, identical with the ruling nation of its state? ... How can it be oppressed by the organism it belongs to? All suffering of nationalities, therefore, would be imaginary and the cure a matter of using the correct terminology. ...

Verily, it is not for the clarification of concepts that we treat nation and state as identical, but for their clouding.

Clarification of concepts—but are concepts really the issue here? Can the question of Jewish peoplehood really be settled by terminology? Can "naturalness and sincerity of national feeling" really be tested by definitions?...

Whether nation or nationality, Judaism is a particularly poor example for definitions. There are strata within German Jewry that can hardly evoke a feeling of "nationality" in me; they are not supranational, as one might think, but "under-national"—the characterless [*artlos*], memoryless, insubstantial marginal brood [*Randgezücht*]. But when I read a verse by Bialik[3] or a letter from Eretz Israel,[4] I feel—here is nation; no, here is more than nation—here is a people....

The Jewish people—this is not a fact of nature but a unique historical reality; not a concept but an immense living and dying before your and my eyes; not a means for the propagation of religion, but the dust-humbled bearer of this religion and all its Jewish ideologies and Jewish ethos. Even though there may be Jews in all places who feel at home in this or that fatherland, the Jewish people at large is homeless....

Messianism

Regarding the blessings and consolations of messianism, is it not you who charges Zionism and its literature with "indulging in frivolous derision of the most sublime idea in Jewish religiosity," that is, the idea of messianism?

Where and when did Zionism indulge?

I believe I know the literature of Zionism well, but I cannot recall a passage that might substantiate your claim. Rather, from Moses Hess[5] up to my own writings (to choose an example from the recent generation at hand) messianism has been presented as the leading idea of Judaism....

What Zionism fights against is not the messianic idea but its misrepresentation and distortion as it is found in a considerable portion of liberal Jewish and anti-Zionist literature. It is a misrepresentation and distortion that glorifies, in the name of messianism, the dispersion, debasement, and homelessness of the Jewish people as something of absolute value and fortune that ought to be preserved to prepare a messianic mankind.

The goal of Zionism, too, is the "redemption of the human spirit and the salvation of the world."[6] But, to us, the right way leads through the "liberation of the tormented people and its gathering around God's sanctuary."[7] ... Let Judaism merge and blend with a messianic mankind! But why should the Jewish people dissolve into the mankind of *today* for the messianic age to be ushered in only later? Rather, if the Jewish people must remain in the midst of mankind, it must do so not as a decaying fact of nature among a steadily spreading confessionalization of religion, but as a people pursuing its ideal for the sake of, yet free from and unhindered by, mankind.... The striving for a homeland is a national one. But the struggle *of* the homeland—of the Jewish communal existence—will have to be a supranational one. We want Palestine not "for the Jews." We want it for mankind, because we want it for the *realization* of Judaism....

Zionism and Religion

The coalition between Zionism and Orthodoxy is unnatural, you say.... Now, I do not know of a "coalition" between Zionism and Orthodoxy.... But even without a formal and organized coalition, and despite their major differences,... there undoubtedly exists a certain commonality, not between Zionism and Orthodoxy as such, but between a truly enthusiastic Zionist and a truly enthusiastic Jew of Law [*Gesetzesjude*]: What they have in common is their passionate rebellion against fictitious Judaism and their passionate longing for real Judaism.

What is fictitious Judaism?... The Judaism that until now has only consisted of negation and opposition still claiming the name of Judaism for itself—this I call fictitious. Real Judaism is lived Judaism.... And, therefore, an authentic Jew does not proclaim Judaism—be it religious or national—any more than a real Zionist uses Zionism as a phrase or confession. On the contrary, the authentic Jew takes the Judaism in his life and his actions seriously.... I only know of two attempts to reach this [goal]: One is the enthusiastic Torah-true Jew whose observance is neither inherited habit nor piety but the submission, out of true religiosity, of his whole life to the forms of old. This attempt is called the preservation of manifest Judaism. The other one is called liberation of buried Judaism. And this is the way of Zionism. This task, which alone will lead to a new *whole* Judaism, can only be fulfilled in Palestine, in the national forms of a supranational striving that I mentioned before. Every authentic Zionist accepts this task in his personal life, for every authentic Zionist is, in the innermost sense of the word, *on his way*....

Hebrew

You, Professor Cohen, say that Hebrew is not a profane vernacular for us German Jews but not a dead language either. You call it the language of our prayer....

I cannot see, of course, the danger and misfortune of reviving Hebrew as a vernacular. But most Zionists will agree with me that Hebrew is not first and foremost a vernacular but the single language that can fully absorb and express the sublime values of Judaism. We do not see in it a "profane" language but, rather, a worldly one in its highest sense that can encompass the spiritual too—a language of the powerful historical continuity, of the entire peoplehood, including our prayers—if only as one chapter in this giant book.... Thus, Hebrew clears the way to buried Judaism in a twofold sense: in content, for it can transmit the essential and lost values;... and in form, for it can revive the pristine Jewish patterns of thought that have been suppressed by the cultured European languages, or "mother tongues."... In this way, the fallow land in us will become arable; real Judaism will grow, piece by piece, and will be torn from the hands of fictitious Judaism. In this way, and by similar means, we have begun to educate young people; and in the same way we will continue to educate many more—an elite [*Auslese*] of Jewish spirit, a troop of Gideon,⁸ tried and sifted out in the battle against the inner Midian, against fictitious Judaism. And under normal circumstances, Professor Cohen, you should be fighting with us instead of trying to "overcome" the "danger" and "curse" of Zionism.

Notes

Source: "Begriffe und Wirklichkeit," first in *Der Jude* 1, no. 5 (July 1916); also as an offprint in *Völker, Staaten und Zion—Ein Brief an Hermann Cohen und Bemerkungen zu seiner Antwort* (Vienna: R. Löwit 1917). Sections of the Buber–Cohen exchange translated by M. Gelber and S. Weinstein in *The Jew in the Modern World*, ed. Paul Mendes-Flohr and Jehuda Reinharz (New York: Oxford University Press, 1980), pp. 448–53. Buber's second response to Cohen, Joachim Neugroschel, trans., in *The Jew: Essays from Martin Buber's Journal Der Jude, 1916–1928*, ed. Arthur A. Cohen (Tuscaloosa: Jewish Publication Society and University of Alabama Press, 1980). Asher Biemann, trans., for this volume.

Editor's note: A prominent philosopher and founder of the neo-Kantian school in Germany, Hermann Cohen (1878–1918), taught at the University of Marburg and, from 1912 until his death, at the Lehranstalt für die Wissenschaft des Judentums in Berlin. In June 1916 Cohen published a critique of Zionism in the *K.C.-Blätter* that was consistent with his belief in the moral progress of humanity and the messianic vocation of Judaism in the Diaspora. Like the liberal Jewish movement, Cohen saw in Zionism and Jewish nationalism an obstacle for the evolution of moral universalism and advocated a German–Jewish symbiosis instead (see, in particular, Cohen's *Die Bedeutung des Judentums für den religiösen Fortschritt der Menschheit* [Berlin: Protestantischer Schriftenvertrieb, 1910], and *Deutschtum und Judentum* [Gießen: Verlag A. Töpelmann, 1915]). Buber responded to Cohen's critique with his essay "Concepts and Reality" ("concepts" being an allusion to Cohen's philosophical method), to which Cohen replied with another critique in the *K.C.-Blätter* (July–August 1916). Buber responded with rebuttal of his own, "Zion, der Staat und die Menschheit," in *Der Jude* (September 1916) defending Zionism's role in the messianic plan.

1. Martin Buber is addressing Hermann Cohen by his highest social rank.
2. Headings are not in the original.
3. Haim N. Bialik (1873–1934), pioneering Hebrew poet whose work became standard literature in the Zionist and Jewish Renaissance movement; author of the famous essay "Halakha and Aggadah" (1917).
4. Hebrew: the Land of Israel.
5. Moses Hess (1812–1875), German–Jewish social thinker, who for a short period of time was closely associated with Marx and Engels. In 1862 Hess published *Rome and Jerusalem*, a book that was widely unnoticed at the time but anticipated many ideas of Zionism. In 1893 the Viennese Zionist Nathan Birnbaum suggested that *Rome and Jerusalem* be included in the canon of "Jewish-national" literature (see Nathan Birnbaum: *Die nationale Wiedergeburt des jüdischen Volkes in seinem Lande als Mittel zur Lösung der Judenfrage* [Vienna: Selfpublished, 1893], p. 27). Theodor Herzl considered Hess his spiritual ancestor (although he discovered him only after he had written the *Jewish State* in 1896). Buber frequently referred to Hess and devoted an essay to him ("Der Erste der Letzten," 1945, in Martin Buber: *Der Jude und sein Judentum: Gesammelte Aufsätze und Reden* [Gerlingen: Lambert Schneider, 1993], pp. 398–410).
6. Buber is quoting himself, cf. The Renewal of Judaism (1911) (p. 154 in this volume).
7. Ibid., p. 154.
8. Gideon: Heroic fighter of the tribe of Menasseh who drove out the invading Midianites (Judg. 6:1–8:35). Note that Buber is referring to an "inner" battle here.

Nationalism (1921)

I am addressing you at a very troubled moment in this Congress and do not know how much attention you will be able to give me at this point.[1] Nevertheless, I have decided not to postpone what I have to say. A consciousness of my responsibility urges me to speak before the confusion increases. What I am going to deal with is the unambiguous demarcation of a kind of nationalism, a degenerate kind, which of late has begun to spread even in Judaism.

An unambiguous demarcation—I need not retract anything I have ever said against anational Jewry, against those Jews for whom—when it comes to public life—the concept of Judaism has less reality than the concept of nation. But now we must draw a new, no less ambiguous, line of demarcation within our own national movement.

We have passed from the difficult period of World War [I] into a period that outwardly seems more tolerable but, on closer examination, proves still more difficult—a period of inner confusion. It is characteristic of this period that truth and lies—right and wrong—are mingled in its various spiritual and political movements in an almost unprecedented fashion.

In the face of this monstrous and monstrously growing phenomenon, it is no longer enough to draw the usual distinctions according to general, currently accepted concepts. For in every such concept, the true and the false are now so intertwined, so tangled and meshed, that to apply them as heretofore, as though they were still homogeneous, would only give rise to greater error. If we are to pass out of confusion into new clarity, we must draw distinctions *within* each individual concept.

It is a well-known fact that, *sociologically* speaking, modern nationalism goes back to the French Revolution. The effects of the French Revolution were such that the old state systems that weighed so heavily on the peoples of Europe were shaken and the subject nations were able to emerge from under the yoke. But as they emerged and grew aware of themselves, these nations became conscious of their own political insufficiencies, of their lack of independence, territorial unity, and outward solidarity. They strove to correct these insufficiencies, but their efforts did not lead them to the creation of new forms. They did not try to establish themselves *as peoples,* that is, as a new organic order growing out of the natural forms of the life of the people. All they wanted was to become just such states—just such powerful, mechanized, and centralized state apparatuses as those that had existed in the past. They looked back into past history rather than forward into a future nationally motivated in its very structure.

We shall understand this more readily if we review the *psychological* origin of modern nationalism. European man became more and more isolated in the centuries between the Reformation and the Revolution. United Christendom did not merely break in two; it was rent by numberless cracks, and human beings no longer stood on the solid ground of connectedness. The individual was deprived of the security of a closed cosmic system. He grew more and more specialized and, at the same time, isolated, and found himself faced with the dizzy infinity of the new world image. In his desire for shelter, he reached out for a community structure that was just putting in an appearance—for nationality. The individual felt himself warmly and firmly received into a unit he thought indestructible because it was "natural"—sprung from and bound to the soil.

He found protection in the naturally evolved shelter of the nation, compared to which the state seemed man-made and even the Church no more than the bearer of a mandate. But since the strongest factor in this bond he had just discovered was awareness that it had evolved naturally, the horizon narrowed and—even worse—the fruitfulness of the national element was impaired. In the individual, the original feeling of allegiance to a people, alive in the depth of his soul long before modern national awareness, changed from a creative power to the challenging "will to power" of the individual as a member of the community. The group egoism of the individual emerged in its modern form.

A great historian has asserted that power is evil.[2] But this is not so. Power is intrinsically guiltless; it is the precondition for the actions of man. The problematic element is the "will-to-power"—greedy to seize and establish power, and not the effect of a power whose development is internal. A "will-to-power," less concerned with being powerful than with being "more powerful than," becomes destructive. Not power but power hysteria is evil....

Modern nationalism is in constant danger of slipping into power hysteria, which disintegrates the responsibility to draw lines of demarcation.

The distinction between the two kinds of nationalism that I am concerned with depends entirely on the right understanding of this responsibility and this danger. But to arrive at this understanding, we must first analyze the phenomenon of nationalism and its relation to peoples and nations; or, to be more exact, we must define what "people" means. What, in this relation, is a nation? What is the significance of nationalism in relation to both people and nation?

The word "people" tends, above all, to evoke the idea of blood relationship. But kinship is not the *sine qua non* for the *origin* of a people. A people need not necessarily be the fusion of kindred stems; it can be the fusion of unrelated stems just as well. But the concept "people" always implies unity of fate. It presupposes that in a great creative hour throngs of human beings were shaped into a new entity by a great molding fate that they experienced in common. This new "coined form" [*geprägte Form*], which in the course of subsequent events "develops as living substance," survives by dint of the kinship established from this moment on; it need not be exclusive but must retain unquestioned preponderance even in eras where there are strong admixtures of other strains. The physical factor of this survival is the propagation of the species in more or less rigid endogamy; the spiritual factor is an organic, potential, common memory that becomes actual in each successive generation as the pattern for experience, as language, and as a way of life. The people constitutes a particular sort of community, because new individuals are born into it as members of its physical and spiritual oneness, and they are born into it naturally, not symbolically, as in the case of the Christian church. The people survives biologically, yet it cannot be fitted into a biological category. Here, nation and history combine in a unique fashion.

A people becomes a nation to the degree that it grows aware that its existence differs from that of other peoples (a difference originally expressed in the sacral principle that determines endogamy), and acts on the basis of this awareness. So the term "nation" signifies the unit "people," from the point of view of conscious and active difference. Historically speaking, this consciousness is usually the result of some inner—social or political—transformation, through which the people comes to realize its own peculiar structure and actions, and sets them off from the actions of others. It is decisive activity and suffering, especially in an age of migrations and land conquests, that produces a *people*. A *nation* is produced when its acquired status undergoes a decisive inner change that is accepted as such in the people's self-consciousness. To give an example: The great shift that made ancient Rome a republic made it a nation, too. Not until Rome became a republic did it become a nation aware of its own peculiar strength, organization, and function, differentiating itself in these from the surrounding world. This dynamic state of nationhood can then reach its height in a peculiar formulation of its historic task. The French state people, for instance, did not attain to complete national existence until in its great revolution it became a missionary for the idea of revolution.

At certain moments in national life a new phenomenon makes its appearance. We call it nationalism. Its function is to indicate disease. Bodily organs do not draw attention to themselves until they are attacked by disease. Similarly, nationalism is, at bottom, the awareness of some lack, some disease, or ailment. The people feels a more and more urgent compulsion to fill this lack—to cure this disease or ailment. The contradiction between the immanent task of the nation and its outer and inner condition has developed or been elaborated, and this contradiction affects the feeling of the people. What we term nationalism is their spiritual reaction to it. Being a people may be compared to having strong eyes in one's head; being a nation, to the awareness of vision and its function; being nationalistic, to suffering in connection with a disease of the eyes from the constant preoccupation with the fact of having eyes. A people is a phenomenon of life; a nation, one of awareness; nationalism, one of overemphasized awareness [*Überbewußtheit*].

In a people, assertiveness is an *impulse* that fulfills itself creatively; in a nation it is an *idea* inextricably joined to a task; in nationalism, it becomes a *program*.

A nationalist development can have two possible consequences. Either a healthy reaction will set in that will overcome the danger heralded by nationalism, and also nationalism itself, which has now fulfilled its purpose, or nationalism will establish itself as *the* permanent principle; that is, it will exceed its function, pass beyond its proper bounds, and—with overemphasized consciousness—displace the spontaneous life of the nation. Unless some force arises to oppose this process, it may well be the beginning of the downfall of the people—a downfall dyed in the colors of nationalism.

We have already said at the outset that original nationalism is the indication of a fundamental lack in the life of the nation—a lack of unity, freedom, and territorial security—and that it warns the nation to mend this situation. It is a demand upon the world for what it needs, a demand that the unwritten *droits de la nation* [rights of the nation] be applied to a people to enable it to realize its essence as a people and thus discharge its duty to mankind. Original nationalism inspires the people to struggle for what they lack to achieve this. But when nationalism transgresses its lawful limits, when it tries to do more than overcome a deficiency, it becomes guilty of what has been called hubris in the lives of historical personalities; it crosses the holy border and grows presumptuous. And now it no longer indicates disease but is, itself, a grave and complicated disease. A people can win the rights for which it strove and yet fail to regain its health, because nationalism, turned false, eats at its marrow.

When this false nationalism, that is, a nationalism that has exceeded the function that it was destined to and persists and acts beyond it, and prevails not only in *one* people but in an entire epoch of world history, it means that the life of mankind, pulsing in its stock of peoples, is very sick indeed. And that is the situation today. The motto that Alfred Mombert,[3] a remarkable German Jewish poet, prefaced to the third part of his *Aeon* trilogy, takes on new significance. It is *Finis populorum*.[4]

Every reflective member of a people is in duty bound to distinguish between legitimate and arbitrary nationalism and, in the sequence of situations and decisions, to refresh this distinction day after day. This is, above all, an obligation imposed on the leaders of a nation and of national movements. Whether or not the people probe deeply into their conscience, and do this unremittingly, will determine not only the fate of a movement that must inevitably disintegrate if it becomes an end in itself but, often, that of the nation, its recovery, or decline. Thus, drawing this distinction is not a mere moral postulate that entails no other obligations but a question of life or death for a people that is irreparably impaired when its spontaneity, fed on the primordial forces of natural—historical existence—is thrust aside and strangled by an apparatus activated by an exaggerated self-awareness.

But the criterion that must govern the drawing of this distinction is not implicit in nationalism itself. It can be found only in the knowledge that the nation has an obligation that is more than merely national [*übernationale Verantwortung*]....

Peoples can be regarded either as elements or as ends in themselves and can regard themselves either as elements or as ends in themselves.

For him to whom peoples are elements, they are the basic substances that go to build mankind and the only means to build up a more homogeneous mankind, with more form and more meaning. But such elements cannot be compared to chemical elements, which can enter into solution and be separated out again. Spiritual elements must maintain themselves because they are threatened with the loss of themselves. But just because they are elements, they are not preserved for their own sake, but to be put to use. A people fully aware of its own character regards itself as an element without comparing itself to other elements. It does not feel superior to others but considers its task incomparably sublime, not because this task is greater than another, but because it is creation and a mission. There is no scale of values for the function of peoples. One cannot be ranked above another. God wants to use what he created, as an aid in his work. In an hour of crisis, true nationalism expresses the true self-awareness of a people and translates it into action.

He, on the other hand, who regards the nation as an end in itself, will refuse to admit that there is a greater structure, unless it be the worldwide supremacy of his own particular nation. He tries to grapple with the problem of the cracked and shattered present by undermining it instead of transcending it. He does not meet responsibility face to face. He considers the nation its own judge and responsible to no one but itself. An interpretation such as this converts the nation into a *Moloch*,[5] which gulps the best of the people's youth.

National ideology, the *spirit* of nationalism, is fruitful as long as it does not make the nation an end in itself; as long as it remembers its part in the building of a greater structure. The moment national ideology makes the nation an end in itself, it annuls its own right to live; it grows sterile.

In this day and age, when false nationalism is on the rise, we are witness to the beginning of the decline of the national ideology that flowered in the nineteenth and early twentieth centuries. It goes without saying that it is perfectly possible for this decline to go hand in hand with the increasing success of nationalistic politics. But we live in the hour when nationalism is about to annul itself spiritually.

It is an hour of decision—a decision that depends on whether a distinction will be drawn and how sharply it will be drawn. We all play a part—we can all play a part—in such a distinction and decision.

I need not discuss in detail the application of these ideas to Judaism and its cause.

Judaism is not merely being a nation. It is being a nation, but because of its own peculiar connection with the quality of being a community of faith, it is more than that. Since Jewry has a character of its own and a life of its own, just like any other nation, it is entitled to claim the rights and privileges of a nation. But we must never forget that it is, nevertheless, a *res sui generis* [thing of its own kind], which, in one very vital respect, goes beyond the classification it is supposed to fit into.

A great event in their history molded the Jews into a people. It was when the Jewish tribes were freed from the bondage of Egypt. But it required a great inner transformation to make the Jews into a nation. In the course of this inner change, the concept of the government of God took on a political form, final for the time being, that of the "anointed" kingdom, that is, the kingdom as the representative of God.

From the very beginning of the Diaspora, the uniqueness of Judaism became apparent in a very special way. In other nations, the national powers in themselves vouch for the survival of the people. In Judaism, this guarantee is given by another power, which, as I have said, makes the Jews more than a nation: the membership in a community of faith. From the French Revolution on, this inner bond grew more and more insecure. Jewish religion was uprooted, and this is at the core of the disease indicated by the rise of Jewish nationalism around the middle of the nineteenth century. Over and over this nationalism lapses into trends toward "secularization" and thus mistakes its purpose. For Israel cannot be healed, and its welfare cannot be achieved by severing the concepts of people and community of faith but only by setting up a new order including both as organic and renewed parts.

A Jewish national community in Palestine, a desideratum toward which Jewish nationalism must logically strive, is a station in this healing process. We must not forget, however, that in the thousands of years of its exile, Jewry yearned for the Land of Israel, not as a nation like others, but as Judaism (*res sui generis*), and with motives and intentions that cannot be derived wholly from the category "nation." That original yearning is behind all of the disguises that modern national Judaism has borrowed from the modern nationalism of the West. To forget one's own peculiar character and accept the slogans and paroles of a nationalism that has nothing to do with the category of faith means national assimilation.

When Jewish nationalism holds aloof from such procedure, which is alien to it, it is legitimate, in an especially clear and lofty sense. It is the nationalism of a people without land of its own, a people that has lost its country. Now, in an hour rife with decision, it wants to offset the deficiency it realized with merciless clarity only when its faith became rootless; it wants to regain its natural holy life.

Here, the question may arise as to what the idea of the election of Israel has to do with all this. This idea does not indicate a feeling of superiority but a sense of destiny [*Bestimmungsgefühl*]. It does not spring from a comparison with others but from the concentrated devotion to a task—to the task that molded the people into a nation when they attempted to accomplish it in their earlier history. The prophets formulated that task and never ceased uttering their warning: If you boast of being chosen instead of living up to it, if you turn election into a static object instead of obeying it as a command [*Weisung*], you will forfeit it!

And what part does Jewish nationalism play at the present time? We—and by that I mean the group of persons I have belonged to since my youth, that group which has tried and will continue to try to do its share in educating the people—have summoned the people to turn, and not to conceit, to be healed, and not to self-righteousness. We have equipped Jewish nationalism with an armor we did not weld, with the awareness of a unique history, a unique situation, a unique obligation, which can be conceived only from the supernational standpoint and which—whenever it is taken seriously—must point to a supernational sphere.

In this way we hoped to save Jewish nationalism from the error of making an idol of the people [*Volksvergötzung*]. We have not succeeded. Jewish nationalism is largely concerned with being "like unto all the nations," with affirming itself in the face of the world without affirming the world's reciprocal power. It too has frequently yielded to the delusion of regarding the horizon visible from one's own station as the whole sky. It too is guilty of offending against the words of that table of laws that has been set up above all nations: that all sovereignty becomes false and vain when, in the struggle for power, it fails to remain subject to the sovereign of the world, who is the sovereign of my rival, and my enemy's sovereign, as well as mine. It forgets to lift its gaze from the shoals of "healthy egoism" to the Lord who "brought the children of Israel out of the land of Egypt, *and* the Philistines from Caphtor, *and* Aram from Kir" (Amos 9:7).

Jewish nationalism bases its spurious ideology on a "formal" nationalistic theory that—in this critical hour—should be called to account. This theory is justified in denying that the acceptance of certain principles by a people should be a criterion for membership in that people. It is justified in suggesting that such a criterion must spring from formal common characteristics, such as language and civilization. But it is not justified in denying to those principles a central normative meaning—in denying that they involve the task, posed in time immemorial, to which the inner life of this people is bound, and together with the inner, the outer life as well.

I repeat: This task cannot be defined, but it can be sensed, pointed out, and presented. Those who stand for the religious "reform" that—most unfortunate among the misfortunes of the period of emancipation—became a substitute for a reformation of Judaism that did not come, certainly did all they could to discredit that task by trying to cram it into a concept. But to deny the task its focal position on such grounds is equivalent to throwing out the child along with the bathwater. The supernational task of the Jewish nation cannot be properly accomplished unless, under its aegis, natural life is reconquered. Formal nationalism disclaims the nation's being based on and conditioned by this more than national task; it has grown overconscious and dares to disengage Judaism from its connection with the world and to isolate it. By proclaiming the nation as an end in itself instead of comprehending that it is an element, formal nationalism sanctions a group egoism that disclaims responsibility.

... A foundation on which the nation is regarded as an end in itself has no room for supernational ethical demands because it does not permit the nation to act from a sense of true supernational responsibility. If the depth of faith, which is decisive in limiting national action, is robbed of its content of faith, then inorganic ethics cannot fill the void, and the emptiness will persist until the day of the turning.

We, who call upon you, are weighed down with deep concern lest this turning may come too late. The nationalistic crisis in Judaism is in sharp, perhaps too sharp, relief in the pattern of the nationalistic crises of current world history. In our case, more clearly than in any other, the decision between life and death has assumed the form of deciding between legitimate and arbitrary nationalism.

Notes

Source: "Nationalismus" (address at the Twelfth Zionist Congress at Karlsbad, 5 September 1921) first in *Wiener Morgenzeitung* (3 September 1921). See also *Stenographisches Protokoll der Verhandlungen des XII Zionistenkongresses in Karlsbad* (1–14 September 1921) (Berlin: Jüdischer Verlag, 1922). Olga Marx, trans., in *Israel and the World: Essays in a Time of Crisis* (New York: Schocken, 1948), pp. 214–26.

Editor's note: The Twelfth Zionist Congress (the first after the Balfour Declaration of 1917) began with high expectations for a Palestine under the British mandate but was soon disrupted by many disagreements on matters of finance and organization. Buber represented the *Hitachduth* [union], which had been formed in 1920 in Prague as a coalition of non-Marxist, Socialist Zionist parties. On behalf of the *Hitachduth,* Buber also proposed a resolution on the Arab question (in response to the Arab riots of May 1920), which was first rejected by the committee but eventually adopted in a much "diluted" version. Buber's address "Nationalism" was delivered at an extraordinary meeting sponsored by the *Hitachduth*. On Martin Buber and the Twelfth Zionist Congress, see Hans Kohn, *Martin Buber—Sein Werk und seine Zeit* (Cologne: Joseph Melzer, 1961), pp. 177 and 341f., and Robert Weltsch's "Nachwort" to H. Kohn, p. 435f. For the text of the resolution, see *A Land of Two Peoples: Martin Buber on Jews and Arabs* (New York: Oxford University Press, 1983), p. 60f.

1. See Editor's note above.
2. Jakob Burckhardt (1818–1897), Swiss cultural historian and pioneering scholar of the Italian Renaissance. Buber took issue with this statement about forty years later in a brief essay devoted to the Swiss historian Carl Burckhardt (1891–1974), "Zu zwei Burckhardt Worten" ("On Two Burckhardt Sayings," Maurice Friedman, trans., *A Believing Humanism: My Testament 1902–1965*

[New York: Simon & Schuster, 1967], pp. 181–82). See also Carl Burckhardt's letter to Buber of 11 November 1961 (Grete Schaeder, ed., *Martin Buber. Briefwechsel aus sieben Jahrzehnten* [Heidelberg: Lambert Schneider, 1973], vol. 3, no. 465).
3. Alfred Mombert (1872–1942), German–Jewish poet of mystical and mythical themes.
4. Latin, literally, the end of the peoples (nations). The motto actually is *de fine populorum* (cf. Alfred Mombert, *Aeon. Dramatische Trilogie,* part 3 [Aeon vor Syrakus] [Berlin: Schuster und Loeffler, 1907]).
5. Semitic god who is sometimes imagined as devouring children.

*Zionism and Nationalism (1929)**[1]

There are not only two fundamental views regarding the national problem and the national reality, as it is often claimed, but three: The first view, the view of the so-called non-Zionists, argues that Israel is less than a nation in the modern sense. The second view argues that Israel is identical with a nation. And the third argues that Israel is more than a nation; in other words, the national characteristics of the modern concept of a nation apply also to the reality of Israel but do not suffice. Israel is a unique creation [*Gebilde*] that includes all characteristics of a nation in the modern sense, without being defined by them; rather, it carries its own laws....

Zionism is not identical with Jewish nationalism. We are very right to call ourselves Zionists and not Jewish nationalists; for Zion means more than nation. Zionism is the belief in a uniqueness. "Zion" is no generic term like "nation" or "state," but a name that denotes something unique and incomparable. Nor is it a mere geographical expression like Canaan or Palestine. Rather, it has always been a name for something that ought to *come into existence* at a certain geographical place on this planet; something that once should have developed, and still ought to develop, or in the words of the Bible, the beginning of the kingdom of God for the human people.

To be sure, whoever believes in and identifies with Zion also believes in a national fact, but even more so does he believe in a supranational task. The vital law of Israel that we can understand from every aspect of our history says that self-assertion is not enough for Israel.... The watchword of the *sacro egoismo* that modern nationalism has coined has no validity for us. It is true that a healthy portion of self-help is necessary for a group no less than for the individual, but this self-help must not deteriorate into selfishness. No matter what goals others might pursue, our

---

* From an address to the Sixteenth Zionist Congress in Zurich (1 August 1929).

principle (which is neither only ideological nor only moral, but based on reality) says that *if we fail to aspire to more than survival, we will not even come to life.* . . .

This is no "new" Zionism. It is the Zionism of all our spiritual leaders—the Zionism of Moses Hess,[2] Ahad Ha'am,[3] the Zionism of Herzl's *Old–New Land*[4] and of A. D. Gordon.[5]

But having said so, we also must take caution not to say that this is something we will realize one day, but first we must create the securities of our life. Nothing is worse than such "sooner or later." You are familiar with our Jewish teaching: All those who turn, who complete their turning, God will forgive, save for those who say, "Let me sin, for there is always the option of turning." . . .

You might object: If we do not participate in the necessary politics of power, how can we secure ourselves? How will we secure this settlement, the beginning *Volksland* in Palestine? To this, I reply, "No conceivable security is as real as this: to become a power in spirit that can sustain the forms of life among the nations, that can become a living example of relations between the nations, that can help prepare a true covenant between Orient and Occident and from there, on the basis of this work, form an alliance with the future elements of all nations." . . .

Again, no "sooner or later!" If we do not begin in the "here and now," under the conditions and decisions of the everyday hour, we will not succeed in fulfilling the task. This, it seems to me, is the only legitimate answer to the Jewish youth of our days; not a form of nationalist assimilation that limps behind all other nationalisms, but a national pioneer spirit that blazes their trail.

I cannot discuss in detail here how this is to be implemented in all realms of life. There are no general formulas. Everyone in his everyday surroundings will experience responsibility. But there are two major examples I would like to offer you. . . .

The first is the Arab question. I shall speak of it in all earnestness and clarity, facing the facts, harsh and cruel as they are. I am afraid that despite these [facts]—no, precisely because of them—growing nationalist assimilation has affected us in this matter. Remember—but I do not need to remind you, for every hour of our life bears witness—how the nations looked down upon us and continue to look down upon us at all places, as strangers, as an inferior group. Let us beware of regarding and treating as inferior what is foreign to us and not sufficiently known! Let us be careful not to commit ourselves what has been committed against us! And let it be said again that while self-assertion is a natural precondition of all our actions, it is not enough. It also requires imagination, the ability to imagine the soul of the other—of the stranger—from within the realities of our own. I must not hold back a confession: It was appalling for me to see in Palestine how little we know the Arab man. I am not deceiving myself into believing that at present a harmony of interests exists between the Arabs and us, or that such harmony could easily be established. And yet, despite all our differences of interest (which result from illusion rather than politics) a political consensus is possible, for there is love for the land there and here, for there is a will for the future of this land there and here. And as we share this common love and common will, it is possible to work together for this land....

Do not, however, ask me for prescriptions in a matter that demands the difficult exercise of personal responsibility in countless small decisions; No more declarations, no more general resolutions! The practical reality of every hour shall show what our intentions are.... I would like to suggest that as a sign of our intentions there be established a permanent commission in Palestine that can function as an advisory board to the Palestine executive in all matters pertaining to the Arab question....

Now, let me briefly address another important issue—the education of youth in Palestine. I believe that in my lifelong work I have demonstrated my awareness for the overall importance of the formal aspects of a nation. I know what the renewal of Hebrew means. But the [renewal of] forms is not enough. Forms can even have a destructive effect if there is no content.... It is not enough to say "renewal" and to talk about forms. One has to approach renewal with utter seriousness. That is, as nurturing forces once emerged from tradition, they now have to emerge from renewal as well and guide our lives. What I would like to see as determining education in Palestine is a Hebrew humanism in the most real sense.[6] It should not be left to the course of development but determine the program, the curriculum, the structure of schools and of the entire education. I have gotten to know the condition of our youth in Palestine a little, and I must not withhold from you that it too is affected by a great *sacro egoismo*. What I mean by Hebrew humanism is that the youth in Palestine will move away from the nationalist assimilation of *sacro egoismo* and turn toward a national pioneer spirit; that it will be educated to fulfill with uncompromising humanness the world-historical task [*geschichtliche Menschheitsaufgabe*] of Judaism at the eternal gate to the nations.

Notes

Source: ["Rede"], first in *Protokoll der Verhandlungen des XVI. Zionistenkongresses und der konstituierenden Tagung des Council der Jewish Agency für Palästina* (London: Zentralbureau der Zionistischen Organisation, 1929). Also in *Selbstwehr* 33 (6 August 1929). Sections translated by Paul Mendes-Flohr in *A Land of Two Peoples: Martin Buber on Jews and Arabs* (New York: Oxford University Press, 1983), pp. 79–80. Asher Biemann, trans., for this volume.

Editor's note: Buber's speech was delivered on behalf of the *Hitachduth* Party (see Nationalism [1921], Editor's note, p. 275) in an attempt to confront the rising Revisionist movement and its leader Vladimir Ze'ev Jabotinsky (1880–1940). In choosing Buber for this task, the *Hitachduth* hoped to "raise the moral and cultural level" of the congress and to reemphasize the spiritual education of Jewish youth (cf. the letter of 11 July 1929 written to Buber by the Zionist politicians Georg Landauer [1895–1954] and Gershom Chanoch [1894–1956]; in Grete Schaeder, ed., *Martin Buber. Briefwechsel aus sieben Jahrzehnten* [Heidelberg: Lambert Schneider, 1973], vol. 2, no. 298). Indeed, Joseph Sprinzak (1885–1959) and Robert Weltsch (1891–1982), both writing on behalf of the *Hitachduth,* expected that Buber's "mere presence" at the congress would help control "Revisionist aspirations" (letter of 17 July 1929; Schaeder, ed., *Briefwechsel*, vol. 2, no. 299).

1. Title not in the original.
2. Moses Hess (1812–1875), see Concepts and Reality (1916) (p. 267, note 5, in this volume).
3. Ahad Ha'am (Asher Ginzberg, 1856–1927), Hebrew essayist and founder of cultural (spiritual) Zionism as a movement that aimed for an above all "spiritual center" of Judaism in Palestine. Buber followed many of Achad Haam's ideas, albeit critically, and sought Achad Haam's cooperation in the opposition against the factions of political Zionism.
4. Theodor Herzl (1860–1904) was often considered the father of modern Zionism. A correspondent and literary editor for the Vienna daily *Neue Freie Presse,* by profession, Herzl tried himself as a playwright ("The New Ghetto," 1894) before he began promoting the idea of a Jewish national state. In February 1896, Herzl's pamphlet *The Jewish State* appeared, and in August 1897 Herzl convened the first Zionist Congress in Basel, which was attended by over 200 delegates from all over the world. In 1902 Herzl published his utopian novel *Old–New-Land* (*Altneuland*). Buber joined Herzl's movement in 1898 and published his first pieces in its journal, *Die Welt*. At the Fifth Zionist Congress in 1901, however, Buber and Herzl split over the question of cultural Zionism (i.e., the revival of Judaism as a national–cultural entity versus the revival of Jews in a national–political entity), and in 1903 again, over the Uganda proposal. That Buber mentions Herzl here as his "spiritual leader" in a line with Hess, Achad Haam, and Gordon, should not be a surprise: For one, Buber had reconciled himself with Herzl's work after 1910; second, he qualifies Herzl's Zionism as the "Zionism of *Old-New-Land*", referring to Herzl's essentially utopian and secular messianic vision of a future (Jewish) State in Palestine that would not depend on the powers of nationalism.
5. Aaron David Gordon (1856–922), pioneer of the labor Zionist movement, moved to Palestine in 1904 to work on various early Jewish settlements and to organize the *Hapoel Hazair* (the young worker), a non-Marxist, Socialist party. In his writings, Gordon emphasized the bond of manual labor between the Jews and their homeland. Buber and Gordon represented the *Hapoel Hazair* at the 1920 founding conference of the *Hitachduth Hapoel Hazair ve Zeirei Zion* in Prague (see also Nationalism [1921] [p. 275 in this volume]).
6. Cf. Biblical Humanism (1933) and Hebrew Humanism (1941) (p. 46 and p. 159 in this volume).

The National Home and National Policy in Palestine (1929)

...It is necessary to consider first of all what Judaism has to do with Palestine. First, the problem of the relations between the Jews and the Arabs in Palestine can be understood only if it is considered against the background of the close connection between the Jewish nation and Palestine. We, who have been considered by others to have betrayed the national ideal, feel more than other sections of the Zionist movement, that this connection between the Land of Israel and the people of Israel is a historical fact and even more, and that the connection is of supreme importance. And we maintain that this cannot be expressed by a national economic formula. It is unjust to speak in the same terms about this nation and this land and the interrelations between them that are used for ordinary nationalism, for this is an exceptional case, in which the accepted ideas are irrelevant. Our position rests on this uniqueness. The Jewish nation remained in existence in opposition to the laws of history because it was the organic bearer of a mission, which it bore not consciously or willingly, but by its very existence; it is the mission for which it was created and by which it lives. The view that a belief in a mission is not the empty consolation of the masses, comforting them for the fact of our dispersion, but something on which our very existence depends, is the underlying motif of what we call Zionism. One thing can be said about this undefinable task: It cannot be maintained by a spiritual undertaking but only through the life we live, and not by the individual's life but through the life of the community. The fulfillment of this task includes, therefore, the creation of a society that establishes a way of life for itself in the country where this task is closely and organically connected with the nation, just as it has been since this nation came into existence as a result of this task.

Not so long ago the yearning for Zion was expressed in the defined and delimited form of the labor of resettling Palestine. This labor had a double implication: the revival of national life and, at the same time, the inception of the fulfillment of a task, which was indissolubly connected with national revival. Anyone who regards our undertaking as one of [pioneering] settlement in Palestine simply to maintain our existence ignores the uniqueness of our activities. This misconception of our task may have grave repercussions.

Zionism affirms the right of the Jewish nation to return to its country and put down roots there. This requires explanation, and we are obliged to delineate our threefold right [to the Land of Israel].

The first right rests on the ancient link [*Urverbundenheit*] between us and the land. This right differs from what is customarily called our "historic right." A historic right in this overall sense does not exist at all: Every chapter in world history that is used as an authority for justifying a given right was preceded by another chapter, which in turn can support a different right. Consequently, it is impossible to claim a right in terms of time. Would not the remnants of those ancient peoples who were dispossessed by the Israelites have the right to question our "historic right?" The ancient link to which I refer is something totally different. What I mean is something evolved from that link, not the complex that we call "culture"—even if it is of an extremely high level, "culture" is no more than one of the various objects that have been the property of nations since the world began. What I am referring to is and will always be a perpetual good for all of humankind; and anyone who recognizes this will also acknowledge our right.

Our second right rests on a proven fact: After thousands of years in which the country was a wasteland, we have transformed it into a settled country, where it was open to us to do so, by years of labor. The right deriving from creation and fertilization [*Recht der Produktivität*] is in fact the right of settlers.[1] The historical approach that rules in these times regards historical events such as the distribution of forces and their influence—the clash of ordered armies—as indisputable proof. This perspective, however, is by no means adequate. Obviously, it is impossible to do anything of historical importance without "power," that is, without the ability to do whatever it is you want to do. However, this is vastly different from the superior power that has been held in such high esteem by contemporary political historians. The vital aspect of the great situations in history has not been which side has "more" power when forces clash with one another, but who has a certain ability to conquer the confusion of the situation and the period after it—who can fulfill the hidden requirements. There are victories that are the outcome of physical superiority alone, but these invariably end in chaos. The right of settlement in Palestine belongs to those who are able to cope with a specific settlement situation. And let us state quite openly that the situation of our settlement includes the lives of the Arab inhabitants of the country, whom we do not intend to expel, and that therefore we must include them in our undertaking if we really wish to conquer the specific confusion that exists here.

The third right applies to the future. The activities that we have begun in Palestine are not directed toward creating just another small nation in the family of nations, another tiny people in the world of peoples, another creature to jump and intervene in world disputes. No, our aim is to start something new; to begin the fulfillment of a task. Within the small groups that exist in our Palestine something is being quietly created that hints at the establishment of a new type of individuals—people who will bear the burden of fulfilling an ancient purpose, leading to the revival to which the Jews have borne witness and which they have bestowed on all nations. It is an error to regard these attempts at communal living merely as an experiment; for these attempts, which will probably give rise to a new kind of society, are, in my opinion, more important than the vast Russian experiment, which must inevitably end in political centralization. Even those who regard these communities as romantically utopian have themselves been blinded by contemporary doctrines, since more than anywhere else in the world, in these Palestine *kibbutzim* there is a healthy realism. And let us not be blinded or struck dumb by the abstract concept of realism that derides all spiritual romanticism and adheres to concrete facts only. More than anywhere else in the world there is here a *topos*—a place where there is a concrete social transformation, not of institutions and organizations, but of interpersonal relations. At the same time, roots are being struck in the land of the ancient, chosen homeland. The social revolution, however, is an indispensable precondition for this striking of roots.

Something is being created here that is of unprecedented importance, an example for all mankind marking out the path for it, by trial and error, and even by missing the way from time to time. We thereby demand justice, in the fullest sense of the word, from humanity, provided it is aware of its real troubles and its genuine needs.

We are now faced, however, with the added responsibility for the nation that has become our neighbor in Palestine and that, in many respects, shares a common fate with us. No contradiction could be greater, if we continue to preserve the idea of our internal mission, than for us to build a true communal life within our own community while, at the same time, excluding the other inhabitants of the country from participation, even though their lives and hopes, like ours, are dependent upon the future of the country.

... It is said that when the Zionist leader Max Nordau[2] first heard that there were Arabs in Palestine, he rushed excitedly to Herzl, proclaiming: "I didn't know that! If that is the case, then we are doing an injustice." In recent years I heard people who generally support Nordau's ideas maintain, "Life cannot exist without injustice; anyone who is not prepared to commit injustice is forced to deny his own existence. As regards a nation—it is inconceivable that a nation should behave in such a manner!"

It is indeed true that there can be no life without injustice. The fact that there is no living creature that can live and thrive without destroying another existing organism has a symbolic significance as regards our human life. But the *human* aspect of life begins the moment we say to ourselves: We will not do *more* injustice to others than we are forced to do to exist. Only by saying that do we begin to be *responsible* for life. This responsibility is not a matter of principle and is never fixed; the extent of the injustice that cannot be determined beforehand but must be reassessed each time, must be recognized anew in the inner recesses of the mind, whence the lightning of recognition flashes forth. Only he who acknowledges it, as the result of serious examination that leaves no room for pricks of conscience, only he can live a human life; and a nation that does so, its life is that of a humanitarian nation [*Menschenvolk*]. The group's responsibility for life is not qualitatively different from that of the individual; for if this were not the case the members of the group would truly fulfill their responsibility only as individuals. The collective element within them would necessarily oppose the individual aspect within them and would undermine and even destroy it; anyone who is [morally] severe with himself as an individual and lenient with himself as a member of a group will eventually, whether consciously or not, falter when he has to fulfill personal responsibility.

Every responsible relationship between an individual and his fellow begins through the power of a genuine imagination [*aktuelle Phantasie*], as if we were the residents of Palestine and the others were the immigrants who were coming into the country in increasing numbers, year by year, taking it away from us. How would we react to events? Only if we know this will it be possible to minimize the injustice we must do to survive and to live the life to which we are not only entitled but obliged to live, since we live for the eternal mission, which has been embedded within us since our creation....

Our relations with the Arabs ought to be developed positively in every respect; economically, by developing a practical community of interests and not, as we have done in the past, by giving assurances of an existing solidarity of interests. Everywhere and at all times when economic decisions have to be made, the interest of the Arab people should be taken into account. This has not been done often enough. Everyone who knows the situation is aware of the many opportunities that have been missed.

As regards internal policy, it is a matter of establishing a combination between national independence and possible coexistence—what is called a binational state. The question of the political representation of the [two] peoples would mean the first stage in the institution of the idea. It is a terribly difficult decision that has confronted us over the years, but we have evaded it. You will ask whether we are sufficiently mature to make this decision. I believe so. If we were to assure the Arab people that we are demanding popular representation together with them, our right to exist would of necessity be safeguarded. This means that a parliament can only be established with the consent of both peoples on the basis of a Magna Carta—of a primary constitution guaranteed by the competent authorities of the world, securing our basic rights, as well as those of the Arabs, that is, above all, the right to immigrate [to Palestine]. There may be many who think otherwise. To me it is a question of a parliament and that this matter of life or death cannot simply be decided by a majority.

As regards external policy, I remember having raised the question—in 1921 in the Political Commission of the Twelfth Congress—whether we should not take into consideration the beginnings of a development toward an alliance between us and the Arab states and whether we should not also include this possibility in our perspective.[3] At the time, I was told by a competent source that this was not an actual possibility. I do not want to investigate how actual it has become now, but it seems beyond doubt that in our policy and calculations, as well as in our discussions and negotiations, we must declare unambiguously that we would not stand in the way of such a development and that we would not be the forerunners of any power that would wish to prevent it.

As to the question of religion, Islam is a much greater reality than we would wish to admit. It is our duty to get to know this reality. I must confess to you that the present religious reality of Judaism is less evident to me. I mean to say that the Arab population is much more strongly conditioned by Islam than the Jews in general are by Judaism. Religion for the Arabs is also a matter of culture; hence, we have been remiss in not acquainting ourselves with Islam and in establishing contacts with its religious authorities. In Palestine I have often observed that Jews who are conversant with Islam are beloved and honored by the Arabs. But there are only a handful of such Jews. The prime necessity for personal contact is a knowledge of the Arabic language. Mutual understanding is only possible through language. As far as socializing is concerned, surely there are social contacts between Jewish and Arab villages, which even take very beautiful, genuine oriental forms. But in the towns there exists much less genuine social intercourse between the two peoples. The situation is better in proletarian circles; but real socializing between Arabs and Jews is still the exception. In this context the cultural question is relevant. Nationally there can be no merging of cultures, but there could be a cultural accommodation with Arabism as a whole, cultural exchange in educational institutions, exchange of cultural values and achievements, and real cooperation....

It especially disgusts me when people speak against the politics of mutual understanding in the name of "national pride." True national pride would logically bring us closer to the Arabs, for it is only on the basis of agreement with them that we can expand and assure our enterprise—building up the land—whose guarantee is our national honor. What distances us from the Arabs is our national arrogance.

A few years ago I spoke about the Arab question with the director of a great cultural institution of the *Yishuv*. The man spoke similarly to this effect: "You know me, and you know that I am no chauvinist, but they are an inferior race." We are spoken of in similar terms in several parts of

Europe. Who is right? As long as we have not imagined to ourselves the inner reality of a nation whose life is motivated by other factors and whose principles are different in nature from our own, as long as we do not come to know and understand what goes on in that nation's heart of hearts and what is expressed by those factors and principles, we shall always consider what is different as inferior. The inner reality of every nation has its own value, and any external criterion by which you come to judge it can only be erroneous.

... The closed-minded attitudes inform the dominant type of nationalism, which has gained so many adherents among us—the most worthless assimilation—which teaches that everyone must consider his own nation as an absolute and all other nations as something relative; that one must evaluate one's own nation on the basis of its greatest era, and all other nations on the basis of their lowest points. If this idea continues to gain acceptance it will lead to a worldwide disaster.

The open-minded attitude of humanitarian nationalism, which claims supporters from our midst who have been "fighting for the Arabs" as long as Zionism has been a political doctrine, demands of us that we judge other nations as we would wish to be judged ourselves, not by our own basest deeds, nor by our greatest acts, but by those that are characteristic of us, which reflect our character. Only a system of this nature can educate mankind, guaranteeing its stand in face of the dangers that are likely to assail it in the generation to come and that no words can express.

Assuredly there are many aspects of the Palestinian Arabs that are annoying to us (just as there are things in us which, in certain respects, are displeasing to me); but we must not ignore the fact that among them the connection with the land—something that will take us a long time still to accomplish—has taken a positive, even organic, form; it is an accepted fact that is no longer even considered. They, not we, have something that can be called a Palestinian style; the huts of the village *fellahin*[4] have grown out of this earth, whereas the houses of Tel Aviv were built on its back. The prostration of Abraham the Patriarch when he invited the passersby into his house can be seen still today but not among us....

There is another attitude that should be given greater attention by us than "national pride:" I would call it an attitude of turning [*Umschwungs-Standpunkt*],[5] and this is the essential point to which many of our workers faithfully hold.

This attitude is based upon the conception of Palestinian society as being divided into classes. It is claimed that the masters, the *effendis*, incite the proletarians, the *fellahin*, against us to divert their attention from the class-consciousness awakening among them—from their revolt against social suppression; the Arab nationalist movement is, therefore, an artificial creation and should be evaluated as such. It is unjust on our part to negotiate with the *effendis*,[6] who cannot be considered to be representatives of the nation; it is our duty, however, to pierce the unnatural front that they have established together with the proletariat, and we will achieve this by making the proletariat aware of their class and uniting them in a socialist front that includes members of both nations. Then they will no longer be led astray by nationalist slogans.

It cannot be disputed that this second attitude does embody an important element of the truth, and that those things that it upholds are of the utmost importance, both now and in the future: cooperation between the two bodies of workers, the enhancement of the organizations and institutions of the Arab proletariat, and the influence of socialist education. But this view also embodies an oversimplification without an adequate basis in fact.

First of all, we must make it clear to ourselves that the nature of things is such that the class consciousness of the Arab masses will develop very slowly and that it will need far more time to develop than has their national awareness, part of which is nothing but old religious fanaticism in a new guise. The socialist process is indeed preferable from the standpoint of feasibility; but the political process is preferable as regards the pace, and in the prevailing circumstances this is of supreme importance for us.

Moreover, the idea that the Arab Nationalist movement in Palestine is artificial is basically unsound. In discussing this from a historical point of view, beginning with the development of the concept of Arab independence, which takes on different forms according to the political conditions in each country and conducts each battle differently, one reaches the conclusion that the internal revolution that has taken place in Palestine [among the Arab population] is only one expression of this general movement. We have our *effendis,* not only since the establishment of the expanded Jewish Agency but since the rise of Zionism, which rests on the alliance between the Jewish bourgeoisie and the proletariat. We know that despite this alliance we have a genuine national unity and real nationalist movement; why should we assume that these do not exist among the Arabs? It is true that in general our *effendis* in Palestine do not evince the tendency of their Arab counterparts to undermine society through class warfare; but are not their feelings of social egoism accompanied by a measure of national enthusiasm? Have we not seen, alongside those shadow figures, honest national politicians who will eventually weaken the position of the former?

I do not know of any political activity more harmful than regarding one's ally or opponent as if he were cast in one fixed mold. When we consider him as "like that," we fall victim to the irrationality of his existence; only when we pay attention to the fact that human nature is much the same all over the world will we be able to come to grips with reality.

We have not settled Palestine together with the Arabs but alongside them. Settlement "alongside" [*neben*], when two nations inhabit the same country—which fails to become settlement "together with" [*mit*], must necessarily become a state of "against." This is bound to happen here, and there will be no return to a mere "alongside." But despite all the obstacles in our path, the way is still open for reaching a settlement "together with." And I do not know how much time is left to us. What I do know is that if we do not attain [such a relationship with the Arabs of Palestine], we will never realize the aims of Zionism. We are being put to the test for the third time in this country.

Notes

Source: "Jüdisches Nationalheim und nationale Politik in Palästina" (lecture at the Berlin chapter of B'rith Shalom, 31 October 1929). Manuscript from *Martin Buber Archive,* ms. var. 350, vav 14 (now in *Ein Land und zwei Völker—Zur jüdisch-arabischen Frage,* ed. Paul Mendes-Flohr [Frankfurt/M.: Insel Verlag, 1983], pp. 115–29). Revised and abridged in *Kampf um Israel—Reden und Schriften, 1921–1932* (Berlin: Schocken, 1932). Gabrielle H. Schalit, trans., in *A Land of Two Peoples: Martin Buber on Jews and Arabs,* ed. Paul Mendes-Flohr (New York: Oxford University Press, 1983), pp. 82–91; 93–95. Schalit's translation, which is printed here, incorporates sections from both the published essay and the manuscript (as published in 1983).

Editor's note: After a series of disturbances of Jewish worship at the Western Wall by the Supreme Muslim Council beginning in May 1929, the Revisionist-affiliated youth group *Betar* (B'rith Yosef Trumpeldor) staged a major demonstration at the site during *Tisha be'Av* (the Jewish commemorative day for the destruction of the temple in 70 C.E.), which was answered by an Arab counter-demonstration. At the end of August 1929, violent clashes between Arabs, Jews, and the mandatory police force broke out in Jerusalem, Safed, and Hebron. Although it is doubtful that the Western Wall incident was the immediate cause, the left-leaning Zionists still held *Betar* and Jabotinsky's Revisionists responsible for the Arab riots. Two months after the event, Buber was invited to speak at the Berlin chapter of B'rith Shalom (covenant of peace; see Introduction, p. 13) and to clarify the goals of "true" Zionism and its perception of the Arab–Jewish conflict.

1. Martin Buber uses the rather misleading term "kolonisatorisches Recht."
2. Max Nordau (1849–1923), important Zionist thinker closely associated with Theodor Herzl; best known for his promotion of physical education among Jews ("Jews of muscle").
3. Following the Arab riots of May 1920, Buber addressed the Twelfth Zionist Congress with a call for rapprochement with the Arabs in Palestine: "By establishing a just alliance with the Arab peoples, we wish to turn our common dwelling-place into a community that will flourish economically and culturally, and whose progress would bring each of these peoples unhampered independent development." ("Rede auf dem XII. Zionisten-Kongress in Karlsbad," trans. Paul Mendes-Flohr in *A Land of Two Peoples,* p. 61).
4. Arab peasants.
5. Not in G. Schalit, but in both essay and manuscript. Note that "turning" (*Umschwung*) does not have the usual positive connotation for Buber.
6. Arab land-holding aristocrat.

Zionism and "Zionism" (1948)

From the beginning, modern Zionism contained two basic tendencies that were opposed to each other in the most thoroughgoing way—an internal contradiction that reaches to the depths of human existence. For a long time this contradiction was not felt except in the realm of ideas. However, since the political situation has grown increasingly concrete and the need for decisive action has arisen alongside it, the internal contradiction has become more and more real, until, in recent years, it has attained shocking actuality.

One can comprehend the two tendencies at the origin as two different interpretations of the concept of [national] rebirth.

One tendency was to comprehend that concept as the intention of returning and restoring the true Israel, whose spirit and life would once again no longer exist beside each other like separate fields, each one subject to its own law, as they existed during the nation's wandering in the wilderness of exile but, rather, the spirit would build the life, like a dwelling, or like flesh. Rebirth: Its meaning is not simply the secure existence of the nation instead of its present vulnerability but, rather, the experience of fulfillment instead of our present state of being, in which ideas float naked in a reality devoid of ideas.

On the other hand, the second tendency grasps the concept of rebirth in its simplest meaning: normalization. A "normal" nation needs a land, a language, and independence. Thus, one must only go and acquire those commodities, and the rest will take care of itself. How will people live with each other in this land? What will people say to each other in that language? What will be the connection of their independence with the rest of humanity? All of these questions are of no interest to this interpretation of rebirth. Be normal, and you've already been reborn!

In fact these two tendencies are only a new form of the pair that have been running next to each other from ancient times: the powerful consciousness of the task of maintaining truth and justice in the total life of the nation, internally and externally, and thus becoming an example and a light to humanity; and the natural desire—all too natural—to be "like the nations." The ancient Hebrews did not succeed in becoming a normal nation.

Today, the Jews are succeeding at it to a terrifying degree.

Never in the past have spirit and life been so distant from each other as now, in this period of "rebirth." Or maybe you are willing to call "spirit" a collective selfishness that acknowledges no higher standards and yields to no uplifting decree? Where do truth and justice determine our deeds, either outwardly or inwardly? (I say "inwardly" because unruliness [*Verrohung*] directed outward inevitably brings on unruliness directed inward.) This sort of "Zionism" blasphemes the name of Zion; it is nothing more than one of the crude forms of nationalism, which acknowledge no master above the *apparent* (!) interest of the nation. Let us say that it is revealed as a form of *national assimilation,* more dangerous than individual assimilation; for the latter only harms the individuals and families who assimilate, whereas national assimilation erodes the nucleus of Israel's independence.

From the clear recognition of these tendencies, which stand in opposition to each other, derives the principal political question confronting us as we dig out the roots of the political problems of our day.

The self-realizing tendency says that we wish to return to the earth to acquire the natural foundations of human life [*Volksleben*] that make the spirit real. We do not wish to return to any land whatsoever, but to that land in which we first grew up, since it alone may arouse historical and metahistorical forces into action, coupling spirit with life, and life with spirit. This land is not, today, devoid of inhabitants, as it was not in those times in which our nation trod upon it as it burst forth out of the desert. But today we will not tread upon it as conquerors. In the past we were forced to conquer it, because its inhabitants were essentially opposed to the spirit of "Israel." Moreover, the danger of Baalization,[1] that is, the danger of subjugating the spirit to the rule of the instincts, was not entirely averted even by conquest. Today we are not obliged to conquer the land, for no danger is in store for our spiritual essence or our way of life from the population of the land. Not as in ancient days, today we are permitted to enter into an alliance with the inhabitants to develop the land together and make it a pathfinder in the Near East—a covenant of two independent nations with equal rights, each of whom is its own master in its own society and culture, but both united in the enterprise of developing their common homeland and in the federal management of shared matters. On the strength of that covenant we wish to return once more to the union of Near Eastern nations, to build an economy integrated in that of the Near East, to carry out policies in the framework of the life of the Near East, and, God willing, to send the "living idea" forth to the world from the Near East once again. And the path to that? Work and peace—peace founded upon work in common.

In contrast to this view of Zionism, the "protective" tendency makes only one demand: sovereignty. That demand was expressed and presented in two different forms, one beside the other. The first form crystallized around the "democratic" concept of the majority: We must endeavor to create a Jewish majority in a state that will include the whole Land of Israel.[2] It was evident that the meaning of that program was war—real war—with our neighbors and also with the whole Arab nation: For what nation will allow itself to be demoted from the position of majority to that of a minority without a fight?

When that program was revealed to be illusory, a program of tearing off took its place; that is, tearing one part of the land away from the rest, and [establishing] in the torn off portion—once again, a majority—a Jewish State.[3] They frivolously sacrificed the completeness of the land that the Zionist movement once set out to "redeem." If only we can attain sovereignty! The life concept of "independence" was replaced by the administrative concept of "sovereignty." The watchword of peace was exchanged for that of struggle.

This has been done during a period when the value of the sovereignty of small states is diminishing with frightening rapidity. Instead of the aspiration of becoming a leading and active group within the framework of a Near Eastern union, there has come the goal of establishing a small state that is endangered in that it stands in perpetual opposition to its geopolitical environment and must apply its best forces to military activity instead of applying them to social and cultural enterprises.

This is the demand for which we are waging war today.

Fifty years ago, when I joined the Zionist movement for the rebirth of Israel, my heart was whole. Today it is torn. The war being waged for a political structure risks becoming a war of national survival at any moment. Thus, against my will I participate in it with my own being, and my heart trembles like that of any other Israeli. I cannot, however, even be joyful in anticipating victory, for I fear lest the significance of Jewish victory be the downfall of Zionism.

Notes

Source: "Zionut ve-'Zionut'," first in *Be'ayot ha-Zman* 7, no. 8 (27 May 1948). "Zweierlei Zionismus," first in *Die Stunde* (Jerusalem) (28 May 1948). Jeffrey M. Green, trans., in *A Land of Two Peoples*, ed. Paul Mendes-Flohr (New York: Oxford University Press, 1983), pp. 220–23.

Editor's note: On 14 May 1948, under the leadership of David Ben-Gurion, the *Yishuv* unilaterally declared independence and statehood, rendering the binational aspirations of B'rith Shalom and *Ichud* (see Introduction, p. 13 of this volume) an anachronism at best. With the young State of Israel still in a state of euphoria (albeit most seriously threatened by the immediate invasion from the bordering Arab countries), Buber warned not to regard independence as a value in itself but to continue the pursuit of "true" Zionism and "true" independence. Like many religious leaders before him, however, such as Rav Kook (1865–1935), the first Ashkenazic Chief Rabbi during the British mandate, or Yitzhak Breuer (1883–1946), one of the ideologues of the Orthodox Agudat Israel, Buber began to see political Zionism as a "necessary evil" for higher, spiritual goals.

1. J. M. Green: "paganization." Martin Buber's reference to the pagan god Baal, whose cult was widely followed in the biblical land of Canaan and posed a constant threat to early Judaism is, of course, deliberate.
2. The reference is to the Biltmore Program (named after the Biltmore Hotel in New York City), which David Ben-Gurion initiated in May 1942. The program demanded unlimited immigration to Palestine (especially for Jews from Europe) and the establishment of a "Jewish Commonwealth." On Buber's opposition to the program, see *A Land of Two Peoples,* p. 160f.
3. Buber is referring to the United Nations partition plan of 29 November 1947, which proposed a Jewish state (including the coastal plane between Ashkelon to Acre, the eastern Galilee and most of the Negev) and an Arab state (with Jerusalem as internationalized enclave). The proposal was accepted by the Zionist leadership, but opposed by Buber and the small *Ichud* (Unity) organization of which he was a part.

Bibliographical Guide

Books and Anthologies by Martin Buber in English Translation

For a complete bibliography through 1978, see Cohn, Margot, and Buber, Rafael, *Martin Buber: A Bibliography of His Writings, 1897–1978*. Jerusalem, Munich, London, New York, and Paris: Magnes Press and K.G. Saur, 1980.

A Believing Humanism: My Testament 1902–1965. Translated by Maurice Friedman. New York: Simon & Schuster (Credo Perspectives), 1967.

A Land of Two Peoples: Martin Buber on Jews and Arabs. Edited, with commentary by Paul Mendes-Flohr. New York: Oxford University Press, 1983.

At the Turning: Three Addresses on Judaism. New York: Farrar, Strauss & Young, 1952; also in *On Judaism*.

Between Man and Man. Translated by Ronald Gregor Smith. London: Routledge & K. Paul, 1947. New, expanded edition with an introduction by Maurice Friedman. New York: Macmillan, 1965.

Buber's Way to "I and Thou": The Development of Martin Buber's Thought and His "Religion as Presence" Lectures. See "Religion as Presence."

Chinese Tales: Zhuangzi: Sayings, Parables, Chinese Ghost and Love Stories. Amherst, N.Y.: Prometheus Books, 1998.

Daniel: Dialogues on Realization. Translated with an introduction by Maurice Friedman. New York: Holt, Rinehart & Winston, 1964.

Eclipse of God: Studies in the Relation Between Religion and Philosophy. Translated by Maurice Friedman et al. New York: Harper, 1952.

Ecstatic Confessions: The Heart of Mysticism. Edited by Paul Mendes-Flohr. San Francisco: Harper, 1985.

Encounter—Autobiographical Fragments. La Salle, Ill.: Open Court, 1972; also as *Meetings*. Edited with introduction and bibliography by Maurice Friedman. La Salle, Ill.: Open Court, 1973.

The First Buber: Youthful Zionist Writings of Martin Buber. Edited and translated by Gilya Gerda Schmidt. New York: Syracuse University Press, 1999.

For the Sake of Heaven. Translated by Ludwig Lewisohn. Philadelphia: Jewish Publication Society, 1946. Now as *Gog and Magog*. New York: Syracuse University Press, 1999.

Gog and Magog. See *For the Sake of Heaven*.

Good and Evil: Two Interpretations. Translated by Ronald Gregor Smith and Michael Bullock. New York: Scribner's, 1952.

Hasidism. New York: The Philosophical Library, 1948; also in *The Origin and Meaning of Hasidism*.

Hasidism and Modern Man. Edited and translated by Maurice Friedman. New York: Horizon Press, 1958.

I and Thou. Translated by Ronald Gregor Smith. Edinburgh: T. & T. Clark, 1937. Now, New York: Scribner's, 2000.

I and Thou. Translated with prologue and notes by Walter Kaufman. New York: Scribner's, 1970. Now, New York: Simon & Schuster (Touchstone), 1996.

Images of Good and Evil. Translated by Michael Bullock. London: Routledge & K. Paul, 1952; also in *Good and Evil*.

Israel and Palestine—The History of an Idea. Translated by Stanley Godman. New York: Farrar, Strauss and Young (London: East and West Library), 1952. Also as *On Zion—The History of an Idea*, with a new foreword by Nahum N. Glatzer. London: East and West, 1973.

Israel and the World: Essays in a Time of Crisis. New York: Schocken, 1948.

Kingship of God. Translated, with a foreword by Richard Scheinmann, New York: Harper & Row, 1967. Now, Brill Academic Publishers, 1990, and Amherst, N.Y.: Prometheus Books, 1990.

The Knowledge of Man. Edited by Maurice Friedman. London: George Allen & Unwin, 1965.

The Legend of the Baal-Shem. Translated by Maurice Friedman. New York: Harper, 1955.

The Letters of Martin Buber: A Life of Dialogue. Edited by Nahum N. Glatzer and Paul Mendes-Flohr; translated by Clara Winston and Harry Zohn. New York: Schocken, 1991.

Mamre: Essays in Religion. Translated by Greta Hort. Melbourne and London: Melbourne University Press, in association with Oxford University Press, 1946.

Martin Buber and the Theatre. Edited and translated, with an introduction by Maurice Friedman. New York: Funk & Wagnalls, 1969.

Meetings. See *Encounter*.

Moses: The Revelation and the Covenant. Oxford: East and West Library, 1946. Now, Amherst, N.Y.: Prometheus Books, 1998.

On Intersubjectivity and Cultural Creativity. Edited with an introduction by S. N. Eisenstadt. Chicago and London: Chicago University Press, 1992.

On Judaism. Translated by Eva Jospe; edited by Nahum N. Glatzer. New York: Schocken, 1967.

On Psychology and Psychotherapy: Essays, Letters, and Dialogue. Edited by Judith Buber-Agassi. New York: Syracuse University Press, 1998.

On the Bible: Eighteen Studies by Martin Buber. Edited by Nahum N. Glatzer. New York: Schocken, 1968.

On Zion. See *Israel and Palestine*.

The Origin and Meaning of Hasidism. Edited and translated by Maurice Friedman. New York: Horizon Press, 1960.

Paths in Utopia. Translated by R. F. C. Hull. London: Routledge & K. Paul, 1949.

Pointing the Way: Collected Essays. Edited and translated by Maurice Friedman. New York: Harper & Brothers, 1957.

The Prophetic Faith. Translated by Carlyle Witton-Davies. New York: Macmillan, 1949.

"Religion as Presence" (lectures of 1922), first published in Rivka Horwitz, *Buber's Way to "I and Thou": The Development of Martin Buber's Thought and His "Religion as Presence" Lectures*. Philadelphia, New York, Jerusalem: Jewish Publication Society, 1988 (German 1978).

Right and Wrong: An Interpretation of Some Psalms. Translated by Ronald Gregor Smith. London: S.C.M. Press, 1952; also in *Good and Evil*.

Scripture and Translation (Martin Buber and Franz Rosenzweig). Translated by Lawrence Rosenwald and Everett Fox. Bloomington: Indiana University Press, 1994.

Tales of Angels, Spirits, and Demons. Translated by David Antin and Jerome Rothenberg. New York: Hawk's Well Press, 1958.

Tales of Rabbi Nachman. Translated by Maurice Friedman. New York: Horizon Press, 1956.

Tales of the Hasidim—Early Masters. Translated by Olga Marx. New York: Schocken, 1947.

Tales of the Hasidim—Later Masters. Translated by Olga Marx. New York: Schocken, 1948.

Ten Rungs: Hasidic Sayings. Translated by Olga Marx. New York: Schocken, 1947.

To Hallow this Life—An Anthology. Edited, with an introduction by Jacob Trapp. New York: Harper, 1958.

Two Types of Faith. Translated by Norman P. Goldhawk. London: Routledge & K. Paul, 1951.

The Way of Man According to the Teachings of Hasidism. London: Routledge & K. Paul, 1950. Now, Carol Publishing Group, 1995; also in *Hasidism and Modern Man*.

The Way of Response: Martin Buber, Selections from His Writings. Edited by Nahum N. Glatzer. New York: Schocken, 1966.

The Writings of Martin Buber. Edited, with an introduction by Will Herberg. New York: Meridian Books, 1956.

INDEX

Abel, 36
Abraham, 27–28
  as biblical leader, 34–35
  dialogues of, 41
Absalom, 37
Action, dialogical principle and, 101
Aggadah, 121
Agnon, Shmuel Yosef, 16n7, 179n
Amos, 23–24, 120, 147
Anthropology
  Buber's interest in, 213n
  integrative, 12
  normative, 14
Anti-Semitism, 3
Apperception, synthesizing, 208
Arab nationalist movement, 286–287
Arab-Jewish conflict, 12–13
Arabs
  Jewish relations with, 281, 291
  Zionism and, 278–279, 281–288
Art
  as dialogue, 199
  encounters with, 173–174
Asceticism, 228
Assimilation, 142
  alternatives to, 3
Autonomy, false *versus* God-willed, 222
Avodah (service)
  evil urge in, 67
  and flow into *hitlahavut,* 77–78
  versus hitlahavut, 76
  in life of hasidim, 74–78
  priorities of, 66–67

Baader, Franz, 108, 114n4
Baal-Shem Tov, 2, 69, 116
  parables of, 76–77, 83, 89–90
  on priorities of service, 66–67
Bakunin, Mikhail Aleksandrovitch, 246, 246n2

Barth, Karl, 220, 222n3
Ben-Gurion, David, 13, 291n, 292n2
Ben-Zakkai, Yohanan, 151, 157n9
Berdichevski, Micha Yosef, 6, 16n7
Between *(Zwischen),* art in realm of, 210
Bialik, Haim N., 265, 267n3
Bible *(see also* Hebrew scriptures; Torah)
  Buber-Rosenzweig translation of, 10
  chasm between modern man and, 55
  context of events in, 52–53
  creation, revelation, redemption in, 55
  as documentation of effect of unconditional on Jewish people, 136
  Hebrew humanism and, 160
  law in, 53
  theme of, 51
Biblical humanism *(see also* Hebrew humanism)
  language in, 49
Biblical leadership, 33–42
  characterization of, 35–36
  failures of, 36–37
  and foreshadowing of dialogical man, 41
  by judges, 39
  by kings, 39–40
  by patriarchs, 38
  by prophets, 40–42
  removal from community, 42
  theocracy and, 39
  types of, 37–38
  by younger sons, 36
Bildung (education), 1, 15n1
Bloch, Ernst, 2
Body, in Hasidism, 67–71
Böhme, Jakob, 4
British mandate, 275n

Buber, Martin
    academic career of, 8, 10
    background of, 1–2, 15n2
    relationship with Zionism, 291n
    shift from religious to philosophical orientation, 10
    in United States, 13–14, 19n58
    writings of, 5
Burckhardt, Carl, 275n2
Burckhardt, Jakob, 4, 144n, 275n2
Burdach, Konrad, 46–47, 49, 158, 160–161, 165n5
Burning Bush (see also Sinai)
    dialogical principle and, 24, 28, 108
    unconditionality and, 120

Christianity
    and distortion of Jesus's message, 117
    early, 154
    and fusing of revelation-redemption, 55
    versus Judaism, 113
    as original Judaism, 151
    soul of, 108
    transformation of "turning" in, 121
Cohen, Arthur, 14
Cohen, Hermann, 12, 263, 267, 267n
Collective, idea of, 243
Commandments (see also Ten Commandments) 613, 133, 138n12
Commune, 4
    rebirth of, 245
Communication, silence as, 189–190
Community (Gemeinschaft), 8, 247–251
    Abraham's role in, 27–28
    as by-product, 253
    center of, 244
    creating, 252–257
    decline of, 248
    as destiny, 256
    dialogue in, 200–202
    essence of, 243–246
    Essene, 121, 155
    experiments with, 4–5
    of faith, 254–255, 273
    in Hebrew humanism, 46
    Judaism and, 255
    loss of, by biblical leaders, 41–42
    mystery of, 76
    national, 254
    need for, 137
    in Palestine, 237
    in progress, 255–256
    rebirth of, 249
    social philosophy and, 11

    versus society, 247, 252
    of spirit with spirit, 130
    studies of, 12
    of work, 254
    youth's relationship with, 128, 130, 134
    of zaddik, 70
Community soul (Gesamtseele), 34
Communization (Vergemeinschaftung), 252
Conversation
    genuine, 211
    with opponent, 202–205
Covenant (berith)
    of absolute with concrete, 229–230
    in Deuteronomy, 30–31
    faith as, 108
    revelation as, 24
Creation
    man as partner in, 118
    meaning in biblical story, 57
    revelation as perception of, 56–57
    speech as act of, 99
Creation story, second, 26–27
Culture, Jewish, 3–4

David, 36
    dialogues of, 41
    failures of, 37
Decalogue (see Ten Commandments)
Decision
    as encounter, 174
    as religious act, 116, 117–118
Deed
    centrality in Judaism, 236
    versus faith, 150–151
    in Jewish renewal, 150–153
    teaching and, 234–239
    value of, 237
    wisdom in excess of, 237
Delitzsch, Franz Julius von, 114n
Descartes, René, 228–229, 233n9
Deuteronomy, eagle passage elucidated in, 29
Dialogical principle (see also I-Thou/I-You relationship)
    in biblical Jewish thinking, 8
    biblical leadership and, 41–42
    in biblical word, 48–49
    early manifestations of, 8
    evolution of, 12
    in I and Thou, 188n
    in language, 49–50
    revelation and, 9
    in Rosenzweig's thought, 32n6
    in writings, 10

Dialogue (*see also* I-Thou/I-You relationship)
art as, 199
with being, human life as, 86
Buber's concept of, 5–6
at Burning Bush, 24–25, 28
in community, 200–202
between Divine and human, 25
genuine, 214–215
genuine *versus* technical, 196
in giving of Ten Commandments, 43–45
history as, 37–38
invasion of semblance in, 215
outside content, 190
realms of, 196–197
in religious disputations, 190–191
responsibility in, 194–196
in silence, 189–190
turning toward other in, 191, 197–198
Diaspora
corroding forces in, 238
revival of Judaism in, 2
Dilthey, Wilhelm, 4, 6, 158, 165*n*4
Distance
in man's relationship with things, 209–210
primal setting at, 207
relation and, 206–213
Divine (*see also* God; Shekhinah)
relationship with, 223–224
Dogma, 140
Dov Baer of Mezritch, 71*n*
Duality
inner, 116
Iranian conception of, 99, 105
of man, 136
Dubnow, Simon, 16*n*7
Dühring, Karl Eugen, 4

Ebner, Ferdinand, 9, 18*n*40, *n*42
Ecstasy (*hitlahavut*) (*see* Hitlahavut [ecstasy])
Education (*Bildung*), 1, 15*n*1
Egoism
versus bending back, 198
national, 7
Egotism, national, 3
Eisenstadt, Shmuel N., 12
Election (*see* Israel/Israelites, election of)
Elijah, 116
Encounter (*Begegnung*), 8
as biblical theme, 51
decision as, 174
human, 172

with nature, 173
Thou in, 174–176
with work of art, 173–174
with You, 184
End of days, 111–112
Enlightenment
European, 1
Jewish (*see* Jewish Enlightenment [*haskalah*])
Epicurus, 232*n*1
Eschatology, Jewish, 111–112
Essene community, 121, 155
Ethics, religious life and, 101, 102
Events, in conscious life, 170
Everyday (*see also* Profane)
religion as, 193–194
Evil urge (*yezer hara*)
failure to transform, 116
inertia as root of, 100
Jewish concept of, 99
power as, 269
serving God with, 67
Exodus story, significance of, 25–26
Experience (*Erfahrung*)
in conscious life, 169–170
It, 169–172
lived (*Erlebnis*), 170–171
primeval, 109
through feeling, 171
world as, 183

Failure, biblical glorification of, 36–37
Faith, 97–106
community of, 273
covenant and, 108
versus deed, 150–151
dialogical situation and, 98–99
nontheological concept of, 97
as relationship to Being, 224
in syncretistic Christianity, 151–152
Fall
act of decision and, 118
Jewish concept of, 99–100
Family, community and, 253
Farber, Leslie H., 14
Fear of God, 109–110, 227
Feiwel, Berthold, 3
Feuerbach, Ludwig, 6
Free will, 110
Friedman, Maurice, 12
Future, in Jewish renewal, 153–156

Gideon, 36
Gnosis, religious entanglement with, 102–104

Index

God (*see also* Divine)
  duality of, 75–76
  fear of, 109–110, 227
  growth in image of, 98
  man as realization of, 28, 118–119
  man's responsibility for, 64
  as transcendent *versus* immanent, 224
  way of, 226
Goethe, Johann Wolfgang von, 1, 15*n1*
Gordon, Aaron David, 3, 278, 280*n5*
Grünewald, Matthias, 202, 205*n6*

Ha'am, Ahad, 3, 146, 148, 157*n3*, 280*n3*
Halakha (*see* Law [*Halakha*])
Halaska (*see* Jewish Enlightenment [*halaska*])
Harnack, Adolf von, 104–105
Hart, Henrich, 4
Hart, Julius, 4
Hasidic legends, 86–87 (*see also* Baal-Shem Tov)
  Buber's adaptations of, 2
  Buber's translations of, 5
Hasidim, life of, 72–84
Hasidism
  antiascetic character of, 9
  antihierarchical position of, 70–71
  avodah (service) in, 74–78
  body in, 67–71
  Buber's interpretation of, 6
  Buber's relationship with, 1–2, 86
  Buber's writing on, 16*n6–7*
  emergence of, 140
  final objective in, 153
  hallowing of everyday in, 67
  hitlahavut (ecstasy) in, 72–74
  illumination of tradition in, 64, 140
  imagery in, 90
  Jewish tradition and, 85
  Kabbalah in, 66, 103–104
  kavanah (intention) in, 78–81
  law illuminated by, 122
  life and legend in, 85–87
  mediation of *zaddik in*, 117
  merging of sacred and profane in, 87–91
  message of, 92–93
  original, 152–153
  shiflut (humility) in, 81–84
  spirit of, 63–67
  and synthesis between spiritual and worldly, 130
  unitary tendency in, 150
  western man and, 91–92
Haskalah (*see* Jewish Enlightenment)
Hebrew, revival of, 266–267, 279

Hebrew humanism, 7, 46–50, 158–165
  defined, 46
  versus national humanism, 162–164
  in Palestine, 279
  Zionism and, 160–162
Hebrew scripture (*see also* Bible; Torah)
  Buber-Rosenzweig translation of, 10
  centrality of, 121
  ossification of, 122–123
Hegel, Georg W. F., 228, 233*n8*
Heraclitus, 224, 232*n3*
Herberg, Will, 14
Hertzka, Theodor, 4
Herzl, Theodor, 2, 278, 280*n4*
Hess, Moses, 3, 265, 267*n5*
History
  approaches to, 54
  biblical understanding of, 37–38
  God's working in, 220
Hitlahavut (ecstasy)
  in life of hasidim, 72–74
  versus service, 76
Hitler, Adolf, 159
Hokhmah, versus sophia, 236, 239*n*
Hosea, 25
Human beings (*see also* Man)
  relationships of, 210–211
Human life, double structure of, 231
Humanism
  Hebrew (*see* Hebrew humanism)
  national, *versus* Hebrew humanism, 162–164
Humanitas (*see also* Hebrew humanism)
  concept of, 159
Humility *(shiflut)* (*see* Shiflut [humility])

I, development of, 176–177
I and Thou, 8, 18*n43*, 181–188
  shift toward language in, 9
Ichud (union), 13
Identity, Jewish, 7
I-I/I-You relationship, 181
  speech and, 9
I-It relationship, 181, 187, 231
  in speech of observation, 9
Imagining, of real, 211–212
Individualism, community and, 248
Indwelling *(Shekhinah)* (*see* Shekhinah)
Intention *(kavanah)* (*see* Kavanah [intention])
Intercommunity, 49
Interhuman *(Zwischenmenschliche)*, 5
  in Buber's thought, 14
  essential quality of, 9
Isaiah, 28, 120, 146, 157
Islam, developing understanding of, 285

Israel (state)
　Arab-Jewish relations in, 281
　binational state of, 284
　and chasm between spirit and life, 290
　as example for mankind, 283
　national humanism and, 162–163
　national-religious character of, 163
　non-Zionist view of, 277
　UN partition plan for, 292n3
Israel/Israelites, election of, 23–32, 274
　as demand, 164
　as destiny, 274
　in Deuteronomy, 29–31
　example of community set by, 27–29
　Exodus story and, 26
　Hosea and, 25
　Jeremiah and, 26
　Moses and, 24–25
　and power in spirit, 278
　and prophecies of Amos, 23–24
　without obligation, 29–30
It experiences, 169–172
It world, 186
I-Thou/I-You relationship, 222, 231
　in biblical speech, 48–49
　in giving of Ten Commandments, 43–45
　in man's relationship to God, 66
　philosophical knowing and, 219
　as religious relationship, 225

Jabotinsky, Vladimir Ze'ev, 12, 279n, 288n2
Jacob, 36
Jacobson, Victor, 13
Jeremiah, 40, 120
　dialogues of, 41
　on duties and privileges, 26
　and speech against the Temple, 31
Jewish Bible (see Bible; Hebrew scripture; Torah)
Jewish culture, debate over, 3–4
Jewish Enlightenment (haskalah), 1
　emergence of, 140
　and opposition to Hasidism, 140–141
Jewish movement, 143
Jewish Renaissance, 139–144, 158
Jewish renewal, 145–157, 255
　basic concepts of, 146–148
　central ideas in, 148–156
　creative synthesis in, 156
Jewish soul
　consciousness of God's redeeming power in, 111–114
　foci of, 107–114
　as pre-Sinaitic, 107–114
　primeval experience of, 109–110

Jews
　Eastern-Western distinctions among, 142
　historical role of, 163–164
　peoplehood of, 273
　secularized, 112–113
　Talmudic, 141–142
Jonah, Book of, 112
Joseph, 36
Judaism
　Buber's relationship with, 1–2
　versus Christianity, 113
　as community of fate and faith, 255
　continuity of, 238
　deed in, 150–153 (see also Deed)
　dialogical situation in, 98–99
　dogma in, 98
　eschatalogy in, 111–112
　eternal types in, 120–121
　faith of, 97–106
　fictitious versus real, 266
　foci of, 107–114
　future in, 153–156
　human action in, 99–101
　Palestine and, 281
　primal forces in, 135–136
　propagation of values in, 234
　prophetic, 147
　redemption in, 105–106
　Reform, 7
　religious development in, 128
　as religious versus national community, 146
　renewal of (see Jewish renewal)
　restraints on, 139
　soul of (see Jewish soul)
　Talmudic, 6
　teaching versus law as essence of, 131
　theologoumena of, 97
　triad of world time in, 104–106
　unity in, 148–150

Kabbalah
　on God's desire for relationship, 65–66
　in Hasidism, 64–65, 93, 103–104
　holy sparks myth in, 89
　and man as partner in creation, 118
Kant, Immanuel, 219, 222n1
Kavanah (intention)
　defined, 78
　and flow into hitlahavut, 77–78
　in Hasidism, 78–81
　in life of hasidim, 78–81
　mission of, 79
　in prayer, 69
　of receiving, 80

Key words, 24–25, 32n3
Kierkegaard, Soren, 38
Kingdom, dialogical principle and, 40
Knowing
  in philosophical world view, 219
  subject-object, 219
Knowledge, religious perspective on, 230
Koznitz, Rabbi of, 111
Kropotkin, Pyotr Alekseyevitch, 251n2

Landauer, Gustav, 3, 4
Language (*see also* Hebrew; Speech; Word)
  as event in mutuality, 49
  in Hebrew humanism, 46–47
  Jewish continuity and, 238
  temporality of, 9
Law *(halakha)*
  Buber-Rosenzweig debate on, 17n34
  versus Buber's concept of doing, 6
  Buber's relationship to, 107
  centrality of, 121–122
  evolving nature of, 135
  Hasidism and, 122
  and importance of deed, 236
  increasing rigidity of, 151
  as Jewish essence, 131
  Jewish soul and, 107–108
  Sinaitic, 116
  tyranny of, 139–140
  zaddikim and, 70
Lazarus, Moritz, 146–147, 157n2
Leadership, Biblical (*see* Biblical leadership)
Lerner, Michael, Buber's influence on, 19n61
Lilien, Ephraim Moses, 3
Lueger, Karl, 3
Luria, Issac, 124n15
Luther, Martin, 147

Magic, religious entanglement with, 102–104
Maimonides, Moses, 138n11
  thirteen principles of, 98, 106n1
Making present, 211–212, 213n8, 214
Malebranche, Nicolas, 230, 233n13
Man (*see also* Human beings)
  as God's partner, 118
  holiness of, 93
  as Torah, 67
  ways of perceiving, 191–192
Marcion, 104–105, 106n16
Marx, Karl, 91–92
Meeting *(Begegnung)*
  genuine, 211
  with God, 103
  in I-Thou relationship, 66
  of repentance and mercy, 28
Memory, 33–34
  in biblical writing, 34–35
  soul, 128
Menachem, Rabbi, 79
Mendelssohn, Moses, 157n11
Mendes-Flohr, Paul, 9, 16n7
Messianic movements, *versus* tradition, 122
Messianism, 40–41
  originality of, 154
  Zionism and, 265
Micah, 120
Michal, 37
Mombert, Alfred, 271, 276n3
Monologue
  bending back in, 198
  realms of, 196–197
  thinking as, 199–200
Monotheism, 98
  myth and, 102
Morality, in religion, 195–196
Moses
  dialogues of, 41
  failures of, 36
  at Red Sea, 38–39
  at Sinai, 24–25, 28, 108
Mystery, and religious *versus* philosophical man, 221
Mysticism (*see also* Hasidism)
  versus tradition, 122
Myth, monotheism and, 102

Nachman of Bratzlav, Rabbi, 2, 81
Nathan, speech of, 29–30
Nation(s), Tower of Babel and, 27
National Socialism, 163
  Buber's persecution by, 8, 10
  rise of, 10
Nationalism, 268–276
  Arab, 286–287
  Buber's interpretation of, 3
  concepts of, 263–265
  consequences of, 271–272
  function of, 270–271
  humanitarian, 286
  in Israel, 290
  Jewish, 274–275
  as obstacle to universalism, 267n
  psychological origins of, 268
  relationship to people, 269–270
  sociological origins of, 268
  Zionism and, 277
Nature, encounter with, 173
Nazis (*see* National Socialism)

Niebuhr, Reinhold, 14
Nietzsche, Friedrich, 2, 4, 59*n*5, 144*n*, 146
Nordau, Max, 283, 288*n*2

Observer, perceptions of, 192
Olam Ha-Tikkun, 66
Old Testament (*see also* Bible; Torah)
    Christian perception of, 104–105
Onlooker, perceptions of, 192
Oppenheim, Franz, 4
Original sin, 110
Otherness
    acceptance of, 211
    speech and, 210–211

Palestine
    under British mandate, 275*n*
    establishing spiritual center in, 148
    Jewish national community in, 273
    national home/national policy in, 281–288
    new society in, 283
Pannwitz, Rudolf, 234, 239*n*1
Partition, 13
Peel Commission, 13
People
    definition of, 269–270
    Jews as, 273
Perception *(Wahrnahme)*
    as becoming aware, 192–193
    of observer, 192
    of onlooker, 192
    of world, 198
Philosophy
    absence of concrete in, 228
    errors of, 225
    religion and, 223–233
    social, in Buber's thought, 11–12
Pinhas of Koretz, Rabbi, 69
Plotinus, 233*n*10
Power
    real security and, 278
    will to, 269
Prayer
    kavanah in, 69
    obstacles in, 76
Presence *(Gegenwart)*, 9
    religion as, 169–180
Present, making, 211–212, 213*n*8, 214
Priest, as eternal Judaic type, 120–121
Profane (*see also* Everyday)
    hallowing of, 67, 71, 79–80, 87–91, 92, 110, 135
Prophecy, in Book of Jonah, 112
Prophet
    as eternal Judaic type, 120–121

    leadership by, 40–42
    revelation through, 58–59
Protagoras, 224, 232*n*2
Protestant theology, Buber's influence on, 19*n*60
Publications (*see* Writings; specific works)

Ragaz, Leonhard, 258, 259*n*
Rathenau, Walter, 2
Realization *(verwirklichen)* of God, man as, 28, 118–119
Rebbe, qualifications of, 70
Redemption
    Christian concept of, 55, 105
    human role in, 112
    in Isaiah, 58
    Jewish concept of, 105–106, 111
    promise of, 25
    and return of *Shekhinah*, 78
    revelation as perception of, 56–57
    through lived moment, 58–59
    unity and, 75–76
Reform Judaism, 7
Relation/relationship *(Beziehung)*
    distance and, 206–213
    entering into, 207–208
    of God and man, 109
    God's desire for, 65
    human *versus* animal, 210–211
    intersection of, in You, 187
    of Israel and God, 23–24
    religious, 225
    spheres of, 183
Religion
    as covenant of absolute and concrete, 229–230
    disputations in, 190–191
    as exception *versus* everyday, 193–194
    history of, 220
    as human expression of life, 220
    morality in, 195–196
    overcoming of, 226
    philosophy and, 223–233
    versus religiosity, 6, 115
    religious *versus* nonreligious elements in, 226–227
    thou shalt not in, 129
    youth and, 125–138
    Zionism and, 266
Religiosity, 115–124
    defined, 6
    form and, 121–122
    reaction against tradition and, 122
    versus religion, 6, 115
    unconditionality and, 123

Religious movements
  founding *versus* reforming, 63
  illuminating, 63–64
Religious socialism, 258–260
Renaissance, Jewish (*see* Jewish Renaissance)
Renewal *(Erneuerung)* (*see* Jewish renewal)
Responsibility, 205n3
  in dialogue, 194–196
  freeing to, 201
  God and, 101
  for God's fate in world, 64
  revelation and, 54–55
  transcendental, 68
Return (*see* Turning)
Revelation
  in Christianity, 55
  as covenant, 24
  dialogical principle and, 9
  of God in world, 66
  and life of man, 103
  as mastery over unconscious, 222
  natural events as carriers of, 56
  and perception of creation and redemption, 56–57
  responsibility and, 54–55
  at Sinai, 54
  unconscious and, 222
Rogers, Carl R., 14
Rosenzweig, Franz, 9, 18n38, 29, 32n6, 108, 113, 114n, n40, n42
  and biblical translation with Buber, 10
  in debate on Jewish law, 7, 17n34, 45n
  on divine truth, 231
  on faith, 233n11
  "Heruth" and, 137n
  I and Thou and, 188n
Rouvroy, Claude Henri de, 4
Ruppin, Arthur, 13

Sacred, separation from profane, Hasidism and, 87–91
Samson, 36
Samuel, kingship demanded by, 39–40
Saul, 37
Schneider, Lambert, 10
Scholem, Gershom, 93n, 179n
Schönerer, Georg von, 3
Scripture (*see* Bible; Hebrew Scripture; Torah)
Service *(avodah)* (*see* Avodah [service])
Shekhinah (indwelling), 65, 66
  fall of, 118–119
  postbiblical conception of, 91
  redemption and, 78
  suffering of, 76
  and union with God, 74
Shiflut (humility), in Hasidism, 81–84
Silence, as communication, 189–190
Simmel, Georg, 4, 6
Sin
  inertia as, 116–117
  original, 110
Sinai (*see also* Burning Bush)
  revelation at, 24–25, 28, 54, 55–56
Socialism
  community and, 247, 250
  Jewish, 3
  psychological origins of, 155
  religion and, 248
  religious, 258–260
Socialization *(Vergesellschaftung)*, 252
Solomon, 30
Soul
  community *(Gesamtseele)*, 34
  Jewish (*see* Jewish soul)
  purity of, 132
Speech (*see also* Language; Word)
  as act of creation, 99
  biblical, immediacy of, 48–49
  conceptual, 222
  and I-It/I-You relationships, 9
  mystical character of, 80
  otherness and, 210–211
Spinoza, Baruch de, 141, 144n5, 154–155, 157n11
Spirit
  in genuine dialogue, 215
  of Hasidism, 63–67
  history of, 208–209
  separation from physical life, 236
Statements, philosophical *versus* religious, 220–221
Strauss, Leo, 179n
Study, without action, 236–237
Symbols, of God, 232

Teaching
  body and spirit in, 236–237
  doing and, 234–239
  evolving nature of, 135
  as Jewish essence, 131
  as process, 132–133
  Talmud and, 234–235
  of values, 234–235
Ten Commandments, 43–45
  as morals *versus* religion, 44–45
Teshuvah, 106n9 (*see also* Turning)
Theocracy, biblical experiment with, 39
Theology, Protestant, Buber's influence on, 19n60

Theophany, changes in, 126
Theurgy, 103–104
Thinking, as monologue, 199–200
Thou (*see also* I-Thou/I-You relationship)
    Absolute Thou and, 178–179
    encounter with, 174–176
    innate, 177
Tönnies, Ferdinand, 4, 251*n1*
Torah (*see also* Bible; Hebrew scripture)
    man as, 67
    613 commandments of, 138*n12*
    as teaching *versus* law, 131–133
Tower of Babel, and history of nations, 27
Tradition
    centrality of, 121–122
    ossification of, 122–123
Transformation *(Umwandlung)*
    concrete, Biblical humanism and, 47–48
    Hebrew humanism and, 161
    in Jewish renewal, 148
Truth, cogitative, 224–225, 231
Tsimtsum, 65
Turning *(Hinwendung),* in genuine dialogue, 214
Turning *(Umkehr)*
    as beginning, 101–102
    community and, 250–251
    teaching of, 117

Unconditionality *(Unbedingtheit)*
    Bible as documentation of, 136
    grounding in, 145
    in Judaism, 119
    religiosity and, 123
    youth's confrontation with, 126, 130
Unification *(yihud),* 68–69, 98, 103
United Nations, 13
    partition plan of, 292*n3*
Unity
    and Buber's concept of religiosity, 7
    of fate, 270
    in Jewish renewal, 148–150
    of man, 136
    thematic importance of, 5
Universalism, national, of early prophets, 23–24
Universalization, in Buber's thought, 8

Values, teaching of, 234–235

Weber, Max, 4, 252
Weizmann, Chaim, 3

Weizsäcker, Viktor von, 7
Wisdom *(hokhmah)*
    deeds in excess of, 237
    Jewish *versus* Greek concept of, 236
Wittig, Joseph, 7
Word
    Greek *versus* Hebrew, 49
    key, 24–25, 32*n3*
World
    It, 186
    layers of, 176–177
    as twofold, 185–186
World view
    philosophical, 219–222
    religious, 219–222
Writings, 10–12
    influence of, 14
    themes of, 14–15

Yiddish, 142–143
Yihud, 68–69, 98, 103
You (*see also* I-Thou/I-You relationship; Thou)
    encounter with, 184
Youth
    community and, 128, 130, 134
    religion and, 125–138

Zaddik
    characteristics of, 67–68
    circles of, 69–71
Zionism, 16*n10,* 263, 264
    Arab question and, 278–279, 281–288, 291
    basic concepts of, 143, 144*n*
    Buber-Herzl differences over, 3
    Buber's relationship with, 2, 4, 5, 12, 13, 17*n13*
    concepts of, 263–267
    cultural, 278, 280*n3,* 280*n4*
    Hebrew humanist opposition to, 7
    Jewish nationalism and, 277
    messianism and, 265
    and national egoism *versus* national humanism, 163
    as obstacle to universalism, 267*n*
    religion and, 266
    spiritual, 3
    tendencies within, 289–292
Zoroastrianism, 106*n6* (*see also* Duality, Iranian concept of)